REALISM, UTOPIA, AND THE
MUSHROOM CLOUD

Michael Bess

REALISM, UTOPIA,
AND THE
MUSHROOM CLOUD

Four Activist Intellectuals and Their Strategies
for Peace, 1945–1989

Louise Weiss (FRANCE)
Leo Szilard (USA)
E. P. Thompson (ENGLAND)
Danilo Dolci (ITALY)

The University of Chicago Press
Chicago and London

Michael Bess is assistant professor of history at Vanderbilt University.

The University of Chicago Press, Chicago 60637
The University of Chicago Press, Ltd., London
© 1993 by Michael Bess
All rights reserved. Published 1993
Printed in the United States of America

02 01 00 99 98 97 96 95 94 93   1 2 3 4 5

ISBN (cloth): 0-226-04420-3
ISBN (paper): 0-226-04421-1

Library of Congress Cataloging-in-Publication Data

Bess, Michael.
    Realism, utopia, and the mushroom cloud : four activist
  intellectuals and their strategies for peace, 1945–1989 : Louise
  Weiss, France, Leo Szilard, USA, E. P. Thompson, England, Danilo
  Dolci, Italy / Michael Bess.
        p.   cm.
    Includes bibliographical references and index.
    1. Szilard, Leo.   2. Dolci, Danilo.   3. Weiss, Louise, 1893–
4. Thompson, E. P. (Edward Palmer), 1924–   .   5. Pacifists—
Biography.   I. Title.
  JX1962.A2B47   1993
  327.1'72'0922—dc20
    [B]   93-9707

                                                                                    CIP

For my parents,
Rina and Donovan

If a man could write a book on Ethics
which really was a book on Ethics,
this book would, with an explosion,
destroy all the other books in the world.

—Ludwig Wittgenstein

CONTENTS

ACKNOWLEDGMENTS

It is delightful indeed to look back over a project nearly six years in the making and to recall, one by one, the dozens of persons who have given me their time, their expertise, or their memories to share and transmit.

The research and writing for this book were funded by fellowships from several sources: a series of dissertation fellowships (1985–86, 1986–87, 1987–88) from the University of California's Institute on Global Conflict and Cooperation (IGCC); a Fulbright Fellowship (1985–86) from the U.S. government for field research in Italy; and a John L. Simpson Fellowship (1988–89) from the Institute for International Studies at the University of California, Berkeley. In addition, the Vanderbilt University Research Council graciously provided funds to cover photograph licensing fees. I would like to thank these institutions for rendering my project financially feasible.

For permission to reprint portions of the following chapters, which had appeared before in article form, my thanks to the *American Historical Review,* the *Bulletin of the Atomic Scientists,* and the *World Encyclopedia of Peace* (Oxford: Pergamon Press, 1986). I would also like to thank Helen Weiss and Egon Weiss for their permission to quote from materials in the Szilard Papers; and Howard Gottlieb, of Boston University's Mugar Memorial Library, for permission to quote from the Dolci Papers. For their permission to reprint the photographs that accompany this book, I would like to thank the Information Bureau of the European Parliament office in Paris (for Louise Weiss's photo); Time, Inc., in New York (for the photo of Albert Einstein and Leo Szilard); the European Nuclear Disarmament (END) London office (for the photo of E. P. Thompson); and the Agenzia Publifoto, of Milan (for Danilo Dolci's photo). All translations are my own unless otherwise indicated.

To the Fellows of the University of California's Institute on Global Conflict and Cooperation, and to the organizers and consultants for the institute's conferences—Herbert York, James Skelly, G. Allen Greb, the late Helen Hawkins, Sanford Lakoff, Jeremy Stone, Johan Galtung, Barton Bernstein, Greg Herken, Tair Tairov, Richard Rockwell, Elise Boulding, and Bruce Larkin—my thanks for all their help and their perceptive comments. While I was in Italy, Cipriana Scelba and Luigi Filadoro, of the Commission for Educational Exchange between Italy and the United States (which oversees the Fulbright Program), provided me with invaluable assistance. At the Institute for International Studies at the University of California, Berkeley, I would like to thank Carl Rosberg, Harry Kreisler, and Karen Beros for their assistance and advice.

My research on Leo Szilard took place in several phases between 1982 and 1987. I am grateful to the following persons, who read various drafts of my writings on Szilard, provided guidance in my research, or otherwise assisted me: Len Ackland, Ruth Adams, Barton Bernstein, McGeorge Bundy, Maurice Fox, Carol S. Gruber, Helen Hawkins, Michael Intriligator, Julius Marmur, Robert S. McNamara, Nancy Myers, Bela Silard (Leo Szilard's younger brother), Nancy Watson, Bruce Wheaton, and Herbert York. I also would like to thank Linda Claassen, Geoffrey Wexler, Kim Palmer, and Brad Westbrook of the Special Collections Department in the Main Library of the University of California, San Diego, for assisting me in working with Szilard's personal archives.

For my research on Louise Weiss, I spent five months in France (December 1986–May 1987). I am grateful to the following persons who consented to be interviewed: Georges Bourdelon, Claude Bourdet, Jean-Marc Brissaud, René Carrère, Pascal Fontaine, Raoul Girardet, Pierre Hassner, Jean Klein, Henri Labrousse, Andrée Martin-Pannetier, Christian de la Malène, Dominique Moisi, Pierre Pflimlin, Alain Poher. I also would like to thank the following persons for their suggestions regarding my research: France Bursaux, Françoise Crouzet, Jean Leclant, Françoise Thom. I extend my thanks to the librarians at the Bibliothèque Marguerite Durand in Paris; to Anne Vitrey, librarian in the Paris office of the European Parliament; to Joëlle Marti, at the Bibliothèque du Parlement Européen in Luxembourg; and to Michelle Sacquin, at the Département des Manuscrits of the Bibliothèque Nationale in Paris.

My primary thanks in my research on E. P. Thompson are due to Thompson himself, and to Dorothy Thompson, who set aside considerable time for interviews, dug up unpublished manuscripts for me to read, and provided detailed comments on a draft of my chapter. I owe a debt of similar magnitude to Mary Kaldor, who allowed me to photocopy thousands of documents amassed during seven years of campaigning in END; her reflections and suggestions have been invaluable to me in shaping my understanding of the movement. During the five months I spent in England (July–December 1986), I was able to interview the following persons, whom I take this opportunity to thank: Paul Anderson, Meg Beresford, Patrick Burke, Basil Davidson, Ken Fleet, Lyn Jones, Louis Mackay, Peter Murphy, John Saville, Cesar Voûte, Fiona Weir. The staff of the Press Library at the Royal Institute of International Affairs (Chatham House) in London provided me with efficient assistance. I also would like to thank Sheila Jones, Harvey Kaye, Carolyn Moorehead, and the staff of the END office in London for all their help.

Danilo Dolci, like E. P. Thompson, generously made himself available to me for interviews and allowed me to photocopy thousands of documents dating back through the past four decades. For assisting my research in Italy (September 1985–June 1986), a special mention is due to Franco LaGennusa, Eliana Riggio, and Justin Vitiello, who helped me to orient my research on Dolci from the very start. I also would like to thank Massimo Margheri and Oddina Lo Presti Seminerio for helping me to find an ancient FIAT 127 which stoically conveyed me and my tape recorder about the Sicilian countryside. The following persons, who consented to be interviewed, deserve my gratitude: Franco Alasia, Paola Buzzola, Amico Dolci, Michael Fähndrich, Francesco Grimaldi, Orazio de Guilmi, Pino Lombardo, Alberto L'Abate, Rosaria Martinetti, Margret and Albrecht Müller-Schöll, Jean-Jacques Peyronnel, Piero Pinna, Carlo Presciuttini, Umberto Santino, Renata Zwick-Rubino. I would like to thank Valerie Andrews, Scott Kennedy, Giacinto Lentini, Mario Molino, Roberto Moscati, and Diana and Don Rothman for the opportunity to discuss Dolci's work in numerous conversations. Howard Gottlieb and his staff at the Mugar Memorial Library at Boston University (where Dolci's private papers are held) provided gracious assistance in my research. I was also very well assisted by the librarians and staffers at the Biblioteca Nazionale, Cassa Per il Mezzogiorno, SVIMEZ, Biblioteca Giustino Fortunato, and the Fondazione Olivetti in Rome.

My views on questions of war and peacemaking were decisively shaped in conversations and classes over the course of many years at U.C. Berkeley. I would especially like to thank the following professors, whose intellectual stimulation rendered my experience of graduate school deeply enjoyable: Reinhard Bendix, Gene Brucker, Ernst Haas, Roger Hahn, Lynn Hunt, John Hurst, Gene Irschick, Thomas Laqueur, Martin Malia, Walter McDougall, Thomas Metcalf, Franz Schurmann, Randolph Starn, Kenneth Waltz, Richard Webster, and Reginald Zelnik. I would like to thank Agnes Petersen at the Hoover Institution on War, Revolution, and Peace at Stanford University for her help in choosing my research topic. I also owe a special debt to Joseph Goldstein, of Barre, Massachusetts, for teaching me how to think about peace in an entirely new way.

To the members of my dissertation committee—my supervisor, Susanna Barrows, Martin Jay, and Michael Nagler—I can only offer the kinds of thanks that one gives to a mentor and a close friend. They have shaped both me and this project through years of intellectual comradeship and exchange. I can only hope that someday I will be able to pass along to my own students some reflection of what my teachers have shown toward me.

As I revised this book for publication, I benefited enormously from critical suggestions by the following persons, who read various parts of my manuscript in draft form or otherwise assisted me with my revisions: Ruth Ben-Ghiat, Charles Delzell, Jean Elshtain, James Epstein, Chiarella Esposito, Carole Fink, Joel Harrington, Joe Mount, Kim Munholland, Wayne Northcutt, Elisabeth Perry, Lewis Perry, Matthew Ramsey, David Ransel, David Roberts, David Schalk, Helmut Smith, Meredith Veldman, Francis Wcislo, Naomi H. Wittes, and Lawrence Wittner. I owe a special debt to Paul Conkin, Barton Bernstein, and W. Warren Wagar for their exhaustive and penetrating comments on the entire manuscript. My literary agent, Mildred Marmur, and Douglas Mitchell, of the University of Chicago Press, have provided the kind of insightful and sympathetic editorial assistance that a scholar can only dream of finding. I also would like to thank my students at Vanderbilt University, graduates and undergraduates, for their persistent questioning of the things I say.

To my mother and father, to my dear friends, to my family, who have shared these past years, I would like to express my gratitude.

The final acknowledgment is to my wife Kimberly, who traveled with me from Trappeto to Greenham Common to the Cinquième Arrondissement and debated endlessly with me over practically every idea. She has been at the heart of the entire project.

INTRODUCTION

At the core of this book lie two images that have haunted humankind since the Second World War—the barbed wire and emaciated figures of Hitler's death camps, and the blinding white flash over the city of Hiroshima. In the starkest possible terms, these images express one of the central dilemmas of contemporary history: the fact that human beings, in the mid-twentieth century, have acquired the technological power both to dominate the earth and to destroy the earth. How can the world's peoples fend off the aggressions of expansionist movements like Nazism except by relying on the ultimate arbiter of physical force? Yet how long can the world's peoples afford to rely on force, now that weapons have become powerful enough to threaten the entire biosphere? It is a dilemma that humankind has yet to resolve in any satisfactory way: how to secure the peace, without risking collective suicide, in a world of such fearsome armaments and belligerent ideologies.

The four intellectuals in this study devoted much of their lives to grappling with this dilemma, both in thought and in concrete action. They were rebels who rejected some of the central tenets of international politics during the Cold War era—the division of Europe, the bipolar "balance of terror"—and offered a vibrant and imaginative array of practical alternatives. What is realistic, and what is utopian? Where does one draw the line? This question recurred like a leitmotiv throughout their turbulent careers. Yet these four individuals, who so brashly challenged the status quo of international politics, were not mere eccentrics or impractical dreamers: their achievements ranged from the creation of the atomic bomb to the mustering of peace marchers in the millions. They were hard-bitten political observers who defied the "conventional wisdom" of statesmen, military leaders, and academic experts, posing troublesome questions of their own: In what ways have the deadly new weapons of the twentieth century changed the ground rules of international politics? To what extent can cooperation replace coercion as an instrument of international security?

Their answers to these questions differed dramatically—as might be expected from four intellectuals who hailed from different countries and who never worked together or knew each other. Nevertheless, I have chosen to juxtapose their stories because their positions also complemented one another, establishing a broad spectrum somewhat similar to the range between two opposed historical figures like Winston Churchill and Mohandas K. Gandhi. At one end of the spectrum lay Louise Weiss, whose career might be summed up as the shipwreck of a youthful idealism, leading to a bitterly pessimistic assessment of political power and human nature. For Weiss, as she grew older, the dictates of a Machiavellian philosophy of power began to seem increasingly compelling: force, hierarchy, and cunning manipulation constituted the central and irreducible elements of politics. At the other extreme lay Danilo Dolci, who never wavered from his conviction that human beings could bring forth a fundamentally gentle and egalitarian social order. Dolci often startled his coworkers with deliberately provocatory articulations of this vision, like the following: "One of the greatest realists in all history was Saint Francis of Assisi."[1] Thus, at one end of this spectrum we have an emphasis on strict hierarchy and the use of force; at the other, an emphasis on the fundamental fellowship among humans and other creatures, and on the tools of nonviolent persuasion and compromise. Weiss, Szilard, Thompson, and Dolci—what I have tried to do in this study is to establish an ongoing "dialogue" or debate among the contrasting worldviews that these figures came to embody. Their careers, in this sense, might be understood as experiments in testing four different "gradations" of hope—four rival wagers upon the human potential.

At the heart of this comparative exercise lies the notion of international politics as a competitive arena in which the ultimate arbiter is physical force. The political theorist Kenneth Waltz uses the nineteenth-century German word *Realpolitik* to describe this conception, and he points out that it has a long and distinguished history:

> Wherever agents and agencies are coupled by force and competition rather than by authority and law, we expect to find . . . the approach to politics suggested by the rubric, *Realpolitik.* The elements of *Realpolitik,* exhaustively listed, are these: The ruler's, and later the state's, interest provides the spring of action; the necessities of policy arise from the unregulated competition of states; calculation based on these necessities can discover the policies that will best serve a state's interests; success is the ultimate test of policy, and success is defined as preserving and strengthening the

state. Ever since Machiavelli, interest and necessity—and *raison d'état,* the phrase that comprehends them—have remained the key concepts of *Realpolitik.*[2]

Throughout this tradition of *Realpolitik,* a profound tension has recurrently arisen between the dictates of "ought" and "is"—between the standards of morality or religion, and the demands of effective action in a competitive struggle for power.[3] Machiavelli, Bismarck, Kissinger—all have drawn a careful line between "what the world is like" and "what we would prefer the world to be like." It would be very nice, they argued, if people were consistently kind to one another and could be trusted to look after each other's welfare. Unfortunately (they continued), experience had shown again and again that human beings could be exceedingly cruel to each other, utterly disregarding the suffering that they caused in their fellow humans, and looking out (more often than not) for their own advantage rather than the well-being of others. In the last resort, some people could only be stopped by brute force, since this was the only language they understood. Individuals like Genghis Khan or Hitler could not be restrained by means of moral or religious injunctions; they could only be stopped by the threat of harsh punishment. Out of this logic had come the old Roman adage, "If you want peace, prepare for war." The best way to keep the peace was to develop a fearsome military capability, for in this way one made it obvious to any potential enemy that the costs of an attack would probably outweigh the benefits. The proponents of this kind of logic usually admitted that it was morally repugnant, but they argued that it had the compensatory virtue, in an imperfect world, of being effective. Better to keep the peace by unpleasant means, they argued, than to risk war because of an excessively rosy and idealistic assessment of one's neighbors.

Herein lies the essential tension animating the present study. Unlike Louise Weiss, Szilard, Thompson, and Dolci all believed that humankind was doomed to self-destruction, sooner or later, unless it could depart dramatically from this age-old tradition of maintaining peace through military deterrence. What was the alternative? All three of them agreed with Weiss that serious conflicts among human beings would always be unavoidable; but each of them offered his own picture of a new world order, in which "is" and "ought" could become more closely integrated, and in which conflicts could increasingly be resolved through the application of reason and compromise. These three men all sought to open a detour around the hard logic of coercion and manipulation that predominates among nation-states—Szilard at the level of international power blocs, Thompson and Dolci at the level of the grass roots. The "spectrum" of their worldviews, therefore, consists in their increasing degrees of distance from the *Realpolitik* of the competitive struggle for power—the position espoused in her later years, with caustic frankness, by Weiss.

The aim of this comparative study is threefold. At the most immediate level, it is simply to lay out the concept of "peace" in its rich diversity, exploring the wide range of meanings that this word can connote. At a deeper level, my goal is to scrutinize the underlying processes through which these four thinkers arrived at their conceptions of peace—to reveal, insofar as it is possible, how their life stories shaped their values and logic, how they learned (or failed to learn) from their experiences. Finally, I try to establish an implicit confrontation among these different visions of peace, so that each thinker can in effect "criticize" the others. My purpose here is not to decide whose perspective was the "winner," nor does it necessarily lead toward any higher synthesis of all four positions. My goal, rather, is to illuminate some of the common moral choices and practical judgments that these intellectuals all faced in putting together their visions of peace. How does the line get drawn, in daily practice, between the "realistic" and the "utopian?" Which hidden assumptions come into play, and which ends do these assumptions serve? These questions lie in the background of my study, informing the way I tell the stories of these four activists' careers. By comparing their hopes and fears, their concrete triumphs and failures, I hope to shed light on the inherent tension between these problematic concepts of "realism" and "utopia," and on some of the powerful ways in which that tension shapes contemporary international politics.

Introductory sketches of these four figures now follow:

Louise Weiss (1893–1983) was the French journalist and political activist who in 1979, at the age of eighty-six, presided over the opening session of the first democratically elected European Parliament. Her career traced a long trajectory through the turbulence of this century: she had been a nurse in World War I, interviewed Trotsky and other Bolsheviks in the chaotic Moscow of 1921, edited a successful journal on foreign affairs during the 1920s, and agitated as a suffragette during the 1930s. Weiss thought of herself as a *femme de combat,* a fighter of causes—and in her pungently written memoirs she relates how her meeting with Trotsky became a loud and table-thumping argument, and how she later staged dramatic street confrontations to promote the cause of women's suffrage in France.

After 1945, Weiss brought the same verve to her campaign for a European resurgence. Like General de Gaulle, whom she deeply admired, she recognized well before the Allied victory in Europe that the preeminent challenge of the following decades would come not from Berlin but from Washington and Moscow. Unlike De Gaulle, however, Weiss was unequivocal in her perception that France could never "go it alone," and that the only way to preserve French influence was to join forces with the other old nations of Europe to form a new superpower. She, therefore, became a devoted advocate of genuine supranational unification, and she spent the last decades of her life campaigning for the creation of a European federal government with a potent military force of its own.

As an ardent champion of a Machiavellian philosophy of power, Weiss provides an important contrapuntal voice within the present study. Whereas Szilard, Thompson, and Dolci all sought to circumvent or subvert the hard logic of *Realpolitik*, Weiss defended this logic as the only reliable means for predicting and controlling the behavior of collectivities. At the heart of Weiss's outlook was a profound pessimism about human nature, a pessimism that had impressed itself upon her through the long succession of betrayals and disappointments that marked her experience of the twentieth century. Like many other French men and women who witnessed the foundering of the League of Nations in the 1930s, the triumph of Hitler in 1940, and the agonizing process of postwar decolonization, Weiss drew conclusions that would endure throughout the postwar period. She rejected bipolar "stability," and frankly described international politics as an irreducible struggle for domination among a plurality of states and races, ideological units and religious groupings.

Leo Szilard (1898–1964) was the brilliant Hungarian physicist who first conceived of a nuclear chain reaction in 1934 and who prodded Franklin Roosevelt to start the atomic-bomb project during the first months of World War II. Szilard (pronounced "Sih-lard") spent the last two decades of his life desperately trying to put the genie back into the bottle—a failure, although his efforts established him as one of the world's first, and most imaginative, nuclear arms-control advocates. From 1945 until his death in 1964, he adroitly used his prestige as a Manhattan Project scientist to promote a sophisticated, two-tiered plan for short-range arms talks between the superpowers and long-range world federation. Because he accepted the superpowers' continued preeminence as a basic "given," his most creative efforts were spent trying to get U.S. and Soviet statesmen (from Khrushchev on down) to reach a "meeting of the minds" on their common interests for the long-term future.

In a letter to Stalin written in 1947, Szilard expressed one of his deepest beliefs, which lay at the root of nearly all his peace proposals and initiatives. "One world," he wrote to the Soviet dictator, "need not necessarily be a uniform world."[4] Szilard was an early proponent of peaceful coexistence between the superpowers, long before Albert Wohlstetter had defined for American "defense intellectuals" that concept of "delicate balance of terror" which eventually shaped the arms control treaties of the 1970s and 1980s.[5]

Szilard tackled the diplomacy of the Cold War from every conceivable angle: from the challenge of orienting a McCarthyite public opinion in support of peaceful coexistence, to the establishment of a "White House–Kremlin hotline"; from the promotion of a spheres-of-influence agreement between the superpowers, to the formation of an effective congressional peace-lobbying group. The task at hand, as he saw it, was to stave off nuclear disaster long enough to allow a gradual transition toward a new international system—a system based on negotiated compromises and the logic of "collective security."

In one sense, therefore, Szilard's ideas were quite far removed from those of Louise Weiss. He was much more "dovish" than Weiss, and placed fervent hopes in the United Nations—an institution to which Weiss scornfully referred as "le Machin" ("the Thing"). He sought to strengthen and rationalize U.S. and Soviet control over international politics, whereas Weiss resented the superpowers' duopoly and continually strove to undermine it. Nevertheless, Szilard's position also bore important similarities to Weiss's position. Like Weiss, he assigned an important role to military force in world politics (although he hoped that in the distant future this role could be gradually diminished). Still more important, he shared Weiss's deep-seated elitism, believing that "popular opinion" should follow the lead of enlightened politicians and far-seeing intellectuals like himself; and he was as hostile as she was to such direct manifestations of grass-roots power as the British Campaign for Nuclear Disarmament or the American student movement of the 1960s.

On the one hand, therefore, Szilard clearly broke with the philosophy of "every man for himself" espoused by persons like Weiss, and he put forth a different ideal based on the logic of long-term cooperation for survival. Still, he shared Weiss's essentially hierarchical conception of politics, both domestic and international; like Weiss, he envisioned a world in which the crucial political and military decisions would ultimately lie in the hands of a few global leaders and their exclusive inner circles.

E. P. Thompson (b. 1924), a British social historian, has been one of the leading figures in the British and European peace movements since the 1950s. After 1956, when he broke with the British Communist party, he became a prominent spokesman for a tenaciously humanistic conception of socialism as well as a key figure in the European Nuclear Disarmament (END) campaign of the 1980s.

Thompson's goal in the END campaign was an undoing of Yalta from the grass roots upward, "rolling back" the influence of both superpowers from the entire European continent, breaking the cycle of militarization that he felt had been foisted upon an unwilling people. Starting in the spring of 1980, he put aside his historical research, finding himself thrust to the forefront of an international political movement whose rapid growth continually surprised him. His mail grew to unmanageable proportions, and he was swamped with requests for public appearances and television interviews. In 1984 he engaged U.S. Secretary of Defense Caspar Weinberger in a blistering debate at Oxford University—an encounter in which both sides claimed a moral victory. He became an impromptu expert on military issues, trading the conceptual tools of cultural and social history for a whole new set of concepts in the fields of military technology and strategic affairs.

Did this mean that Thompson had forgotten his role as a historian, as some critics implied? Hardly. Thompson believed that Europe in the 1980s was traversing a transitional period similar to the one he had described in his book, *The Making of the English Working Class*. Just as English artisans and radical intellectuals had come together in the early nineteenth century to struggle for the vote, redefining their own sense of collective identity in the process, so he now thought the people of Europe were redefining their perception of themselves and of their own future. In October 1983, Thompson addressed a crowd of 250,000 peace activists in London's Hyde Park, reminding them of the traditions they were embodying. "At some point," he told them, "the old structures of militarism must buckle under peaceful, nonviolent pressure, as the railings of this Hyde Park (more than 100 years old) once buckled under the pressure of peaceful demonstrators for the vote."[6]

What would it take to reunify Europe? What kinds of social systems would the European peoples choose, if the influence of both superpowers receded from their continent? With his coworkers in British END and on the European mainland, Thompson was able to push public opinion beyond the prevalent concern with adding and subtracting warheads, toward a much broader debate that embraced the basic political questions of the postwar period.

Thompson's position contrasted more sharply with Weiss's than with Szilard's, for he at least shared Szilard's concern for building a formal system of international security, whereas he shared very little with Weiss. At a more fundamental level, however, Thompson diverged from both Weiss and Szilard in several important respects. He did not think of peace simply as the "absence of major wars" but broadened this definition to embrace a positive (and far more arduous) set of requirements: a full-fledged peace, stable and enduring, would require important changes *within* nations as well as *among* nations. Ultimately, in Thompson's view, it was unrealistic to expect a lasting peace unless the world's peoples had begun seriously to address the deeper social and economic inequalities that plagued global society.

His conception of peace, therefore, entailed precisely the opposite of the elitism that characterized the positions of Weiss and Szilard. Instead, Thompson envisioned an international coalition of grass-roots movements that would gradually introduce social reforms and learn to govern itself, building peace from the local level upward, as it were, rather than from the pinnacles of power downward. For Weiss and Szilard, the most urgent problems facing humankind were primarily military and geopolitical in nature. "Low politics"—the relations between employers and trade unions, for instance, or between local institutions and the bureaucracies of the nation-state—these would have struck Szilard and Weiss as peculiar areas in which to campaign for peace. For Thompson, on the other hand, peace was inseparable from a form of direct popular self-government that required close attention precisely to this area of "low politics." He was not sanguine about the prospects of creating a nonviolent grass-roots democracy, spanning the world's diverse cultures and peoples; but he believed that this distant ideal could provide a vital moral orientation for the peace movements of the present world.

Thompson, however, was not an absolute pacifist. He had fought in World War II, and he believed that a military mechanism of collective security would continue to be necessary for the foreseeable future. His strategy stopped short, therefore, of the adamant nonviolence advocated by Danilo Dolci.

Danilo Dolci (b. 1924) has worked as a community educator in the poorest regions of Sicily since 1952. Deeply devoted to the principles of Gandhian nonviolence, he began his work at age twenty-eight, with a protracted fast to publicize the plight of children who were dying of malnutrition in the isolated villages of Western Sicily. Through three decades of activism, the logic of Dolci's nonviolence steadily led him to broaden the scope of his campaign— moving from the village level to the national level to the international level— until it culminated in a critique of industrial civilization itself.

For Dolci, it was a mistake to focus on the East-West rivalry between the superpower blocs without pushing the analysis further. He believed that the deeper roots of this large-scale military and political competition lay in the values of common citizens, and in the everyday social processes that shaped those values. Increasingly, as he struggled to understand the endemic violence in the Sicilian countryside, he became convinced that this violence was not fundamentally separate from the violence that was taking place among nations. One could point to obvious differences, to be sure; for the violence of the state was more deadly, more complex and impersonal, than the violence among individuals. Yet his experiences led to a growing conviction that getting rid of the missiles would require substantial changes in the whole social order of modern industrialism.

Like E. P. Thompson, therefore, Dolci believed that international peace could only rest upon a foundation of social peace at the local and regional levels; any disarmament plan that failed to take this social and economic dimension into account was based on false premises. Unlike Thompson, however, Dolci directed few of his activities directly against the military and political structures that are usually associated with problems of war and peace. He did not protest at military bases or campaign for a new pan-European politics, as Thompson was doing. His tools, instead, tended to be more local in scope: organizing a community of illiterate peasants to build a major dam (despite fierce opposition from the mafia), creating workers' cooperatives, founding an experimental elementary school devoted to the principle of nonviolence. In all these activities, Dolci explicitly believed that he was laying the foundations for a new society in which superpowers, missiles, and militarism would become obsolete. He conceived of his work in Sicily as experiments in a "laboratory of suffering"[7]—experiments whose results could be adapted to conditions in the dozens of countries he visited, from Brazil to the USSR, from the United States to India. The methods he developed in his remote Sicilian village, he hoped, might eventually spread to other communities throughout the globe, thereby eroding the broader patterns of international violence and hegemony.

Like Gandhi and Martin Luther King, Dolci believed that conflicts among human beings were inevitable, but that any attempt to resolve those conflicts by coercive or manipulative means would ultimately backfire. In the short run, a violent solution might indeed provide one person or group with an advantage; yet in the long run, he believed, all positions built up and defended by such dominative means were bound to collapse in renewed violence. A truly effective policy for peace, therefore, required taking an extremely long-term view of human events; it required penetrating beneath the surface manifestations of violence and cruelty, in order to identify the deeper attitudes and ingrained patterns of behavior that caused them. Not surprisingly, therefore, Dolci gradually came to concentrate his efforts on the education of the young, among whom he hoped to fashion new attitudes and new patterns of behavior. Only in this way, he believed, could an authentic and lasting peace be born.

In essence, these four activists were all asking themselves the same recurring question: To what extent can humankind bring forth a new international order in which cooperation displaces coercion as a means of resolving conflicts? This question proved slippery, of course; for each of them differed significantly from the others in assessing human nature, the patterns of history, the flexibility of social institutions. Their relative positions can be most clearly schematized by comparing their perceptions of two fundamental issues: the role of military force, and the role of social hierarchy.

For Weiss, force and hierarchy constituted the necessary and irreducible basis of human social order, and she painted her picture of global society accordingly—as a vast pyramid with the white Europeans firmly in command at the top. Szilard's position, while similar to Weiss's in some respects, was more moderate and nuanced: he affirmed that the world's political and intellectual elites, prodded by the threat of nuclear catastrophe, might attain a new degree of rationality and cooperation unparalleled in history. Force and hierarchy would still play a crucial role, Szilard believed, but they would not shore up a single pyramid of power; instead, the future world order would be polycentric and fluid—a delicate equilibrium among huge political blocs, carefully maintained by the mediating institutions of the United Nations. E. P. Thompson went one important step further: he applied Szilard's optimism to the majority of the world's common citizens, arguing that they possessed a latent potential for precisely the kinds of self-control and rational cooperation that Szilard envisioned among the elite "global managers." For Thompson, therefore, the roles of force and hierarchy could be mitigated even further. Grass-roots democracy, starting at the local level, might gradually erode the vast power blocs that characterized the Cold War era; and as these grass-roots groups increasingly worked together in cross-cultural networks, they could build their own institutions of collective security, sharply reducing the anarchic use of force that characterized the contemporary state system. Danilo Dolci, finally, envisioned a civilization that whittled away at force and hierarchy until they approached the vanishing point. In the distant future, he believed, education could be designed in such a way as to train the young, from the very beginning of their socialization, to seek compromise and to reach collective decisions on a consensual basis. In the school he founded in Sicily, and in his community work, he sought the concrete methods of pedagogy and conflict resolution that would pave the way for a fully democratic and nonviolent society.

This, therefore, is the basic spectrum of political visions underlying the present study. What remains to be explained is why I chose these four particular individuals as the subjects of my research. Aside from the inevitable element of arbitrariness inherent in any selection of this nature, I would point to three main factors as having affected my decision.

The first factor lies in the basic commonalities that link these four figures together, rendering comparisons among them feasible and interesting. These were, to begin with, four Europeans who rebelled against the prevailing political currents of the Cold War era. Despite their differences, they all rejected (with equal indignation) the Manichaean "either-or" that the East-West rivalry seemed inexorably to force upon them. "The Cold War," wrote E. P. Thompson in 1984, "dragooned people into flocks of Atlanticist sheep or pro-Soviet goats, and blocked off any 'third way.'" [8] Although the four figures in this study differed sharply in their proposals for a "third way," their common refusal to be either a sheep or a goat remains one of the most striking features of their careers. Can one be on the political "Right" and yet be harshly critical of the United States? This was a basic question for Louise Weiss. Can one be on the "Left" and yet be independent of the Eastern bloc? Since the 1950s, E. P. Thompson has doggedly struggled to prove that one could. Can one refuse to be identified with either Left or Right, East or West, and still remain politically effective in a prevailing atmosphere of military and ideological polarization? Leo Szilard and Danilo Dolci both tried to create space for such a nonaligned stance. Confronted again and again with the question, "Are you with us or with them?" these four recalcitrant individuals resoundingly answered, "Neither!"

These were, in other words, four mavericks—four tenacious and indeed often cantankerous persons; and it was here, in their style of activism, that they shared a second basic similarity. Throughout their careers, they all insisted on remaining relative political outsiders. Though they may have supported, or even founded, important social and political organizations, they all bridled at the kinds of unquestioning partisanship, group discipline, and ideological orthodoxy that collective action often entails. At no point did they surrender their right to criticize anybody and anything that they deemed worthy of criticism; and because of this, they often found themselves equally at odds both with those in power and with many others who were contesting that power.

In this sense, my primary reason for selecting this particular "cast of characters" grew out of the central constellation of questions and issues that I intended to explore. I chose four Cold War rebels—four independent-minded political outsiders—because I wanted to chart some of the broad outlines of resistance to the Cold War, the struggles and travails of those who rejected the tense bipolar standoff of the postwar years. Having started my work on this project in 1985, when the Cold War still occupied a dominant place in international politics, I wanted to clarify and compare some of the principal alternatives to that dominant political reality. Yet this initial concern immediately brought me to a second, and equally important question: To what extent did these dissident visions merely represent pious hopes or irrelevant anachronisms, and (conversely) to what extent did they offer practical and plausible alternatives to the Cold War status quo? Here I came to my second main reason for choosing these four figures: their diverse political visions tended to complement each other, falling naturally into the broad spectrum that I have described above. By juxtaposing these four visions of the future, establishing an implicit dialogue among them, I hoped to clarify some of the fundamental assumptions underpinning the tension between "realism" and "utopianism" in the nuclear age. Did the meaning of the word "realism" undergo a fundamental shift, now that atomic weapons had brought unparalleled destruction within the reach of growing numbers of statesmen? Would the world's peoples have to open up their minds (and their lives) to radically new alternatives and possibilities under these dramatically changed circumstances? The writings and practical struggles of these four intellectuals returned again and again to these basic questions, answering them in ways that dovetailed quite strikingly with each other, and thus affording me a chance to make systematic comparisons of their assumptions and judgments.

Louise Weiss plays perhaps the most distinctive role within this study, precisely because of her pessimistic conception of human nature and her brash emphasis on military force as the most effective arbiter among peoples. Her pugnacious vision of a world beyond the Cold War provides a continual counterweight to the more optimistic assumptions and speculations of the other three. Hers is the voice of tough-minded, world-weary experience, admonishing the other three figures to keep in mind humankind's foibles and limitations.

Szilard, Thompson, and Dolci, on the other hand, all shared an ardent belief that the world's peoples *could* move toward greater levels of cooperation. However, within this common framework, they, too, developed distinctive and complementary strategies that took each of them, from Szilard to Dolci, farther away from Weiss's hard-nosed *Realpolitik*. Szilard sought to open up alternative channels of communication among the superpowers' elites, working frantically to exert a moderating influence upon the pinnacles of state power where control over the Bomb resided. Seeking to reform the Cold War diplomatic establishment from behind the scenes, he nonetheless accepted many of the underlying assumptions and ground rules of traditional interstate relations. Thompson, by contrast, rejected Cold War diplomacy outright, and called for a new international politics founded upon direct contacts among common citizens and local self-governing councils. Unlike Szilard, he concentrated on the slower and more cumbersome processes of mass politics, mobilizing vast demonstrations against the Cold War and the division of Europe, and harking back to pre-Yalta traditions of European independence. Dolci, finally, perceived both the existence of the missiles and the division of Europe, but chose in his campaign to explore the underlying social causes of these unfortunate realities. His effort to invent a new way of wielding power among individuals and groups necessarily fell into a still longer time frame, in which gentler values would almost imperceptibly come to permeate industrial civilization.

One would not need to go far afield, of course, to find other individuals whose careers and ideals might have fit very nicely into a study of this nature. Figures like Alva Myrdal, Bertrand Russell, Petra Kelly, E. F. Schumacher, or (in Weiss's case) Raymond Aron might have provided an equally compelling focus for comparative discussion. Such figures certainly grappled just as hard with the central issue around which this book revolves: the reassessment of *Realpolitik* by a new generation of intellectuals, in the aftermath of Hiroshima. Nevertheless, I eventually settled on these four individuals for one final reason: their stories had not been told before, and yet they possessed a particularly direct relevance to some of the most important currents in postwar European history. Weiss's designs for a European superpower anticipated the growing speed with which the nations of the European Community have pushed toward their integration goals of the 1990s and beyond. Szilard's search for an *entente cordiale* between the Americans and Russians appeared almost hopeless during the 1950s and 1960s, but it no longer seemed nearly so farfetched in the post–Cold War world of the 1990s. Thompson envisioned a phased disengagement of both superpowers from their European commitments, and this was a theme whose centrality in European and American political discussions has been steadily increasing since the mid-1980s. Danilo Dolci's move from the prosperity of Northern Italy to the impoverished South, finally, allowed me to explore (in a sort of microcosm) some of the broader problems of uneven development that also characterize global North-South relations—problems whose importance has persistently grown since the Second World War.

Naturally, the ending of the Cold War has dramatically changed the historical backdrop of this book, for these four activists all sharpened their skills, and fashioned their distinct identities, out of opposition to the rigid bipolar rivalry and militarized "peace" that typified the Cold War. Yet it should not surprise us if the beginning of a more fluid era in world politics renders their visions of peace even more relevant than before. Precisely because they all tried to picture a world beyond the Cold War, and to show how such an international order might work, their struggles and experiments have become all the more directly pertinent to the "new world order" that statesmen and citizens are striving to build today. As the global arena opens up to alignments and conflicts that had remained suppressed during the bipolar "balance of terror," there is room for a new creativity in international politics, but there is also room for new misunderstandings and disastrous failures. Under these changed conditions, the reflections and experiences of four rebels, who struggled for several decades to chart a safe pathway into a post–Cold War era, acquire a special relevance all their own.

At first, the task of undertaking a four-nation study seemed unnecessarily complicated, both from a logistical and from a theoretical point of view. Gradually, however, I became convinced that cross-cultural comparisons would enhance, rather than diminish, the vividness of the basic issues I wished to investigate; for I began to see how each of these careers made particular sense within its own national setting. Weiss had a vision of the future whose "Euro-Gaullist" overtones exerted a special appeal for a people like the French; her muscular advocacy of "peace through strength" was deeply conditioned by her country's bitter experiences with the Versailles treaty, the debacle of 1940, and the humiliating retreat from colonial preeminence after World War II. Szilard, who wanted to make an immediate impact on the way the superpowers perceived and communicated with each other, established his base of operations directly in the policy-making environment of Washington, D.C. Thompson has been described by one of his close friends as "an English radical" straight out of the "moral tradition going back to Tom Paine;"[9] his voice within the nuclear disarmament movement has been especially powerful because it drew deeply upon this moral tradition, pushing beyond the technical concerns of disarmament and probing for the much broader political preconditions of a European reunification. Unlike some of the highly talented members of the German peace movement, moreover, Thompson (as an Englishman) was in a position to broach the extremely controversial subject of East-West reunification without being suspected of harboring nationalistic motives. Dolci, finally, left behind a relatively comfortable existence in Northern Italy to devote his life to the desperately poor and ignorant peasants who populated the southern half of his country. Italy, with its chronic disparity between North and South, was a uniquely appropriate European nation for the pilot project of nonviolent social change and development of resources that Dolci had in mind.

It would certainly be an exaggeration to argue that these activists could *only* have pursued their particular strategies within these specific national and historical contexts; yet it is nonetheless true that strategy and context are deeply related. To live in a Sicilian fishing village, for instance, is to experience tangible problems that have lain upon the countryside for centuries and centuries, becoming as ingrained in people's minds as they have in the stark landscape. In this sense, it was as fitting for Dolci to think in the long term as it was for Szilard, bustling around the capital of a superpower, to look nervously ahead at the coming months and years.

In the chapters that follow, I narrate each of these four stories separately, only occasionally offering direct comparisons and contrasts among them. These were, after all, historically separate careers; it seemed potentially misleading (as well as tedious) to subsume every single project or episode within a broader comparative framework of my own invention. The "points of dialogue" among these activists' positions—the underlying parallels, the instructive divergences—will, therefore, remain more or less implicit until I take them up for extended discussion in the concluding chapter.

Louise Weiss addresses the opening session of the European Parliament (Strasbourg, 1979).
Courtesy of Information Bureau of the European Parliament.

Albert Einstein and Leo Szilard in 1946, reenacting the signing of their fateful 1939 letter to Franklin Roosevelt: "It is conceivable that extremely powerful bombs of a new type . . ." March of Time. Copyright Time Life Films, Inc. Courtesy SFM Entertainment.

E. P. Thompson speaking before a London peace rally (1981). Courtesy of
END/European Dialogue.

Danilo Dolci (in handcuffs) being led from Palermo's *Ucciardone* prison to his trial (March 1956). Courtesy of Agenzia Publifoto, Milan.

Peace through Strength: Louise Weiss's Global *Realpolitik*

To whom will the power go?
To whom the right to live?
To the strongest!

—Louise Weiss, 1975[1]

In the summer of 1944, the French journalist Louise Weiss returned to what was left of her home in Paris. Only a few weeks before, the Nazi officers who had lived there for three years had finally fled northward with the last of Hitler's troops. They had not left much behind: her paintings were gone, her furniture ransacked or missing. Most painful of all, for Weiss, was the loss of several cartons containing all her personal correspondence and writings from the 1920s and 1930s. Unpublished interviews with Léon Blum, notes describing late-night conversations with Paul Valéry, long manuscripts detailing her ongoing debates with Aristide Briand—these documents, now irretrievably lost, had testified to an entire era in her life. For nearly twenty years, Weiss had been a passionate advocate of the League of Nations and of the liberal internationalism that it incarnated. In 1920 she had advocated sending humanitarian aid to the starving Soviets, and until the mid-1930s she had repeatedly supported all efforts for a Franco-German rapprochement. Yet as she looked back on those well-intentioned efforts from the perspective of 1944, she felt an uncontrollable bitterness: she had been nothing but a fool. In her memoirs, written many years later, she argued that if any universal trait characterized human beings, it was not a higher capability for justice but rather the will to dominate others. Hitler had proved, with shattering finality, that what ultimately carried weight in the shaping of history was not tolerance or the spirit of compromise but rather brute force and blind conviction.

Such principles as these did not come easily to a woman like Weiss, and it took nearly half a century of harsh lessons before her innate passion turned definitively from fervent idealism toward the more aggressive outlook of her later years. In the aftermath of World War II, Weiss was continuously haunted by the image of the French debacle of 1940 replayed on a larger scale, with the entire West as the bewildered victim of overwhelming aggression from without. This fear did not turn Weiss into a mainstream Cold Warrior, however, for her interpretation of postwar events led her to scorn the narrowly bipolar rivalry between the superpowers as only one aspect of a much broader struggle for supremacy among many nations, ideologies, and racial groups.

Weiss's primary distaste for the Cold War sprang from the fact that it raised Russia and America into a position of hegemony, turning her fellow Europeans into "dishonest and beggarly vassals" who no longer aspired to shape the world's future.[2] From her peculiarly French perspective, she emphasized the eclipse of Europe (and a fortiori of France) within a world where the dominant tensions of geopolitics and ideology had gravitated into the exclusive control of Washington and Moscow. Within her own alternative vision of the future, the United States and Soviet Union would gradually become elements in a broader, multipolar arena of world power; and the ideological tension between capitalism and communism would resume its place alongside other forms of collective bonding such as those of race and religion. The Cold War had stifled this diversity of alignments, but the diversity was inexorably re-emerging: it was this process that she sought to encourage and hasten among the elite circles of European politics.

1893–1940: The Weakness of Liberal Internationalism

Louise Weiss was born in 1893 in the small town of Arras, near the English Channel and the Belgian border in the French region of Picardy. Her entire family had fled there one generation before, after Germany seized their native province of Alsace in the Franco-Prussian war of 1870. Throughout Weiss's childhood, the annexation of Alsace and Lorraine remained a source of serious friction between France and Germany, and the name of Otto von Bismarck (who had presided over the German victory) evoked a deep-seated mood of *revanchisme* among most Frenchmen. Weiss's father, a mining engineer, took Louise and her three brothers on long bicycling trips through the two "lost provinces," so that they would never forget the injustice done to the land of their ancestors.[3] Louise certainly did not forget, but her austere father might have disapproved of the way she savored historical irony: eight decades later, his daughter was elected to the first Parliament of Europe, which met in the Alsatian city of Strasbourg. The two "lost provinces" had returned to France in 1919, but in the 1980s Louise Weiss was far more interested in forging the union of France and West Germany than in the anachronism of *revanche*. She acquired a pet cat and named it after a man whose ruthless empire-building inspired her: Bismarck.[4]

The France of the *Belle Epoque,* in which Weiss grew up, was a world perhaps nearer in spirit and structure to the Europe of Napoleon than to that of De Gaulle. In 1900, France was still the world's largest exporter of iron ore and the third-largest producer of wheat. France's principal rivals were Germany on land and Great Britain overseas. A central issue in French politics was the right of the state to control the Catholic Church, and monarchists only recently had lost their position as key contenders for governmental power. Peasants working on the land made up 40 percent of the French population, and in 1900 a new piece of "progressive" legislation restricted child labor to ten hours per day.[5]

The situation for women, as Weiss rapidly discovered, was still conditioned by the rigid values of the nineteenth century. Although women comprised 37 percent of the French work force, they were paid only half as much as men, and they were restricted to such areas of work as domestic service, textiles, clerical work, and elementary school teaching.[6] As late as 1914, a mere 10 percent of all university students were women; and unfortunately for the young Louise, her father regarded that 10 percent with stern disapproval. He had raised his daughter with all the genteel appurtenances of the *haute bourgeoisie*—from domestic servants to summers in England and Belgium—and he thought that a woman's education should be oriented exclusively toward the satisfaction of a future husband and the raising of a family. Louise's mother, however, had a different opinion. She herself was descended from a long line of Alsatian Jews, but she held convictions that ran counter to tradition: anticlerical, rationalistic, strong-willed, she taught her daughter to cherish independence of spirit above all other things. Thus, while Louise's mother preserved the outward forms of deference to her Protestant husband, she was not entirely displeased when she heard that Louise, at age ten, had punched a classmate in the nose for calling her a Jew and a freethinking *Dreyfusarde*.[7]

The Weiss family moved to Paris in 1899, and Louise attended an elite private school in the elegant quarter of Auteuil. She soon distinguished herself as a student of such exceptional promise that one of her teachers offered to give her private lessons for free. After receiving her *baccalauréat,* Weiss began preparing for the rigorous state examination known as the *Agrégation,* which qualified one to teach in France's secondary schools. She chose as her field of specialization the broad field of Literature and Culture (or *Lettres*). Since her father would have adamantly opposed any such ambitions in his daughter, she patiently waited every night for the rest of the family to go to bed and then, in great secrecy, began her readings and compositions. She kept up this double existence for three years, and in July 1914—amid the mounting tensions of a continent preparing for war—she took the exam and came out first in her class. Her father, presented with a fait accompli, grudgingly accepted his daughter's defiance of paternal authority; by way of congratulations, however, he curtly told her that he would have preferred to see such an achievement in one of his sons.[8]

She was twenty-one years old and had only begun to discover what a high price one paid to defy social conventions and succeed as a woman in a man's world. Constantly torn between the accepted ideals of femininity and her passionate desire to affirm herself in public life, she was to face bitter choices that nearly always resulted in the sacrificing of her feelings and personal relationships. Only a few years later, when she had become a successful journalist, she fell in love with Milan Stefanik, a young Czech nationalist who had come to Paris to drum up French support for his country. They developed a strong intellectual and affective bond, yet the relationship ended badly, in 1919, when the young man admitted to Weiss that he did not know how he could live beside a forceful woman who was his equal. "I will never be your master," he explained: "I've never been able to teach you anything."[9] Looking back on the sorrowful episode in her memoirs, a half-century later, Weiss wrote with typical frankness:

> Suddenly I understood the strange visits I sometimes received from the wives and mistresses of my journalistic colleagues. They wanted to see for themselves how attractive I was—and they all left my office reassured. Was I really such a monster? Probably.
>
> Political ambition was not what moved me. What I loved was exploration, intellectual discovery. How could I accept the ordinariness of a family life? What a defeat! . . . The alternative before me: to devour the planet or devour myself.[10]

Unfortunately, while she tried hard to channel the energies of her lonely personal life into the passion of her public endeavors, Weiss's memoirs often convey a sense of regret or bitterness, as if she suspected by moments that her independence had been dearly bought indeed. Although she felt sure that she could have followed no other path, the character trait she bluntly described as "my feminine inadequacy" remained a source of anguish throughout her long life.[11]

The First World War provided Weiss with a valuable opportunity to express this strong sense of independence and personal initiative: at age twenty-two she organized a small field hospital for the survivors of the trenches. In the northwestern countryside of Brittany, well behind the battle lines, the women and children of the Weiss family had settled to wait out the war. Weiss decided she could best help the war effort by taking care of the more lightly wounded soldiers who needed a place to convalesce. After a good deal of pleading and bargaining with the harried officials of the government and the Red Cross, she obtained enough rations and medical supplies to support a few dozen men. It was here, in direct contact with those who had fought in the trenches, that she began to form a new picture of war, a concrete and human picture far removed from the abstract conceptions of her university readings. The dreadful wounds, the pitiful cries of the soldiers through the night, the simple stoicism of these predominantly lower-class men—these realities contrasted sharply with all her received ideas about nationalism, virtue, and glory. She began to hate this war even more than she hated the Germans, and she resolved to do everything in her power to prevent its ever happening again.[12]

Three years later, in 1917, a chance to make a broader impact on the war presented itself. The French population was becoming deeply demoralized by the stalemate that was killing off a generation, and rumors began to circulate about negotiating a separate peace with Germany. On the Eastern front, Russia had been taken over by the Bolsheviks and was withdrawing from the war. The

United States had declared war on Germany, but few American troops could be expected until the following year. It was in these uncertain circumstances that Weiss was approached by a distant acquaintance from Paris, a man with the odoriferous name of Hyacinthe Philouze, with the idea of founding a new weekly magazine. Philouze had received a generous bequest from a rich friend in the trenches, and his aim was to create a regular forum in which to debate the ideas and policies that would shape the postwar world. He needed the help of someone well-educated and willing to work hard for low pay; he was not bothered by the fact that she was a woman. Delighted at this rare opportunity, Weiss overrode her family's objections and returned to Paris to begin her new job.

The first issue of *L'Europe Nouvelle* ("The New Europe") came out on January 12, 1918. The journal was oriented toward an international readership interested in foreign affairs, but during its early years it clearly reflected the lack of experience and still vague ideas of its founders. High-flown rhetoric about international cooperation was the order of the day, but it remained unclear on what tangible foundations this cooperation could be built. Gradually, however, Weiss consolidated her control over the journal, becoming the editor-in-chief by 1923 and imparting a greater coherency to its articles. Interviewing politicians, traveling throughout Europe, learning to defend her journal's finances from unscrupulous businessmen, she built up a formidable network of contacts and friendships, and established herself as a respected figure in the male-dominated world of French journalism and politics.

Weiss published her first major series of articles in the fall of 1921, when she traveled to Moscow by train to see for herself what the Bolsheviks were doing in Russia. What she found was a country still caught up in a spirit of war—war against the encircling capitalist powers, against the White Russian counterrevolutionaries, against anarchists and Mensheviks, and above all against the widespread famine that threatened the Russian people after seven years of fighting and political turmoil. Weiss spent five weeks in the near chaos of Moscow, closely tailed by agents from the dreaded *Cheka* (the early forerunner of the KGB). She interviewed several Bolshevik leaders, including Kamenev, Radek, Chicherin, and Trotsky—and her exchanges with Trotsky revealed her lively journalistic style:

> TROTSKY: The French *petite bourgeoisie* controls your government. And when they hear about the misery in Russia, they say to themselves: "Patience, patience. This will be the death of communism. We, the bourgeois, will hold on longer than them . . ."
>
> WEISS (interrupting): You're biased. When your government called for emergency aid, . . . I assure you that many Frenchmen sincerely believed we should rush to the assistance of the starving.
>
> TROTSKY: Perhaps. But that's not the French government's atti-

tude. Your government's information about Russia is gotten from White Russian exiles and from French citizens with vested interests over here: you don't have a true picture of what's happening in Russia.

WEISS: You reproach the French government for this, . . . but you have a great advantage over us, because we cannot make our voice heard here in Russia. You, on the other hand, exercise control over several communist publications appearing in France. Our leaders read those publications, and you can hardly blame them for relying on the picture they convey . . .

TROTSKY (interrupting): Excuse me. Is it an interview that you want, or a political argument?[13]

Despite the critical tone of her articles, however, Weiss was impressed by the Bolsheviks. She noted with approval the strong morale and discipline that Trotsky had created, by sheer force of will, within the Red Army; and she was enthusiastic about Lenin's New Economic Policy (NEP), which was just being launched. The Soviet Foreign Affairs Commissar Chicherin had explained to her that the NEP—a scaling back of pure communism in favor of a mixed socialist-capitalist economy—was not just a tactical move but a logical development in the revolutionary struggle. "We are now entering a phase of peaceful consolidation," Chicherin argued; "we need to make an internal compromise with the Russian peasants and *petits-bourgeois,* and an external compromise with the capitalists, who would invest their money in Russia." [14] This apparent tendency toward moderation appealed to Weiss, and she closed her series of articles with an urgent appeal for Western aid to Russia:

> If we conclude that the leaders in Moscow are not *entirely* responsible for the famine; if we admit that many of those leaders truly desire to better the conditions of the Russian masses, while *giving up their incendiary plans for a worldwide revolution;* if we believe that they are capable of understanding the requirements of coexistence on the planet; then why should we not come to the assistance of this people whose blood was so recently flowing along with ours on the field of battle?[15]

This sentiment of generosity toward a regime she clearly disliked was typical of the tolerant internationalism that Weiss espoused during the 1920s and early 1930s. Like many other intellectuals, particularly in France and Britain, she fervently hoped that the League of Nations might bring into common practice a new principle of international arbitration; and she developed *L'Europe Nouvelle* into an increasingly sophisticated instrument of advocacy for this ideal. Paralleling the work of the League of Nations Union in Britain, Weiss's influential magazine embodied a strong current in French opinion that regarded the hard-nosed pursuit of "national self-interest" as a dangerous anachronism.[16] The causes of World War I, according to this perspective, did not lie in the aggression of any single nation but in the broader system of selfish imperialist rivalries that had governed the prewar world. This did not mean, however, that internationalists like Weiss necessarily advocated a dismantling of all colonial structures and the emancipation of the non-European peoples. For the 1920s and 1930s, such beliefs were still considered too radical by many French and British citizens;[17] and since France and Britain wielded preponderant influence within the League, this nominally 'internationalist" body accordingly perpetuated many of the old institutions of imperialism under the euphemism of "mandated territories."[18]

Weiss's internationalism, rather, possessed a more sharply circumscribed meaning: it focused primarily on Europe's internal divisions and conflicts, seeking a new mentality, and new legal mechanisms, that might avert another continental war. In the editorials Weiss wrote through the 1920s, she showed a particular sensitivity to the grievances of nations like Germany and Russia that had been excluded from the League. Her great fear was that a majority of Germans, Italians, or Russians might come to view the League as nothing but an administrative device for preserving Anglo-French domination over Western and Central Europe. At the same time, however, she understood the dilemma of French statesmen who felt abandoned by Britain and the United States and who became obsessed as a result with the question of national security. In the absence of British support, it was not surprising to her that France should choose to act unilaterally, as it did in the forcible occupation of the German *Ruhr* in 1923.[19]

The great difficulty of building a new international system, she gradually realized, was that a single vision of a desirable postwar order had to animate the statesmen of different nations *simultaneously;* the tragedy of the 1920s, in her view, lay in the failure to achieve such a consensus. While she applauded the Locarno Treaty of 1925 for the compromise it created between France and Germany, she still sensed that German statesmen were far from satisfied.[20] She strongly approved the Kellogg-Briand pact of 1928, which sought to outlaw war as a means of settling international disputes; yet she pointed out that this purely juridical and moral treaty was still far from providing a reliable means of enforcing the peace.[21] As long as Britain remained suspicious of France, and Germany remained fundamentally resentful of the Versailles Treaty, the League of Nations would be crippled.

After 1929, Weiss's worst fears began to come true. The onset of the Great Depression drove each member of the League into increasingly narrow and self-interested policies of economic autarky. In Germany, the economic collapse rapidly brought Hitler's xenophobic nationalism from the fringes to the center of political life. Deeply alarmed, Weiss decided in 1930 that publishing *L'Europe Nouvelle* was not enough; she had to participate more directly in the shaping of public opinion—before it was too late. As far back as 1925, she had already been thinking about a new discipline, halfway between academics and contemporary politics, that she called the "science of peace."[22] Now, in October 1930, she founded an institution that would focus exclusively on the building of such a science: an Ecole de la Paix, or "Peace Academy."

Drawing upon the full resources of *L'Europe Nouvelle* and her many connections in politics, she secured the regular support and participation of such diverse figures as France's Prime Minister Edouard Herriot, the poet Paul Valéry, the scholars Elie Halévy and André Siegfried, along with dozens of French government officials and industrial leaders, foreign ambassadors, and key functionaries from the League of Nations.[23] The academy met once a week in the Théâtre Richelieu at the Sorbonne; its conferences usually featured a prominent guest speaker, followed by a panel discussion. Although they were open to the general public, these conferences were explicitly designed to provide a meeting ground for an elite group of influential international figures. Weiss's records indicated an average attendance of about four hundred persons, roughly a fifth of them foreigners, with professional ties ranging from banking to diplomacy, from journalism to the military.[24]

The goal of the Ecole de la Paix was to create a neutral platform where experienced individuals could speak, not as Frenchmen or Germans or Britons but as witnesses testifying as impartially as possible on the major problems facing Europe and the world. Weiss founded her Ecole, in other words, upon a desperate gamble—a gamble that European elites might still find a moderate common ground, across national boundaries and outside party politics. Speaking before the Ecole in May 1931, a professor from the University of Berlin (identified only as Mr. Becker) told the assembled group that most Germans regarded their country's recent admission to the League not as a step toward peace but only as a painful reminder of Germany's inferior status.[25] Following Becker, French Foreign Minister Anatole de Monzie warned the group that it was not possible, in the long run, to exclude Soviet Russia from the new European order they were seeking to build. "Precisely because our formula of justice is incompatible with that of Soviet society," he said,

> we must find a way to bring our mutual differences before a tribunal of arbitration. Such a tribunal would have to start out as a group of experts, of specialized negotiators and technicians; but it might gradually expand its purview from the narrower economic issues to broader questions of national importance. . . . As long as entire peoples remain excluded from the postwar system of peace, those peoples may someday cause the peace to fail.[26]

Grappling with difficult political matters such as these, but also focusing on the technical, economic, and administrative obstacles confronting the League, the members of the Ecole de la Paix met regularly from 1930 until 1936. During these six years, however, the spirit of moderation and conciliation in international politics suffered one serious blow after another. Japanese incursions into China, Hitler's rise to power in Germany, Italian aggression in Ethiopia—these ominous developments, which the League proved powerless to prevent, steadily poisoned the atmosphere that had given Weiss's Ecole its broader meaning. After 1932, moreover, as the full impact of the depression made itself felt in France, the internal political life of the country became dangerously polarized. Fascist groups on the extreme right battled in the streets with increasingly militant leftists and trade unionists. On February 6, 1934, Weiss herself wandered by accident into a massive right-wing demonstration in the Place de la Concorde, and was clubbed into unconsciousness by clashing rioters.[27] "The final conferences of the Ecole de la Paix," she wrote in her memoirs,

> took place amid fear, confusion, tumult, and absenteeism. . . . The totalitarianisms on our eastern and southeastern borders irradiated a sort of darkness that had ended up engulfing Paris. . . . Members of the Ecole heckled at guest speakers, regardless of their arguments, and the speakers heckled back. I was forced to shut down my school.[28]

Already, two years earlier, Weiss had also resigned from *L'Europe Nouvelle*. The three underlying principles of the League—disarmament, collective security, arbitration—had all foundered on the rock of a resurgent nationalism that horrified and bewildered her. Disarmament, she wrote in her memoirs, was impossible to achieve except under strict international controls that no nation was willing to accept. Security seemed to mean something drastically different when one crossed the border from one country to another. Arbitration was futile unless a tribunal could be created with the clout to enforce its own decisions—but all the nations agreed that they wanted no such thing.[29] Editing a journal that incarnated these failed ideals had become too frustrating for Weiss to bear.[30]

Weiss, however, also had personal reasons for leaving *L'Europe Nouvelle*. "I had become an abnormal woman in the eyes of my contemporaries," she wrote,

> a sort of monster of intelligence and authority—someone to be defied, or if possible used, but certainly not loved. Beneath the surface, though, I had remained a ridiculously pale and innocent flower, and I desired nothing more than to be cherished by someone, and mastered.[31]

In 1934, Weiss turned forty-one years old. She felt an irrepressible anguish at the thought of becoming an arid creature who had utterly sacrificed her womanhood for the sake of a career. Shortly after leaving *l'Europe Nouvelle,* she married a young architect of humble origins; but the marriage was not a success and ended soon afterward in divorce. Although she devoted less than a single page of her memoirs and diaries to this episode, it was clear that Weiss's independence of spirit rendered marriage an insufferable solution to the dilemmas of her personal life. "All in all," she pragmatically concluded,

> my marriage did not bring me pleasure but it ultimately provided me with a new legal status as a divorcee. This made my existence a good deal smoother, and opened up romantic possibilities that I would certainly not have encountered as a spinster.[32]

Faced, early in 1934, with the collapse of her political ideals and with a deep anxiety about her own womanhood, it is not surprising that Weiss should have come to channel her prodigious vitality into the causes of feminism and women's suffrage. She was understandably resentful of the social order that had made things so difficult for a talented woman like herself, forcing a cleavage between her personal and public life. At a deeper level, moreover, she was the kind of person who instinctively looked toward high ideals for orientation—an inveterate campaigner who could not help being outraged by the sexist double standard at the heart of French politics. She had had enough of hearing politicians—many of them her personal friends—begin their speeches with the grand flourish, "Ladies, and Citizens!"[33]

It was thus only a matter of eight months between Weiss's resignation from *L'Europe Nouvelle* and her founding of a new feminist organization, La Femme Nouvelle ("The New Woman"), in October 1934. Although she would continue to be occupied with the disintegrating remains of the Ecole de la Paix for another year and a half, the better part of her energy was devoted henceforth to the cause of women's rights. These rights were surprisingly narrow and restrictive in 1934, particularly for a country like France, where the Declaration of the Rights of Man in 1789 had paved the way for an unprecedented broadening of political freedoms throughout the Western world. Whereas women had obtained the right to vote in many European countries in the wake of World War I, French women not only failed to obtain this right until 1944 but remained in the grip of a profoundly discriminatory civil code whose direct roots went back to the *Code Napoléon* of 1803. A married woman was not allowed to travel freely or to take up a profession without the prior consent of her husband; she was similarly constrained in the owning of property and the exercising of commerce; her husband, designated officially as "head of the household," had final say over the schooling and raising of her children. On the other hand, women paid taxes at the same rates that men did and were equally as liable as men to prosecution and punishment for criminal offenses.[34] "We are," Weiss wrote in 1934, "adults in our faults and liabilities, but minors in our rights."[35]

Thus, during the second half of the 1930s, Weiss effectively turned her back on the crescendo of violence that was threatening the peace of Europe, and plunged instead into the intricacies of French domestic politics. Hitler's remilitarization of the Rhineland, the Spanish civil war, the Austro-German *Anschluss,* the Munich crisis—these international events left her with a feeling of powerlessness and bewilderment, but within her own country she at least hoped to bring about a constructive social reform that was long overdue. Weiss did not make a direct connection between the causes of peace and of feminism, as a later generation of activists was to do.[36] Rather, she felt that she had reached a dead end in her campaign for a new international order, and was turning her attention to a separate area where she thought her efforts might prove more effective.

In the fall of 1934, La Femme Nouvelle opened a small office on the Champs-Elysées, where passers-by were soon presented with a controversial exhibit: a huge world map, emblazoned with the words, "American women vote, English women vote, German women vote, Austrian, Czechoslovakian, Hungarian, Chinese women vote. French women do not vote."[37] Weiss organized meetings and rallies, collected funds, and tenaciously lobbied among the halls and committee rooms of the French Senate.[38] When this failed to produce any effect, she mobilized the several hundred active members of La Femme Nouvelle for a political campaign in the Paris quarter of Montmartre, with Weiss herself running as a "symbolic candidate" for the Paris city council. On May 5, 1935, as local gendarmes moved in to arrest the suffragettes for this illegal incursion into politics, the women, at a prearranged signal, doused the men of order with large amounts of rose-scented talcum powder. "Vive les suffragettes!" shouted the women of Montmartre and the newspaper photographers, who knew how to appreciate this peculiarly French adaptation of Gandhian nonviolence.[39]

The following year, when the Popular Front came to power, Weiss was one of three women chosen by Léon Blum to hold ministerial positions in his government; but she turned him down. Blum had made the offer on the condition that Weiss would abandon her suffragist campaign—to which she bluntly responded: "I have struggled, not for the sake of being nominated, but for the right to be elected.[40] After coming tantalizingly close to bringing the issue of women's suffrage to a successful vote in the Chamber of Deputies in 1937, La Femme Nouvelle met its final defeat in 1938, when it failed to win the right for women to participate in noncombatant forms of military service. Indefatigable, Weiss spent the last remaining months of peace organizing emergency aid for the streams of Jewish refugees who were pouring out of Germany and Eastern Europe.[41]

Nevertheless—as if in counterpoint to the general darkening of horizons—Weiss met a man in 1939 who was to become the great love of her life. In her memoirs, she called him *Le Chevalier de Saint-Magloire,* preferring not to divulge his real name lest the details of their love affair might embarrass his surviving relatives[42] The *Chevalier,* who had distinguished himself in the trenches of the last war, was a gentleman farmer who owned land in the countryside of Brie, southeast of Paris. Like Weiss, he was in his late forties when the Germans invaded Poland in September 1939, and the two lovers spent the winter and spring of the "phony war" feverishly enjoying the sort of passion that is usually attributed to couples in their teens and twenties. Weiss had a terrible foreboding that he would be killed in the coming war, for he had insisted on signing up for frontline combat duty, despite her pleas to take a more cautious assignment. In early May 1940, Weiss regularly went to stay with him during visitors' hours at the front, amid the eerie atmosphere of apparent calm while the Nazis made final preparations to attack. On one weekend, Weiss relates in her memoirs, she and her *Chevalier* went out for a last picnic together, in the fields filled with flowers and new leaves. "What I desire," he told her,

> "is that there should be no more French army. In the future, if we had to continue raising troops, Germany would be forced to do the same, and a third war would inevitably come. What I desire is an international army, to guarantee universal order. In such an army, the heroism of the French would be well employed. Do you approve of this wish, my dear one?"
>
> "Not at all. Find something else!" I said.
>
> I held back a sob. My *Chevalier* was still holding on to the idealism of the "war to end all wars," the idealism of the League of Nations for which I had crusaded and which had failed.[43]

On May 10, the German assault finally came, with a blitzkrieg into Belgium and a surprise attack through the Ardennes Forest. On June 9, the *Chevalier* was killed at his artillery position by the banks of the Seine, northwest of Paris. The French government fled to Bordeaux the next day, as it had done in 1914. On June 22, France surrendered to a jubilant Hitler, the ceremonies carefully orchestrated by Nazi officials in the same clearing of the Compiègne Forest where the Germans had signed their armistice in 1918.

1940–1965: The Weakness of European Nation-States

For Louise Weiss, as for so many other French men and women, the following five years became a struggle for physical and emotional survival. In her war memoirs, she resorts to a semifictional form of narrative to capture the feeling of utter disorientation and despair, as millions of personal tragedies—great and small, secret and notorious—came together to form an enduring national trauma. During the first period of the war, when the Germans appeared to be masters of Europe, the French collaborationist regime at Vichy ruled with a relatively light hand, concentrating mainly on the conservative social revolution that its leaders hoped to carry out.[44] Weiss wrote to General Philippe Pétain, the Vichy leader, in July 1940, requesting his permission to travel to the United States in search of badly needed medical supplies for the French war wounded.[45] With Pétain's blessing, she left France through the Spanish border on July 14, 1940, and spent the next six months shuttling between New York and Washington, D.C., struggling to convince American politicians that the pharmaceuticals would not fall into German hands. In the end she succeeded, returning to Vichy in December 1940 with several hundred kilos of materials from the American Red Cross. When Vichy officials promptly asked her to return to the United States—only this time as a spy—she indignantly refused, and became persona non grata in the collaborationist capital.[46]

Weiss then returned to Paris, which was under direct Nazi control. By playing on her Germanic-sounding name and her father's Protestant background, she managed to trick a French bureaucrat in charge of Jewish affairs into issuing a document certifying her as a pure Aryan, thereby fending off deportation to a concentration camp. The remainder of the war became an increasingly dangerous cat-and-mouse game with French and German authorities. In August 1943, her brother André was arrested by agents of the French *milice* (the Vichy regime's equivalent of the Gestapo), on vague charges of aiding the Resistance; but Louise was able to capitalize on the vacillating loyalties of a local prefect and secured his release. She herself was acquainted with several highly placed members of the Resistance; but her own role remained quite limited, for the Gestapo had amassed a large file on her prewar activities and sympathies and began keeping her under surveillance.[47] She was thus forced to spend the final months of the Occupation moving from one hiding place to another under a pseudonym.[48]

On August 26, 1944, Charles De Gaulle made his triumphant reentry into liberated Paris, marching from the Arc de Triomphe down the Champs Elysées. Weiss, crushed against a tank by the wildly joyous crowd, managed to catch a glimpse of him as he passed by. Looking back on that day thirty years later, she wrote in her memoirs that the image of this remarkable man striding tall and alone down the broad avenue had produced a strange distortion of perspective, as if France had truly survived through to victory on her own. This was an illusion, Weiss wrote,

> because France would never rediscover its ancient glory and power. It was only a nation of middling strength and resources. Charles de Gaulle, by infusing the French with this sentiment of triumph—a triumph actually won by the Americans and Rus-

sians—was leading them into error. Knowingly. For what he wanted was to give back to a defeated people the sense of their fundamental value.[49]

Nearly all French citizens agreed in 1945 that the political structures of the prewar Third Republic needed to be replaced with something more vigorous, more effective. Such hopes, however, proved unrealizable. Although the extreme Right was largely eclipsed through its association with Fascism, the new Fourth Republic, which was born in October 1946, reflected many of the same parliamentary cleavages, and ultimately the same Left-Right stalemate, that had plagued its predecessor. Even the charisma of General De Gaulle, and the participation of the Communists in government until mid-1947, proved insufficient to tip the balance of internal politics decisively in one direction or the other.[50] The result was a feckless pattern of shuffled cabinets and grumbling compromises painfully similar to those of the 1930s. After 1947, moreover, this inherently mediocre political process, dubbed *immobilisme* by contemporaries, was further buttressed and stabilized by the massive infusion of dollars provided to Western European countries under the Marshall Plan; for the U.S. government, accurately gauging the political polarization in Europe as an opening for increased Soviet influence, quickly offered military guarantees and financial resources of its own. By 1949, only four years after the unspeakable turmoil and volatile hopes that surrounded the German surrender, the tense bipolar order of the Cold War had settled upon the continent.

For Louise Weiss, the decade following the debacle of 1940 marked a profound transformation. Although she herself did not speak of this period as a major turning point, it is clear from her writings that her ideas and emotions were powerfully realigned by the war. The Louise Weiss of the 1930s had certainly been passionate about her ideals, but she had still written in an earnest, questioning, and cautiously optimistic tone. By the late 1940s, when she again took up journalism, Weiss's articles were cynical and bitingly sarcastic, her mood often fey. From the broad-minded internationalism of the interwar years, her thinking hardened and sharpened until it gradually took shape as a militant ideology of Western supremacy over other cultures. She no longer pleaded, mediated, and argued; she either championed or excoriated. "I inscribe the League of Nations upon the gravestone of things that have died in my lifetime," she wrote in 1975, "but I do not salute it. . . . No, I do not. With all the force of my youthful hopefulness—a shattered hope which still wounds me today— I spit on its tomb."[51] This radical shift was probably due to the fact that a deep personal trauma had been superimposed upon an already acute crisis of intellectual ideas and values. The German invasion of 1940 was the culminating event in a series of political disillusionments that had caused growing anguish for Weiss since the early 1930s; and the violent death of her first requited love had only underscored this anguish with the raw immediacy of bereavement.

In 1945, Weiss was fifty-two years old. The Nazis had looted her home in Paris; she had abandoned her career as a journalist a decade before, and she was once again alone. Briefly, in May 1945, she considered going into politics and ran for the city council of Magny-les-Hameaux, a small town northwest of Paris where her family had long owned property. She affiliated herself with the prewar centrist party of the Radicals but was soundly defeated by the Communist candidates, who swept many such local elections in the early postwar years.[52] After this experience, Weiss shifted her allegiance firmly to the Right, where it was to stay for the rest of her life. At the same time, although she became a staunch supporter of General de Gaulle, she resolved to abandon politics and to establish herself once again as a journalist.

Between 1946 and 1965, Weiss criss-crossed continuously through Asia, the Middle East, Africa, and the Americas, writing articles for prominent French newspapers and magazines.[53] She learned the art of filmmaking and hired a permanent cameraman, turning out a total of thirty-seven documentary films for French television. She went on speaking tours for the Académie Française, met regularly with foreign dignitaries, and founded a short-lived political journal, *Le Fer Rouge* ("The Red Iron") in 1957. Her cameraman, Georges Bourdelon, was repeatedly amazed by her tenacity and energy. On one trip through Northern Africa in 1964, when Weiss was seventy-one years old, she drove with him for twelve hours in a jeep, crossing the fringes of the Sahara on a dirt track under the scorching sun, only to arrive at an old colonial outpost and spend half the night fiercely discussing politics with the local residents.[54]

A good deal of this frantic energy came from Weiss's conviction that she was witnessing a historic shipwreck: the foundering of her native Europe in an increasingly hostile and alien world. Three main themes dominated her thought: the dwarfing of European nations by such giants as China, the Soviet Union, and the United States; the weakness of Western liberal values before a rising tide of authoritarian practices and ideologies; and the demise of European colonial empires under the onslaught of Third World nationalism.

These three themes were closely linked in Weiss's mind; and the key to them all, for her, lay in the troubled history of colonialism. By 1945, France had been acquiring and governing overseas possessions for roughly two centuries, and its empire encompassed territories twenty times larger than the metropolitan nation itself. Second only to the British empire in size and importance, the French empire had provided fighting soldiers for the two world wars, valuable raw materials, and a substantial market for French industrial products during the depression. It embraced extremely diverse cultures—from Vietnam to such North African Arab countries as Algeria and Morocco; from black African territories like Senegal, Gabon, and Madagascar to tiny Pacific or Caribbean islands like Tahiti or Martinique. These far-flung lands were governed by a complex hierarchy of French administrators and indigenous elites, all of whom looked to Paris for the setting of basic policy.

Although the empire was openly authoritarian in structure, and had been consolidated through military conquest, it was not regarded by most French citizens as an object of spoliation or outright subjugation. Rather, the ideology that made colonialism palatable (and even honorable) for many French men and women was that of the *mission civilisatrice*—the duty of the White Man to introduce an inherently superior form of civilization to the unfortunate peoples whom progress had passed by. From religion to sanitation, from natural science to agriculture, the metropolitan culture became the self-appointed educator and protector of the non-European peoples.

To Louise Weiss, this ideology seemed fundamentally valid and reasonable. In February 1954, at a time when her travels focused on Northern Africa and the Middle East, she gave an important speech before the prestigious Academy of Moral and Political Sciences in Paris. She had been nominated for membership in the academy, and her lecture was designed to impress an audience of renowned scholars and experts. "I ask you to follow me," she said,

> to Helouan, on the right bank of the Nile. . . . The year is 1948. A young Italian scholar, Fernand de Bono, had recently discovered a group of tombs dating back to approximately 6,000 B.C. The dryness of the sand had perfectly preserved the bones of these ancient Egyptians, their cereal grains and bouquets of flowers, symbols of their elementary religious convictions. Fernand de Bono assured me that certain Chillouk tribes, living nearby today in the Anglo-Egyptian Sudan, still bury their dead in the same way. I inferred from this that 8,000 years of mental evolution separate us—you and me, gentlemen, and Europe in general—from these illiterate Chillouk tribes. And yet, in order to resolve the conflict between the British crown and the Egyptian government, these tribespeople have been given the right to vote—our European right to vote, conquered after so many struggles and so many hard-won shifts in public and private consciousness. . . .
>
> Paternalism—which has recently been denounced as an infamous and outdated form of governance—appears to be the only psychologically valid type of relationship with such primitive peoples. Practiced in many different forms, while these peoples advance step-by-step from one mental age to another, paternalism has given excellent results from the human point of view.[55]

In this speech, Weiss was synthesizing two opposed currents of French thought on colonial relations—the position of "Assimilation" and that of "Association."[56] The former viewpoint had its roots in the radical egalitarianism of the French Revolution. Its proponents, who dominated French colonial policy until the 1880s and 1890s, fervently believed that the colonized peoples were ultimately entitled to the same rights as French citizens, and that every effort should be made to assimilate them into French culture and nationhood. Therefore, while these assimilationists reluctantly approved of paternalistic rule as a temporary measure, they only justified the colonial relationship as an apprenticeship that would eventually transform other races, quite simply, into Frenchmen of a different color. Toward the end of the nineteenth century, however, this optimistic vision came increasingly under attack. Thinkers like Gustave Le Bon, Ernest Seillère, and Jules Harmand, heavily influenced by Social Darwinism, began to argue that some races were inherently better suited to think, plan, and behave like leaders. Other races, they argued, were intrinsically prone to the unclear thinking and disorderly, emotional behavior that impaired effective social action. This inequality was not something that education could rectify, for it presumably rested on such inalterable qualities as cranial capacity, manual dexterity, and other genetically determined characteristics. It was useless, in this view, to seek the cultural assimilation of other races. The best that one could do, rather, was to associate the colonial peoples as permanently unequal partners, establishing a benignly lopsided relationship with them, bringing order and plenty into their lives, while ruling them indefinitely with a firm hand.[57]

Louise Weiss's notion of "mental age" was closely related to the racial theories of the late-nineteenth-century "associationists." It rested on the same use of metaphors—such as "older," "younger," "higher," "lower," "advanced," "backward"—to express a cultural and political bias as if it were a scientific fact.[58] Where Weiss differed from the associationists, however, was in the fluidity of her particular metaphor, which allowed her to incorporate the assimilationist prospect of long-term emancipation, once the tutelage of the white peoples bore fruit at some point in the future.

How could a woman like Weiss, who had so vigorously rejected the racism of the Nazis and the sexist paternalism of French society in the interwar years, adopt such an explicitly racist ideology? The essential difference, as she saw it, was that Hitler's racial theories were exclusive and nihilistic in nature, whereas her own were both inclusive and constructive.[59] While the Nazis justified the mastery of one race and the perpetual subordination or killing of all others, Weiss regarded her own vision as a frank recognition of the inferiority of other cultures, coupled with a profoundly humanitarian impulse to elevate and to edify them.

Many of Weiss's documentary films and travel writings were accordingly designed to show the French public what a positive impact the colonial endeavor had produced. In one pair of films, for instance, she juxtaposed two stark images from black Africa: the ritual (practiced by tribes in Madagascar) of unearthing and reburying dead bodies after they had been in the ground for one year; and, by contrast, the solemn testimonial of an aged black tribal chief from the Comoro islands, impeccably dressed in a French officer's uniform: "I was born French. I fought for France. I do not want to die anything but French."[60] The ghoulish details of the first film were calculated to elicit a response of disgust and contempt from European audiences; while the dignified loyalty of the assimilated tribal chief provided a reassuring impression of colonial harmony and progress. Like classic advertising photographs of "before" and "after," these two images tried to demonstrate the success of the French *mission civilisatrice.*

Weiss admitted, of course, that colonialism was not a purely humanitarian enterprise. "It goes without saying that private fortunes have been made," she told a group of reporters at the Paris Anglo-American Press Club in 1950,

> but those who made these profits by-and-large had a high conception of their duties toward the indigenous peoples. . . . It is not the Europeans who have created the unspeakable misery of the Asians and Africans, their epidemics and ignorance; it is not the Europeans who invented their petty despotisms and their rotten systems of feudal government. On the contrary, the Europeans . . . built schools, hospitals, libraries, and churches.[61]

Had the colonial powers committed any serious errors or transgressions? Yes, Weiss thought: they had failed to accord the indigenous elites a sufficient opportunity for upward mobility. "Equal treatment for equal diplomas," she wrote in her personal notes on the Vietnamese situation in 1950:

> this principle, followed to the letter, would have won our victory for us. It would have provoked such a strong assimilation in the long run that the Vietnamese would eventually have come to hold the true reins of power in their country—all without clashes and dramatic confrontations. . . . But when a Vietnamese clerk or manager perceived that he was getting paid only slightly more than the coolies and manual laborers, while the French bureaucrats received three times as much, he concluded: "The system allows Whites to live the grand life, at the expense of the Yellow race."[62]

What Weiss tenaciously ignored in her films and writings were the countless gradations of violence inherently involved in colonial paternalism—from the loss of a distinct cultural identity, to the humiliation of enforced obedience, to the outright brutality that defined the final limits of compliance and resistance. Those who saw her documentaries and read her books were not told about the traditions of "exemplary repression" through which native populations were terrified into submission: the burning alive of Haitian ex-slaves in sulphur-impregnated shirts by Napoleon's general Rochambeau (1802);[63] or the 1903 public execution of a black prisoner in French Equatorial Africa "by discharging a stick of dynamite attached to his body."[64] Weiss's audiences did not hear about the widespread institution of corporal punishment, the forced resettlement of populations, and the techniques used well into the twentieth century by colonial officials to coerce natives to work on the plantations—from taking hostages to burning their villages.[65] Between 1922 and 1934, for example, the construction of the Congo-Ocean railroad was carried out by 120,000 forced laborers under conditions that made a mockery of the International Labor Organization's guidelines: "I have need of 10,000 dead for my railroad," remarked the French governor in charge.[66]

Weiss's confident vision of the *mission civilisatrice* also flew in the face of readily available statistics. Far from educating the native peoples, the French colonial schools were designed to turn out compliant indigenous minorities who would mediate between the metropolitan power and the local populations. The result was that only 1 or 2 percent of the indigenous populations tended to receive some form of European education.[67] As for economic investment in the empire, it remained below 15 percent of French foreign investments until the late 1920s, and sharply accelerated only after 1945 (as pressures for decolonization mounted).[68]

These kinds of facts apparently eluded Louise Weiss; they constituted a major "blind spot" for this woman who, in other areas of politics, had shown herself capable of lucid attention to empirical realities. Like the vast majority of white colonialists, she focused only on those achievements that reinforced the legitimacy of the White Man's power: the curtailing of epidemic diseases, the orderly settlements, the roads and plantations that appealed to European conceptions of efficiency.[69] The idea that Africans and Vietnamese, Arabs and Polynesians, might feel the same forms of deep humiliation and indignation that she had felt as a woman in interwar France—this idea, if it occurred to her, was never acknowledged. She addressed French-speaking black men in the familiar "tu" form, as one addresses a child, and clung to her concepts of native backwardness and French generosity.[70]

Weiss was not alone, moreover, in holding fast to the ideology of the *mission civilisatrice* well after World War II. On the contrary, she was articulating the convictions of a clear majority of French citizens at least until the mid-1950s. A public opinion poll conducted as late as April 1956 showed that 75 percent of the French population considered it very important (48%) or fairly important (27%) to maintain the close association between France and her colonies or ex-colonies, while only 11 percent thought this was unimportant. Similarly, in a nationwide poll conducted in 1957, 70 percent of the respondents believed that France's colonial endeavor had produced very good results (25%) or fairly good results (45%), whereas only 19 percent regarded French colonialism as having produced fairly bad results (15%) or very bad results (4%). "These sentiments," the authors of the 1957 poll observed, "are fairly evenly distributed among all categories of the population, regardless of age or social *milieu*. They are dominant even among the working classes, and become still more intense as one reaches the higher socio-cultural levels."[71] Even the French Left, which might be expected to have followed Lenin's bitter denunciation of imperialism, either remained ambivalent about colonial rule (as in the case of the Blum government) or actively supportive of it (like the government of the Socialist Guy Mollet in 1955). Apart from the danger of abruptly liberating subject peoples who might promptly fall under the influence of other nations, most French Socialists (and many Communists) believed that the populations of the non-European countries would not become good socialists unless they first acquired a solid sense of European values and social organization.[72]

As a result of this complex consensus which spanned French society from Left to Right, the process of decolonization proved far more difficult and lacerating for France than it did for England. Ever since the mid-nineteenth century and the Franco-Prussian War, many Frenchmen had come to regard their Empire as a compensation for a perceived decline in France's European power and prestige. Perhaps even more than the British, moreover, the French tended to perceive the abandonment of their colonies not only as a military or economic issue but as a moral humiliation. To let go of the *mission civilisatrice* was to question all those self-confidently Eurocentric values that had made possible the French projection of power from the start. In the fifteenth century, the center of the universe had not easily been displaced outward from the earth to the sun; and decolonization required an analogous, and equally disturbing, rearrangement of mental horizons.

The Second World War, however, had irreparably destroyed the image of invincible European superiority upon which all colonial power ultimately rested. Not only had France itself undergone forcible occupation, but it had been ignominiously driven out of Asia by the Japanese. When Algerian and Vietnamese nationalists rebelled against the postwar reassertion of French dominance, therefore, the French military establishment responded with a vengeance. It put down a revolt in Algeria in May 1945 with full-scale armored assaults and aerial bombings, causing deaths in the thousands.[73] A year later, when the Vietnamese proved recalcitrant, the French navy bombarded the Haiphong harbor, killing over fifteen thousand people.[74] In both of these cases, the act of "exemplary repression" failed to produce its traditional effect and instead kindled an even fiercer nationalist movement. Since the Vietnamese leader, Ho Chi Minh, was a Communist both trained and supported by the Soviet Union, the French government was able to rely on massive financial and tactical aid from the United States; by 1954, the United States was paying for over 70 percent of the French military budget.[75] To no avail. After a climactic surrender at Dienbienphu in the Vietnamese hinterland, the French were driven out of Vietnam in 1954, and the fate of this divided country henceforth depended increasingly on Washington.

As for Algeria, the long-simmering revolt among Arab nationalists gradually escalated into all-out war by 1958, with bloody atrocities committed on both sides, and the systematic employment of torture by the intelligence personnel of the French army.[76] Since Algeria had been far more closely tied to France than other colonies, both by extensive white settlement and by its legal status as an integrated *Département* of the metropolitan nation, the issue of Algerian independence brought France to the very brink of civil war. In June 1958, under threats of a military mutiny against the civilian government in Paris, the French Parliament dissolved the Fourth Republic and called up General De Gaulle from retirement to restore national unity.

Charles De Gaulle was an ardent believer in the *mission civilisatrice,* and had consistently sought to restrain or absorb the centrifugal forces in the French empire, ever since the imperial conference at Brazzaville in 1944.[77] He was also a pragmatist, however, and in 1958 he apparently concluded that the costs of colonialism had become too high for France to bear. During the following decade, he presided over a steady and rapid liquidation of empire, using his singular prestige to draw the majority of French people toward a new vision of their world role. By the mid-1960s, when Louise Weiss completed the last of her world travels, France was no longer an imperial power but merely a middle-sized nation like Italy, Spain, or West Germany.

Weiss grudgingly agreed with De Gaulle that France really had no choice but to abandon colonialism. For her, however, this defeat was not caused by any internal contradiction or inherent deficiency in French overseas rule; it was the expression, rather, of a far broader readjustment of global power—a steady weakening of the liberal West, in contrast to the growing influence and resoluteness of Russia, China, and the new nations of the Third World. Weiss's worldview had changed dramatically since the 1920s, and she now deeply believed in Hitler's lesson that there was no choice in world politics but to master others or be mastered by them. Decolonization, from this perspective, did not represent a liberation of subject peoples but merely the gradual replacement of one imperial hegemony by another. The only remaining questions for the twenty-first century were: Who would lead the new empires, and according to what principles?

In this global struggle for dominance, Weiss believed, the West was doing badly mainly because it was divided against itself—and the primary blame for this division she laid at the door of the United States. Precisely at the moment when the Second World War had rendered France and Britain most vulnerable, she argued, the United States had begun to undermine their global influence through a policy of intransigent anticolonialism.[78] Deprived of U.S. support, and confronted by a militant Third World nationalism that Russia and China actively encouraged, the French and the British had been forced to dismantle their empires. The result, in her view, was an immense power vacuum in the Third World, which the United States sought to fill by incorporating many of the ex-colonies into its own network of economic and military ties. Yet by the late 1960s this "informal empire" of the United States was falling apart on all sides. Unlike the Chinese and the Russians, who understood quite well how to consolidate political power among alien peoples, the Americans remained torn between their own ideology of political freedom and the authoritarianism required to run a successful empire.

Having eliminated the French and the British from the game, Weiss argued, the Americans had lacked the essential self-confidence to move aggressively in steering the rest of the world toward their own camp. The future now belonged to those global actors who had no such qualms: Russia, China, and perhaps others. What was taking place could be summed up as a *"Tempête sur l'Occident"*—a "Storm over the West," as she entitled the final volume of her memoirs.

In 1957, at the height of the Algerian war, Weiss briefly interrupted her travels and returned to Paris to found a small political journal, *Le Fer Rouge* ("The Red Iron"). Her aim was to galvanize French opinion around the colonial idea; and although the journal only survived for seven months, its feverish articles gave a fair measure of Weiss's mood:

> Our maps have not ceased to demonstrate the crumbling system of transoceanic defenses set up by the United States. Our editorials have not ceased to decry their moral weakness in the United Nations and in the Middle East. But what can we do? France is their vassal—their dishonest and beggarly vassal. France has chosen, for the sake of living in laziness, corruption, and abundance, to envision no other politics than that of NATO. Our present decomposition will take us through a period of indescribable agony, toward a final collapse in favor of an Asiatic Europe which will wipe us off the map.[79]

American anticolonialism, for Weiss, resulted from two distinct factors: hypocrisy and self-delusion. The United States, she argued, had merely dislodged the colonial hegemony of the French and the British so as to replace it with a more subtle commercial hegemony of its own. "The Americans," she wrote in 1975, "these latecomers on the international scene, needed a moral doctrine to conceal their appetite for world power. . . . Karl Marx had well understood in his day the equivocal nature of American anti-colonialism, and had drawn the right conclusions about it."[80]

This hypocrisy, however, was not in itself what aroused Weiss's anger the most, for she could understand well enough the Machiavellian logic of using a moral ideology to cloak a deeper will to power. What really enraged her was the apparent inability of the Americans to make up their minds: Did they want to be a dominant world power, or not? In their stubborn idealism, she argued, they refused to accept that running an empire required a massive and direct intervention in the affairs of other peoples, as the French and British had once done, and the Russians and Chinese now sought to do.[81] Instead, the Americans tried to influence other governments by increasing or decreasing aid, or by backing certain local elites; and when it came to the use of force, the U.S. leaders remained relatively cautious and indecisive, fearful as they were of alienating their easily isolationist public opinion.[82] This kind of "imperialism at an arm's length," Weiss argued, was fraught with internal contradictions; for it constituted a sufficiently disruptive form of foreign intervention to arouse the hostility of local nationalists, but failed to bring with it the strong civic order and impressive public works that might counterbalance that hostility among the native populations.[83]

The United States was not entirely to blame, however, for the "Storm over the West." Weiss's travels had taken her to China in 1955 and 1958, and it was there, as she made a film about the building of a large earthen dam, that the relative weakness of the West struck her most forcefully. In her film she skillfully conveyed her own sense of awe as multitudes of laborers placidly moved to and fro, guided as if by telepathy, their actions coordinated from some invisible center, while fervently chanting the praises of their leader, Mao Zhe-Dong.[84] The unquestioning conviction of these tens of thousands of minds was a force that easily made up for the lack of heavy trucks and bulldozers. Working with nothing but their hands and voices and creaking wicker baskets, these ardent citizens of the People's Republic raised a huge, looming mass of brown earth across a broad river valley. They lived on rice and faith, Weiss observed; and it was precisely this faith in themselves and in their future that the nations of the West sorely lacked. When Albert Camus received the Nobel Prize for Literature in 1957, Weiss wrote in *Le Fer Rouge:*

> He has only given life to men and women who are alienated from their social environment, strangers to their own instincts, to their fellow men, to their past. . . . After Camus, there remains little to be said about the fierce negations of a Marquis de Sade or a Nietzsche. Always the same disaffected geniuses. Always the same epic of disintegration. Now we understand the symbiosis that unites Camus with the young people of the western world—these youths who . . . wallow in the spiritual destruction that surrounds them. Both Camus and the youth of the West have gone to the extreme limit of disintegration. They are either ignored or regarded with amusement by the millions of young builders who are constructing the Russo-Asiatic world.[85]

Decolonization was particularly important, Weiss believed, because it re-vealed at the heart of Western culture the deepest source of weakness that can afflict a society: it had ceased to believe in itself. This could not be blamed only on the United States; it stemmed from a profound loss of nerve that had run through all of Western civilization since 1945. Weiss did not profess to understand the reasons for this loss of nerve until almost a decade after her travels had ended. She gradually concluded, however, that the Western democ-racies were poisoned by their own success. Their free-market economies produced an overabundance of material goods that encouraged softness and self-indulgence; their political freedoms allowed even the avowed enemies of democracy to work openly in undermining the social consensus that made de-mocracy possible.[86] Compared with the unquestioning discipline, austerity, and self-confidence of the Chinese citizens whose labors she had witnessed, the citizens of Europe and North America seemed hopelessly effete and divided. "A planetary government is imposing its presence," she wrote in 1975,

> [and this] government will not belong to those who possess the best weapons, but rather to those who have succeeded in rallying the minds of others to their own vision of the future: whether freely or by force. I would prefer freely.[87]

Was it possible for a free society to compete with the world's various totalitar-ian ideologies, fanatical religious alignments, and resurgent racial groupings in this global struggle for popular allegiances? This was the question that marked the final years of Louise Weiss's lifetime.

1965–1983: The Strength of a European Superpower

Two decades had elapsed since the end of the Second World War. Weiss, now in her seventies, returned to Paris and began writing her memoirs, which were to occupy her for the next eleven years. Memoir writing, however, did not im-ply a winding down of her active life. On the contrary, Weiss's ambition and vitality continued in all their intensity until a few months before her death in 1983, when she was ninety years old.[88]

Weiss felt certain that her memoirs constituted a testimonial of exceptional literary value, and she pressed her more influential friends to nominate her for a Nobel Prize in Literature and a membership in the Académie Française—both of which eluded her.[89] She was singularly concerned about achieving pub-lic acclaim for her work and seemed to think of herself as a *Grande Dame* of Europe, an emblem of her continent.[90] In 1976, after publishing the last volume of her memoirs, she was awarded the title of *Grand Officier de la Légion D'Honneur* by President Valéry Giscard-D'Estaing, and a few years later re-ceived the Robert Schuman Prize for eminent service to the European ideal.

Yet she remained restless and unsatisfied. Her intelligence and fiery spirit allowed her to move freely among the elite circles of Parisian politicians and intellectuals, but she never quite attained the full stature and eminence to which she felt entitled.[91]

In 1976, at eighty-three years of age, Weiss found (to her surprise) that she was still brimming over with energy and needed a new project to fill her life.[92] During the following three years, she embarked on a continuous series of lectures throughout France and Western Europe, like a missionary ardently preaching a new religion. She traveled back and forth, from Hamburg to Brussels, from Nice to Strasbourg to Bonn.[93] By 1979, she had become well-known as a champion of European unification and was accordingly chosen by the neo-Gaullist leader Jacques Chirac as a candidate for the European Parliament. This would be the first time that a pan-European deliberative body was directly elected by universal suffrage, and Weiss happily joined the campaign, stepping up the pace of her lectures. In June 1979 she was elected on the neo-Gaullist slate and began drafting the opening speech that she had been assigned to give, as the eldest member of the new assembly.

For Weiss, this late entry into politics could not have happened at a better time, for it allowed her to become an official and legitimate representative of a new conception of Europe. This conception had already emerged in her writings during the early 1950s but in a still tentative and embryonic form. Only now, after twenty-five years of evolution in European politics, did it represent something relatively feasible and coherent. Her vision rested on three central currents of postwar history: the European integration movement, the ideals of Gaullism, and the problems posed by decolonization.

The first of these currents—the European integration movement—had won Weiss's allegiance as early as the 1930s, when Edouard Herriot and other statesmen had discussed before her Ecole de la Paix the possibility of creating a European federation of nations.[94] After World War II, however, Weiss's attention had shifted to the colonial question, for she apparently felt that the imminent collapse of the French and British empires took precedence over the distant construction of a united Europe. It was not until the 1970s, therefore, after decolonization was practically complete, that Weiss returned to the "European Idea" as a possible remedy for Western decline. The long and complex trajectory of European integration now became central to Weiss's career, for it was on the rapid acceleration of that supranational process that she staked all her hopes.

European unification was an idea that had captured the imagination of such illustrious thinkers as Kant, Nietzsche, and Ortega y Gasset.[95] Both in the interests of curbing the periodic wars that had ravaged the continent, and in the prospect of marshaling a new strength by abolishing frontiers, these isolated visionaries had become advocates of a supranational Europe long before 1945.

It took the unprecedented destruction of the Second World War, however, as well as the looming power of Russia and America, to impress upon the minds of many Europeans that their ancient national divisions had become more of a burden than an asset. Starting with the anti-Fascist resistance fighters of World War II, therefore, and gradually gaining force during the early postwar years, a substantial movement of European federalists began to emerge as a major political grouping within most of the European nations.

The institutional development of European integration followed a tortuous and irregular rhythm.[96] In 1949, the creation at Strasbourg of a pan-European deliberative body, the Council of Europe, marked the first major step toward unification; and it was followed in 1950 by the highly successful European Coal and Steel Community (ECSC), which pooled key industrial resources of France, West Germany, Italy, Belgium, the Netherlands, and Luxembourg under a single supranational authority. These two successes, however, were followed by a clamorous failure in 1954: the rejection by the French National Assembly of a proposal to unify the armies of the ECSC countries into a single military body (the European Defense Community, or EDC). Five out of the six ECSC nations had formally accepted this radical idea; but the French parliament, after a bitter debate over the trustworthiness of Germany, ultimately defeated the EDC by 309 votes against 250.[97] A United States of Europe—or what amounted to a small but potentially enlargeable superpower—had come remarkably close to realization.

Instead, the proponents of European unification had to settle for a less ambitious creation: the European Economic Community (EEC), which came into being in 1957. The EEC (comprised of the same six nations as the ECSC) bore a certain resemblance to the *Zollverein,* or customs union, that had bound together the tiny German states during the early nineteenth century, paving the way for German nationhood in 1870. Unlike the *Zollverein,* however, the EEC was bringing together peoples with drastically different backgrounds and cultures, from Hamburg to Palermo. Its development was, therefore, a slow and arduous one, fraught with crises, standoffs, and interminable negotiations. The long-term goal, as stated in the founding treaties, was to unify the economies of the member nations as much as possible, breaking down tariff barriers and allowing free movement of workers and goods throughout the community. A gigantic bureaucracy of technicians and lawyers quickly built up in Brussels, Luxembourg City, and Strasbourg, the three cities where the EEC conducted its daily business. During the 1960s, President De Gaulle repeatedly frustrated the more ardent "Europeans" by vetoing the admission of Britain and demanding special concessions to France's farmers.

By the mid-1970s, the EEC had made steady progress toward abolishing trade barriers and had expanded to a membership of nine, adding Denmark, Ireland, and Britain in 1973 (it would later expand again, accepting the membership of Greece, Spain, and Portugal by 1986). Nevertheless, the mid-1970s energy crisis graphically demonstrated the underlying disarray of the community, as member nations flagrantly fended for themselves in cutting separate deals with the petroleum-exporting countries. In July 1979, therefore, when Louise Weiss delivered her inaugural address before the newly elected European Parliament, the achievements of the EC (now formally rebaptized as "European Community") remained rather ambiguous. If one considered that these nations had been at each other's throats only a few decades earlier, then the transformation in European politics seemed remarkable indeed. If one considered, on the other hand, that the goal of the early European federalists had been the creation of a fully integrated supranational entity, then the progress of unification seemed much more disappointing. There was something sadly comical about the European Court in Luxembourg, where nine judges sat in crimson robes, with simultaneous translations and great ceremony, deciding on such momentous issues as the transportation of goat cheese.

This irony was not lost on Louise Weiss. "The institutions of the EC," she told the European Parliament at its opening session, "have made European beets, European butter, European cheeses, wines, veal, and even European pigs. They have not made European people."[98] How to accelerate the process of European integration, forging a higher "European identity" among the new generations? This became a key issue for Weiss in her final years; for Europe's strength vis-à-vis the outside world depended directly on the degree of its internal unity and self-confidence. She lobbied hard in the European Parliament for the creation of a Museum of Europe, and headed the Parliamentary Commission on Youth, Culture, Education, Information, and Sports. In 1980 she traveled to Rome to discuss the promotion of this "European identity" with Pope John Paul II and reported herself fully satisfied that he understood her views.[99] She even created a small institution, the Fondation Louise Weiss, which awarded an annual prize to prominent individuals who advanced the cause of European unity.

Spiritual unity was not enough, however. In Weiss's view, what Europe needed was a sense of its own independent world role, as well as the material means to play that role effectively. "I am no friend of euphemisms," she had said in an honorary speech before the French Senate in 1978:

> let us observe something clearly, once and for all. The two super-powers share a common interest: they do not want a Europe that speaks with a single voice. Although on the surface their [ideological] reasons are opposed, they are secretly in agreement that the fate of the world must be decided by only two nations: themselves. . . . But the long teeth of their power would be dulled if we could create a Third Superpower—all that is lacking for this is the will to grow and impose ourselves.[100]

It was here that the second of the three main components of Weiss's vision—that of Gaullism—came to complement that of European unity.

What did Gaullism represent, as a current of postwar history? General De Gaulle had come to power as president of the newly constituted Fifth Republic in 1958, at the peak of the Algerian crisis. His presidency has been criticized from many angles—as an authoritarian rule in the French tradition of Strong Men like Napoleon, Napoleon III, Boulanger, Clémenceau, and Pétain; as a presidency of show and appearances, lacking in real purpose or substance; and as a remarkable period of inconsistency in foreign affairs, alternating between policies of courtship and of alienation toward Germany, Russia, China, the United States, and the movement for European unification.[101] All these criticisms may contain significant elements of truth, but it is equally important to note, as some historians have done, that De Gaulle always kept one goal foremost in his mind: making the best of France's diminished resources to give her the greatest possible independence and weight in world affairs.[102] Only the harshest of critics, moreover, would seek to deny that De Gaulle's handling of the Algerian crisis between 1958 and 1962 showed all the marks of great statesmanship: courage, flexibility, and a far-sighted commitment to the French national interest that rose well above the bitter sectarian divisions of contemporary French politics.[103]

European integration, in De Gaulle's view, represented both a danger and a valuable opportunity; for he greatly feared the loss of France's unique identity, but always hoped that Europe's growing stature might provide new scope for French world leadership. Above all, he deeply resented the hegemony of the superpowers and did all he could to make a show of independence from them. In the Berlin Crisis of the late 1950s, he took a harshly anti-Soviet position, only to travel to Moscow with great fanfare a few years later. In the mid-1960s, he withdrew the French military from NATO, announcing his displeasure at American dominance over that organization; but he always took pains not to push the Americans toward a full-scale breach. Although his room for maneuver was undeniably limited by the relative decline of French power, his dramatic style was first to deny and then to bestow again those favors of diplomacy and influence over which he still retained control.

For Louise Weiss, all this certainly constituted a step in the right direction, but it was still not enough. Like De Gaulle's successor, Georges Pompidou, she felt that France would inevitably remain a paper tiger—if it was a tiger at all—so long as it tried to dominate Western Europe or to pursue a "politics of grandeur" on its own.[104] Even more than Pompidou, moreover, she deliberately enlarged her sense of patriotism to include all of Europe as her "home," and she regarded the traditional nationalism of many French conservatives as a dangerous anachronism. In her view, what was necessary was a militant "Euro-Gaullism"—a united Europe both fiercely independent from the superpowers and intensely preoccupied with influencing the political development of the Third World. It was here that the third element in her vision—military force—became significant. "Ah, the European Defense Community!" she exclaimed before a West German audience in 1980:

> Today we could begin to undertake military cooperation sector-by-sector. Germans and Frenchmen would work together to design our own missiles analogous to the [American] Pershings and the [Soviet] SS-20s. . . . The recent accords allowing Germany to build its own naval vessels would permit us to develop a European Agency for the Defense of Energy Resources and Strategic Metals. In this way, we could assure our Community its indispensable supply of primary resources. . . .
>
> Rapidly, other members of the community would adjust themselves to such a Franco-German team. . . . In this way, with its own defenses at last, and with a political will of its own being reborn, the weight of Europe would really count in the calculations of force. Better late than never![105]

Unlike Szilard, Thompson, and Dolci, Weiss did not believe that "the calculations of force" in world politics had undergone a major revolution in 1945. In her speeches and memoirs, she coolly acknowledged the potential destructiveness of warfare in the nuclear era;[106] but she contended that the risks of possessing nuclear weapons were far outweighed by the advantages they would offer in the competitive struggle for world power. She apparently did not perceive a nuclear holocaust as a very likely eventuality; what worried her far more were such problems as overpopulation, depletion of natural resources, and, above all, the rise of an aggressively self-assertive Third World. For Weiss, therefore, nuclear weapons did not inaugurate a new and qualitatively different epoch in world politics; on the contrary, they merely constituted the most recent tools invented by human beings in their age-old struggle for domination. Just as statesmen had done throughout history, today's leaders would inevitably continue to vie with each other in seeking the greatest strategic advantage from all the military and psychological factors at their disposal. The possibility that this ancient struggle for supremacy might lead, under contemporary conditions, to a devastating nuclear war, appeared only dimly and fleetingly in her writings. In the entire sixth volume of her memoirs (devoted to the period 1945–75), for instance, Weiss only took up the subject of nuclear war three times—each time devoting no more than a few sentences to it. The following is a representative sample: "Atomic weapons have deterred human beings from fighting each other, because the earth's peoples are simply too afraid [to use these weapons]; but this has not anesthetized their desire to dominate each other."[107] Weiss apparently assumed that the destructiveness of these new weapons would force a sufficient degree of caution upon the world's statesmen and that the risk of accidents or miscalculations remained minimal.[108]

It would be a mistake to say, however, that nuclear weapons did not figure prominently in Weiss's thought. Arguing along the same lines as China's Mao Zhe-Dong, she contended that these weapons were essential to national sovereignty and to independence from the hegemonic pretensions of the two superpowers. If a united Europe possessed its own nuclear missiles, she argued, these would simultaneously serve three essential functions: they would deter Soviet aggression; they would free Europe from the debilitating protection of America's nuclear umbrella; and (perhaps most important) they would increase the leeway for Europe's *nonnuclear* forces to be used against smaller adversaries in the Third World.[109] The possession of nuclear weapons granted one's nation admission to the club of great powers; it accorded the status, and instilled in one's neighbors the fearful respect, that Weiss considered essential to true leadership.

Weiss was too pragmatic to advocate a resurrection of outright colonialism; she understood that the era of direct overseas rule had irrevocably passed away. Consequently, she couched her old paternalism in a new terminology that would appeal to "moderates" of all political stripes: defensive military intervention to "protect Europe's vital interests," and "selective use of economic power" to provide diplomatic leverage. "Until now," she wrote in 1981,

> only American, Russian, and French naval vessels have patrolled in the Indian Ocean to secure the Strait of Hormuz and the other sea lanes. A European effort in this area could be undertaken, with German, Italian, Greek, and English cruisers complementing the work of the French Navy. . . . Other measures of this sort could be undertaken in Europe, before opening negotiations for a full-fledged common defense.[110]

These kinds of "police actions," Weiss thought, would help to galvanize the people of Europe, showing them that supranationality meant more than just haggling over tariffs. In 1976, after Israeli commandos had freed a group of hostages held in Uganda by Palestinian terrorists, Weiss had commented:

> French public opinion totally approves of the Israeli operation. A certain regret has even been expressed concerning the petroleum-producing emirs: for there are some among us who think they could just as easily be brought to heel. Israel is reawakening the values of the West.[111]

As for economic aid, Weiss argued, it was being handed out indiscriminately to both friends and enemies of the Western democracies. In a lengthy proposal to the European Parliament in 1980, she set forth her idea of a new policy:

> The European Community should take into account the absurd situation that has developed at the United Nations, where the bulk of expenses is paid by a minority of democratic nations, and policies

are determined by an anti-European majority of totalitarian nations which pay nothing. With this in mind, the European Community should take back its aid programs into its own hands, overseeing them directly. . . . It should cut off assistance to those nations which only use it to fight against our freedoms.

And she added, almost casually, an open-ended clause for military expeditions: "In those cases where a direct intervention became necessary, a European force should act to save as many lives as possible." [112]

The picture that Weiss painted was, perhaps intentionally, a rather vague and impressionistic one. She was suggesting a broad new spirit rather than spelling out the concrete details of a future foreign policy. European civilization faced a decisive challenge from the Arabs, from the Asians, from the Russians; it had been badly let down by the myopic policies of the United States. A Western European superpower, armed with missiles, a strong navy, and a resolute will, might still defend itself. It could do so most effectively by taking the counteroffensive, channeling the weaker nations of the world (especially in Africa) back toward a modern version of the tutelage that had begun with colonialism. The imperative toward which Weiss had groped in the 1950s now possessed a solid base from which to be realized. "What we are called upon to do," she had written, "is not only to *save,* but to impose upon the world, those moral values that have constituted the greatness of humanity until today." [113]

This worldwide projection of power could never succeed, moreover, unless drastic corrective measures were taken on the domestic front as well. Here, indeed, lay one of the great paradoxes of Weiss's career: she became an increasingly strident champion of liberty and democracy at the same time as her political views were veering more and more openly toward authoritarianism. During the 1930s, she had seen the world's three leading democracies demonstrate an unimaginable weakness before the aggressive provocations of Germany, Italy, and Japan; and it was Stalin, not Blum, who had come to the aid of the Spanish anti-Fascists. She concluded that democracy was becoming inherently unfit for survival, and regarded the vigor of the left-wing and right-wing dictatorships with a sort of horrified admiration. Those who still believed in liberalism would have to make up their minds: either to adapt the structures of liberal democracy for a protracted struggle against these new kinds of enemy, or to stand blindly upon their traditional principles of liberal tolerance and face eventual extinction.

What the democracies needed, in Weiss's opinion, was a stiff dose of governmental authority, to counterbalance the internal division and confusion that had paralyzed them since the 1930s. Throughout her postwar writings and speeches, she inveighed against the Western trade unions, which weakened economic output with their irresponsible and selfish strikes; [114] against the political parties, which placed a higher priority on their own petty rivalries than on the welfare of the social whole; [115] against the universities, whose teachings undermined traditional values of patriotism and authority without offering any constructive synthesis for the young to follow;[116] against the welfare state, which removed the essential incentives to compete and produce;[117] against the abolition of the death penalty, which demonstrated the declining self-confidence of Western society in imposing its own moral values.[118]

For Weiss herself, the tension between democratic ideals and paternalistic power had already come to a head as early as 1953, in a heated conversation with Vincent Auriol, the French president, about education in Morocco.

> WEISS: We have opened admirable colleges where we teach the Moroccans the principles of the French Revolution. . . . We should reconsider this kind of education, . . . for what we are teaching them is precisely how to rebel against us.
>
> AURIOL: But then we would have to prevent them from reading the French classics!
>
> WEISS: Certainly not. But I would stop emphasizing a form of nationalism which . . . does not coincide with French interests.
>
> AURIOL: . . . We can't keep them in ignorance about the history of France . . .
>
> WEISS: No, but we could comment on it from a different perspective.[119]

If education interfered with authority, then education must be restricted, modified. Here Weiss espoused the same principle of "guided education" and one-sided propaganda that she denounced in the totalitarian countries.

Weiss never went so far as to call for the dismantling of representative government in France. Rather, she seems to have hoped that her writings would contribute to a dramatic shift in French public opinion, arousing and alarming a sufficient majority in the electorate to cause a major reorientation in national politics. As with De Gaulle's "crisis investiture" in 1958, she evidently hoped that French citizens would vote overwhelming powers to a new leadership; and that this leadership would then proceed, legally, to impose the necessary restraints on French constitutional rights. "In the dictatorships there is no opposition," she wrote at the conclusion of her memoirs.

> This permits their leaders to execute their long-term designs with great patience, taking advantage of the enemy's liberties to go about methodically sapping his strength. On the other hand, it has become impossible to govern the liberal democracies in the interest of their stability and expansion. . . . Certainly, the voters select their leaders. Yet while giving their leaders power, they hold back the authority to use it.[120]

Democracy, she reasoned, must be strong and unified in order to survive; and in order to become strong, democracy must submit to certain restrictions. A greater degree of direct state control over education, trade unions, and political dissent; a willingness to make strategic alliances with authoritarian but anti-Communist regimes like South Africa;[121] a resolute commitment to project military force wherever the various enemies threatened to advance: these were the kinds of policies that would render democracy strong once again.

Weiss never quite recovered from the trauma of World War II. Throughout the postwar years, the imagery in her writings and the emotional tone of her political views revealed that she had remained fixed in the mentality of wartime. As she became more and more absorbed by questions of geopolitics and the global balance of power, she felt a proportionate distaste for Western political culture with its divisions, stalemates, and perpetual compromises. Instead, she held on tightly to the wartime picture of strong leaders like De Gaulle and Churchill, who had known how to take command and be followed; and she apparently ignored the fact that these same statesmen had quickly adapted themselves, after 1945, to the more arduous exigencies of compromise and democratic consultation that peacetime brought to the fore. By the final decades of her career, she had imperceptibly drifted away from the pluralistic values that she claimed to defend, and was advocating a return to the characteristic social and political structures of a society at war. In the name of defending Western freedom, she was ready to urge that many of the West's essential freedoms be curtailed.

The American political scientist Hans Morgenthau, author of the influential study *Politics among Nations,* had observed the process of European integration with some anxiety as early as 1961. "The time has passed," he wrote,

> when the French or the Germans could dream of making the world over in their own image. Yet if the nations of Western Europe were able to unite and form a new political and military unit of considerable potentialities, they would then have acquired the power basis for a new crusading spirit, common to all of Western Europe, to compete with the nationalistic universalism of other nations.
>
> That the traditional nation-state is obsolescent in view of the technological and military conditions of the contemporary world is obvious. Yet, while trying to replace it with a larger unit, better attuned to these conditions, it is well to take care that it not be replaced simply by a more efficient vehicle for the crusading nationalism of our age.[122]

What Weiss had in mind was precisely what Morgenthau feared: a new crusading superpower. To what extent did this vision correspond to actual trends and serious possibilities in European politics?

Despite the widely publicized abolition of economic barriers among EC nations planned for the 1990s, the political and cultural obstacles to full-fledged supranational integration remain formidable. It remains unclear how the reunification of Germany will affect the already complex internal balance of the EC; nor is it clear how the newly autonomous nations of Eastern Europe will fit into a post–Cold War European order. In Western Europe, the balance of political opinion remains rather evenly distributed around the "moderate" center—a quintessentially pragmatic and cautious center that would find Weiss's vision of European *Sturm und Drang* either abhorrent or impractical, or both. This does not mean, however, that her vision is an insignificant one. On the contrary, the magnifying lens of Weiss's passionate extremism provides a useful glimpse into two rather subtle areas of contemporary European politics. On the one hand, her ideas about European military autonomy are becoming increasingly fashionable among mainstream politicians of both Left and Right. On the other hand, it is interesting to speculate how the emotional appeal of her xenophobic "Euro-nationalism" might grow dramatically if Europe's relative affluence and well-being ever came under serious threat.

The question of building a European defense in separation from NATO surfaced periodically during the decades that followed the collapse of the EDC, but to most Europeans this idea remained nothing more than a pious hope or a chimera.[123] It was not until 1979 that two events—the election of the European Parliament and NATO's decision to place a new class of U.S. missiles in Europe—substantially altered the political prospects of a purely European defense. Widespread popular resentment against the American missiles led many conservatives to reconsider the idea of European military autonomy; and the European Parliament (though it was formally barred from handling military issues) seemed a promising political step toward a future system of common defense. Some politicians publicly considered bringing the Western European Union (W.E.U.) out of mothballs.[124] This organization had been formed in 1948 as a forum for military cooperation between England, France, and several other continental nations in the event of a German resurgence; but it now seemed to offer an even better institutional basis for the inclusion of Germany within a unified Western European command.

All these proposals continued to run into serious obstacles: widespread pacifism in the European Left (except in France), the touchy problem of admitting Germany to the nuclear club, France's reluctance to relinquish its nuclear autonomy, and above all the deep-running *angst* that any advance toward European military independence might produce a concomitant reduction in the U.S. commitment to NATO. Nevertheless, the seed had been planted, and senior French politicians as diverse as Edouard Balladur on the Center-Right and Jean-Pierre Chevènement on the Center-Left began to make concrete proposals that sounded strikingly like a toned-down version of Louise Weiss's grand vision. Balladur (who later became French minister of finance under the premiership of Jacques Chirac) wrote in the *Figaro* in 1980:

Could the nations of Europe—without backing away from their alliances and their ties to the western world—harmonize their armaments, organizing among themselves a permanent system of military cooperation and mutual aid? Our countries, having increased their military capabilities, could intervene together (after having decided together) to defend the peace or their own interests wherever they are threatened—in the Middle East, in the Mediterranean, in Africa, or elsewhere. They could carry weight in the evolution of the world.[125]

Similarly, at a conference in 1987 entitled "Europe Faced by the Empires," the prominent French Socialist Jean-Pierre Chevènement made a ringing plea of his own:

We must explore whether France and Germany are capable of defining together a concept of *European Defense* . . . , and we must see which European nations could join them. . . . The key is to bring forward the consciousness of our European identity, and the ideal of a Europe fully capable of playing its global role. . . . Collectively, we have a heavy responsibility toward the countries of the Third World, to allow each of them to find its own way independently of the models imposed by one or the other of the two superpowers.[126]

Although both these mainstream politicians would no doubt have strongly rejected Weiss's neocolonial ambitions, their publicly articulated yearning for a Europe that would once again "carry weight" signaled the crossing of a significant psychological threshold.[127] Nor were these politicians alone in their longings, for throughout Western Europe the concept of military autonomy was exerting a growing popular appeal—even *before* the ending of the Cold War in 1989–90. In a public opinion poll conducted by the French newspaper *Libération* in 1987, the citizens of Britain, Italy, and West Germany joined the French in pronouncing some startlingly rebellious views about the future of NATO. Should existing relations with NATO be maintained? An average of 35 percent thought they should. Fully 29 percent, however, believed that a united Europe should develop its own military forces separate from NATO; while 25 percent thought that each country should resume its own defense on a purely national basis.[128] Thus, while Louise Weiss's ideas about creating a new military superpower would certainly require the surmounting of many complex obstacles, it would be a serious mistake to underestimate the potential appeal of those ideas in coming decades.

If a European superpower did come into being, what global conditions would tend to push it toward the aggressive shape that Weiss envisioned? Among the many possibilities, a prolonged depression or an acute energy crisis, coupled with a sense of military insecurity, might effectively awaken that assertive European identity for which Weiss had campaigned. One of the uglier precedents lies in the decade of the 1930s, when Europe most recently faced a period of severe hardship. At that time, the instinct of nationalism had still provided the primary point of reference, and Europeans had thrown themselves into a continental "civil war" even more violent than that of 1914. By the year 2000, however, after half a century of peace and quiet economic integration, that narrow force of traditional nationalism may no longer possess its old attraction. The European peoples, no longer finding it plausible to blame each other for their woes, might compensate for this loss of traditional enemies by projecting their collective hostilities outward. A new "Other" might take shape, vaguely sensed beyond the familiar confines of their old continent. If this timeworn mechanism of cultural bonding were indeed to assert itself, then the terrain would be fertile for Hans Morgenthau's fears to begin coming true.

There is no reason, of course, why the tragic history of the interwar years should necessarily repeat itself. On the other hand, Europe's past gives little reason to be smug about Europe's future. Far from being the radiant center of light and humanism that Weiss liked to portray, European civilization has shown the same deep ambiguities as other cultures. Spectacular advances in science and civil rights have gone hand in hand with commensurate refinements in the capacity to brutalize nature and other human beings. Under propitious conditions, those racist and militaristic forces that had proved so strong in European culture from the 1880s to the 1930s might come to the fore once again: from the White Man's Burden in England to the German thirst for *Lebensraum,* from the French *mission civilisatrice* to the Italian myth of a new Roman Empire. Many contemporary Europeans, having witnessed the catastrophe of World War II and the ordeals of decolonization, tend to think of these aggressive ideologies as relics out of a remote past. They are not at all remote, however, nor are they necessarily dead. Although Weiss's extremist vision of a crusading Europe may never come close to full realization, it is useful to be aware of the direction in which she pointed, and of the subtle gradations by which that vision might be approached.

Only two months before she died in a Paris hospital in May 1983, Louise Weiss had still been actively engaged in her writings and speaking-tours on behalf of the "European idea." After her death, most of her contemporaries chose to ignore the more authoritarian aspects of her views, and to emphasize instead the remarkable fusion that she had embodied between a pronounced "Frenchness" and a higher European identity. A page-one obituary in *Le Monde* noted that Helmut Schmidt, when he had been chancellor of West Germany, had referred to Weiss as "the grandmother of Europe," and the obituary went on to narrate in detail the long entanglement of Weiss's life with the key individuals and events of twentieth-century France.[129]

According to former French Prime Minister Pierre Pflimlin, who had become well acquainted with Weiss during his term as president of the European
Parliament, she sincerely thought of herself as a "woman of peace."[130] This
might appear strange, given the blunt aggressiveness of her language and her
ideas; yet it is only strange if one fails to identify the particular current of
"peace through strength" that Weiss had come to represent after World War II.
Like many other French men and women, Weiss regarded the history of the
twentieth century as an object lesson in the need for maintaining unassailable
military power. From the deceptive victory of 1918 to the failure of appeasement, from the debacle of 1940 to the ringing colonial defeats in Vietnam and
Algeria, the French experience of war during Weiss's lifetime resulted in a
deeply rooted sense of national insecurity. As late as the 1980s, Western European peace activists who had mustered vast demonstrations for a denuclearized
continent found themselves repeatedly perplexed by the relative indifference
or hostility that their efforts inspired within France. The overwhelming popularity of the national *force-de-frappe* (nuclear striking force) among French
citizens testified to a desire for absolute military autonomy that cut across all
political and generational boundaries.[131] Weiss's career, therefore, may be best
understood within the context of this peculiarly French tradition of fears and
aspirations. Although many of her authoritarian ideas would have been quickly
repudiated by a majority of French public opinion, other currents in her
thought, if purged of their extremism, came closer to expressing the sentiments
of a nation acutely conscious of its own relative decline.

It would be a mistake, however, to regard the phenomenon of the *mission
civilisatrice* as a purely French cultural product. From ancient Rome to
nineteenth-century Britain, from Japan and Germany in the interwar years to
the United States and Soviet Union after World War II, great powers in their
ascendancy have consistently tended to create a gratifying image of themselves
as bearers of unprecedented peace, justice, and prosperity. As one writer for
Time magazine observed in 1980, Weiss's ideas could easily be applied to other
nations possessing a sense of their own mission abroad:

> [The United States] remains militarily, economically, and morally
> powerful—in the aggregate, far more powerful than Russia. The
> problem is not lack of strength but a bewilderment of will. The
> U.S. must decide how its strength should be applied, and if it is
> willing to pay the inevitably high price for applying strength.
> French author Louise Weiss believes that the present American
> predicament began in a "search for a false popularity," a product of
> the chagrin over the Vietnam years. The quest [for such popularity]
> should be abandoned.[132]

This vision of history as a lusty competition for paramountcy remains the ultimate legacy of Louise Weiss. She had started out her career as an idealist, preaching cooperation, tolerance, and the sanctity of international law. By the mid-1930s, she had seen these principles evaporate into impotent words; and a decade later, she emerged from the dust of a cataclysmic war, deeply embittered. "Never again!" she vowed to herself; and she took up a stance akin to that described by Thucydides in his celebrated Melian dialogue: "[T]he powerful exact what they can, and the weak grant what they must."[133] Her hierarchical style of globalism raises sobering questions even for those who might deeply disagree with it, questions that cannot be avoided by all the idealists of the world who place a certain automatic faith in notions of "global community" and "world federalism." Can processes of supranational unification be divorced from ancient patterns of cultural domination and from hegemonic imbalances in economic and military power? Would the emergence of a European superpower—even if it eschewed Weiss's imperial designs—actually constitute a step toward stable world peace?

Louise Weiss made "hard" questions like these almost impossible to evade, because she had a refreshing quality of calling things by their true name. As she toured the planet, making her films and writing her articles, she painstakingly recorded what she saw: the starving, the power-hungry, the ignorant, the affluent, the cunning, the fanatical, the desperately violent, the abysmally apathetic. Far from the rather pious and legalistic formalism of many advocates of "world order"—yet equally far from acquiescing in the Cold War status quo—Weiss found her own solution in a conception of paternalistic world empire.

This vision may not be dismissed as a mere reactionary anachronism. On the contrary, Weiss clearly understood two fundamental facts of postwar globalism. First, she came squarely to grips with the awesome diversity of the world's cultures, confronting head-on the problem of maintaining order in this pullulating mosaic of human wills. And second, she observed the empirical fact that power in the present world all too often took the shape of domination by some people over others. Even in the Western democracies, she saw signs that deeply worried her: masses of voters more interested in soccer games, Hollywood movies, and a guaranteed pay raise than in having a real say over the affairs of their government. At the global level, she tallied up with consternation the billions of individuals whose minds swayed to and fro in vast ideological tides; and she wondered how liberal values could possibly survive in a planetary climate increasingly hostile to all critical thinking.

Paradoxically, her solution to these problems rested on an authoritarianism and a cultural double standard that contradicted her own liberal values from the start. Nevertheless, she had raised in an unusually clear way the one question that all proponents of a "new globalism" would necessarily face: What shape would power have to take if it was *not* to rest on fear and manipulation? A central problem, for Leo Szilard, E. P. Thompson, and Danilo Dolci, was how to answer this question concretely, while taking into account the harsh but undeniable realities so incisively underscored by Weiss.

Peace through Cooperative Diplomacy: Leo Szilard's Vision of a Superpower Duopoly

Nobody should renounce even the boldest
hopes before human nature has been given
every opportunity to demonstrate its limits.

—Leo Szilard, 1930[1]

Like Louise Weiss, the Hungarian phys-
icist Leo Szilard experienced the ending of the Second World War as a singularly traumatic and ambiguous moment. Weiss had returned to her shattered
home in Paris during the summer of 1944, following on the heels of the fleeing
Nazis. For Szilard, the point of dark and transformative insight did not come
until a year later, in August 1945.

Szilard, too, had suffered personally at the hands of Nazism. As a Jewish
university professor in Berlin, he had been forced to flee, eventually making
his way like so many others to the United States. With the help of his friend
Albert Einstein, he had persuaded Franklin Roosevelt in 1939 that the Germans
might be well on the way to building an atomic bomb; and he had devoted
himself for three frenetic years to the production of plutonium in the Manhattan Project. Like so many other scientists, he had agonized over his moral
responsibility in creating this fearsome new weapon, but he had reasoned that
if *somebody* was going to possess nuclear bombs, it had better be the United
States rather than Hitler's Germany. Now, in August 1945, he saw emblazoned
in the newspaper headlines the news about Hiroshima's obliteration. Never one
to avoid unpleasant truths, he knew that in a very real sense the bomb had been
his idea: his own hands had leveled that city.

For several months Szilard had been urgently seeking to promote discussion
among Manhattan Project scientists and to contact the policymakers in Washington, for he feared that within a few short years a deadly nuclear arms race
would take shape between the United States and the Soviet Union. In one far-
sighted letter to Roosevelt, he predicted the coming era of nuclear-tipped inter-
continental missiles and the potential for unlimited destruction that they
implied.[2]

For Szilard, therefore, the experiences of World War II led to conclusions
that were equally as pessimistic (in one sense) as those reached by Weiss; yet
they thrust in a fundamentally different direction. If the mushroom cloud over
Hiroshima conveyed any clear meaning to him, it was that the modern world
must forever abandon the idea of securing political goals by military means.
Along that path, he ardently believed, lay collective suicide—not this year,
perhaps, nor the next, but someday, inescapably. This was the fundamental
premise of Szilard's reasoning, and from this premise flowed a series of infer-
ences that diverged sharply from those drawn by Weiss. The only rational goal
of statesmanship, under these new circumstances, was not just to build up national strength or to avoid war but to pave the way for something truly unprece-

dented: a permanent peace. The task ahead—an arduous one, he admitted—was to construct a new system of international security in which all the world's peoples would *voluntarily* participate, because it was manifestly in their best interest to do so.

1898–1949: From Science Fiction to the Nuclear Arms Race

Szilard's life story falls unavoidably into two parts: on one side lie all the events leading up to his August 1939 letter to President Roosevelt about making an atomic bomb; on the other side lie all the events that sprang from his letter, as he struggled desperately to bring under control the immense forces he had helped unleash.

Born into a prosperous Budapest family of Jewish merchants in 1898, the eldest of three children, Szilard made an early impression on those around him as an exceptional child.[3] His younger brother, Bela, later told an interviewer that in

> all his youthful pictures—school pictures in high school, six years old, four years old even—[Leo was] dead serious. He wanted always to be different. How consciously I can't tell you. But he [even] dressed differently from his schoolmates.[4]

A frail and sickly child, Leo spent most of his time up to the age of ten at home; he received his early education from his mother and from governesses who taught him German and French. "Very often it is difficult to know where one's set of values comes from," Szilard later observed, "but I have no difficulty in tracing mine to the children's tales which my mother used to tell me. My addiction to the truth is traceable to these tales and so is my predilection for 'Saving the World.' "[5]

One such tale was *The Tragedy of Man,* a dramatic poem written by the Hungarian writer Imre Madach. Four decades later, Szilard could still vividly remember the deep impression that this story had made on him—prodding him to think in broad, eschatological terms that were unusual in a ten-year-old:

> In that book the devil shows Adam the history of mankind, with the sun dying down. Only Eskimos are left and they worry chiefly because there are too many Eskimos and too few seals. The thought is that there remains a rather narrow margin of hope after you have made your prophecy and it is pessimistic.[6]

As an adult, Szilard delighted to think of himself as a brilliant and prescient eccentric; he deliberately cultivated this self-image in his daily actions, and also (not surprisingly) projected it backward onto his own past. It is difficult, therefore, to know just how early in his life he really began thinking of "saving the world." In any case, this picture of a precocious child thinking earnestly about the fate of the earth was the one that Szilard himself carried with him throughout his life.

When he was ten years old, Leo's health improved, and he began attending public school. He easily excelled, eventually winning the Eötvös mathematics prize in a nationwide competition; but his schoolmates apparently did not resent his brilliance.

> For some reason, ... I was always a favorite of the class. ... Perhaps my popularity was ... due to my frankness, which was coupled with a lack of aggression. One of the favorite sports of the class at that time was playing soccer. I was not a good soccer player, but because I was liked there was always a rivalry between the two teams: On whose side would I be? I was sort of a mascot. ... So up to the age of fifteen, when I finally refused, I played every soccer game on one side or the other, very often on the losing side.[7]

Szilard was sixteen when the First World War broke out, and his reaction (as he later recalled it) was characteristically detached and impartial:

> From reading the Hungarian newspapers, it would have appeared that whatever Austria and Germany did was right and whatever England, France, Russia, or America did was wrong. ... Somehow, it seemed to me unlikely that the two nations located in the center of Europe should be invariably right, and that all the other nations should be invariably wrong.[8]

Despite his skepticism, Szilard was drafted into the Austro-Hungarian army in 1917. Before his regiment could reach the front, however, he fell ill with Spanish influenza and arranged to be sent home to Budapest for hospitalization. This illness probably saved his life, for he later received word that his regiment had been all but annihilated in battle.

As the war ended, and the Austro-Hungarian Empire disintegrated, Hungary briefly became a Soviet-style republic under the leadership of the Communist Bela Kun; but in August 1919, the Kun regime was crushed in a violent coup d'état and replaced by the Right-wing dictatorship of Admiral Nicholas Horthy. Szilard decided that Hungary's chaotic political situation did not bode well for his future studies, and he applied for admission to the Engineering School at the University of Berlin. In December 1919, he boarded a train and headed west, beginning the long series of international peregrinations that was to mark his restless career.

Berlin in 1919 was one of the world's foremost centers of theoretical physics; the faculty at the university included such Nobel laureates as Albert Einstein, Max Planck, and Max Von Laue. Szilard could not resist the lure of this intellectual milieu, and within a few weeks he switched from engineering into physics. He learned quickly, moreover, and soon impressed his professors as a student of exceptional talent. During the Christmas holidays of 1921, he spent three weeks taking long walks and feverishly jotting down notes on a particularly vexing problem in thermodynamics. When school began again, he approached Einstein after a seminar and told him that he had solved the problem: he had found a way to reconcile the two prevailing (and radically different) theories describing thermodynamic fluctuations. Einstein responded: "That's impossible. This is something that cannot be done."

"Well, yes," Szilard replied, "but I did it."

Szilard showed his manuscript to his professors, and the following week Max Von Laue telephoned him at home: "Your manuscript has been accepted as your thesis for the Ph.D. degree."[9] He was twenty-three years old.

During these Berlin years, Szilard also became acquainted with the science fiction writings of H. G. Wells, which made a profound impression upon him. In particular, Szilard was struck by a prediction that Wells had made in 1914 concerning the release of atomic energy, its revolutionary consequences for warfare, and the inevitable world government that "atomic survivors" would establish among the radioactive ashes of a devastated civilization. At first, Szilard did not regard Wells's books "as anything but fiction."[10] However, after the Frenchman Frédéric Joliot announced the release of artificial radioactivity in 1933 (the very year, by a strange coincidence, for which Wells had predicted it), Szilard began to think seriously about the possibility of atomic weapons.

It was also in April 1933, three months after Hitler became chancellor of Germany, that Szilard fled from Berlin to Vienna, catching one of the last unrestricted trains out of the country before Nazi controls were clamped down. He had been observing events in German politics with growing anxiety throughout the 1920s, and had first reached the conclusion "that something would go wrong in Germany" in February 1929, before the onset of the depression.[11] Hjalmar Schacht, the president of the German *Reichsbank,* had made the startling announcement that Germany could not pay any more war reparations unless it got back its former colonies. "I was so impressed by this," Szilard later recalled, "that I wrote a letter to my bank and transfered every single penny I had out of Germany into Switzerland."[12] After this event, Szilard had prepared himself for the worst: "I had two [packed] suitcases standing in my room . . . ; the key was in [them], and all I had to do was turn the key and leave when things got too bad."[13]

From a hotel in Vienna, he mobilized an international campaign to help find new academic posts for the hundreds of Jewish intellectuals who he knew would be fleeing Hitler's Germany as he had done himself. Later in 1933, this project brought him to England; and it was here, as he was crossing a London street one autumn day, that he made the most momentous theoretical breakthrough of his career:

> [It] suddenly occurred to me that if we could find an element which is split by neutrons, and which would emit *two* neutrons when it absorbed *one* neutron, . . . [it] might become possible to set up a nuclear chain reaction, liberate energy on an industrial scale, and construct atomic bombs. The thought . . . became a sort of obsession with me.[14]

Szilard's idea, as it turned out, was still too far ahead of its time. Lord Ernest Rutherford, who dominated British physics during the 1930s, had recently dismissed the notion of tapping the atom's power as "moonshine."[15] Thus, because no one would provide financial backing for experiments based on so adventurous a conception, Szilard was forced to abandon his plans for research. Nevertheless, he took out a secret patent on his idea in 1934 and assigned it to the British admiralty for safekeeping.

Szilard was still living in London in March 1936 when Hitler's troops reoccupied the demilitarized Rhineland territories, unopposed by France or Britain. From that point on, Szilard later recalled, "I knew that there would be war in Europe."[16] Although he had been offered a lectureship at Oxford University, it was time once again to prepare the suitcases. He had told his friend Michael Polanyi half-jokingly in 1935: "I would stay in England until one year before the war, at which time I would shift my residence to New York City. That was very funny, because how can anyone say what he will do one year *before* the war?"[17] In September 1938, Szilard was visiting a friend in Illinois when British Prime Minister Neville Chamberlain returned to London from the Munich Conference, trading the fate of Czechoslovakia for "peace in our time." Szilard brooded for three months, then wrote a most characteristic letter to the director of the Clarendon Laboratory at Oxford:

> It seems to me that the Munich agreement created, or at the very least demonstrated, a state of international relations which now threatens Europe and in the long run will threaten the whole civilized world. . . . I greatly envy those of my colleagues at Oxford who in these circumstances are able to give their full attention to [scientific works] . . . without offending their sense of proportions. To my great sorrow I am apparently quite incapable of following their example. . . . I may therefore return to England if I can see my way of being of use, not only in science, but also in connection with the general situation. . . .
>
> Please excuse the three months' delay of this letter. Immediately after the Munich agreement it did not seem possible for me to have

a sufficiently balanced view, and I had to allow some time to elapse
before I was able to write without bitterness of this event.[18]

Shortly after Szilard had written this letter, the eminent Danish theoretician
Niels Bohr arrived from Europe with a piece of startling news: nuclear fission
in uranium had just been discovered by two German scientists. Szilard immediately perceived the implications of the discovery and set up experiments (on
borrowed equipment) to determine whether uranium, under appropriate conditions, would sustain a nuclear chain reaction. The experiments, conducted with
Walter Zinn at Columbia University in March 1939, indicated that it would.
"All we had to do," Szilard later recalled,

> was to turn a switch, lean back, and watch the screen of a television
> tube. If flashes of light appeared on the screen, that would mean
> that neutrons were emitted in the fission process, . . . and that the
> large-scale liberation of atomic energy was just around the corner.
> We turned the switch and we saw the flashes. We watched them
> for a little while and then we switched everything off and went
> home. That night there was very little doubt in my mind that the
> world was headed for grief.[19]

Since it was clear to Szilard that war was approaching, he decided that Franklin
Roosevelt himself must be apprised of these scientific developments and of
their possible military consequences. To this end, he drafted a letter to the
president, persuaded Einstein to sign it, and had it dispatched directly by a
friend who had good connections in the White House. Out of these events the
two-billion dollar Manhattan Project gradually developed. Szilard was assigned to the so-called Metallurgical Laboratory at the University of Chicago,
the branch of the Manhattan Project devoted to the production of plutonium in
an atomic pile.

Albert Einstein later referred to his signing of Szilard's letter to Roosevelt
as the one great mistake of his life.[20] On the other hand, when they were faced
at the beginning of World War II with the serious possibility of a Hitler
wielding atomic weapons, most scientists did not hesitate to contribute their
energy and ingenuity to the wartime cause. The Manhattan Project eventually
became a top military priority for the United States, especially after the Pearl
Harbor attack of 1941; and it steadily grew into a complex industrial effort
with a plodding momentum of its own. For Szilard, the strict regimentation
and requirements of secrecy represented the opposite of the scientific openness
he considered essential to creative research. He soon grew restive, and complained repeatedly to his superiors that excessive restrictions on interdepart-
mental communications were slowing the project down. His initial fears were,
on the one hand, that Germany would procure a bomb first and subjugate the
entire planet; or, on the other hand, that if the United States could not quickly

develop its own bomb to use against Germany, the peoples of the world would never comprehend the weapon's revolutionary destructiveness, and would hence lose the incentive for a radical postwar arms-control agreement.[21]

Then, as it became increasingly clear toward the end of 1944 that Germany could be vanquished by means of nonnuclear weapons, Szilard's fears turned toward Japan. By this point, the issues had all shifted, for there could be little doubt any longer of a U.S. victory. Was it still necessary to use the atomic bomb against Japan, and if so, in what manner? Szilard became deeply concerned about the total isolation of the scientists, who were making the bomb, from the relatively small group of policymakers who would decide how to use it. He worried not only about the moral issues involved in using the bomb but about the consequences that it would have for the balance of power in the postwar world. Specifically, Szilard later wrote, he "was concerned at this point that by demonstrating the bomb and using it in the war against Japan, we might start an atomic arms race between America and Russia which might end with the destruction of both countries."[22]

Not being one to mince words, Szilard appealed vigorously to the project's administrators with various schemes to end the scientists' isolation, but he received only superficial reassurances. He then circulated petitions among the various Manhattan Project installations, requesting permission for the scientists to engage in open debate concerning the use of the bomb. The debate's proceedings, he suggested, should be sent to the president. This proposal was quickly blocked by the military security personnel, who had already grown suspicious of Szilard's independent temperament as early as 1940, and had ordered him shadowed by detectives for the duration of the war.[23] (The agents duly recorded: "Subject is of Jewish extraction, . . . usually eats his breakfast in drug stores and other meals in restaurants, . . . occasionally speaks in a foreign tongue, and associates mostly with people of Jewish extraction. He is inclined to be rather absent-minded and eccentric, and will start out a door, turn around and come back, go out on the street without his coat or hat. . . . Subject's actions are very unpredictable and if there is more than one entrance or exit, he is just as apt to use the most inconvenient as not.")[24]

Undaunted by the failure of his petitions, Szilard drafted a long letter to President Roosevelt and had it transmitted directly to the White House by a friend. "The strong position of the United States . . . in the past thirty years," he wrote,

> was essentially due to the fact that the United States could out-produce every other country in heavy armaments. . . . The existence of atomic bombs means the end of the strong position of the United States in this respect. From now on the destructive power which can be accumulated by other countries as well as the United

States can easily reach the level at which all the cities of the "enemy" can be destroyed in one single attack. . . .

If there should be great progress in the development of rockets after this war it is conceivable that it will become possible to drop atomic bombs on the cities of the United States from very great distances by means of rockets. . . .

. . . [Should] our "demonstration" of atomic bombs and their use against Japan be delayed . . . so that the United States shall be in a more favorable position in negotiations aimed at setting up a system of [international] controls?[25]

A few days later, Szilard had just received word of being granted an appointment with Eleanor Roosevelt when the news broke that the president had died of a stroke. He then requested to see Harry Truman in person. Truman was not available, but he directed Szilard to discuss his concerns with James F. Byrnes, who (unbeknownst to Szilard) was slated to become Truman's new secretary of state. In May 1945, Szilard visited Byrnes at his home in Spartanburg, South Carolina, but the ensuing discussion left both men dissatisfied. Byrnes disapproved of Szilard's "general demeanor and his desire to participate in policymaking,"[26] while Szilard was "completely flabbergasted" by Byrnes's assumption that "rattling the bomb might make Russia more manageable."[27] In particular, Szilard was appalled when Byrnes made a pointed reference to the destiny of Hungary, implying that Szilard should worry less about long-term relations between the United States and Soviet Union than about keeping his native country free from domination. "I certainly didn't want Russia to stay in Hungary indefinitely," Szilard later wrote, "but what Byrnes said offended my sense of proportion."[28]

Troubled by this revealing encounter with one of the senior officials of the incoming administration, Szilard returned to Chicago. During the next two months, he desperately sought to circulate another round of petitions, pushing the Manhattan Project scientists to demand greater control over the use of their creation—but to no avail. On August 6, Hiroshima was bombed and the new weapon's existence most starkly revealed to the rest of the world.

Szilard's fundamental ideas about politics as the art of conciliation and mediation were born long before the nuclear era, amid the decaying democracy of Weimar Germany. It was here, during the 1920s and early 1930s, that he first witnessed the blind force of ideological partisanship as it dragged a nation toward anarchy. His earnest and imaginative response to the internal polarities of Weimar Germany clearly prefigured the way he would later respond to the great polarity between Russia and America.

Szilard had come to Berlin in December 1919, just as the defeated German people were first making their rather sullen and half-hearted departure from the authoritarian grandeur of Kaiser Wilhelm's Second *Reich*. The new republic, which had its birthplace at Goethe's native city of Weimar, was regarded by many Germans—both on the Left and the Right—as an alien political model imposed on a helpless nation by the victors of the First World War. One of the great paradoxes of Weimar democracy was that its principal supporters were the allegedly Marxist members of the Social Democratic party, whose leaders dominated German politics during the early postwar years. Flanked on the left by militant Communists and on the right by reactionary or proto-Fascist groups, the liberal center rested on an increasingly fragile coalition of Social Democrats, Catholics, and so-called *Vernunftrepublikaner* (republicans by rationalization), reluctant liberals like Thomas Mann who yearned for a uniquely German synthesis of traditional and modern political forms, and who supported the Weimar government only because all immediate alternatives seemed far worse.

Acutely sensitive to this volatile atmosphere of clashing political views, and alarmed by the economic turmoil and strident racism of the 1920s, the young physicist Szilard tried to sketch a solution of his own. He wrote in 1930,

> If we possessed a magical spell with which to recognize the "best" individuals of the rising generation at an early age, . . . then we would be able to train them to independent thinking, and through education in close association we could create a spiritual leadership class with inner cohesion which would renew itself on its own. . . . [Such a group could] exercise a potent influence on the shaping of public affairs even without any particular inner structure and without any constitutionally determined rights. . . . It would also be conceivable that such a leading group would take over a more direct influence on public affairs as part of the political system, next to government and parliament, or in the place of government and parliament.[29]

This organization, which Szilard called *Der Bund* (meaning "a closely bonded alliance"), may have been directly modeled after the contemporary proposals of H. G. Wells, whose science-fiction writings had already awakened in Szilard's imagination the fateful vision of an atomic bomb. Szilard greatly admired Wells, and even met briefly with him in 1929—yet he never mentioned any explicit connection between his "Bund" and the book Wells published in the same year, *The Open Conspiracy: Blue Prints for a World Revolution*.[30] Whatever the actual relation between them, however, the "Bund" and the "Open Conspiracy" represented the same bold conception of political renewal—with the difference- that Szilard focused upon the concrete circumstances of Germany in 1930, whereas the mind of Wells roamed more freely across the continents and decades.

For both Szilard and Wells, the growing political and economic disarray of the 1920s and '30s suggested that twentieth-century society was no longer governable by traditional forms of leadership. They proposed that the citizens of the Western democracies gradually transfer the reins of governance to a new elite, made up of the "best minds" from all fields and trained to act with decisiveness amid the incipient chaos of the era. Szilard's plan was more detailed than that of Wells, for it specified the methods of selection, training, and education for his ideal elite, whereas Wells preferred to leave such details up to the initiative of the participants. For both of them, however, the key element was the inner cohesion of this new group of leaders. Although its members would be drawn from diverse backgrounds and encouraged to hold contrasting views, the new elite must be united by a spiritual esprit de corps which transcended all the ideological, national, and class distinctions that were threatening to tear modern society apart. Both the Hungarian scientist and the English novelist were rather vague about details, but they explicitly pointed to an underlying "religious spirit" as the foundation for their proposals.[31] Like the Guardians in Plato's *Republic,* these new leaders must represent exactly the opposite of the rapacious trafficking that had been associated with the word "politics" since ancient times. In Szilard's "Bund," they were to

> demonstrate their devotion through particular burdens which they take upon themselves and through a life of service. . . . They must hand over to the Order all monies they earn above the base minimum necessary for their existence. . . . For a part (about a third?) of the members of the Order, celibacy may perhaps be prescribed.[32]

The "Bund" and the "Open Conspiracy" were frankly elitist conceptions, but neither of them was intended as a blueprint for a modern form of oligarchical government. What Szilard and Wells had in mind, rather, was to inject a strong dose of meritocracy into the processes of contemporary mass democracy. They envisioned a group of enlightened leaders with sufficient moral authority to persuade large numbers of citizens, but they refused to accept any Leninist notions of a vanguard party that could force the masses to follow their "objective" interests. "Care must be taken," Szilard wrote,

> that the prevailing opinion of the leading group be safely and freely communicated to a wide public so that the two may never diverge to a significant degree. . . . Whether one should ever give the Order an opportunity to exercise a more direct influence on public affairs is a question that can be postponed until experience has shown . . . to what degree it has succeeded in remaining closely bound to the general public.[33]

In proposing such a new form of governance, Szilard and Wells were drawing directly or indirectly from all three of the major ideologies that competed for dominance during the interwar years. From classical liberalism—which remained central to their proposals—they adopted the principle of the free exchange of goods and ideas as a basic tenet. They mitigated this liberal principle, however, with an emphasis on centralized planning for public welfare, as espoused by contemporary communists and socialists. Wells referred to himself as a nonmarxian socialist, while Szilard (who abhorred all such labels) was attracted to the idea of social planning less from any ideological conviction than from his ingrained penchant for rational and well-ordered solutions. Finally, their proposals also reflected a critique of parliamentary democracy somewhat similar to that which was emerging among the ideologues of Fascism; for both Szilard and Wells saw little hope in the polarized and ineffectual parliaments of England, France, and Weimar Germany. Like the Fascists, they urgently sought new sources of resolute leadership outside the traditional organs of national public life; but they were drastically different from the Fascists in everything else, for they based their solutions on reason, tolerance, and a deep respect for the virtues of diversity. Indeed, the "Bund" and the "Open Conspiracy" were deliberately designed to forestall a decline into Fascism by addressing and remedying precisely those weaknesses in parliamentary government that the Fascists tended to exploit.[34]

Szilard's proposed "Bund" also bore many similarities to Louise Weiss's Ecole de la Paix, which was meeting during these same years in Paris. Both these institutions were designed to provide a neutral platform, from which enlightened individuals might gain insight into each other's contrasting positions, thereby moving closer to mutual understanding and to producing a common plan of action for the future. "In today's bureaucracy," Szilard wrote in 1930, "there is no structure whatsoever that would offer a guarantee of a well-thought-out, large-scale definition of aims."[35] This had been precisely one of Weiss's main reasons for founding her Ecole: the idea that an elite group of individuals, endowed with the respect of the broader population, might step forward to offer a democratic society the sense of direction that it so badly needed to survive. Szilard's "Bund," however, never went beyond the initial planning stages; for in the growing polarization of Weimar Germany, he was unable to find enough persons willing to participate in his unorthodox experiment. Still, he did not grow disillusioned by the harsh setbacks of the 1930s (as Weiss did), and later revived his elitist proposals for consensus building and mediation in the new context of the postwar era.

"If you are a scientist," Robert Oppenheimer told a gathering at Los Alamos, New Mexico in November 1945,

> you believe that it is good to find out how the world works; that it is good to find out what the realities are; that it is good to turn

over to mankind at large the greatest possible power to control the world. . . . It is not possible to be a scientist unless you believe that the knowledge of the world, and the power which this gives, is a thing which is of intrinsic value to humanity.[36]

Oppenheimer's audience, which consisted largely of Manhattan Project scientists and technicians, did not include Leo Szilard. Had he been present, though, Szilard would doubtless have found it troubling to hear such a straightforward assertion about the value of knowledge in dominating the environment. Szilard expressed his more ambiguous assessment of the relation between knowledge and power in a 1946 contribution to the pamphlet *One World or None.* "Atomic bombs," he wrote, "are the product of human imagination applied to the behavior of inanimate matter; [we] cannot cope with the problems that their existence has created unless we are willing to apply our imagination to the problems of human behavior."[37]

Here was a scientist who clearly understood that Oppenheimer's phrase, "power to control the world," actually concealed an unbridgeable qualitative difference between controlling things and controlling people. Implicit in Szilard's statement was a paradox lying at the heart of industrial civilization: while human mastery over nature steadily increases, humanity's control over its own destiny becomes more and more problematic. This twentieth-century paradox of growing power and diminishing control is all too familiar to the postwar generations, who have learned how to conduct their everyday lives in a strangely insecure atmosphere of global ecological crises and economic disequilibrium, political turmoil, and fearsome armaments. For Szilard, Hiroshima and Auschwitz could only be followed by humility. "I am not particularly qualified to speak about the problem of peace," he wrote in 1947 for the newly created *Bulletin of the Atomic Scientists;*

> I am a scientist and science, which has created the bomb and confronted the world with a problem, has no solution to offer to this problem. Yet a scientist may perhaps be permitted to speak on the problem of peace, not because he knows more about it than other people do, but rather because no one seems to know very much about it.[38]

Szilard was too sophisticated to think that the inductive logic of natural science could be transferred to the infinitely more obtuse and intractable questions of politics, and he readily acknowledged the rift between physical problems and social problems. Nevertheless, it is impossible to understand Szilard's vision of peace without understanding his vision of science, for both were derived from the same reservoir of fundamental values. Like his great masters, Einstein and Bohr, Szilard did not find any rigid cleavage between "scientific" and "humanistic" categories of thought. He approached basic scientific problems with an undisguised reverence that bordered on rationalistic mysticism; and, conversely, he tried to keep his personal life and political ideas as clear and unfettered as he kept his scientific creativity. In 1940, when the A-bomb project was still a small and tentative undertaking, he wrote down for himself a list of the personal ideals that moved him. He was evidently embarrassed enough by their openly emotional tone to feel the need to entitle them—with typical wry self-mockery—"Ten Commandments." On science, Szilard wrote:

> Do not destroy what you cannot create.
> Speak to all men as you do to yourself, with no concern for the effect that you make, so that you do not shut them out from your world; lest in isolation the meaning of life slips out of sight and you lose the belief in the perfection of the creation.

On the conduct of his personal life, he wrote:

> Do your work for six years; but in the seventh, go into solitude or among strangers, so that the recollection of your friends does not hinder you from being what you have become.
> Let your acts be directed towards a worthy goal, but do not ask if they will reach it; they are to be models and examples, not means to an end.
> Honor children. Listen reverently to their words and speak to them with infinite love.[39]

Szilard did not need to "obey" these commandments, for (in the words of his widow) they already reflected his spirit "like a portrait."[40] Scientific inquiry, personal life, and social action were inseparable for him; he brought the same intellectual habits and moral values to all three.

On the other hand, although he took his work very seriously, Szilard's style of thought continually revealed a certain playful lightness. His friends remarked that he could labor night and day for several months on a scientific experiment, than abandon it suddenly with complete serenity, saying, "Oh, it was not a good idea."[41] He preferred to act as a catalyst and innovator, concentrating all his effort on a problem in its early stages when the frames of reference were not yet clear-cut; and then, once the general outlines had emerged, his attention would wander and he would move on to something else. The drudgery of finishing a project, as well as the subsequent recognition for it, he cheerfully left to others.[42] "Had he pushed through to success all his new inventions," observed the Nobel Prize-winning physicist Dennis Gabor in 1973, "we would now talk of him as the Edison of the twentieth century."[43]

With gentle irony, Szilard relentlessly criticized the statesmen and political trends of the Cold War period, yet he did not hesitate to turn the same dry bemusement upon himself: "I must confess," says the main character in one of his stories, "that with Szilard I never know when he is serious and when he is joking, and I suspect that often he does not know himself."[44] He could be brusque and impulsive at times, or extraordinarily patient and cautious; he was as understated about his own achievements as he was unintimidated by the achievements of others; he plunged vigorously into scientific and political arguments, yet his friends and colleagues marveled at his apparent incapacity for acrimony or ill will.

Szilard was not exactly a humble man, but it would be misleading to say that he had a "big ego." He was egocentric, in the sense that he appears to have felt personally responsible since his childhood for affecting the fate of humankind in some decisive way; and he would let nothing come between him and this responsibility. His vision of his own stature was neatly captured when he looked back with irony on his unsuccessful 1945 meeting with Truman's secretary of state, James Byrnes:

> I was rarely as depressed as when we left Byrnes' house and walked toward the station. I thought to myself how much better off the world might be had I been born in America and become influential in American politics, and had Byrnes been born in Hungary and studied physics. In all probability there would have been no atomic bomb, and no danger of an arms race between America and Russia.[45]

Having lived in Hungary, Germany, and England before settling in the United States, Szilard was perhaps less a Hungarian emigré than a rootless *citoyen du monde:* "Leo's home," according to a friend, was "wherever his intellectual interests [happened] to be at the moment."[46] During the postwar years, he lived mainly in hotels and faculty clubs, ate his meals in "horrible restaurants frequented by students," and "owned no property, very few books."[47] In 1951 he married "an old friend of Berlin days," Gertrud Weiss; but his wife was knowingly taking on a relationship with a man who could never be tied down.[48] Whenever possible, he affiliated himself with academic institutions only on the most tenuous and temporary basis. Although he was officially a professor at the University of Chicago through most of his postwar career, he regularly sought (and received) research grants which permitted him to rove continuously among major American universities, staying in each location for a few months or years at a time. Among scientists, something of a "Szilard legend" eventually developed, and he was noted not only for his "uncanny ability to conceive ideas before their time," but also as "an intellectual adventurer, likely to embark at any moment on some excursion far beyond the boundaries of science . . . unpredictable just because his behavior [was] so devastatingly rational."[49]

Even in physical appearance, Szilard seemed a striking and unusual figure.

The sociologist Edward Shils, a close friend of his, was left with the following impression after they first met in 1945:

> From my window, I could see him approaching, roly-poly; he walked smoothly and rapidly, the swift and regular agitation of his legs contrasting with the serenity of his bearing. . . . Very shortly thereafter, he came to my room. He was short and plump; he had a large head, a high, broad, somewhat sloping brow, and small, fine, neatly curving features. His hair, dark and combed back, had a broad grey streak running almost from the center of his forehead, and surmounted a ruddy face. It was the face of a benign, sad, gentle, mischievous cherub. The whole formed a picture of unresting sensitivity and intelligence, immensely energetic and controlled, and yet with great ease and gentleness of manner.[50]

In 1946, Szilard astonished his colleagues by abandoning physics altogether and starting over anew in the fledgling field of molecular biology. This radical break, according to one of his friends, signified "a turning from death to life that seemed to reflect his deep revulsion after Hiroshima."[51] Szilard himself, however, attributed the switch more simply to an intuition that physics had been intellectually exhausted by mid-century and that it was time to move on to something truly new. He was especially disgusted by what he perceived as the co-optation of theoretical physics by the demands of large-scale technology. "Nowadays," he wrote,

> a physicist has to go to the army or navy and get himself a million dollars or if necessary ten million, and build a cyclotron for a few hundred million volts at least, but preferably for a billion volts or even ten billion volts, and after he has gone through the trouble of spending a few million dollars, which usually takes a few years, he can then sit down and observe phenomena which no one could predict and about which he can then be astonished.[52]

On the other hand, Szilard believed that "while physics appears to be on the way out, biology does not seem to exist yet." He suspected that "there must exist universal biological laws just as [there] exist, for instance, physical laws [like] the conservation of energy or the second law of thermodynamics."[53] Like Einstein and Bohr, Szilard tended to approach scientific questions with an eye to their bearing on the fundamental mysteries of nature; he was actually more at ease with those answers that bordered on mathematical or metaphysical paradox than with straightforward, one-dimensional models projecting mere mechanical laws. Not surprisingly, his early biological research, which focused on the phenomenon of aging, was guided by questions about the subtle reciprocal interaction of the whole and part within a living organism:

> [Does] aging occur in a cell of the animal body because it is not
> placed in a constant environment, but in an environment deter-
> mined by all the cells of the body, and because that environment
> changes as the result of the interaction of the cells of the body with
> each other? . . . Even if we understood all the phenomena that a
> muscle or nerve fiber may exhibit in terms of the underlying physi-
> cal and chemical analysis, we will not have made an appreciable
> step towards the understanding of what life is.[54]

The fact that Szilard should have been thinking in such speculative and anti-reductionistic terms in his postwar scientific work is not without significance for his political activities. He repudiated physics because he believed that it had succumbed to the lure of technology and was, therefore, enduring a slow death of massive institutionalization. He embraced biology, on the other hand, precisely because it did "not seem to exist yet"—because it was an uncharted territory that still offered opportunities for small-scale, flexible research into areas that one chose because they were intrinsically interesting, not just poten-tially lucrative or useful. What motivated Szilard's choice was probably not so much an explicit value judgment that physics, in Robert Oppenheimer's words, had "known sin,"[55] whereas biology was untainted because it focused on life. Such a comparison, given the historical circumstances of the Manhattan Proj-ect, apparently did not strike Szilard as entirely fair; for few could know better than he what it had been like to make the agonizing decisions of 1939. Rather, the essential problem for Szilard appears to have been much simpler: postwar physics was being harnessed like a workhorse for the utilitarian ends of indus-trial society, whereas biology still seemed relatively free to roam wherever the human imagination beckoned. Both in his aversion for what he perceived as the physicist's submission to the ends of power and in his attraction to the biologist's independence, Szilard the scientist was no different from Szilard the humanist.

Thus, if there was a common thread running through Szilard's personal life and scientific ideals, it was the peculiar movement he always made between passionate involvement in some problem or endeavor, and abrupt disen-gagement so that he could move on to something new. "[A] man's clarity of judgment," he told an interviewer in 1960,

> is never very good when he is involved, and as you grow older, and
> as you grow more involved, your clarity of judgment suffers. This
> is not a matter of intelligence; this is a matter of ability to keep
> free from emotional involvement.[56]

This vigilant and continuous effort of emotional disengagement was also cen-tral to Szilard's conception of peace; for war, as he saw it, flowed essentially from strong emotional attachments to particular national or ideological positions. Human beings, he believed, would not engage in the insane destructiveness of modern war unless they had been blinded by irrational impulses and narrow affective allegiances. There is no sign that Szilard read or was directly influenced by the writings of another Hungarian, Karl Mannheim, whose *Ideology and Utopia* was first published in Bonn in 1929. Yet Szilard would almost certainly have shared that work's urgent preoccupation with "the prospects of rationality and understanding" in an era of violently clashing nationalisms, racisms, and hardened ideologies.[57] Like Mannheim, Szilard believed that the intellectual's role in the twentieth century was to help other groups of people get along with each other—to stand apart from all limited or parochial interests, providing a neutral ground from which those conflicting positions might be harmonized, or at least allowed to coexist.

Szilard apparently never doubted that such a neutral ground could be created. He believed that lasting peace was a remote but real possibility, and he based this belief on the deeper faith that clear and open-minded communication could lead to successful compromises on all the major conflicts that divided human beings from each other. The nature of the conflicts, per se, did not trouble Szilard, for he believed that no social problem would prove so intractable as to resist indefinitely the efforts of intelligent and rational negotiators.

1945–1964: The Urgent Utopia

On September 23, 1949, the U.S.-Soviet arms race which Szilard had long foreseen became a public fact, as President Truman made the dramatic announcement that the Soviet Union had just exploded its first nuclear device. The news defied all those confident forecasts of a fifteen-year U.S. nuclear monopoly—forecasts that had impelled James Byrnes, four years earlier, to brush off Szilard's pleas for U.S.-Soviet cooperation. Szilard himself, three days before Truman's announcement, had been reading ancient Greek history. His notes recorded that he was "considerably frightened" by what he read, for he saw a clear historical parallel between the U.S.-Soviet rivalry and the deadly conflict that had brought Athens and Sparta to ruin. The logic of arms races, it seemed to him, had not changed substantially in 2,500 years.

> Sparta and Athens did not want to go to war, but both looked upon war between themselves as a possibility which could not be disregarded. Therefore each one felt impelled to take steps which would make it more likely that it should win the war if war came. Each such step which Sparta took to improve her chances in case of war, and every such step which Athens took to improve her

chances in case of war, was of necessity a step which made war more likely to occur.[58]

Szilard had remained unconvinced by the stark picture of the Soviet Union that gained currency during the early postwar years. For many Westerners, he knew, the Soviets were similar to the Nazis in their ideological fanaticism and single-minded pursuit of world domination: they only understood the logic of superior force, and could not be kept at bay by means of reasonable compromises, but solely by fear. For Szilard, however, this conflation of two peoples like the Germans and the Russians, each of which possessed its own unique heritage and culture, could only result from a hopelessly muddled and superficial understanding of European history. In his view, it was far more accurate to interpret Soviet actions as stemming quite simply from the logic of self-interest. "Soviet Russia," he wrote in 1949,

> is a dictatorship no less ruthless perhaps than was Hitler's dictatorship in Germany. Does it follow that Russia will act as Hitler's Germany acted? I do not believe so. . . . To my mind anything that Russia has done in the past four years can be fully understood as the action of a nation pursuing her national interests, guided largely, though not solely, by strategic considerations.[59]

Szilard met regularly with Soviet scientists and officials during trips to Europe and at international scientific conferences, and he once chided his friend Edward Teller, the father of the American hydrogen bomb, for his rigidly anti-Soviet position:

> I doubt that Teller would find it easy to hold on to the premises of his political thinking if he had had adequate personal contact with our Russian colleagues and had made an extended visit to Russia. . . . The set of values of our Russian colleagues is not exactly the same as the set of values of the man in the street in Moscow or Leningrad, and of course the Soviet Government is no more a human being than the Government of any other great power. Still, the Soviet Government does not operate in a vacuum and the members of the Soviet Government who are, after all, human beings are not likely to remain unaffected by the set of values which pervades most of Russia.[60]

Unswayed by the dehumanizing rhetoric of the Cold War, Szilard insisted on assuming that the majority of Russians were not beastly aggressors but normal human beings like the citizens of other nations. The Soviet government, he believed, was a ruthless dictatorship; but it was amenable to reason, and it was certainly not interested in committing national suicide. On this basis, he felt, there was room for fruitful bargaining and long-term accommodation.

Unfortunately, however, the international atmosphere during the first five years after World War II could hardly have been less propitious for advancing ideas like Szilard's. The mentality of James Byrnes, which had so dismayed Szilard in 1945, also characterized most of the powerful individuals who helped shape the postwar world—from Truman to Acheson and Dulles, from Stalin to Zhdanov and Molotov. Even before Roosevelt's death, Western suspicions had been fueled by the Soviet betrayal of the Polish wartime leadership in Warsaw, just as Russian suspicions were fueled by the Anglo-American delay in establishing a second front in Europe. After 1945, the two erstwhile allies—each unfurling the banner of a rival ideology—scrambled to gain control over the postwar world before control was preempted by the other. Soviet and American actions followed upon each other in rapid succession: on the Soviet side, the vain attempts in 1946 to control Iran and Turkey; Communist takeovers and purges in Poland, Hungary, and Czechoslovakia; and the sudden blockade of Berlin. On the American side: Truman's abrupt cancellation of Lend-Lease in 1945; U.S. manipulation of the United Nations as an instrument for opposing Soviet policies;[61] the Truman Doctrine and anti-Communist intervention in Greece; U.S. moves to establish pro-Western governments (and military bases) around the vast perimeter of the Soviet land mass, in Asia, the Middle East, and Western Europe; and the formation of NATO in 1949. Within the Soviet Union, these international events went hand in hand with a further hardening of the already paranoid and brutal excesses of Stalinism;[62] while in the United States, Truman's government loyalty investigations (inaugurated in March 1947) paved the way for the collective hysteria of McCarthyism.[63]

Which side was to blame for this self-aggravating cycle of fear and provocations? Who started it? Szilard regarded such questions as naive and misleading, because they implied that one side had been the exclusive aggressor while the actions of the other had been uniformly defensive. He did not see the Cold War this way. For him, rather, the Cold War was like a lethal game that could either be observed from the outside or "played" from the inside. From the perspective of the inside, one heard people in one bloc passionately describing those in the other bloc as "evil" or "primarily at fault." From the outside perspective, however, one saw a polarized configuration of international politics that could be logically expected to express itself in precisely this kind of hostile repartee between two self-righteous camps. Szilard easily admitted that one side or the other could be primarily responsible for any given international incident, but he refused to accept the idea that the Cold War as a whole was triggered by unilateral action. The Cold War, in his view, was an interactive relationship based on a dynamism of fundamental symmetry: the reciprocal logic of the arms race, and the reciprocal distrust of two alien peoples.

Szilard truly considered nuclear war a day-to-day possibility, and he occasionally urged his friends "to leave the United States, and go to live in Australia or New Zealand or perhaps a small island in the Pacific, in order to be away from the danger." [64] Although he himself continued to bustle about such prime nuclear targets as New York and Washington, D.C., Szilard took precautions in the same way as he had done during the crisis years between 1929 and 1933: he carried with him his essential patents and documents in two bags known as "BBS" and "SBS" (Big Bomb Suitcase and Small Bomb Suitcase). In 1962, at the height of the Cuban missile crisis, Szilard fled by plane to Geneva until the duel between Kennedy and Khrushchev had clearly been resolved. "I have been getting more and more convinced that the country will come to grief," he later explained to a friend. "If I were to stay in Washington until the bombs begin to fall and were to perish . . . I would consider myself on my deathbed, not a hero but a fool." [65]

It was this grim appraisal of humankind's prospects that set the tone for Szilard's radical solutions to the Cold War. Szilard's vision of peace—like everything else about him—evolved continuously as new ideas and new events stimulated his imagination. Nevertheless, he forced himself twice during the postwar period (in 1955 and 1961) to sit down and bring together his far-ranging thoughts into a fairly comprehensive "blueprint" for a pathway out of the Cold War. The first effort was a long article for the *Bulletin of the Atomic Scientists,* entitled "Disarmament and the Problem of Peace." [66] The second eventually took shape as a humorous fictional essay, "The Voice of the Dolphins," designed to convey the complex ideas of his 1955 article to a much broader audience. [67] The narrator of this essay, a historian of the 1990s, describes the steps through which a demilitarized world federation has emerged out of the international anarchy of the 1950s. Crucial to the transformation was the "Vienna Institute," where Soviet and American scientists (working together as a team) had learned to communicate with superintelligent dolphins. Acting as arbiters between the global power blocs, the dolphins devised ingenious disarmament plans which preserved national sovereignty and identity while leading gradually toward global disarmament. The story ends with the narrator's well-founded suspicion that the dolphins never really existed, but that they were a convenient fiction used by the scientists to enhance their credibility as neutrals promoting peace.

Szilard started from the assumption that two major incentives might push the superpowers toward a political settlement: the danger of nuclear annihilation, and the tremendous economic benefits of reducing military expenditures. Pragmatically anticipating the lobbying of arms-manufacturing corporations and military groups, he suggested that the U.S. and Soviet governments each set up a special fund to compensate those who possessed vested economic interests in the military establishment. These funds, he thought, could be financed from current defense budgets and could subsidize the conversion of arms industries to peaceful purposes. Military personnel would be given extremely generous allowances, over a period of years, to train for a new career; but they would not be the only ones to reap the benefits of disarmament. Szilard calculated that the billions of dollars in annual savings would enable the superpowers (depending on their priorities) to abolish hunger in the Third World, or to double their own domestic standards of living. "Leisure," he wrote, "could take the form of . . . two months' additional paid vacation for everybody."[68]

With incentives like these, it was hard to consider disarmament uninteresting: But what about national security? In Szilard's view, disarmament was meaningless—even dangerous—unless it was preceded by a fundamental political agreement that both superpowers strongly supported. In "The Voice of the Dolphins" (1961), he asked his readers to imagine a world patrolled by "multinational police forces" created with the blessing of the United States and the Soviet Union. These regional military forces would operate under the aegis of the United Nations; their assignment would be to deter aggression in their designated areas of the globe and to punish any nation that disturbed the status quo by violent means. The actions of these U.N. police forces would be governed by regional committees of nations endorsed in advance by the superpowers. "America," Szilard thought, "might agree not to veto a slate favored by Russia for a certain region if Russia would agree not to veto a slate favored by America for a certain other region."[69]

Szilard's reasoning here was straightforward. He believed that the superpowers would continue for the foreseeable future to project their influence to the far corners of the globe, as their national interest and ideology ordained; and it seemed far safer to have this influence regulated by the interposed institutional structures of the United Nations. For the sake of international stability, he argued, it was better to cushion the rivalry of the superpowers through a tacit division of the planet into regional spheres of influence, rather than to have Russia and America intervening unilaterally and erratically in the affairs of lesser nations, as dictated by the flux of international crises and fickle public opinion.

Szilard's vision, therefore, was not based on some vague and pious conception of world government that simply cancelled out national sovereignty. Instead, he proposed a flexible and decentralized structure in which international bodies could modulate the preponderant influence of major nations, while smaller nations could acquire a limited but nonetheless real capability to govern their own local regions. In "The Voice of the Dolphins," Szilard wrote:

> When the possibility of setting up regional police forces under the control of various "groups" of nations was first discussed, many people opposed it on the ground that each such region would be likely to become the sphere of influence of one or the other of the

great powers. . . . It turned out, however, that the regions under the control of the various groups of nations were spheres of non-influence, rather than spheres of influence. For instance, Central America was under the control of Uruguay, Canada, Austria, and Australia, and this did not place Central America in the sphere of influence of the United States, but it did exclude Central America from the sphere of influence of the Soviet Union. Similarly, the Middle East was excluded from the sphere of influence of the United States without falling into the sphere of influence of the Soviet Union.[70]

Why should the superpowers allow these lesser nations to take over their own roles as international constables? Why, for instance, should the United States cede its traditional dominance over the political fortunes of Central America to "Uruguay, Canada, Austria, and Australia?" The answer lay in the broader advantages of the global settlement with Russia—of which the Central American and Middle Eastern "regional police forces" were an integral part. For the sake of defusing the nuclear powderkeg and greatly increasing their own economic prosperity, the superpowers might be willing to barter some of the direct influence that they currently exercised over various regions of the planet. The fact that such an agreement would require both the superpowers and the world's smaller countries to surrender some of their sovereignty to the United Nations did not deter Szilard, for to him it offered the only path toward a safer, more stable world.

A crucial flaw in this vision, of course, lay in Szilard's rather sketchy depiction of the regional police forces themselves. What if Uruguay and Austria, for instance, could not agree on how to respond to a crisis within their sphere? What if the regional police force in the Middle East began implementing a policy that one (or both) of the superpowers strenuously opposed? Szilard did not directly address these kinds of thorny questions, and his articles accordingly failed to attract much attention.

In another sense, however, these questions are somewhat unfair; for Szilard never hoped to provide an infallible blueprint for peaceful international relations. His aim, rather, was to depict a global political system governed by an entirely different set of assumptions and ground rules. It was obvious that such a picture would seem highly unrealistic if judged by contemporary standards; but Szilard's goal was to imagine what such a world might look like and to specify the changes that would have to occur in order to get "from here to there."

Szilard could see plainly that the vast majority of human beings was still hemmed in by the divisive allegiances of nation, class, religion, race, and local community. All these divisions constituted the substance of human culture, he believed, and could not be simply overruled or ignored. The trick to steering this imperfect world toward sanity, as he saw it, lay in a concept that he called "predetermined gradualism." The idea underlying this cumbersome term was fairly ingenious, for it simultaneously addressed two profoundly conservative tendencies in human society. On the one hand, Szilard observed, most people were inherently slow to change, and stubbornly resisted drastic alterations in their established patterns of life and thought. On the other hand, the political, economic, and military problems of the postwar world were so complex and interconnected that every attempt at piecemeal change in one of these domains invariably ran afoul of major obstacles in the other domains. The solution, in Szilard's view, was to bring together a wide range of problems and disagreements and resolve them as part of a single package of long-term compromises and trade-offs. Rather than immediately implementing the whole set of deals, however, the negotiating teams would lay out a steady progression through prearranged stages, which each step coming a little closer to the desired final goal. In this way, he reasoned, the outcome would be predetermined, but the steps along the way would be gradual enough to ease the shock of transition.

Moreover, foreseeing the reluctance of political leaders to embark on sweeping negotiations over the shape of the distant future, he added another interesting twist: either side should be able to withdraw from the agreement at any time with complete impunity. If the agreement was truly sound, he argued, it would be strongly in the interest of both sides to keep it in force. Rather than seeing the whole settlement abrogated, they might, therefore, be willing to make partial concessions when particular (and unforeseeable) conflicts arose. Naturally, such a comprehensive political settlement would have to rest upon a "gentleman's understanding" not to engage in political subversion outside one's own indirect spheres of influence; and once again, the primary enforcer of this "understanding" was nothing more than the self-interest of the superpowers in keeping the overall agreement in force.

What Szilard envisioned, therefore, was a world where the positive incentives of cooperation had replaced the negative sanctions of fear and punishment in keeping the peace. It was at this point, and only at this point, that he began to discuss disarmament. Szilard thought that the superpowers would have to accept three basic principles if they sincerely wanted disarmament. First, they would have to agree to maintain their weaponry at levels of rough parity or equilibrium. Second, they would keep a portion of their strategic nuclear forces as "insurance" against being double-crossed, an "insurance" that would presumably be required for a long time. Finally, with each diminution in levels of armament, they would have to agree to concomitant reductions in the secrecy that cloaked their military establishments; for secrecy implied the possibility of betrayal, and fear of betrayal would block all progress.

The key to the entire procedure, of course, lay in the gradual transfer of peacekeeping functions to the regional police forces established under a spheres-of-influence agreement. It was essential to avoid creating a power vacuum at any point in the disarmament process; for in the absence of an effective arrangement for settling conflicts and enforcing the peace, the disarmament of the superpowers would become a dangerous descent into vulnerability and possible chaos.

Szilard envisioned three broad phases of disarmament. During the first stage the superpowers would destroy three-quarters of their conventional military forces, while retaining their full arsenal of nuclear weapons. At this point, the regional police forces would begin to operate as enforcers of the peace, and other great powers like France, China, and Great Britain would also reduce their conventional forces. If the first stage proved workable over a period of years (Szilard did not specify how many), then the more drastic reductions of the second phase would begin. Here, all conventional arsenals would be gradually eliminated, including those of the lesser nations, and only the multinational peacekeeping forces would remain. Then, in the third stage, the last stockpiles of nuclear weapons would be destroyed. At the heart of this final step was the establishment of a foolproof method of inspection, so that no nation could secretly accumulate a nuclear arsenal and blackmail the rest of the world.

Szilard's solution to this difficulty was directly connected to the broader political settlement between the superpowers. If the world's nations truly desired to keep the global settlement in force, he wrote, then they "might have to adopt a fresh attitude toward the problem of inspection, and decided to legalize the position of the informer."[71] Each nation, in other words, would adopt an official policy of actively encouraging its own citizens, government employees, and scientific researchers to report any violation of the overall disarmament plan. Indeed, he argued, each nation would allow all the other countries to employ local citizens as secret informers, providing large cash rewards and immunity from prosecution to anyone who discovered a violation. Why? Because, if it was true that the participating states had a strong interest in keeping the international settlement in force, then it would also be in their interest to convince other states that they were not cheating. Accordingly, they would do everything in their power to establish a credible system for reassuring their neighbors that any major violation would be reliably discovered and reported.

This picture represented a perfect reversal of the reasoning that characterized traditional international politics. Szilard had taken the logic of competitive self-interest and gradually subverted it, in steady increments, until he had pushed through to an entirely different logic of cooperative self-interest. He was fully aware of the utopian tension between his final vision and the harsh world of the Cold War; but he believed that the articulation of such a long-range vision was an essential first step—even for much more modest programs of change.

Thinking about the distant future, however, did not make much sense to Szilard unless it was coupled with prompt action to create a "breathing space" within the all-too-real Cold War of the present. Disregarding the fact that a scientist, in the 1940s, was expected to stick to laboratory experiments and graduate students, he began stepping with increasing confidence into the limelight of politics and the mass media.

Already during the fall of 1945, while the nation was still in disarray from the war, Szilard received his first lesson about maneuvering for success in American politics. The occasion was a bill being rushed through congress to form a new, military-controlled U.S. Atomic Energy Commission (AEC). Alarmed by the prospect of military officers obtaining preponderant authority over peacetime nuclear-policy decisions, Szilard immediately established a lobbying headquarters in a Washington hotel. He enlisted the support of fellow scientists, congressmen, and members of the press, and was thus able to persuade the House Military Affairs Committee to reopen its hearings on the bill. After being the first to present testimony, he began to contact everyone he knew to mobilize a solid opposition. Edward Shils, Szilard's friend from the University of Chicago, later wrote:

> I remember going to his suite in the building where we were staying. He was simultaneously on two separate long-distance calls on telephones in two rooms, going back and forth, putting down the receiver in one room while he went to take up the conversation in the other.[72]

Szilard was particularly effective in this early phase of the struggle, when prodigious outbursts of energy were required to build up a momentum of dissent. Gradually, however, as more and more atomic scientists pledged their support, founding a national federation in Washington to represent their new movement, Szilard began to withdraw toward the sidelines. Although he continued to work for the scientists' cause, he clearly preferred the role of catalyst to that of administrator and left the orchestration of the final lobbying drive to others. Eventually, the scientists won a major victory, and the AEC began functioning in 1947 under strictly civilian control.[73]

At the same time, Szilard was becoming increasingly alarmed by the anti-Communist hysteria that he saw reflected in the press and in the rhetoric of politicians. The only way out, in his view, was to embark on a campaign of education among the American public, breaking the psychological patterns of blind mistrust and setting new terms for the debate on foreign policy. In a letter to Einstein in March 1950, as Senator Joseph McCarthy was loudly accusing the U.S. State Department of being riddled with Communists, Szilard described in detail a proposed Citizens' Committee which would serve to clarify U.S. diplomatic aims by holding mock American-Russian debates. According to the plan, a group of well-educated U.S. citizens would study carefully a specific topic of international concern and then divide into two groups. One side would argue as if they were Russians, while the others would defend the "American" position. A transcript of the debate would then be made public. In this way, Szilard believed,

> if we could at least achieve that the public discussion of the Russian-American conflict will be henceforth carried on more in terms of the real conflicting interests which are involved and less in the irrational terms in which it has largely been conducted in these last four years, then we would already have achieved something of importance.[74]

Szilard proposed the Citizens' Committee for sponsorship by the Emergency Committee of Atomic Scientists, of which both he and Einstein were members; but the outbreak of the Korean War two months later forced him to postpone his project indefinitely.

Judging from the much lower profile that he kept during the remainder of the 1950s, it appears that Szilard reluctantly came to grips with McCarthyism, acknowledging the strength of this pervasive and irrational phenomenon, and recognizing that an immigrant like himself was in no position to launch an effective opposition. As a result, he focused more on his biological research and confined his political ideas to the relatively safe platform of the *Bulletin of the Atomic Scientists*. He continuously readapted his thinking, moreover, as the Cold War waxed and waned. The Korean War, between 1950 and 1953, had spurred the United States to a new level of involvement in the affairs of distant nations—a level unprecedented in the nation's history. From Iran to French Indochina, from Formosa to Guatemala, the U.S. government intervened to block what it perceived as a rising tide of global communism.[75] It signed security treaties with Australia and New Zealand in 1951, with Francisco Franco's Spain in 1953, and with the Southeast Asian nations in 1954. The U.S. defense budget grew dramatically during the 1950s (independently of the specific costs incurred by the Korean War), and the first U.S. hydrogen bomb cast its glaring light over the Pacific atoll of Eniwetok in 1951. Over half of the U.S. citizens in a 1954 nationwide poll declared that they "regarded favorably" the efforts of the senator from Wisconsin, Joe McCarthy.[76]

The Soviets, too, were thinking in global terms, but their means of projecting influence were not yet comparable with those of their rivals. In March 1953, four months before the Korean armistice, the death of Stalin abruptly shook the power hierarchy in the Eastern bloc. As the reins of governance passed into the hands of an uneasy oligarchy, some of the tighter controls of Stalinism were relaxed; but only two months after Stalin's death, the new rulers unflinchingly used tanks in great force to crush an anti-Soviet insurrection in

East Germany. By 1955, Nikita Khrushchev had emerged as the new Soviet leader, and it was he who presided over the formation of the Warsaw Pact, a mirror image to NATO in the Eastern bloc. Under Khrushchev's strong leadership, the Soviet Union began to acquire a new reputation as a modern superpower fully capable of challenging the leading role of the United States. By the end of the following year, the Soviet Union had concluded fourteen economic and military pacts with Third World countries.

A meeting between Eisenhower and Khrushchev in 1955 brought few substantial agreements but contributed to perceptions of a "thaw" in the Cold War; this perception was reinforced early in 1956, when Khrushchev astounded the world at the Twentieth Congress of the Soviet Communist party by denouncing Stalin's criminal excesses. The "thaw" abruptly ended, however, in November 1956—a month in which the overwhelming predominance of both superpowers became plain for all to see. On the Western side, a rash military action by France, Britain, and Israel to wrest the Suez Canal from Egypt's control turned into a humiliating fiasco after Washington issued peremptory instructions to place the matter before U.N. arbitration. On the Eastern side, a successful reform movement in Poland had led to growing hopes for independence and self-rule in Szilard's native Hungary; yet when the Hungarian reformers moved into outright revolution, troops from the Warsaw Pact poured in from all sides under Soviet orders. Although more than three thousand of his countrymen perished during the Soviet-sponsored invasion, Szilard maintained a strict silence on the subject. He may have feared that any public protest on his part would destroy his carefully cultivated position as an intermediary between East and West.[77]

The period of the mid-fifties "thaw," however, had provided an important opportunity for Szilard to emerge from his relative isolation. In 1955, Bertrand Russell and Albert Einstein had issued a joint "manifesto" on the nature of future wars, calling for a meeting of scientists from around the world to discuss the problems of atomic energy and international cooperation. The meeting, which became the first in an ongoing series, was held in 1957 in Pugwash, Nova Scotia, and started what gradually became known as the Pugwash Movement. Szilard participated with guarded enthusiasm. Although he attended eight of the eleven conferences held during the following seven years, and often presented long papers specifically written for each occasion, he remained skeptical that any conference held on so large a scale could really promote a "meeting of the minds" (as he called it). He realized that it would be unlikely for Soviet scientists to speak freely in so widely publicized and formal a context, and he disapproved of the vague and noncommittal proposals which were all that such a huge congregation could agree upon as its common platform. Accordingly, when the seventy participants of the third conference issued in 1958 a fundamental declaration that was to be "considered the tenet of the

Pugwash Movement," it was ratified unanimously—"with only Szilard abstaining."[78]

By the late 1950s, the United States and the Soviets had reached a tense modus vivendi. Although it would take another decade before Western military experts would begin talking of "parity" or "equivalence" in the military capabilities of the superpowers, the Soviets had made a huge impression in 1957 with the launching of Sputnik (the first man-made satellite) aboard a powerful rocket. Suddenly the fearful prediction that Szilard had made to President Roosevelt in 1945 was coming true: nuclear technology had been coupled with aeronautics and ballistics, threatening entire nations with a rain of destruction from one moment to the next. The mainland of the United States, long protected by vast oceans, was no longer a sanctuary but a naked and vulnerable target. Although initial U.S. fears of a "missile gap" later turned out to be exaggerated, the Soviets had succeeded in establishing what one American strategic expert described as a "balance of terror."[79]

Szilard's periodic articles in the *Bulletin of the Atomic Scientists* during the late fifties and early sixties clearly reflected these new strategic realities. Although he still clung to his long-term hopes for a comprehensive settlement between the superpowers, he devoted several extended essays to the more pressing problem of stabilizing the U.S.-Soviet rivalry, so as to mitigate the inherent dangers of the arms race. In one article, entitled "How to Live with the Bomb and Survive" (1960), he pragmatically accepted the rationale of nuclear deterrence, or mutually assured destruction, that was gradually becoming the cornerstone of the superpowers' strategic policies.[80] Nevertheless, he characteristically pushed this rationale much farther than most "defense intellectuals" of the period.[81] If the superpowers' statesmen truly believed in nuclear deterrence, Szilard argued, then their primary goal should be to reach an explicit understanding about how to handle conflicts and crisis situations without triggering a disastrous escalation that neither side wanted. They should establish formal procedures for handling such crises well in advance, so that neither side would be likely to misread the other's actions; and they should promptly scale back their nuclear forces to low and equal levels, since it was far easier to monitor a small and stable number of weapons than a constantly changing and proliferating arsenal.[82]

At the heart of Szilard's thinking, in these short-term proposals for stabilizing the arms race, just as in his long-range hopes for disarmament, lay the goal of enhancing communication between the two enemies. Without effective communication, even the most modest attempts at cooperation were bound to fail; yet the existing points of contact between the superpowers in the late 1950s struck him as hopelessly inadequate. Official diplomacy consisted mainly of mutual accusations and posturing; such informal channels as the

Pugwash conferences seemed too far removed from the realities of power to accomplish much. It was here, therefore, that Szilard decided to embark on a bold attempt at conducting diplomacy on his own. Starting early in 1959, he began to write a series of letters directly to Nikita Khrushchev, describing his plan for orchestrating a more far-reaching "meeting of the minds" between the Americans and Russians. To his astonishment, the Soviet leader wrote back; and for the next four years, Szilard and Khrushchev traded proposals back and forth. These contacts with the Soviet leader represented the culmination of ideas that Szilard had developed for his "Bund" in the early 1930s, and they ultimately came to constitute one of the more important episodes in his career.

What Szilard envisioned was a small, unofficial forum for Russian-American discussions on arms control; the novelty in his idea was to seek official approval for the informal talks and to have off-duty government experts as well as scientists participating. A delicate balance had to be struck, Szilard thought, between the rigidity of official negotiations among the powerful, and the relative flexibility (but proportionate impotence) of discussions among mere outsiders. Since the participating Russian and American experts would not speak as representatives of their governments, they would be freed from the need to use bargaining tactics and could thus communicate more clearly. At the same time, since these persons would have close informal connections with decision makers who were actually in power, the discussions' impact on official policy might still prove considerable.

Szilard knew that the Soviet government in recent years had issued several resounding proclamations calling for "General and Complete Disarmament." Western defense experts had routinely dismissed these Soviet proposals as mere propaganda, pointing to the fact that the Soviet government refused to allow on-site inspection of its weapons facilities as proof that it made its offers in bad faith.[83] Szilard, however, decided to take the Soviet offers more seriously. Although he doubted that "General and Complete Disarmament" could ever take place, except as the final development in a much broader process of political accommodation, he nonetheless believed that a propitious moment had arrived for taking the first step.

Szilard's major opportunity arose in October 1960, when Khrushchev traveled to New York, flanked by representatives of all the Eastern-bloc countries, to attend the Fifteenth General Assembly of the United Nations. In addition to frequent diplomatic receptions and vigorously combative press conferences, Khrushchev met the Cuban leader Fidel Castro for the first time, mended fences with Yugoslavia's Tito (with whom relations had been severely strained), and conferred privately with world statesmen from Ghana's President Kwame Nkrumah to Britain's Conservative Prime Minister Harold Macmillan.[84] Amid the hectic schedule of engagements, the Soviet leader set aside fifteen minutes for an interview with Szilard. Their talk, once it had begun, actually lasted two hours.

Szilard and Khrushchev met under awkward circumstances, for the international atmosphere in the fall of 1960 was not a propitious one for conducting diplomacy—whether openly or behind the scenes. An American presidential campaign was reaching its climax, as candidates Richard Nixon and John Kennedy fiercely vied with each other in presenting images of patriotism and anti-Communist toughness.[85] Only five months earlier, the Soviet leader and President Eisenhower had abruptly scuttled a scheduled summit meeting after Soviet antiaircraft rockets shot down an American U-2 spy plane near the Russian city of Sverdlovsk. "We came to New York," Khrushchev later wrote, "determined to show that American imperialism isn't all-powerful and that we knew our rights, despite the anti-Soviet howling and growling that was stirred up against us."[86] At one point during the U.N. sessions, the Soviet leader even took off his shoe and angrily banged the podium in front of him to interrupt a speech by a Western diplomat.[87] Large motorcades escorted Khrushchev to and from the U.N. skyscraper, for Manhattan's streets bristled with demonstrators waving placards and shouting slogans to denounce the Communist system and its representatives. When Szilard arrived at the Soviet U.N. mission headquarters at 11 A.M. on October 5, he had to pass through a barricade of two hundred New York policemen who had formed a protective *cordon sanitaire* around the entire block.[88]

Szilard brought to the interview a seven-page letter in Russian, summarizing his views on the burning issues of contemporary international politics. Through an interpreter, he told Khrushchev that although time was short, he wanted first to "take a minute and talk in a somewhat lighter vein."

I said that I had brought him a sample of the Schick Injecto razor, which is not an expensive razor but is very good. The blade must be changed after one or two weeks and the blades I brought with me should last for about six months. Thereafter, if he would let me know that he likes the razor, I would send him from time to time fresh blades, but this I can do, of course, only as long as there is no war.

K. said that if there is a war he will stop shaving, and he thinks that most other people will stop shaving also. I said that I was somewhat distressed to see that, during his stay in New York, he stressed only the points where he was in disagreement with American statesmen and that I thought he might have found a few points on which he was in agreement. . . . K. asked what points I had in mind and I told him that he might have said, for instance, that he was in agreement with Senator Kennedy on everything that Kennedy was saying about Nixon, and he could have added that he was in agreement with everything that Nixon was saying—about Kennedy.[89]

Szilard's record of the interview does not say whether Khrushchev was amused, but the length of the ensuing conversation suggests that the Soviet premier had seen through the devices of the razor and the political wisecrack and understood that Szilard was more interested in peace than in political partisanship.

Three main themes dominated the conversation. First and foremost in Szilard's mind, of course, was the subject of rational communication between the superpowers. He reiterated the proposal he had made in his letters for creating an informal forum of discussion among superpower "insiders." Khrushchev had no objection to this idea, adding "that Topchiev, the General Secretary of the Academy of Sciences of the USSR, will be able to arrange all the contacts that we might want."[90]

Encouraged by Khrushchev's response, Szilard next proposed that a direct phone link be set up between the White House and the Kremlin. Apart from its potential usefulness in times of international emergency, Szilard told Khrushchev that "the installation of such a telephone connection would dramatize the continued presence of a danger which will stay with us as long as the long-range rockets and bombs are retained."[91] The Soviet leader then alarmed Szilard by revealing that, just before leaving the Soviet Union, "an American manoeuvre was reported to him, about which there was some doubt, which forced him to order 'rocket readiness,' and he added that, incidentally, this readiness [had] still not been rescinded."[92] Khrushchev told Szilard that if the U.S. president approved of the idea, then he, too, would be willing to have the special phone line installed.[93]

The remainder of the conversation dealt with the two interlinked themes of picturing how a disarmed world might work, and figuring out how to get "from here to there." Szilard chose to confront Khrushchev first with one of the more pressing short-term issues. During the preceding two years, relations between the superpowers had been dangerously strained by disagreements over the fate of Berlin. Khrushchev had issued an ultimatum in 1958, threatening to turn the divided city over to East German control if diplomacy failed to produce a final agreement on the city's future status. John Foster Dulles, U.S. secretary of state, had responded that NATO would meet such a move "if need be with military force."[94] Tensions were still high in the fall of 1960, and Szilard had come up with a solution that must have raised Khrushchev's eyebrows:

> East Germany might offer to shift its capital from East Berlin to Dresden on condition that West Germany shifts its capital from Bonn to Munich. If that is done, then it would be possible to create two free cities: East Berlin and West Berlin with a view of perhaps

forming, at some later time, a similar confederation between East Germany and West Germany.[95]

The proposal typified the more utopian and fanciful side of Szilard, for it was highly reasonable in an abstract way, and yet seemed deliberately to ignore the immense political obstacles that would rapidly block any such act of international sleight of hand. Khrushchev immediately rebuffed the idea, saying "that he could not very well ask [the East German Premier] to shift the capital of East Germany away from East Berlin."[96] Here, Szilard had clearly underestimated the political pressures impinging on both Soviet and American statesmen, blocking them from any moves that could remotely appear as "backing down."

Just as they did not see eye-to-eye on the Berlin question, Szilard and Khrushchev also failed to reach substantial agreement on a long-range vision of a disarmed world. Reading through the detailed letter in which Szilard explained his views, Khrushchev agreed that the power balance in the U.N. General Assembly would gradually shift away from its predominantly pro-U.S. stance. He praised Szilard's perceptiveness for predicting that "a world police force, under the central command of the Secretary-General of the United Nations, would not be acceptable to the Soviet Union in the present circumstances, and it might not be acceptable to the U.S. in circumstances that might prevail a few years hence."[97] Khrushchev disagreed, however, with Szilard's proposal to get around this obstacle by creating regional U.N. police forces whose actions would be governed by committees of nations specially selected by the superpowers. To Khrushchev, this proposal appeared (correctly) as a return to the traditional conception of dividing the world into spheres of influence belonging to the various Great Powers. He told Szilard "that the nations in the region where such a regional force operates would come under the control of the nations who controlled the police force."[98]

Szilard explained to Khrushchev that "while the Great Powers might be able to exert a certain amount of influence in such regions, at least their control would not be direct but rather indirect."[99] The Soviet leader, however, whose nation was just beginning to come into its own as a real superpower, apparently did not find this voluntary shackling of the Great Powers attractive. He brought the conversation to an end, asking Szilard how he would feel if he were to send him a case of vodka. Szilard answered "that I wondered if I couldn't have something better than vodka."

> "What do you have in mind," said Khrushchev, and I said, "Borjum." A few days earlier when Khrushchev delivered one of his long speeches before the United Nations, he had a glass of mineral water in front of him from which he drank from time to time and several times he pointed to it and said, "Borjum, excellent Russian

mineral water." When I said, "Borjum," Khrushchev beamed. "We have two kinds of mineral water in Russia," he said, "they are both excellent and we shall send you samples of both." [100]

After their meeting, Szilard and Khrushchev continued to correspond with growing frequency. Having received a formal go-ahead from the Soviet leader, Szilard began contacting prominent Americans to enlist their support for a series of high-level but informal discussions. He called his undertaking the "Angels Project," and explained his choice of this name in a letter to Khrushchev:

> Contrary to what one might think, most people closely connected with the [Kennedy] Administration are keenly aware of the need of avoiding an all-out arms race. Moreover, there are a number of men among them who are "on the side of the angels" and who have consistently taken the position that the United States should be prepared to give up certain temporary advantages it holds, for the sake of attaining an agreement with the Soviet Union that would stop the arms race. [101]

Between October 1960 and October 1962, Szilard worked tirelessly to bring his project together. He obtained the sponsorship of the National Academy of Arts and Sciences, sought (and received) substantial pledges of funding from major foundations, and vigorously promoted his idea with high officials in the Kennedy administration. Among the "Angels" who tentatively agreed to participate were Henry Kissinger (then a professor at Harvard), Marvin Goldberger (Princeton), Roger Fisher (Harvard), George Rathjens (a former advisor to President Eisenhower), and Herbert York (later to be chief U.S. negotiator in the Comprehensive Nuclear Test Ban talks). These figures were typical of Szilard's chosen "constituency": scientists with good connections in government, ex-diplomats, liberal or "centrist" academics, all of whom shared Szilard's faith in the intrinsic value of international communication and compromise. It was to this relatively small but influential elite that Szilard regularly turned when he needed support for his projects.

Not all those whom Szilard approached responded favorably. "Your letter," wrote back one indignant professor at the Stanford Linear Accelerator, "identifies the individuals whom you are asking to join you in these discussions in effect as a minority of men of good intent working in an otherwise hostile environment of the U.S. Government. This I feel is grossly unfair." [102] Szilard responded (by return mail) that even though everyone in the government might indeed want to stop the arms race, there was still a valid distinction to be made between those who were willing to make compromises (the Angels) and those who were bent on negotiating from a position of superiority. "It is the very essence of the proposed project," he went on to explain,

that the American and Russian participants would not be representative samples, composed of both angels and non-angels. [If they
were,] they would not be likely to reach a consensus that would
be far-reaching enough to be interesting. But if they are samples
biased in favor of the angels, the group might come up with the
image of a disarmament agreement that America and Russia might
conceivably be prepared to accept at some future date. Such an
agreement would presumably not be currently acceptable to either
of the two governments; nevertheless, the image could be very useful because it could focus attention on the goal towards which we
might want to move.[103]

And he could not resist further ruffling his critic, as he closed his letter, with a
typical volley of playful mischief:

Of all those with whom I have consulted, you were the only one
so far who objected to the basic concept of the project. This does
not necessarily mean, of course, that the others are right and that
you are wrong; you might well be very much brighter than some
of those others with whom I have consulted, but I am certain that
you would not expect me to concede that you are brighter than
I am.[104]

During the months before the Cuban missile crisis in 1962, Szilard sent
Khrushchev regular reports on the progress of the Angels project. In mid-
October, as terse ultimatums went back and forth between the superpowers and
the U.S. navy prepared to intercept several Soviet ships carrying nuclear missiles to Cuba, Szilard suddenly flew to Switzerland (presumably taking "Big
Bomb Suitcase" and "Small Bomb Suitcase" with him on the plane). He was
still there in early November, waiting for the tense international atmosphere to
calm down, when he received a letter through the Soviet legation in Geneva. It
was from Khrushchev, who began his letter by speaking in a strange tone of
awe about "the international crisis that we have just survived." Without giving
any details, the Soviet leader admitted to Szilard just how close to a "devastating thermonuclear war" Russia and America had come: "during those days
the world was practically on the brink of such a war."[105] Khrushchev then went
on to speak with surprising fervor about the Angels project:

I like this proposal. . . . My understanding is that the participants
of the meeting . . . are to hold their discussions without . . . [outsid-
ers], without representatives of television or radio corporations.
And the conclusions to which they come are to be considered as
their personal views. But at the same time they are to be people
enjoying the respect and confidence of public opinion in their
countries. . . . Their conclusions could greatly influence public

opinion, and even officials and governments would have to listen to them.[106]

Unfortunately, the Angels project—and especially its creator—had not been faring so well in the eyes of the Kennedy administration. A year before, during the early months of Kennedy's presidency, Szilard had moved to Washington to get acquainted with the new wielders of power and sound out their receptiveness to his own way of thinking. "I was stopped in my tracks," he wrote, "by the invasion of Cuba by Cuban exiles" in April 1961.[107] The U.S.-sponsored invasion at the Bay of Pigs so outraged Szilard that he drafted a petition to President Kennedy and secured signatures from "about one in six" members of the National Academy of Arts and Sciences. "In deciding whether to use force," the petition read,

> our Government must give due regard to the [United Nations] Charter and it must not adopt a double standard of morality; it must not apply one yardstick to the actions of the Soviet Union, England, or France and another one to the actions of the United States.[108]

This kind of stinging rebuke, duly delivered to the White House with a cover letter from Szilard, was not likely to win friends in high places—particularly with a president unusually sensitive to the judgment of America's intellectual elite. In December 1962, Szilard showed his recent letter from Khrushchev about the Angels project to McGeorge Bundy, Kennedy's special assistant for National Security Affairs; but Bundy remained unimpressed and made it clear that he was not in favor of the scheme. "Szilard," Bundy later wrote, "was not the kind of man for this truly unofficial but well-connected process."[109] During the spring of 1963, Szilard continued to correspond with Bundy's assistant at the White House, Carl Kaysen, but he made little progress. Although President Kennedy himself "wished the project success" in a note to the prospective Angels in June 1963, a disheartening blow came shortly afterward, on July 1.[110] William Foster, head of the U.S. Arms Control and Disarmament Agency, ruled that none of the agency's consultants would be permitted to participate in "Angels" discussions at any time. This not only excluded one of the more influential "Angels," Herbert York, from participating, but also created a significant imbalance in the American and Russian teams. "I am uncertain in my own mind," Szilard admitted to Khrushchev two weeks later,

> just how useful the proposed conference would be in the present circumstances. . . . No official of the American Government would directly participate, yet it would be necessary for some of the junior officials of the Soviet Ministry of Foreign Relations or the Ministry of Defense to participate in the conference, and the con-

ference could hardly be useful if Soviet participation were limited to the Academy of Sciences of the USSR.[111]

Confronted with this clear reluctance on the part of the U.S. government to provide the project with serious support, the Russians too drew back. Through a Kremlin spokesperson, Khrushchev told Szilard that the Russians henceforth would rely on the informal channels of communication already established among scientists at the Pugwash conferences.[112] The Angels project had failed, and Szilard admitted as much in a letter to Secretary of Defense Robert McNamara in February 1964: "I myself shall make no further attempts to engage the Russians in 'private discussions' on the subject of arms control."[113]

Was Szilard surprised by the disappointing outcome of his efforts? Probably not. "It is not possible," he had written only a year before, "to get the Government to do something that no one inside the Government wants done."[114] He did not believe that the government was full of warmongers, but simply that it was dominated by a rather short-sighted view that the United States should only negotiate with the Russians from a position of superior strength. Since an analogous constituency on the Russian side manifested this same attitude with perfect symmetry, the arms race went forward in an endless spiral. The Angels project had rested on a gamble that enlightened minorities on both sides of the Cold War could break the ongoing deadlock, if only they were given official approval for trying. Here, however, lay the key ambiguity in Szilard's plan: Was it equally in the interest of the U.S. and Soviet politicians to embark on such a gamble? How did the Angels project figure in the calculus of the superpowers' statesmen?

In 1963, the Soviet Union was still weaker militarily than the United States, both in conventional and nuclear weapons. Kennedy had used the widespread (and erroneous) perception of a "missile gap" in 1961 to launch a massive American arms buildup; yet the military superiority of the United States at the time of the Cuban missile crisis had constituted a decisive factor in Kennedy's resolution to face the Soviets down.[115] Khrushchev, keenly aware of these facts, was under intense domestic pressure to show that the Soviet position had not been seriously undermined by his Cuban blunder.[116] Amid this configuration of political pressures, the appearance of Szilard with his Angels scheme may well have seemed tantalizing to the Soviet leader. Szilard would choose the American "Angels," while Khrushchev himself could handpick the Soviet ones; this would conveniently exclude the U.S. government from the process of shaping the meetings. Furthermore, if the American "Angels" truly believed that "the United States should be prepared to give up certain temporary advantages," it was hard to see how such talks could go badly for the Soviet Union. Since disarmament talks reinforced the image of a negotiation between equals, while possibly mitigating or at least obscuring the Soviets' actual military inferiority, Khrushchev had every interest in encouraging discussions of this nature. The Kennedy administration, however, which had gained power in 1961 precisely on the platform that the United States was falling *behind* the Soviets, most manifestly did not. In 1963, Kennedy and McNamara were in the process of increasing the U.S. defense budget by 25 percent, while reorganizing the Pentagon and articulating their new military-diplomatic policy of containment through "flexible response." They were not uninterested in arms control, but they had already defined for themselves a much narrower set of agreements to be sought with the Soviets; and they had been painstakingly guiding their own team of negotiators toward precisely such a limited but tangible goal in the Atmospheric Test Ban talks. Few things could have been more disruptive of their plans than to enter unpredictable discussions of far-reaching disarmament—discussions orchestrated by a well-intentioned scientist over whom they had little or no control. Thus, while "wishing the project success," they allowed it to fall by the wayside.

Szilard did not see Kennedy and McNamara as dark figures deliberately impeding the progress of peace. He did, however, regard them as being far too deeply embroiled in the day-to-day problems of running the government to provide real leadership for the long-term safety of the nation. He earnestly believed in their good intentions as they sought to stabilize the strategic arms race, edging away from former Secretary of State Dulles's policies of "massive retaliation" and diplomatic "brinksmanship." All this was reasonable in itself, he thought, but it was not nearly enough to bring about the drastic changes that were needed in the long run. "I do not believe," he had written earlier,

> that the problem which faces the world today can be solved at the level of foreign policy in the narrow sense of the term . . . , nor do I believe that it is within the power of the [U.S. government to tackle] this problem without the full support of the American people for a bold and constructive solution.[117]

Therefore, at the same time as he was piecing together the Angels project in 1961, Szilard began a much broader political experiment to see how many "Angels" existed among the American population as a whole, and to organize these grass-roots "Angels" into an effective political force.

This political experiment—the last in Szilard's career—began in the fall of 1961, when he delivered a gripping speech about the nuclear peril at nine universities and colleges throughout the United States. He had recognized that the atmosphere of McCarthyism was truly over, and that the widespread docility of the American public before governmental authority had been left behind with the coming of the new decade. Blacks in the South were first stirring, in what were to be triumphant years of nonviolent activism for civil rights, while university campuses experienced the prickling beginnings of nonconformism and revolt against "the Establishment." A novel about nuclear Armageddon, Nevil Shute's *On the Beach,* was a troubling bestseller; and President Eisenhower himself, in a memorable farewell speech the preceding January, had warned his fellow Americans:

> This conjunction of an immense military establishment and a . . . permanent armaments industry of vast proportions . . . is new in the American experience. The total influence—economic, political, even spiritual—is felt in every city, every state house, every office of the federal government. . . . The potential for the disastrous rise of misplaced power exists and will persist.[118]

Szilard was apparently struck not only by the content of Eisenhower's speech but especially by the fact that such a speech could be made at all. Disappointed by the international actions and prevailing attitudes of the new Kennedy administration, he decided that his Angels project would not be enough. He wrote a speech of his own entitled "Are We on the Road to War?" and embarked on a nationwide speaking tour to see how his ideas would fare at the grass-roots level. The response he received was so enthusiastic that he began devising plans to transform this diffuse antiwar sentiment into a coherent political movement.

The organization he founded for this purpose, the Council for a Livable World, is still functioning three decades later. As Szilard conceived it, the Washington-based council would receive pledges of money from a wide variety of members whose common concern was to encourage a departure from the foreign policy of the Cold War. These funds would then be directed to the electoral campaigns of congressional candidates whose voting records had demonstrated an unequivocal commitment to peace and arms control. "As far as federal elections are concerned," Szilard wrote, members of the movement "would be pledged to cast their vote, *disregarding domestic issues,* solely on the issue of war and peace." [119] By thus concentrating exclusively on the peace issue, Szilard apparently hoped to avoid the fragmentation and internecine strife that prevented many pacifist organizations of the period from wielding political clout.

By February 1961, Szilard had received over one thousand letters from persons throughout the nation pledging 2 percent of their annual incomes for campaign contributions. "I am overwhelmed by the mail that pours in," he admitted.[120] From the *New York Times* to the *San Francisco Chronicle,* Szilard's speaking tour had received detailed and sympathetic coverage, and his appeal for collaborators stirred up a surprisingly hopeful and eager response. In the words of one Chicago newspaper columnist:

> Szilard . . . proposes something that can be done. I strongly recommend it to those . . . who despair, to those who have already turned

away from these words because they fear and feel they are impotent in the face of [the threat of war]. . . . Whatever help he can use from this citizen, he will get.[121]

Here, then, was the "Bund" of the 1930s making its appearance in a new form, after being adapted by Szilard to fit the political style of American democracy. The Council for a Livable World was not an explicitly elitist organization, as the proposed "Bund" would have been, for it relied directly on the support of progressive public opinion. Like the "Bund," however, the council was led by a core group of prominent individuals—many of them scientists, not surprisingly—who would define the council's platform and choose the candidates to be funded. This "Board of Directors" would provide the long-range sense of direction that Szilard found sadly lacking in American politics. "Whether such a movement," he wrote, "could grow further and come to represent not only a decisive amount in campaign contributions but also a significant number of votes, would . . . depend on the future course of world events."[122]

By March 1963—less than a year after founding the council—Szilard was able to send out the following report to council members:

During the [1962] election the Council did fairly well. . . . We received and transmitted to George McGovern checks totaling over $20,000 and to Senator [Joseph] Clark over $10,000. McGovern was elected with a margin of a few hundred votes and it is generally recognized here that the Council was instrumental in his election.[123]

Thus, at the same time as the Angels project was approaching collapse, the council was beginning to take off. It had proved impossible for an "outsider" like Szilard to make a direct impact on the diplomacy of the superpowers, but his indirect approach of influencing the U.S. electoral process was ultimately more effective. Although the council did not grow into the major political organization that Szilard had envisioned, it continued to provide a focal point for the energies of concerned citizens throughout the following decades. Szilard himself died less than two years after founding the council; but he had established a lasting prototype for the conversion of widely dispersed popular sentiment into hard political currency. Long before the "Political Action Committee" became a standard vehicle for the lobbying efforts of countless special-interest groups, he had pioneered this idea to promote the special interest of a "livable world."

Was Szilard unrealistic? Did he have an overly optimistic view of human nature and of politics—and was it this that prompted his quixotic efforts to nudge the superpowers beyond the diplomacy of the Cold War?

It is worth noting that Szilard was not alone in advocating an arduous kind of "realism," oriented toward a radical transformation of world politics. In May 1950, the *Bulletin of the Atomic Scientists* printed a pithy article, "On Negotiating with the Russians," by the eminent political scientist Hans Morgenthau. Szilard already knew Morgenthau, for they both held positions at the University of Chicago; and he so strongly approved of Morgenthau's article that he later quoted a long excerpt from it in a letter to Secretary of State Dean Acheson.[124] Morgenthau declared himself a firm believer in the "realist" current of political theory—the current of *Realpolitik,* which conceived international politics as an unregulated competition for power among nations pursuing their own self-interest.[125] Yet in his article, Morgenthau started from the same premise as Szilard: "[T]he choice before the world is between negotiated settlement and war, that is, universal destruction."[126] Like Szilard, he argued that the Russians would live up to any political agreement as long as it was in their interest to do so—and he strongly attacked the typical Cold War view that any arrangement advantageous to the Russians must automatically be disadvantageous to the United States. He then proposed, as the basis for a comprehensive settlement between the superpowers, a return to the traditional practice of dividing the world into spheres of influence. Morgenthau cited Winston Churchill and Arnold Toynbee as fervent contemporary supporters of this idea, and his closing quotation from Toynbee must have particularly gratified Szilard:

> In 1904 France and Great Britain went into consultation, worked over the map of the world, and wherever there was friction between them they ironed it out and made a bargain on a fifty-fifty basis: "You have this, we keep that; and we will forget about that old quarrel of ours." In 1907 Great Britain and Russia did the same. This is a difficult thing to do, in view of the traditional rivalries and dislikes of nations, and we succeeded in doing it in those cases only under strong pressure; we had a common aggressive enemy of whom we were all afraid, and that was Germany. But, after all, in the present situation America and Russia have a common enemy too, of whom I am sure they are likewise afraid, and that is atomic energy.[127]

Unlike Toynbee, however—whose proposal sounded like a revival of old-style European imperialism—Szilard's spheres of influence were not based on "You have this, we keep that." Instead, his own plan was to modify this traditional notion by gradually shifting military control to regional police forces, thereby submerging the preponderant influence of the superpowers within a broader system of collective security.

The question of Szilard's realism was directly taken up in 1950 by the eminent French political philosopher Raymond Aron, in response to a provocative article on European security by Szilard. In 1949, shortly after President Truman had announced the successful detonation of a Soviet atomic weapon, Szilard predicted in the *Bulletin of the Atomic Scientists* that this qualitative change in the strategic equation would drastically undermine the credibility of the American nuclear "umbrella" which protected Western Europe. Suddenly, he reasoned, it had become possible for the Russians to incinerate Western Europe overnight, without directly threatening the United States. Although he acknowledged that the existence of NATO would probably continue to deter Russian aggression, he posed a difficult question for Europeans to answer: "[Can] anyone seriously expect the French, Belgians, and the Dutch thus to accept, for the sake of a lessened probability of war, the absolute certainty that in case of war their cities will be utterly destroyed?"[128] This question penetrated to the key psychological weakness of the NATO alliance: the serious possibility that a "limited" nuclear war might be fought on European soil, without involving the territories of the superpowers. Szilard proposed a fairly straightforward solution to this problem: NATO should be dismantled, but the United States should conclude defense pacts with each of the Western European countries separately; Western Europe should be neutralized, and the United States should cease to prepare "those nations in peacetime as bases for possible future military operations against Russia."[129] In this way, the Western Europeans would be encouraged to build up their own defenses, while continuing to rely on the deterrent effect of a U.S. defensive guarantee; but NATO bases in Western Europe would no longer constitute a potential military threat to the Soviet Union—thereby removing a basic incentive for Soviet aggression.

Within six months, Aron's response to this ambitious proposal arrived from across the Atlantic and was also published in the *Bulletin*.[130] Aron recognized that Szilard was the first to speak openly and clearly about the upcoming vulnerability of Western Europe; yet he entirely disagreed with Szilard's solution. According to Aron, Szilard's idea was *politically* unrealistic because, unlike Switzerland or Argentina during World War II, Europe was itself a primary object of superpower contention and hence intrinsically nonneutral; Szilard's idea was *strategically* unrealistic, because to have a neutral Europe on its huge Western flank would be intolerable for the Soviet Union; it was *ideologically* unrealistic, because the rival social theories governing the Soviet Union and Western Europe would inevitably lead to reciprocal antagonism in a crisis. Aron contended that Szilard was far too optimistic about the possibility that open dialogue with the Soviet Union would lead to an international understanding—and concluded, with regret, that the only realistic option for the United States and Western Europe was to continue waging the Cold War until the Russians began to behave themselves.

Much of the disagreement between Szilard and Aron stemmed from a deeper opposition between two *kinds* of realism. Underlying Aron's form of realism was the basic question, *"What is it possible to achieve, given the record of the past?"* As Aron reconstructed it, the record of the past clearly demonstrated that force, and the threat of force, must remain the ultimate arbiters within the international arena. In his view, moreover, this fundamental fact of politics did not necessarily bode ill for the U.S.-Soviet rivalry. "As long as the Soviet Union is afraid of general war," he predicted, "she will refrain from creating a *casus belli,* and the cold war will retain the same limited character which distinguishes it at present."[131]

Szilard's realism, however, reflected an entirely different type of question: *"What is it necessary to achieve, given the prospects of the future?"* Unlike Aron, Szilard did not believe that the Cold War could continue indefinitely without breaking down at some point into all-out war. "The traditional aim of foreign policy," he wrote, "is to prolong the peace; that is, to lengthen the interval between two wars. What is the use of postponing war if we know—as we know today—that it will be all the more terrible the later it comes?"[132]

From Aron's perspective, which was quite similar in this respect to Louise Weiss's, Szilard was engaging in wishful thinking: for even if it was true that the survival of humankind depended upon a long-term settlement between America and Russia, this did not in itself render such a settlement likely, or even possible. The fact that something was urgently needed for survival did not necessarily bring it any closer to realization.

On the other hand, Aron's perspective also was open to criticism: for in Szilard's view, the hardline mentality of persons like Aron and Edward Teller could not help but have the effect of a self-fulfilling prophecy. Aron had ended his article with the conclusion that the "best that Americans can do is to maintain their superiority in armaments and every time a particular problem arises, not to leave the slightest doubt as to the attitude they intend to adopt."[133] By refusing to see a way out of the Cold War, Szilard believed, one entered a mechanical spiral of logic that could only result in steady escalation of armaments and continuation of hostilities.

Both lines of argument involved specific risks. Szilard's "realism" rested on a wager that human beings, under the threat of nuclear destruction, would succeed in drastically reshaping their military relations, building a formal international system of stability and cooperation. Aron's "realism" rested on a wager that no such radical institutional transformation was necessary: rather, the fear of nuclear war would automatically impose self-restraint upon the world's statesmen, and this self-restraint could be counted upon to last indefinitely. In a sense, therefore, both positions were pinned upon a similar hope: that the nuclear peril would force statesmen to learn how to govern their behavior with an unprecedented rationality and self-control.

Here, in the end, lay the two principal flaws in Szilard's reasoning—flaws that Louise Weiss might have pointed out, had she confronted him in direct debate: Szilard deliberately avoided discussing the need for a global "arbiter"; and he assumed, like Aron, that rationality would prevail.

The first of these flaws stemmed from Szilard's repugnance for most visions of "world government," as they had emerged since the early years of the twentieth century. The idea of a single world government had vaguely attracted him in the 1930s and mid-1940s, but he eventually came to the conclusion that such a centralized institution—even in the unlikely event of its establishment—would constitute a cumbersome and potentially oppressive monstrosity. Instead, he put forth the alternative vision of a more decentralized world order in which the United Nations would function only as a coordinating body, while actual policy-making was left to regional subgroups of nations.

This vision, however, left Szilard open to some tough questions: Supposing two or more of his proposed "regional police forces" developed opposing positions in a crisis? Supposing two member nations in a single regional force took strongly conflicting views? What would prevent them from coming to blows, and who would arbitrate between them? Szilard never addressed these kinds of questions, because he believed that no single authority of arbitration was likely to be accepted by all the world's peoples for the foreseeable future. And yet the logic here remained inescapable: any formal system of "collective security" clearly required the recognition by all participants of some higher authority, like a World Court, before which conflicting members might negotiate their respective claims. If such a court was to have real clout, then each national or regional government would first have to surrender a portion of its own sovereignty to it, subordinating certain aspects of its power to the authority of the court. No "halfway solution" to this problem existed: either the nations could agree upon a higher authority to defend their vital interests, or they would have to continue to defend them on their own behalf. Like Weiss, of course, Szilard knew from personal experience what the fate of such international arbitrating bodies had been during the 1930s; but he failed to address this crucial problem in clear terms and pinned his hopes, instead, on a rather vague notion that the nuclear menace would force even the most intractable opponents to behave reasonably and reach a compromise.

Here, indeed, lay Szilard's second key weakness: his elitist and overly rationalized view of politics. A passage from "The Voice of the Dolphins," written in 1961, revealed the problematic assumptions underlying his position:

> Political issues are often complex, but they are rarely anywhere as deep as the scientific problems which were solved in the first half of the century. These scientific problems were solved with amazing rapidity because they were constantly exposed to discussion among scientists, and thus it appears reasonable to expect that the solution of political problems could be greatly speeded up . . . if they were subjected to the same kind of discussion.[134]

Szilard was perfectly aware that partisan political issues could not be reduced to the clearer terms of scientific discourse; but he never appears to have relinquished a lingering hope of prodding politics *closer* to the norms of scientific truth. Perhaps, he reasoned, it was impossible to cleanse political conflicts of the inherent bias that pervaded them, but at least it might be possible to reduce that bias to much lower levels. Thus, in his earnest desire to find a common ground, he tended to exaggerate the capacity for people to act rationally and disinterestedly where vital interests were concerned; and he overlooked the blind self-destructiveness of human beings in a state of passion. Louise Weiss would probably have reminded him, if she had had the chance, of Adolf Hitler's stance when the Second World War began to turn against him. Far from taking a rational and prudent course, he had said, in effect: "I *will* succeed in my designs, or I will bring down utter ruin upon my *Reich* and the rest of the world!"

This last consideration applied to Raymond Aron's position as well: for on what did Aron base his rather sanguine assumption that the militarized peace of the Cold War could continue indefinitely? Had there ever been a peace that rested on mutual threats and that did not degenerate at some point into bloody conflict? Aron could reply that nuclear weapons had raised the stakes so high that the ground rules had fundamentally shifted: nobody, not even Hitler, would want to attack a nuclear-armed foe. And yet, Hitler *had* been willing to risk the future of his nation, as well as his own life, on a wild military gamble—attacking powers whose demographic and economic base vastly outstripped those of Germany. How could Aron be sure that no more gamblers of this sort would be born, or that miscalculations, malfunctioning machines, or some other imponderables might not someday come into play? Aron's notion that the nuclear menace would somehow force a fundamental rationality upon international relations for the foreseeable future seems equally as problematic, in this sense, as Szilard's.

Nevertheless, Aron's "realism" had the advantage of advocating a continuation of existing patterns of behavior, whereas Szilard called for a radical departure from contemporary assumptions and habits. For this reason, it was Aron's vision that prevailed, and has continued to prevail, even in the multipolar political context of the post–Cold War era. Neither Aron nor Szilard offered a fully satisfactory solution to the problems of power and domination that Louise Weiss so bluntly articulated. Aron's stoic version of "muddling through," while it certainly has "worked" since the 1950s, does not offer a very comforting prospect for the coming century. Szilard's vision of thoroughgoing international cooperation, on the other hand, still seems rather far-fetched and idealistic.

This does not mean, however, that the two positions are fruitless or uninteresting; for they both contained elements that, when combined, offered some promise of a path to follow for the long haul. Aron insisted (quite plausibly) that military deterrence would have to form the basis of international politics for the foreseeable future; in the absence of a higher arbiter, there was simply no other option available. Yet this logic was by no means incompatible with Szilard's proposals for pushing and prodding the world toward greater cooperation. Although deterrence unavoidably rested upon fundamental distrust, Szilard rightly pointed out that it did not *have* to rest upon mutual hatred; and it was here that many of his proposals made a great deal of sense. The principle of cooperative self-interest could (and did) provide the basis for fruitful action among the Great Powers—as evidenced by the successful U.S.-Soviet Atmospheric Test Ban treaty of 1963, and by even broader international accords like the 1989 treaty to protect the earth's ozone layer. Szilard's fervent advocacy of cooperative self-interest, therefore, was not necessarily "utopian." Above and beyond the clash of national interests, religious worldviews, and political ideologies, Szilard was correct to point out that vital interests remained in common, and that these interests provided a powerful incentive for keeping open the lines of communication, and for reducing the role of emotional and moralistic posturing.

In the long run, moreover, Szilard was also correct to insist that military deterrence posed awesome risks, and that the only path away from military deterrence lay in the direction of ever-increasing levels of international cooperation. Today's generations, he argued, needed to adopt the same rationale as a young person saving money for the (seemingly distant) future of old-age retirement: they had to start resolutely making small changes in their current mental habits—paving the way, bit by bit, for a different era in which cooperative habits and assumptions might no longer seem so strange.

Did Szilard's efforts make a difference in the Cold War? At the level of the arms race and the superpowers' diplomatic relations, his various projects and proposals clearly failed to have much impact. At a less tangible level, however, Szilard's lonely voice during the bitter years of Stalinism and McCarthyism helped to articulate a more hopeful vision of rational and stable relations between the world's foremost powers. He traveled, he wrote letters, debated on television, organized meetings, gave speeches, and published more than forty articles on the "problem of peace" between 1945 and 1964. Not many people listened to Szilard during these difficult years, when the nations were trying to regain their equilibrium after the cataclysm of World War II. What is probably true, however, is that for an influential minority of scientists, academics, and politicians, Szilard persuasively embodied the counsels of tolerance and compromise, in a time of widespread hysteria and ideological Manichaeanism. The "White House—Kremlin hotline," the Angels project, the Council for a Livable World—these were powerful reminders of the danger that loomed over the world; they directly and tangibly strengthened the hand of all those who feared for the future of humankind, and who struggled to exert a moderating influence upon international politics.

Szilard's precociousness as a scientist-activist was due both to his own unruly personality and to the extraordinary circumstances of the Manhattan Project, which suddenly thrust upon him the prestige he needed to make his opinions heard. He was destined for a solitary and uphill journey, partly because his political views contradicted the prevailing public opinion, and partly because his adopted social role contradicted the prevailing image of the scientist. "In one generation," writes the historian Rae Goodell,

> the role of scientists in politics has been transformed, not once but twice. In the 1940s most scientists stuck to their laboratories and avoided the taint of politics. In the 1950s it became fashionable to make occasional trips to Washington and give behind-the-scenes advice to government officials. In the late 1960s the behind-the-scenes "inside" advisory system lost its enchantment and effectiveness, giving way to a rash of alternative, "outside" activities in Congress, courts, and the press.[135]

At least twenty years before such activism became fashionable and influential, Szilard's role as a socially concerned scientist had already prepared the ground for others who would come later.

Szilard himself would readily have admitted that his ever-flowing torrent of plans and proposals sometimes contained extremely far-fetched ideas. In one short story, he urged the superpowers to establish "rules" of nuclear war, methodically evacuating specific cities in times of crisis and then blowing them to smithereens.[136] Yet there was also an element of deliberate choice in Szilard's unorthodox stance; for in this absurd-sounding story, he was in effect pointing at the gross absurdity of "controlled" nuclear deterrence. Was it not absurd, he implied, to carry on business as usual in cities that were preprogrammed into actual guidance mechanisms of real missiles waiting to be fired from one moment to the next? The ending of this particular story revealed the deeper intent underlying many of his proposals and projects: after the superpowers had established a list of twelve equivalent cities that they might evacuate and destroy during a confrontation, a political insurrection occurred.

> Within a few days after the receipt of the first Russian note which listed the twelve cities, people began to register in Washington as lobbyists for one or another of the twelve cities, and ten days later there was not a hotel room to be had in the whole city. It was the most powerful lobby that ever hit Washington.[137]

At some point, Szilard implied, people might wake up to the tangible fact that it was truly their own cities, their own homes, their own families and futures that were on the line. If such an awakening occurred, then perhaps the political pressure might become sufficient to compel a reevaluation of what was realistic and what was absurd.

Seen from this perspective, Szilard's life and works take on a singular consistency. From the spirit of his scientific research to the concrete aims of his political lobbying, Szilard's goal was always to disrupt established patterns and to reaffirm new models and examples of the possible. Where he saw government institutions rising up with their huge, cumbersome power and impersonal facades, he fought back with an appeal for direct international contacts and small-scale exchanges. Wherever he saw public opinion passively accepting the narrow parameters of choice offered by officials and experts, he proclaimed a bewildering array of alternatives and urged people to question their own deepest assumptions. It was only by *pushing* the limits, he believed, that the limits could be made to budge.

In 1959, five years before his death, Szilard was informed that he had cancer of the bladder; but he did not die of cancer. Compelled to transfer his base of operations to a room in a New York hospital, he sat down and devised his own course of radiation therapy. His friend Norman Cousins, hearing that Szilard's days were evidently numbered, rushed up to visit him and later recorded his impressions:

> Szilard was out of bed. The top of the bed had been converted into a working desk suffocated by papers, scientific journals, and manuscripts. Szilard was seated on a straight chair against one side of the bed, one hand holding the telephone receiver, the other making notes. . . . He finished his phoning, then grinned. . . .
>
> "These radiologists don't know x-rays," he said in feigned despair. "I find myself having to give a course in radiology to these fellows. Anyway, I'm the chief consultant on my own case. It's quite fascinating."
>
> I asked how he felt.
>
> "Fine. Say, have you heard the story about Senator Margaret Chase Smith? It seems she was asked by a reporter how she would like to be president and told the reporter the question was too hypothetical to be taken seriously. 'Come now,' the reporter said, 'this is an age for new traditions. We may not be far away from the time when a woman will be president.' Senator Margaret Chase Smith still refused to comment. Finally, the reporter said, 'Very well, Senator, suppose you wake up one morning and find yourself in the White House, what would you do?' Replied Margaret Chase Smith: 'I'd apologize to the First Lady and go home.'"
>
> Szilard let out a roar of delight at his own story, [then] told two more. . . . I found myself adding to the laughter that was reverberating down the hospital corridor. What was happening was clear.

Leo Szilard was not only running the doctors; he was also running his visitors, creating the mood, governing the conversation.[138]

A few months later, Szilard's radiation therapy had proved so successful that he was able to leave the hospital for good. When he died four years later (in May 1964), he had added the Angels project and the Council for a Livable World to his list of endeavors, and had accepted a research position in La Jolla, California, at the Jonas Salk Institute for Biological Studies which he had helped to found during 1963. He died in his sleep of a heart attack—which is not too surprising, since he had conducted his personal life with the same gleeful disregard for moderation that characterized his public struggles. ("A great favorite for lunch," recalled his friend Edward Shils, "was a glass of buttermilk into which he poured the entire contents of the sugar bowl, followed by sherbet.")[139]

Who was this man, who cracked jokes in the face of deadly illness, who reveled in eccentricities—and yet who so earnestly and doggedly built his life around the clash of empires and the spectral vision of a mushroom cloud? Among the many extremes that found expression within the character of Leo Szilard, his reputation for inordinate rationality and self-control stands out perhaps the most. He deliberately tried to cultivate an image of cool detachment, and his younger sister Roszi later recalled his response to a family crisis:

> When my husband was gravely ill, Leo came to see us from the other end of the world. He gave us money and took care of us. At the same time, he protested that he was not doing it for a relative. "I did it for a man in trouble," he insisted. "I would have done it for anybody."[140]

He struggled to maintain clear and impartial judgment, but the tone of his writings was far from aloof; he tried hard to keep his personal life unencumbered, but the tenderness he evoked in his numerous friends could not be denied. This tension within his character was never resolved, for he had fixed his will upon difficult and abstract ideals, while in his daily life, not far beneath the surface, flowed a current of vibrant emotions. Like many persons of acute sensitivity, he strove to master himself by building walls made of concepts, logic, and rational principles; but in Szilard's case, those walls clearly resonated with what was moving behind them.

Did Szilard feel guilt for his role in the creation of nuclear weapons? His own explicit answer, given in a nationally televised interview in 1961, was that he did not: "I thought we must build the bomb, because if we don't, the Germans will have it first. . . . I never blame myself for having guessed wrong."[141] His writings, however, revealed a more complicated set of feelings. In one of his short stories he depicted a physicist who abruptly went mad a few years after having helped invent the world's first atomic bomb. This "neurotic condition," Szilard suggested, "was brought about by his pessimistic outlook on world affairs, coupled with his manifest sense of guilt." [142] In one article written in 1947, Szilard referred to himself and fellow atomic scientists as peculiar advocates of peace, since there was a sense in which they were "mass murderers." [143] Edward Shils later recalled a poignant occasion in the early 1950s, after Edward Teller had succeeded in his efforts to promote the hydrogen bomb: "Szilard said in a sighing aside, 'Now Teller will know what it is to feel guilty.'" [144]

Although it was reasonable to feel that there had been no alternative to working on the bomb in 1939, the enormity of the consequences also made it reasonable to feel an anguish of uncertainty. "Are you a religious man, Dr. Szilard?" asked the television interviewer Mike Wallace in 1961.

> SZILARD: Well, look, I don't believe in the personal God, but in a sense, I am a religious man. I think that life has a meaning. . . .
> WALLACE: When you say life has a meaning, you mean . . .
> SZILARD: Well, this is difficult to define what it means that life has a meaning, but if you press me for a definition, I will say that life has a meaning if there are things which are worth dying for. [145]

He was not a religious man in the conventional sense, but on August 11, 1945, five days after Hiroshima and two days after Nagasaki, he wrote a quiet letter to the Rev. Alfred Painter, chaplain at the University of Chicago:

> Presumably, if the war should end within the next few days, there will be a service in your chapel. . . . I wondered whether you thought that provisions could be made in this service for a special prayer to be said for the dead of Hiroshima and Nagasaki. . . . I also wondered whether it would be possible to arrange for an offering at the end of the service for the survivors of Hiroshima and Nagasaki, with the idea of transmitting the collected sum to the survivors when conditions permitted. [146]

It is painful to imagine the emotion Szilard must have felt, knowing that he was personally responsible not just for the dead in Japan, but—thinking in broad historical terms as was his wont—for the possible end of the human species. Yet, as he was later to do with his cancer, he found a peculiar strength in such a moment. Keeping his struggle to himself, he was able to channel his emotion from guilt to hope, from despair to playful and tenacious commitment. In this simple act, perhaps, lay the heart of Szilard's legacy.

Peace as Grass-Roots Internationalism: E. P. Thompson's Campaign against Bloc Politics

It is not just that we are preparing for war: we are preparing ourselves to be
the kind of societies which go to war.

—E. P. Thompson, 1981[1]

The British historian E. P. Thompson shared Szilard's most basic assumptions about the threat of nuclear disaster and the need for a transformation in world politics. On one vital point, however, his logic diverged from Szilard's. Cooperative diplomacy, he felt, would not in itself bring about a lasting peace; the changes would have to cut much deeper than that. "Some Soviet ideologists," wrote Thompson in 1984,

> have recently been attempting to re-baptise us as an "anti-war movement." But that will never be enough. By an "anti-war movement" they intend a movement which is limited in its agenda to matters of military posture and procurements only and from which all matters of ideology, polity, and culture are excluded. . . .
> Certainly nuclear weapons are the most odious symbols of our predicament. . . . But the peace movement, . . . if it is to *make* peace and not only make protest, must set itself an agenda which extends into every nook and cranny of our culture and our polity. It has to be an affirmative movement of an unprecedented kind.[2]

The logic behind Thompson's position was straightforward. In any future world—even a disarmed one—the "military solution" would always continue to exist as an ultimate possibility; any nation or region that became radically unsatisfied with its lot could revert at any time to building weapons in secret and threatening its neighbors. If the use of force were to be avoided, therefore, it was essential to make sure that every group within the world community continued to see greater benefits in "playing the game" than in becoming a renegade. The implication of this fact was that the peoples of the world would have to begin thinking of "security" in truly collective terms. The basic goal of each nation or region would no longer be merely to look after its own needs; now, it would also have to ensure that the minimal conditions for every other region's existence had been met. There could be no desperately poor peoples, no persecuted racial or religious minorities, no power-hungry governments dominating their neighbors.

Thompson's conception of peace, therefore, extended to a qualitatively different level of society than Szilard's. It was not enough, Thompson felt, to manipulate the large political blocs of humanity, rearranging them and working through the United Nations to reduce the friction with which they rubbed against each other. Instead, Thompson called for a widespread change in the way human beings distributed power among themselves, a transformation of political and economic relationships that started at the local level and ran all the way up to the highest pinnacles of government. This vision was, in one sense, even more brashly "utopian" than Szilard's—for it rested on the premise that international peace could not be separated from the intractable problems of political repression and the uneven distribution of wealth. In another sense, however, Thompson could argue that this broader conception of peace stemmed from a more "realistic" analysis of the causes of war; for as long as large portions of humanity continued to live in conditions of desperate hunger and absence of the most basic human rights, how could large-scale violence ever be far away? This was the problem that drew Thompson steadily away from the elites and "global managers" who typically preoccupied Weiss and Szilard, thrusting him into the very different world of "politics from below."

As an independent Marxist, moreover, Thompson eventually found himself challenging the ideological orthodoxies of both the capitalist West and the Communist East. On both sides of the Iron Curtain, he argued, the ideals of authentic democracy were being betrayed—albeit in different ways. On the Soviet side, the original Marxist goal of transferring power to the majority of society's active citizens had degenerated into a ruthless totalitarianism. On the Western side, he felt, despite the survival of precious civil liberties, the old ideals of popular self-rule were steadily succumbing to domination by a network of powerful institutions: business corporations, "media industries," government bureaucracies, military agencies, and academic think-tanks.

Although the mechanisms of domination were subtler on the Western side than in the East, Thompson argued, they were equally dangerous in both cases; for they embodied a form of power that harked back directly to Machiavelli's prescriptions in *The Prince*. A cunning ruler, for Machiavelli, should regard human beings essentially as "objects" whose actions and volitions he could predict and channel—for the greater welfare and growth of the state as a whole. Like clay in the hands of a skillful potter, the citizens of Machiavelli's polity would assume the shape imparted to them by their shrewd leader. Thompson detested this view of social order, considering it the negation of genuine democracy. In his view of history (and of the future), the "objects" became active subjects, unpredictable, unruly; and actual historical individuals, with their complex array of feelings, allegiances, and moral perceptions, took the reins of social change into their own hands.

Thompson's career, therefore, might be understood in part as a long campaign against the Machiavellian philosophy of power. He rebelled against the notion that the "common people" had to be led manipulatively from above, and that they could never lead themselves, trusting their own ideals to guide them. He rebelled against the cynically instrumental assessment of moral principles evinced by thinkers like Machiavelli—against their emphasis on "getting results" by any means available. Could a moral vision of politics be "realistic"? Was it possible, in other words, to bring together explicit moral values and grass-roots political action, pursuing collective goals democratically *and* effectively? These questions lay at the heart of Thompson's work, both as a historian and as a peace activist.

1924–1956: Liberalism, Fascism, Stalinism

"My father was a very tough liberal," E. P. Thompson told an interviewer in 1976.

> He was a continuous critic of British imperialism, a friend of Nehru's and of other national leaders. So I grew up expecting governments to be mendacious and imperialist, and expecting that one's stance ought to be hostile to government.[3]

Thompson's parents had lived in India from 1912 to 1923. His mother, Theodosia Jessup, was an American whose family had long served as missionaries in Lebanon. His father, Edward John Thompson, was a Methodist educational missionary who had become increasingly entranced with Indian history and culture, writing books about Tagore and other Bengali poets and strongly supporting the Indian Congress Movement in its pressures for decolonization and self-rule.

Edward Palmer Thompson (known as "E. P." to distinguish him from his father) was born in Oxford in 1924, shortly after his family had returned to England from its long sojourn abroad. His older brother, Frank, had been born four years earlier in Darjeeling; the two were to grow up in close affinity with each other.[4] Through the following two decades, Thompson's father divided his time between teaching Bengali at Oxford and writing poetry, historical novels, and political polemics; his passionate opposition to both Fascism and imperialism strongly colored the youth of his two sons. E. P. Thompson later described his childhood home as a place "to which some of the most interesting men of the preceding generation were frequent visitors"—from the poet Robert Bridges to the statesman Lord Lothian, from Tagore to Gandhi and Jawaharlal Nehru.[5] "As a child," he wrote,

> I had no doubt that Indians were our most important visitors: the sideboard loaded with grapes and dates was testimony of this. A little older, I would cadge postage stamps from poets and political agitators. Older again, I stood in awe before the great Jawaharlal, as he asked me about my batting technique.[6]

By the time Thompson was old enough to attend a private school (Kingswood, near Bath), the international atmosphere was already being darkened by the Spanish Civil War, the Italian invasion of Ethiopia, and Hitler's remilitarization of the Rhineland. Two of his brother's close friends joined the anti-Fascist volunteer forces in Spain, and one of them was subsequently killed. In August 1938, Nehru wrote to Thompson's father while on a visit to Prague: "War can be avoided if only England and France made it clear that they would not tolerate any German aggression in Czechoslovakia." And two months later, after the Munich crisis: "The outlook is about as evil as it could be. . . . Still, I suppose one has to go on and fight the monster. . . . And remember that the Himalayas are always there, as a refuge, for a while at least, from Fascism and its friends."[7]

In 1939 Thompson's brother Frank, who was now in his first year as a student at Oxford, dismayed his parents by joining the British Communist party. "From his parents," E. P. Thompson later wrote, "[Frank] had taken the best of the liberal tradition—a respect for the rights and opinions of men of every race and colour, and a will to improve the conditions of the working-classes of England and of the world."[8] Yet this liberal tradition did not push far enough for Frank, and his experience in the Oxford Labour Club had convinced him that communism offered the most effective anti-imperialist and anti-Fascist political stance of all. This conviction must have been badly shaken later in 1939, when the Nazi-Soviet pact caused the Communist parties of all nations to perform an abrupt about-face, suddenly demanding that party members refuse participation in the imminent "imperialist war." Frank was independent-minded enough to resist both the conflicts with his parents and the directives of his newly chosen party: he stayed a Communist but volunteered for war service nonetheless. By March 1940, he was training in the Royal Artillery.

E. P. Thompson was only fifteen years old at the time of these events; yet his brother's principled resoluteness made a deep and lasting impression on him.[9] In 1941 (still too young for military service) he started university at Cambridge, taking up literature and history. He read Vico for the first time, developing a fascination for the subtle interplay between individual choice and collective historical patterns in the philosophy of this eighteenth-century Italian.[10] He wrote poetry and became active in student politics; a little later in the year, he joined the Communist party himself.

The decision caused less conflict than Frank's had done, partly because Frank had "broken open the way,"[11] and partly because by 1941 the Nazis had betrayed their Soviet allies, and it thus became possible for Communists to oppose Fascism without having to defy the party line. Thompson shared his older brother's enthusiasm for a popular and democratic conception of communism that had not yet been crushed by the experiences of Stalinism. "My brother's surviving letters," he later explained,

> are totally at odds with the cardboard ideological picture of what Stalinism was. His commitment was to people and above all to the astonishing heroism of the Partisan movements of southern Europe.[12]

One such letter from Frank, written early in 1944, expressed a seemingly un-quenchable passion and optimism about the future:

> My eyes fill very quickly with tears when I think what a splendid Europe we shall build . . . when all the vitality and talent of its indomitable peoples can be set free for cooperation and cre-ation. . . . When men like these have mastered their own fates, there won't be time for discussing "what is beauty?" One will be overwhelmed by the abundance of it.[13]

In 1942, at a historical juncture in which Fascism seemed everywhere to be advancing in triumph, E. P. Thompson enlisted in the British army. By the following year (at age nineteen), he was a lieutenant in charge of a tank troop in the Sixth Armoured Division, fighting first in Northern Africa and then pushing slowly northward with the Allied armies up the Italian peninsula. Though he deeply believed in the cause for which he fought, his poems and other writings also revealed his own bewilderment and revulsion at the war's raw physical brutality.[14] He later recollected the agony he had felt, having to order young men like himself to advance into deadly ambushes and then facing the task of answering correspondence from their next of kin:

> I was as callous as any young soldier had to be in order to survive (my substitute for emotional responses took the form of outbreaks of skin disease) but I could scarcely bear to read these rather for-mal, self-effacing, ever-courteous letters:
>
> "My brother was all I had in the world we had lived together the last ten years since losing our mother and I would like to know a few more details, if the spot where he is buried is marked or did an explosion make this impossible?"
>
> "Please did one of his friends pick some wild flowers and place on his grave? . . ."
>
> "Will you try and do me a kindness and see that his personal belongings are sent back to me and if you could get me a photo of his grave it would set my wife's mind at rest as she is greatly grieved."
>
> With all the weight of my twenty years I did what I could to offer comfort and to abbreviate the grief of my enquirers by giving to these deaths a definite term.[15]

It was midway through the Italian campaign, in 1944, when he received notice that his brother Frank, who had volunteered for an especially dangerous mis-sion behind Nazi lines into Bulgaria, had been captured and shot along with a band of local partisans.

Thompson returned to England with the victorious British army in 1945, but the war's ending was marred by the absence of Frank and by the serious illness of his father, who died the following year. In 1946, he returned to Cambridge to finish his degree in history, and it was here that he met Dorothy Sale, who later became his wife. Their relationship turned out to be an unusually close one, for she was both a Communist like himself and a talented historian whose studies focused at the time on the nineteenth-century Chartists. The enduring intellectual partnership that they formed was to become a prominent feature in the landscape of the postwar British Left.

During the summer of 1947, Thompson and Sale joined a group of British volunteers who were working in Yugoslavia on an international construction project: the Youth Railway from Samac to Sarajevo. Already, the tensions of the early Cold War were becoming apparent; the momentous break between Tito and Stalin was still a year away, but Winston Churchill's proclamation of an "Iron Curtain" was already more than a year old. In Greece, to the south, the British army was suppressing a Communist insurgency and restoring the monarchy; in Washington, the Truman Doctrine and Marshall Plan were being announced. It was under these conditions that Thompson and Sale, both in their early twenties, decided to see for themselves what it meant to perform hard manual labor alongside fellow socialists in a socialist country.

The Yugoslav Youth Railway was to be 150 miles long, snaking from East to West through the hills and crags along the river Bosna. Its official purpose was to aid industrial reconstruction by providing a badly needed transportation link between Slavonia and Bosnia. In the enthusiastic account that Thompson published when he returned to England, the uniqueness of the project became clear.[16] It was a genuinely socialist endeavor in conception and organization, with centralized planning, political rallies, and volunteers from twenty nations subdivided into labor brigades (Thompson was "commandant" of the British group); yet the collective spirit of the project drew more from the voluntaristic heritage of the Yugoslav Resistance than from the *Führerprinzip* of the interwar youth leagues.

> There was no kow-towing, strutting, bullying, saluting, or segregation of leaders. . . . The leadership was elected, either on a temporary or a permanent basis, by the members of the brigade at its first formation. . . . [Brigade leaders] lived, ate, slept, and worked in the most informal relations with the other volunteers, and anyone critical of their methods or harbouring a grievance could bring the matter forward in open meeting.[17]

Rising early in the morning, the volunteers would spend six to eight hours laying track or excavating tunnels along the mountainside. Women and men worked together, sharing responsibilities on an equal basis. In the late afternoon, the various national brigades began to commingle, inviting each other as guests to their separate camps. Cultural and linguistic boundaries fell by the wayside, as the young workers carried on "long conversations in what sounded like pidgin Irish interspersed with gestures and Spanish expletives."[18] As the sun went down behind the Balkan ridges, huge bonfires sprang up.

> Slogans would be roared back and forth, and one would be thrown up into the air by laughing volunteers. Then, without any signal, one would find oneself with joined arms moving rhythmically round in a circle in the firelight, singing back the words of the leader. And then perhaps more shouting, or a swift and expert Greek peasant dance, led by a girl in working-overalls with her long black hair streaming behind her.[19]

Thompson was particularly seized by the openness and tolerance for diversity that characterized his fellow workers.

> One met the most remarkable medley of political opinions, and some amusing contrasts. A Canadian loudly pro-Soviet arguing with a Roumanian equally loudly anti-Communist, or Swedish Marxists going hammer-and-tongs at Czech exponents of "western democracy."[20]

In this international dialogue, the two most conspicuously absent nationalities were the Russians and Americans, both of whom had been barred by their governments from coming to Yugoslavia.

One of the songs that circulated around the campfires contained a couplet that deeply impressed Thompson:

> We build the railway,
> the railway builds us.[21]

It was precisely this kind of Europe, where the nationalities worked side by side, sharing their work and aspirations as they shared each other's folk songs and cultural traditions, that his brother Frank had envisioned amidst the violence of 1944. The volunteers established their own libraries, concerts, theater, and newspapers, showing that hard physical work could go smoothly together with aesthetic and political education. The mingling of diverse national cultures, Thompson wrote,

> turned out to be something quite different from what we expected. It was not a rather dreary business of . . . not feeling any particular malice towards anyone. It was made up of a number of dislikes, irritations, and fits of anger, as well as laughter, songs, sudden attractions, gratitude, and admiration.[22]

A strong feeling of equality pervaded the camps: "everyone worked, ate, danced, studied, and sang in the same suit of overalls, which were washed, together with underclothes and socks, in the cold mountain streams."[23] Yet this egalitarian atmosphere did not prevent a fierce competition among brigades and individuals to demonstrate their excellence in everything from laying track to writing poetry.

For Thompson himself, the experience on the railway crystallized a set of ideals that would continue to emerge in his writings for decades. The tension between individual initiative and collective purpose, the complex relation between material practice and cultural values, the creative movement between national identity and international communication—all these "dialectical pairs" would subsequently find development as central themes, both in his thought and in his political work. Nearly three decades later, in 1973, Thompson would point to his experiences in Yugoslavia in an open letter to the apostate Marxist Leszek Kolakowski. On the railway, he wrote, he had learned that it was possible "within the context of certain institutions and culture" to "conceptualize in terms of 'our' rather than 'my' or 'their'":

> Young Yugoslav peasants, students, and workers, constructing with high morale their own railway, undoubtedly had this affirmative concept of *nasha* ("our"). . . . The fact that this moment of euphoria proved to be evanescent—and that both the Soviet Union and "the West" did what they could to reverse the impulse—does not disallow the validity of the experience.[24]

The England to which Thompson returned in 1947 was in the midst of a social transformation almost as far-reaching as the one taking place in Yugoslavia. One of the unanticipated effects of the Second World War had been to break down some of the traditional barriers that divided Britain's upper and lower classes, forcing them to work closely together in the desperate struggle against Fascism. As early as 1942, the bipartisan wartime government had committed itself to a substantial expansion of social insurance once victory was achieved; and this had contributed to a widespread radicalization of expectations among the British electorate. The political triumph of the Labour party in the 1945 election (though it astounded many Britons) was a direct expression of this wartime leveling process.[25] Clement Attlee's Labour government, which held power until 1951, promptly set about constructing an elaborate system of parliamentary socialism. It nationalized roughly one fifth of the economy, sharply raised income and inheritance taxes, and offered the British people a comprehensive set of social services "from cradle to grave."

The Achilles Heel of this ambitious reconstruction program was the relative exhaustion of the British economy, which had been strained far beyond its resources by the war. According to one study,

> Britain [in 1945] had lost approximately one quarter of her national wealth . . . ; she had sacrificed approximately two thirds of

> her export trade. . . . Her total merchant shipping had been reduced
> by 28 percent. . . . The national debt meanwhile had tripled, while
> the country's standard of living had fallen heavily.[26]

Despite the Labour government's best efforts, such essential goods as potatoes and bread, gasoline and clothes, were still rationed as late as 1948 and 1949. By 1950, Conservative politicians who blamed these persistent economic woes on nationalization and high taxes began to strike a responsive note among many British voters. It was under these circumstances that Churchill returned to power in the election of 1951, opening a period of continuous Conservative rule that lasted until 1964. Still, despite the setback to Labour, the Conservatives were forced to adapt themselves to many of the structural changes that had been made, and the social reforms of the first postwar government became established features of British life.

For Thompson, as he returned in 1947 from his adventure in Yugoslavia, these changes seemed part of a broader European transformation. "Struggles on housing estates," he later explained to an interviewer,

> or strikes, or the sense of euphoria when the mines were national-
> ized and when the health service was introduced—all these affir-
> mative things were part of one's own experience. So it wasn't just
> going and seeing it all happen over there. One felt that the Yugosla-
> vian partisans were a supreme example, but it wasn't totally dif-
> ferent.[27]

Thompson's own contribution to this broader effort took the form of a daily life divided between teaching and political organizing. In 1948, after getting married, he and Dorothy moved to Halifax, in the northern district of Yorkshire (where they were to live for the next seventeen years). Thompson had secured a job in an adult-education program linked to Leeds University—one of the last of these positions available to Communist intellectuals before a British "mini-McCarthyism" set in.[28] Teaching literature and history to classes of working-class adults posed something of a challenge, for he could not hope to interest such students with dry academic lectures. It was perhaps here that his distinctive style of writing and arguing was born: polemical, laced with witticisms and startling metaphors, interweaving long quotations of poetry with more conventional historical narrative.[29] Thompson was even moved, during his first year in Northern England, to try his hand at writing a war novel (which remained unpublished).

Alongside this professional work, Thompson devoted a solid half of his time to the politics of the Left. He was simultaneously chairman of the Halifax Peace Committee, secretary of the broader Yorkshire Federation of Peace Organizations, editor of a peace journal, and a member of the Yorkshire District Committee of the Communist party.[30] This was to appear, when he looked back on it in later years, as a deeply ambiguous period in his political life. On the one hand, he felt that he was participating in a genuine grass-roots movement: distributing leaflets outside factory gates and housing estates, getting directly involved in the working-class politics of his local area, helping to organize a strong network of contacts and alliances. He was particularly impressed by the quality of many individuals in the local peace movement and Communist party, some of whom were self-educated workers whose keen sense of democratic process evoked profound respect in him. The chairman of the Communist party's District Committee, he later recalled,

> was a former Labour counselor who had been long involved in very interesting fringe causes like the right to keep footpaths open. He conducted the committee in a democratic way, and insisted upon disagreements being argued through—unlike the stereotype. I remember occasions when he said, "I'm not going to take the chair on this issue because I disagree with Bert: will someone come and take the chair and we'll have it out." So I was impressed at a certain sense of collective work, and also by the suppression of mere individualism in the pursuit of a common cause.[31]

On the other hand, however, Thompson repeatedly found himself clashing with the manipulative tactics of the party leaders in London, who wanted to extend their control over ever-broader sections of the non-Communist peace movement. The Yorkshire Federation of Peace Organizations, of which he was the secretary, represented a loose coalition of groups ranging from Methodists and Quakers to Labour party members and trade unionists. Thompson had seen longstanding members of the Labour party face expulsion rather than give up their peace activism, and it galled him to see the Communist party trying to control these independent-minded individuals from the outside.[32]

Nevertheless, he stifled his doubts and resentments in the name of loyalty to the broader cause. In the journal that Thompson edited, the *Yorkshire Voice of Peace,* a typical editorial in 1953 would read:

> Nothing has been clearer in the past two months than that it is America, and not Russia, who has got the bit between her teeth and is galloping downhill to war. Look at the evidence: her refusal to stop the H-blasts; her pressure for German rearmament, with or without France; her post-haste rejection of the Russian offer to join NATO; her threat to enter the colonial war in Indochina and to extend it to China.[33]

Thompson's willingness to condemn the United States for rejecting such a manifest absurdity as a "Russian offer to join NATO" provided a clear example of the Communist "casuistries" that he was to criticize so bitterly in later years.

Alongside these explicitly political pursuits, Thompson participated regularly, with Dorothy, in the meetings of the Historians' Group of the Communist party. This semiformal group included such influential Marxist scholars as Christopher Hill, Maurice Dobb, V. G. Kiernan, George Rudé, Rodney Hilton, Eric Hobsbawm, and John Saville, all of them at various stages of their careers, but all equally eager to discuss the theory of Marxism and what it meant for writing history.[34] "These were the people," recalled Eric Hobsbawm,

> who would make their way, normally at weekends, through what memory recalls mainly as the dank, cold, and slightly foggy morning streets of Clerkenwell to Marx House or to the upper room of the Garibaldi Restaurant, Laystall Street, armed with cyclostyled agendas, sheets of "theses" or summary arguments, for the debates of the moment.[35]

Thompson himself, when he joined the group, had not yet come to think of himself as a historian; it was Dorothy's participation in the group that drew him in. Nevertheless, he had already begun to work upon his first major project, a biography of the British Socialist and artist William Morris:

> I was seized by Morris. I thought, why is this man thought to be an old fuddy-duddy? He is right in with us still. And then I read one or two books *so* dreadful and so ideological about Morris that I thought I *must* answer these. . . . In the course of doing this I became much more serious about being a historian.[36]

The book on Morris, which was first published in 1955, clearly revealed the underlying ambiguity of Thompson's position within communism during the early 1950s. On the one hand, it was an orthodox and obedient expression of the Communist party line, the appropriation of Morris's life by a "true believer" whose political value judgments intruded regularly into the biographical narrative:

> Twenty years ago even among Socialists and Communists, many must have regarded Morris's picture of "A Factory as It Might Be" as an unpractical poet's dream: today visitors return from the Soviet Union with stories of the poet's dream fulfilled. . . .
> Were William Morris alive today, he would not look far to find the party of his choice.[37]

On the other hand, this biography of Morris subtly foreshadowed much of the substantive critique of Marxism that was to develop more openly in Thompson's later work. In the postscript to a revised (and "de-Stalinized") edition that came out in 1976, Thompson described the 1955 edition as "already a work of muffled 'revisionism.'" And he added: "The Morris/Marx argument has worked inside me ever since."[38]

What was this "Morris/Marx argument"? The figure of William Morris—
the figure that so deeply "seized" Thompson—was that of a man consumed by
moral outrage at the shabby compromises of Victorian society, a man who felt
irresistibly drawn by the vision of an egalitarian future in which all could share
meaningful physical labor and aesthetic aspiration. Born in 1834, Morris
started out life as a young Romantic, writing poetry that showed the heavy
influence of John Keats. At Oxford, where his wealthy family sent him to
school, he encountered the biting critique of industrial utilitarianism put forth
by Ruskin and Carlyle. He developed a lasting love for medieval art and culture
and launched into a successful career in the plastic and decorative arts; his
architectural designs and woven tapestries gradually won him widespread re-
nown, while his savage writings and lectures about the soulless world of utilitarianism stirred up far-ranging controversy. In the mid-1880s, however, when
Morris had just turned fifty, he crossed a "river of fire." [39] No longer content to
rail against the cultural barrenness of Victorian England, he began to criticize
systematically the very economic underpinnings of industrial capitalism.
Within the space of a few years, he abandoned many of his "respectable"
middle-class connections and plunged headlong into the Socialist movement.
He spoke at streetcorners, wrangled with anarchists and reformists, and devoted himself single-mindedly to the creation of a genuine working-class
movement that might someday transform society from top to bottom.

Morris had been deeply influenced by Karl Marx, referring to *Capital* as a
"great book" and to Marx himself as a "great man." [40] Where then did Thompson perceive an implicit "Morris/Marx argument"? From his perspective in the
early 1950s, as he looked at his own party, Thompson was beginning to suspect
that something was missing, or had gone awry, in the orthodox Marxist vision
of human life. As early as 1948, when he had narrated his experiences in Yugoslavia, he had already made clear his own rejection of dogmatism and authoritarian methods, as well as his profound attraction for a vision of socialism that
embraced both politics and culture, physical labor and aesthetic cultivation. He
was understandably captivated, therefore, when he discovered in William Morris a Socialist whose values seemed strikingly close to his own. Morris, too,
had rebelled in the early 1880s against the authoritarian tendencies of Henry
Hyndman, a Socialist leader who envied Morris's popularity and influence.
One could easily see, in Thompson's narrative, where his own sympathies and
resentments lay: "[Morris] was enraged at Hyndman's 'sacramental' dogmatism, which seemed to be the means he was employing to throw suspicion upon
all those who were not ready to accept his personal leadership." [41]

Like Thompson in the 1950s, moreover, Morris had been rendered thoroughly uncomfortable by the prevailing tendency among Socialists to raise
economic theory far above all other forms of knowledge, disparaging the moral

and aesthetic aspects of human life as mere epiphenomena. "Morris," Thompson wrote, "was very conscious of his own disabilities in the field of political economy: 'I want statistics terribly,' he had written to Scheu the previous August. 'You see, I am but a poet and artist, good for nothing but sentiment.'"[42] At the heart of Thompson's biography of Morris lay the desire to rehabilitate "poetry," "sentiment," and the importance of each individual's moral courage within a Marxist culture that recognized only the iron discipline of the Party, the "scientific" laws of economic change, and the mechanical contradictions among faceless classes. Morris's struggles with Marxist dogmatism and economism gave Thompson a chance to explore some of his own misgivings, while displacing them onto a historical discussion of events long past.

Of course, these undercurrents of criticism and rebellion were only discernible through hindsight; for in the 1955 edition of *William Morris,* they were overwhelmed by the sometimes shrill partisanship of a young author who wanted to leave no doubt as to his own political allegiances. Thus, it is not surprising that an anonymous reviewer of the book for the *Times Literary Supplement* should have felt provoked to write an intensely hostile and dismissive evaluation, entirely overlooking the substance of Thompson's argument, and pronouncing it "a remarkable feat" that Thompson had managed "to sustain a mood of ill-temper through a volume of 900 pages."[43] It was not until the 1976 edition, in which Thompson excised the intrusive posturing of the 1950s, that reviewers began to acknowledge this book as a masterful biography and a major reconceptualization of the Romantic heritage.[44]

Nevertheless, the years of working on Morris's biography had quietly given strength to Thompson's dissident impulses. Within a year of its publication, the subterranean tensions contained within that work broke through to the surface, as Thompson resigned from the Communist party and set out, with new and old companions, to define a more open and humane conception of socialism. "When, in 1956," he later wrote,

> my disagreements with orthodox Marxism became fully articulate,
> I fell back on modes of perception which I'd learned in those years
> of close company with Morris, and I found, perhaps, the will to go
> on arguing from the pressure of Morris behind me.[45]

In February 1956, at a secret session during the Twentieth Congress of the Soviet Communist party, Nikita Khrushchev officially denounced many of the atrocities that had occurred under Stalin's dictatorship. Khrushchev's motives in making these unprecedented revelations were partly derived from internal intrigues within the Soviet power hierarchy, and partly from a genuine desire to relax some of the Stalinist controls that still gripped Soviet society three years after the dictator's death.[46] Nevertheless, as the news began to leak out to the rest of the world, the impact of the Twentieth Congress proved more far-reaching than Khrushchev had calculated. In Poland, a reform movement under Wladislaw Gomulka promptly began to challenge Soviet domination, while in the West a fierce debate emerged over Stalin's legacy and the future of communism.

For the top leaders of many Communist parties in the West, of course, the traditions of Stalinism proved hard to relinquish; and they nervously made Khrushchev's revelations the object of a systematic cover-up. Jean Pronteau, a member of the French Communist party's Central Committee in 1956, later recalled his own disillusioning experience after a brief trip to Poland, where he had read a copy of Khrushchev's recent speech. Upon returning to Paris, he rushed to see the French party chief Maurice Thorez in his office:

> Straight away, I said to him: "I've just got back from Poland, I've seen the report." He looked at me, expressionless: "The report? What report?" I replied: "The report Khrushchev made in closed session, the secret report." Without turning a hair, Thorez said: "There is no secret report." I started to get worked up, and took out of my briefcase the notes I had taken in Poland. At that point Thorez said to me: "Oh! so you've got it. You should have said so right away." And he added in a pontifical manner: "Anyway, just remember one thing. This report doesn't exist. Besides, soon it will never have existed. We must pay no attention to it."[47]

The attitude of the British Communist party was similar to that of the French. Even after the *Observer* published a full text of Khrushchev's speech in June 1956, the party leadership did its best to explain it away and to suppress discussion of the issues it raised.[48]

For Thompson, on the other hand, and for thousands of other British Communists, this situation was rapidly becoming intolerable. Painful as the self-critique might be, it now seemed impossible to avoid it any longer; and indeed, Thompson and his wife, Dorothy, even felt a certain element of relief in the raising of long-stifled questions.[49] After trying unsuccessfully to initiate an open debate on the Khrushchev revelations in the official Communist party press, Thompson teamed up with another young Communist historian, John Saville, to produce an independent journal of discussion, the *Reasoner.*

In mid-July, the first issue appeared. It was thirty-two pages long, made from stencils typed by Thompson and duplicated by Saville on a borrowed machine. The tone of this first edition was still relatively mild. It announced the editors' aim to criticize "views which have come to be accepted as orthodox," but repeatedly affirmed their continued adherence to the principles of Marxism and loyalty to the party. Nevertheless, to the rigid and thoroughly Stalinist leadership of the British Communist party, the journal's underlying message must have been all too clear. Thompson, in one article, engaged in debate with a prominent party figure over "the uncritical character of our support for the Soviet Union"; a translated poem by a Hungarian writer lampooned the failures of East-bloc Communism; and two short editorials invited the journal's readers to contribute their own ideas about "the ever-present problem of our sectarianism and dogmatism." [50]

The response was immediate. All two thousand copies of the *Reasoner* promptly sold out, and over three hundred letters arrived by early August offering support and articles. [51] With equal alacrity, the Yorkshire District Committee of the Communist party issued a resolution: "This District Committee asks Comrades Thompson and Saville to cease publication of the *Reasoner*." [52] Neither Thompson nor Saville wanted to be expelled from the party or to create a damaging schism within its ranks, but they felt that the closed-mindedness of the party leadership left them no alternative. Late in September, therefore, a second issue of the *Reasoner* came out, with articles along the same lines as before. At this point, Thompson later recalled, he and Saville "were summoned up before Harry Pollitt himself [the chairman of the British Communist party] and all the other bigwigs. John Saville and I were grilled and then we said it was our Communist duty to continue." [53]

Here, however, international events intervened, turning this relatively minor tug-of-war into a much more significant crisis. Throughout the preceding summer, France and Britain had been struggling with Egypt's Nasser over the sovereignty of the Suez Canal. At the same time, in the Eastern bloc, the success of the Polish reform movement had gradually encouraged a similar movement in neighboring Hungary. In the weeks that followed, events in Budapest and along the Suez Canal became peculiarly linked. On October 23, students and workers in Budapest held huge demonstrations against Soviet domination of Hungary; Khrushchev responded by moving Soviet tanks into position around the perimeter of the rebellious city. The Hungarians, however, now poured into the streets in unprecedented numbers, and Khrushchev was forced to back down. On October 28, as the world's attention focused on Budapest, the Soviet leader withdrew his tanks and agreed to open negotiations. The next morning Israel, France, and Britain suddenly launched a long-planned attack against Nasser, driving the Egyptian army from the Sinai. Taken off guard, both superpowers immediately called for a ceasefire in the Middle East, but the Anglo-French forces disregarded all warnings and pressed forward into the canal zone. On October 30, the Hungarians announced their unilateral withdrawal from the Warsaw Pact, and Khrushchev's position hardened dramatically on all fronts. He threatened to use long-range rockets in support of Egypt, and on November 3 ordered Soviet tanks back into Budapest to crush the Hungarian uprising.

Thompson and Saville spent the morning of November 4 on the telephone, putting together an emergency edition of the *Reasoner.*[54] Throughout the Hungarian rebellion, the British Communist party had consistently sided with the Soviet leadership, and it now seemed impossible for these two dissidents to hold back any longer their full sense of betrayal and outrage. "In this crisis," their editorial stated, "when the Hungarian people needed our solidarity, the British Communist Party has failed them." Thompson then went on, in an impassioned essay entitled "Through the Smoke of Budapest," to proclaim his irrevocable break with Stalinist orthodoxy:

> The theory of the all-powerful, centralised state is wrong—our comrades in Poland and Yugoslavia are proving this in life. . . . The Stalinist theory of the dictatorship of the proletariat is wrong. . . . The identification of all disagreement, all opposition, all hesitation, with "objective" counter-revolution is wrong. . . .
>
> It was mechanical idealism such as this, mounted on Soviet tanks, which fired through the smoke at the workers and young people of Budapest.[55]

And Thompson and Saville concluded their last-minute editorial:

> We urge all those who, like ourselves, will dissociate themselves completely from the leadership of the British Communist Party, not to lose faith in Socialism, and to find ways of keeping together. We promise our readers that we will consult with others about the early formation of a new Socialist journal.[56]

During these months, some seven thousand members—roughly a fifth of the total—left the Communist party.[57] Thompson and Saville, who were expelled at the same time as they resigned, immediately began seeking ways to keep their promise and provide a focal point for this large pool of leftists who no longer possessed a common institutional affiliation. Early in 1957 they began publishing the *New Reasoner,* a journal that would bring together dissident voices from the Eastern bloc with those of the non-Communist Left in the West.

1956–1971: New Aims for a New Left

In the six or seven years that followed his break with the Communist party, Thompson entered a period of political activism and historical writing whose intensity would only be surpassed by the years between 1980 and 1984. Apart from coediting the *New Reasoner* with John Saville, he threw himself into the work of promoting New Left clubs in as many British cities as possible. After 1958, he participated in the Campaign for Nuclear Disarmament (CND), sharing in the daily practice of fund-raising and organizing marches, as well as in the writing of articles to help define the campaign's wider goals and strategy.

In 1959, the *New Reasoner* merged with another journal to form the *New Left Review,* and Thompson became an active presence both in the *Review*'s pages and on its editorial board. At the same time, of course, he was still working as a teacher in Halifax; and he had embarked, in the late 1950s, on the historical work that was to render him internationally famous, *The Making of the English Working Class* (published in 1963).[58]

Not surprisingly, the theoretical concerns that motivated Thompson in *The Making of the English Working Class* were intimately related to his political work in the New Left.[59] Indeed, his questions of theory and his questions of practice were really identical: How do people change the structures of the society in which they live? How does a "new consciousness" emerge among specific groups of people, and how is it possible for this "new consciousness" to bring about the transformation of a society? At the heart of Thompson's search lay a new idea of revolution, a new understanding of the "transition to socialism."[60] Little by little, his work as a historian had convinced him that a fundamental misconception underlay the orthodox Marxist picture of how the modern labor movement had been born. Nor was this merely a historian's quibble; for in Thompson's view, the consequences of this misconception extended directly into the mid–twentieth century, robbing the labor movement of its force and—still more important—of its genuine democratic potential. The new conception of revolution that he proposed to his contemporaries derived directly from his reconceptualization of what had happened among English workers a century and a half before.

The traditional Marxist vision, which Thompson now considered obsolete, ran roughly as follows: in the early nineteenth century, a new system of industrial capitalism became dominant, in which large numbers of workers were simultaneously concentrated into urban factory centers and subjected to unprecedentedly exploitative conditions of labor. Brought together in this way, the workers were able to recognize their common interests as an exploited class and to organize. At a propitious moment, they would act in unison, seizing the power of the state and abolishing the economic system based on private property; after this point, it would be possible to begin creating a new society free from exploitation.

Thompson's main objection to this picture, which he expressed most clearly in two articles written in 1960, was directed at the tacit assumption "that the origin and growth of working-class consciousness was a function of the growth of large-scale factory production whose inevitable tendency must be to engender a revolutionary consciousness."[61] The key words here were "inevitable" and "engender." For orthodox Marxists, the particular physical and social conditions of the factory system had inevitably engendered a concomitant form of consciousness which would, in its turn, become instrumental in overturning capitalism. For Thompson, on the other hand, physical and social conditions did not mechanically generate predictable responses in the minds of men and women. Cultural reactions to the factory system were in fact highly diverse and often contradictory—from the nostalgia of the Luddites to the escapism of the Methodists, from the utopian aspiration of the Owenites to the reformism of the Chartists. What united the English working class, he argued, was not a uniform set of experiences "generated" within a ubiquitous factory system, but rather a dogged effort on the part of many diverse individuals to call upon and awaken deeper traditions of equity and justice that were being violated in manifold ways.

Thus, in his research for *The Making of the English Working Class*, Thompson had discovered that

> the most revolutionary "shock troops" of the working class were [often] not factory proletarians at all [as Marx had assumed] but were the depressed handworkers; while in many towns, including large industrial towns, the actual nucleus of the labour movement was made up largely of artisans—shoemakers, saddlers and harnessmakers, building workers, booksellers, small tradesmen, and the like. Further, so far from being vacillating "petit-bourgeois" elements, these were often . . . among the most consistent and self-sacrificing participants in the working-class movement.[62]

Not only was the working class far more heterogeneous than Marx had conceived it to be, but the forging of a sense of unity among these disparate groups had hinged crucially upon the organizational efforts of determined individuals. Class unity, far from being an automatic outcome of a particular mode of production, consisted rather in a new way of perceiving oneself in relation to others: a self-image painfully built up and refined through a long process of tentative advances and humiliating failures. Moral courage, creative reflection upon one's environment, difficult choices in the shifting of one's allegiances—these were among the key factors in the making of class consciousness.

For orthodox Marxists, therefore, the essence of social change lay in the amalgamation of new relations of production; for Thompson, it embraced a more complex reciprocity between relations of production and their construal in human experience. In the former picture, the rise of the factory system and the rise of class consciousness went together like a linear relation of cause and effect; in Thompson's analysis, the connection between the two was far less deterministic, for it hinged upon the "wild card" of human subjectivity. How would people perceive the changing relations of production? What emotions would this arouse in them? How would they choose to act in response? All these questions, which were cultural in nature, provided the crucial mediation between the rather wooden terms of "cause" and "effect."

This reemphasis on culture and human initiative in the shaping of working-class history went hand in hand with a drastically revised notion of revolution. Thompson utterly rejected the elevation of the 1917 Soviet Revolution to the status of a general model or schema for all "transitions to socialism." In a lengthy article entitled "Socialist Humanism" (written in 1957), he attacked contemporary Russian communism as "anti-democratic, inherently bureaucratic, alternately paternalist or despotic towards the people."[63] He painstakingly analyzed this form of statism, tracing its roots not only to Stalin himself but also "to ambiguities in the thought of Marx and, even more, to mechanistic fallacies in Lenin's writings."[64] At the core of the problem he saw a failure by Marx and Engels to understand fully, or to emphasize adequately, "how men's ideas were formed, and wherein lay their field of agency."[65] The crucial ambiguity lay in their use of the pivotal word "reflection," which could either mean a passive echoing, like a mirror, or a much more active and creative process of reworking given information into a new synthesis. The gradual erosion of the second meaning in the transition from Marx to Lenin to Stalin had ultimately resulted in a rigid and brutal ideological orthodoxy intrinsically hostile to popular initiative and the genuine renewal of ideas. "How much easier," he wrote ironically, "if the people had no minds, if the 'superstructure' was cut out and society was all 'base': then this clumsy business of reflection could be done away with."[66]

Thompson insisted, however, that a strong humanist element in the Marxist tradition was still alive, and could be separated from the disastrous dogmatism and authoritarianism with which it had been fused. Steering between the reformist model of the Labour party and the cataclysmic model of orthodox revolutionaries, he sought to define a concept of revolution that would remain true to the values of "socialist humanism." This revolution would be gradual and nonviolent, basing its advance on "unrelenting reformist pressures in many fields" and on voluntary changes in people's values;[67] yet it would be a "revolution" nonetheless, because it would aim not at any accommodation with acquisitive capitalism, but at a thoroughgoing transformation into a society where the logic of community and of reciprocity prevailed over competitive individualism. It would focus not on the seizure of power and the takeover of the State's administrative institutions, but rather on the building of new institutions for popular discussion and self-governance—a process of self-education and self-organization from the grass-roots upward. "It is possible to look forward to a peaceful revolution in Britain," he wrote in 1960,

> with far greater continuity in social life and in institutional forms than would have seemed likely even twenty years ago, not because it will be a semi-revolution, nor because capitalism is "evolving" into socialism; but because the advances of 1942–48 *were* real, because the socialist *potential* has been enlarged, and socialist forms, however imperfect, have grown up "within" capitalism.[68]

Needless to say, this conception of revolution provoked a great deal of criticism among those on the Left who were used to thinking in terms of physical force as the ultimate arbiter in the struggle between classes. As early as 1958, Thompson's "Socialist Humanism" had been criticized by fellow contributors to the *New Reasoner* as "flitting on the perimeter of idealism," and as the work of a "utopian socialist" who believed too strongly in "the power of the word."[69] How, his many critics asked, could this idea of peaceful revolution have any efficacy within an affluent society where the ideological hegemony of the established order was powerful and resilient? What would this "revolution" look like?[70]

Thompson's answer hinged once again upon a historical analogy. Just as in the early nineteenth century, when the determined agency of Chartist organizers had helped to produce an intense collective awareness of common interests and aims, so in the mid-twentieth century a new movement for popular self-organization could make all the difference. "The problem," he wrote in 1960,

> is not one of "seizing power" in order to create a society in which self-activity is possible, but one of generating this activity now within a manipulative society. . . . One socialist youth club of a quite new kind, in East London or Liverpool or Leeds; one determined municipal council, probing the possibility of new kinds of municipal ownership in the face of Government opposition; one tenant's association with a new dynamic, pioneering on its own account new patterns of social welfare—play-centers, nursery facilities, community services for and by the women—involving people in the discussion and solution of problems of town planning, racial intercourse, leisure facilities; one pit, factory, or sector of nationalized industry where new forms of workers' control can actually be forced upon management . . . —a breakthrough at any one of these points would immediately help in precipitating a diffuse aspiration into a positive movement.[71]

Here, therefore, lay Thompson's hopes for the New Left. It would bring together ex-Communists with the left wing of the Labour party, nuclear disarmament activists with trade union members, dissidents in the Eastern bloc with Western rebels against NATO, offering an international grass-roots alternative to the stale orthodoxies and "sterile antagonisms" of state capitalism and state communism.[72] He was not sanguine about the prospects for success, and singled out the ideological hardening of the Cold War as the greatest obstacle to the flourishing of a new socialist humanism.[73] Nevertheless, he plunged into his work in the New Left clubs and the Campaign for Nuclear Disarmament with an ardor that could only have been fueled by genuine optimism as well as political conviction. "This new popular consciousness," he wrote in October 1960, "could develop so swiftly that it would leave [the Labour party leader]

Mr. Gaitskell and his Parliamentary caucus flapping about like fish on dry land."[74]

This remark, which might easily seem more whimsical than realistic, was in fact referring to a remarkable confluence of political developments that had occurred during the preceding three years. Throughout the 1950s, the Conservative party had ruled Britain from a position that seemed unchallengeable. The economy, bolstered by Marshall Plan aid, had grown fairly steadily (although not as quickly as in other nations of Western Europe). British public opinion had accepted the necessity for decolonization much more readily than the French; and even the humiliation of the Suez fiasco had been survived by the Conservative government with relatively little recrimination. British statesmen still prided themselves on their "special relationship" with the United States, and remained aloof from the supranational currents that were carrying the continental nations toward the European Economic Community. Thus, it was not surprising that the new prime minister who took office in 1957, Harold Macmillan, should have felt confident enough to refurbish Britain's image as a great power by announcing the imminent construction of an independent thermonuclear arsenal.

Here, however, an interesting cleavage began to form between British politicians and the British electorate; for although the Labour party leaders promptly swung into line behind the new nuclear policy, a great many individuals on the Left remained profoundly skeptical. To them, the testing of a British hydrogen bomb at Christmas Island in the spring of 1957 seemed like a gratuitous escalation of the arms race. Britain's proper role, they believed, should be to mediate between the two superpowers, not to engage in a vain effort to mimic them.[75] In April 1957, a major policy statement by the British minister of defense, seeking to popularize the logic of nuclear deterrence, had admitted that there was "no means of providing adequate protection . . . against the consequences of an attack with nuclear weapons";[76] and in October, the launching of *Sputnik* by the Soviet Union effectively dramatized this statement, underscoring once again the extreme vulnerability of Britain in the nuclear age. To this hypothetical danger, moreover, was added the very real threat posed by radioactive fallout from weapons tests, increasingly publicized by scientists and by antinuclear groups.[77]

The result, by the end of 1957, was a heightened awareness of the nuclear peril among wide sections of the British public—a growing anxiety which the established political parties showed no sign of addressing. A significant political space had opened up, within which the Campaign for Nuclear Disarmament (CND) would flourish. Founded in January 1958 by a group of prominent intellectuals, including Bertrand Russell, Julian Huxley, and A. J. P. Taylor, the campaign appealed primarily to educated middle-class individuals rather than the working-class constituency favored (at least in theory) by the New Left.[78]

Nevertheless, the connections between these two movements developed at a deep level; for they both reflected the same distrust of political parties, and the same desire to fashion a new kind of politics based on direct popular participation.[79] In April 1958, the first of an annual series of CND protest marches took place, mobilizing between five thousand and ten thousand people for a forty-five-mile trek (over three days) between London and the British nuclear-weapons facility at Aldermaston. By 1960, the Aldermaston March had swelled to approximately 100,000 participants, and CND's aims of bringing nuclear policy to the center of public debate had unquestionably succeeded. During a tumultuous convention of the Labour party at Scarborough in October 1960, the rank-and-file membership overrode the pleas of its leaders and voted for a platform of unilateral nuclear disarmament by Britain.

At the same time as CND had been growing in stature and influence, moreover, the New Left also had come into its own. The first issue of *New Left Review* (circulation 9,000) was published in January of 1960; and by this time approximately twelve "New Left clubs" had formed throughout England. Within a year that number would grow to forty. The purpose of these clubs was closely aligned with the arguments expressed by Thompson in his article on "revolution": to provide focal points for discussion and local initiative outside established party institutions. Organized into a loose network, the clubs held a national convention and a "summer school" each year, seeking to forge a consensus among the many strands of the British Left. Their rapid growth during the year 1960, coupled with the spectacular success of CND, provided the unusual context for Thompson's vision of a grass-roots movement that would leave professional politicians and administrators "flapping about like fish on dry land."

In 1958, Thompson and his wife had taken upon themselves the organization of CND in Halifax—calling meetings, planning marches, and distributing leaflets.[80] By 1960, CND occupied a central place in Thompson's vision of a "revolutionary" shift in consciousness extending far beyond the New Left and involving the whole of the British people. "The opportunity for a revolutionary breakthrough," he wrote in the winter of 1960,

> might as possibly arise from international as from local political or industrial causes. Should the protest in Britain gain sufficient strength to force our country out of NATO, consequences will follow in rapid succession. The Americans might reply with economic sanctions. Britain would be faced with the alternatives of compliance or of a far-reaching reorientation of trade. The dilemma would agitate the consciousness of the whole people, not as an abstract theory of revolution but as an actual and immediate political choice, debated in the factories, offices and streets. People would become aware of the historic choice presented to

our country, as they became aware during the Second World War. Ideological and political antagonisms would sharpen. Non-compliance with America would entail winning the active, informed support of the majority of the people for policies which might bring with them dislocation and hardship.[81]

Thompson stressed that he was not offering a "prediction," but only

> an impression of *one* possible way in which a revolutionary situation could arise, resulting not from disaster but from an active popular initiative. . . . And it is *this* event which could at one blow break up the log-jam of the Cold War and initiate a new wave of world advance. Advance in Western Europe, and, in less direct ways, democratisation in the East, may wait upon us.[82]

With these images, Thompson was prefiguring much of the substantive strategy he was later to adopt in the European Nuclear Disarmament (END) campaign of the 1980s. The key difference would lie in his subsequent insistence that any attempt to dismantle NATO must fit together with a symmetrical dismantling of the Warsaw Pact, so that disarmament and "democratization" would become truly indivisible. In both cases, however, the common element lay in his distinctively "anti-Machiavellian" vision: peace did not just mean an absence of war among nation-states, but rather the *presence* of a new egalitarian politics, arising from among the "common people" themselves, and building its own bridges across the boundaries of culture and territory. Thompson explicitly rejected the state-centric and elitist proposals of intellectuals like Weiss and Szilard, calling instead for a new activism among each of the world's peoples, so that domestic reforms and international cooperation could be directly created by the citizens themselves.

In the end, however, Thompson's vision of 1961 as a potential watershed proved unrealizable. CND, riven by internal dissension over the tactics of protest, gradually began to lose its élan. The goal of unilateral nuclear disarmament, which had provided an effective rallying point for the campaign's diverse supporters, failed to infuse the movement with a sense of long-range political direction. According to Peggy Duff, the campaign's ebullient organizing secretary, the majority of CND activists

> thought that banning the bomb was a fairly simple matter, and they never recognized the revolution in British politics that it required. They wanted to get rid of the bomb, leave NATO and abandon the American alliance without upsetting the pattern of life in Sutton, Totnes, or Greenwich, SE3. . . . Occasional conferences on the positive aims of the campaign were very wishy-washy.[83]

At the 1961 Labour party conference, Hugh Gaitskell succeeded in overturning the previous year's disarmament resolution; and during the following two years, the Cuban missile crisis and the Limited Test Ban Treaty of 1963 served to underscore the marginal role played by Britain and the apparent fact that the superpowers could "deal" successfully with each other.[84] Both these events, coupled with the exhaustion of the campaigners themselves, helped to dissipate the energies that had fueled the movement.[85]

The New Left unraveled for some of the same kinds of reasons. Looking back candidly at the disappointments of 1961 in December of that year, the editors of *New Left Review* gave the following account of the problems that had plagued their work:

> Last winter was a thin time for the Left Clubs. While few disbanded, many became quiescent. The National Clubs Committee, hamstrung by lack of money, found it difficult to meet. The response to [summer] schools was poor. . . . The sales of *New Left Review* had tilted downwards, and every one of our enterprises— books, pamphlets, industrial work—were handicapped by lack of money and personnel.[86]

At a deeper level, the key weakness of the New Left lay in its propensity to explode into innumerable factions, all of which claimed to hold the most pristine vision of genuine socialism. As these factions subsequently looked back on the early 1960s, each offered its own explanation of past failures—from the absence of a genuine base among working-class trade unions to an excessive absorption with CND, from the lack of a cogent revolutionary strategy to an overly intellectualized conception of class struggle.[87] Although there may be elements of truth in many of these interpretations, it is perhaps precisely this acute divisiveness among the New Left's constituencies, and their fratricidal competitiveness, that most seriously undermined its collective efforts. As early as October 1960, Thompson had already testified to the acrimonious atmosphere that sometimes poisoned New Left clubs:

> I cannot forget an appalling meeting of the London Club . . . at which half-a-dozen Covenanting sects were present, each reaching by means of their "Marxist science" diametrically opposed conclusions. The vibrant self-consuming hatred displayed by one sect for another can have left no emotional energy over for concern with the capitalist system or nuclear war; and the air was thick with the sniff-sniff-sniff of "theorists" who confused the search for clarity with the search for heresy. The word "comrade" was employed, in six-foot-high quotation marks, like deadly barbs on the polished shaft of Leninist irony—embellishing devastating witticisms of

the order of "Perhaps *Comrade* Thompson will tell us if he sup-
poses that socialism will come at the behest of the Virgin Mary?"[88]

Thompson himself came to be embroiled in a particularly bitter feud early
in 1962, a conflict that led to his withdrawal from the *New Left Review* the
following year. The immediate cause of the rift lay in the appointment of a new
editor, Perry Anderson, who represented a younger group of New Left thinkers. "We freely spoke of the 'Old Guard' among ourselves," Anderson later
wrote, "at a time when Thompson was just over 35."[89] This split between the
so-called Old New Left and New New Left rested not only on differing generational experiences, but also on profoundly divergent accents of theoretical orientation. To Anderson and his group, "1956" and "Socialist Humanism"
seemed far less important than the new political movements taking shape
within the Third World, and the new currents of existentialist Marxism developing in Paris. Sartre and Fanon were the exciting intellectual figures, in comparison with which William Morris seemed provincial and obsolete. For the
"Old Guard," on the other hand—the Thompsons, Saville, Mervyn Jones, Raymond Williams, Ralph Miliband, and others—this new direction taken up by
Anderson seemed more like a disturbing mixture of hypertheoretical virtuosity
and anti-Western *machismo.* "It seems the fashion now will be," warned
Thompson in 1962,

> to attach ourselves to peasant-revolutionary movements; adopt
> their dismissal of "the West"; [and] tolerate a mystique of vio-
> lence, virility and simplicity, in which men can *only* find their hu-
> manity with a rifle in their hands aimed at a white face.[90]

These arguments went unheeded by Anderson and his group, who wanted
to cut back support for CND and the dwindling New Left clubs, while shifting
the review's emphasis toward Marxist theory and the revolutions in the Third
World.[91] By 1963, therefore, the position of the "Old Guard" within the *New
Left Review* was becoming increasingly untenable; yet the prospect of undertaking a major struggle for control of the journal seemed both senseless and
demeaning. "We were demoralized and tired after six years of it," Thompson
later explained, "and had no money. I remember going down to London [to
consult on the review] with holes in my shoes and sopping socks. It was all a
very dismal time."[92] Early in 1963, the Thompsons and the rest of the "Old
Guard" resigned from the review's editorial board, leaving the field open for
Anderson to undertake a full-scale reorientation of its content and style. The
"row" between Thompson and Anderson became public in 1965, with a ran-
corous exchange of articles in the *Socialist Register* and the *New Left Review;*[93]
yet their deep-running disagreements were to prove fruitful in the long run. In
1980, Anderson would publish *Arguments within English Marxism,* a full-scale
engagement with Thompson's ideas carried out in a considerably more con-

structive tone;[94] and the "Anderson-Thompson debate" would provide a significant crystallization of many latent tensions within Western Marxism.

In his political work after 1963, Thompson continued to refer to himself as a "dissident Communist," and, still later, as a "libertarian Communist."[95] He refused to accept the equation, "Communism = Soviet totalitarianism," and insisted that the genuine roots of the Communist movement lay in the struggles for democratic self-rule among the workers of the early nineteenth century.[96] While ardently espousing his own brand of "peaceful revolution," therefore, Thompson saw no contradiction in joining the Labour party—which he and Dorothy did in 1962.[97] "Is a party necessary?" he was later asked by an interviewer. "Yes," Thompson replied,

> and probably several parties that argue with each other. . . . The thing is that we fight for reforms and make encroachments into all areas of social life, political as well as economic. . . . And while it is true that reforms can legitimise the system to some extent, it is wrong to see only the legitimising aspect, as the left often does, and to ignore the fact that these are genuine gains that the system has to adjust to with difficulty.[98]

While intensely hostile to the existing "system," Thompson preferred to push against its limits from the inside rather than to call for its abrupt dismantling and reconstruction from zero. In 1967, he joined the literary critic Raymond Williams and the Socialist writer Stuart Hall in circulating the May Day Manifesto, a critique of the relatively centrist policies enacted by Harold Wilson's Labour government (which had taken power in 1964). Yet despite its fierce attack on Labour's ethic of "welfare capitalism," the Manifesto refused to abandon the existing traditions of parliamentary rule:

> We would very willingly admit the power and importance of the House of Commons, if it would show some signs of political action . . . against organized private power or established interests; fighting a popular cause against arbitrary authority or secret decision. . . . We are told that we have parliamentary government, but all we can say is that we would like to see some.[99]

Throughout the winter of 1967–68, Thompson, Hall, Williams, and other contributors to the Manifesto traveled around England organizing "Manifesto Groups," which were directly modeled on the New Left clubs of a few years earlier. Before this new movement could take hold, however, it was overtaken and sidetracked by the wave of student revolts that spread through the industrialized countries during 1968.[100]

Thompson's attitude toward these new student movements was a characteristically tortured and multifaceted one. He strongly agreed that British students should protest against the U.S. war in Vietnam, but felt repelled by their confrontational tactics and "punch-ups" with the police. Too many of their actions struck him as "irrationalist, self-exalting gestures of style," and he could not share their belief "that some campus-based revolution would by-pass the working class."[101] Above all, he objected to the position taken by the British "Vietnam Solidarity Committees," which explicitly ranged themselves on the Communist side in the war:

> I thought the objective of the peace movement should be to bring the war to an end—not actually to espouse Vietcong victory. Which I suppose is very liberal and soft of me; but that was my CND training. . . . This left me rather muzzled. A lot of the militant and rather *macho* leftism of that time turned me off completely.[102]

Only two years later, however, Thompson became a central participant in a rather different student movement. In 1965, he and Dorothy had moved south from Halifax to Warwick, where he had been asked to head the Centre for the Study of Social History at the newly formed Warwick University. During his fifth year of teaching there, in 1970, students began to agitate for greater democracy in the educational process; and on the night of February 11 they occupied the campus administration building. Thompson, who "had been arguing for a more reformist course of action," was telephoned at 8:30 in the evening by students who had opened confidential university files.[103] They had found documents clearly establishing that university officials were monitoring the political activities of students and staff, screening prospective students according to their political views, and had apparently sought to secure the deportation of the labor historian David Montgomery, who was visiting from the United States.[104] Thompson responded by photocopying the key documents and distributing them to all faculty members the following morning. In the furor that ensued, Thompson defended his publication of the documents on the grounds that the information they revealed required a full-scale inquiry into the university's administration.[105] Having sided with the students, he found himself caught between two kinds of attack: on the one hand, liberals and conservatives who denounced his breach of the university's right to privacy; and on the other, militant leftists who ridiculed his effort to restore impartiality in the university's official procedures. This impartiality, he argued, was not to be dismissed as a mere sham but represented a crucial principle that one should fight to uphold. "It is here," he wrote,

> that red moles and Maoists, looking down at our contemptible liberal maunderings from the revolutionary heights of North London, tend to go wrong. In so far as they persuade students that *all* the rules, the democratic and constitutional defenses, of the institution are no more than liberal "masks," their analysis could be self-

fulfilling. . . . They can't denounce democracy as a spoof and at the same time help to man its defenses.[106]

Eventually, after an official inquiry and modest reforms, the tumult at Warwick University subsided; yet the impact of this episode on Thompson's thought remained significant. Throughout the following decade, Thompson published a steady series of articles defending the institutions of British liberalism from what he saw as a manifold array of encroachments.[107] On the Left, he observed a tendency to dismiss all "democratic and constitutional defenses" as a mere facade behind which the manipulative rule of power and money went on untrammeled. On the Right, he discerned a growing authoritarianism in British society, in the "Official Secrets Act," the political screening of juries, the spread of wiretapping, and the manufacture of consensus by "a compliant press [and] a managed television."[108] Both these tendencies, Left and Right, contributed to an erosion of precious civil liberties—liberties rooted in historic struggles for democratic self-rule and without which his own vision of a new democratic spirit would become meaningless.

With the confrontation at Warwick University behind him, Thompson decided in 1971 to withdraw from academic teaching and to devote himself full-time to writing history. Dorothy Thompson had begun teaching social history at Birmingham University; and in 1972 they were able to buy a house in the countryside near Worcester, an eighteenth-century property which included its own ghost (Thompson insisted), and where Thompson spent most of his subsequent time as a writer. Yet this new home was far from being a country retreat, as one of the Thompsons's old friends, the writer Mervyn Jones, later observed in his autobiography:

> The Thompsons' house had the intriguing name of Wick Episcopi. Everything about it—the ample high-ceilinged rooms, the shelves crammed with books, the log fires, the affectionately indulged dogs and cats, the noble cedar tree on the front lawn, the big garden where Edward tended his pears and raspberries—gave it the appearance of a scholar's retreat. Here, perhaps, one might find a man labouring patiently on the transcription of runes, while seldom glancing at a newspaper or worrying himself over current controversies. In reality, Wick Episcopi was the base from which Edward fired his salvoes in relentless warfare against the arrogance of power.[109]

1963–1980: The Power of Culture

If the idea of democratic self-rule lay at the heart of Thompson's political work, of course, neither was it ever far from his mind as he continued with his historical writing. In a broad sense, the three major works he published during this period—*The Making of the English Working Class* (1963), *Whigs and Hunters* (1975), and *The Poverty of Theory* (1978)—all revolved around the same common theme: the possibility for human beings to shape their own history. Once again, just as in his political stance of "libertarian communism," Thompson's treatment of this theme rested on the delicate balancing of antagonistic categories. Human agency, he argued, was determined and limited by preexisting conditions; yet it was also capable of transforming those same conditions through conscious action, and it therefore could have a say in shaping its own evolution. Nor was this issue merely a matter of interest for Marxists or specialized historians; both the major reconceptualization of the Cold War that Thompson proposed in 1980, as well as his prominent role in launching a new European peace movement, derived directly from his theoretical reflections on the power of individuals to shape their society.

At the center of Thompson's work lay a rejection of the Marxist model of economic "base" and cultural "superstructure."[110] As early as 1957, he had already begun to question the analytical distinction itself between "economic" and "cultural" categories of events:

> Production, distribution, and consumption are not only digging, carrying, and eating, but are also planning, organizing, and enjoying. Imaginative and intellectual faculties are not confined to a "superstructure" and erected upon a "base" of things (including men-things); they are implicit in the creative act of labour which makes man man. . . . The very category of economics—the notion that it is possible to isolate economic from noneconomic social relations . . . was the product of a particular phase of capitalist evolution.[111]

This line of thinking steadily drew Thompson toward a more complex vision of history. Human lives unfolded on many levels—economic, political, psychological, biological—any one of which might provisionally assume causal priority in determining a given formation of events. These "levels," moreover, continually interacted with each other in ways that defied the traditional Marxist impulse to reduce all historical change to its economic determinants.[112]

As a concrete example, Thompson spent several pages in the essay "The Poverty of Theory" describing the imaginary case of a British woman who was simultaneously a trade-union organizer in her factory, a Labour party activist, a mother of three children, an amateur musician, a member of the Church of England, the wife of one man and the mistress of another. All of these "levels" played crucial roles in determining her life; no single domain could adequately explain the distinctive story that her daily actions gradually formed. "Is the woman," Thompson asked, no more than a point at which all these relations, structures, roles, expectations, norms, and functions *intersect;* is she the carrier of all of them, simultaneously, and is she *acted* by them, and absolutely determined at their intersection?[113]

The only way to find out, Thompson replied, was not to consult some abstract Marxist model or sociological theory but simply to observe her history, which expressed the ineffable totality of the ongoing relations reverberating within her life. Thompson offered two possible scenarios for the woman's story. In the first, she suffered a nervous breakdown under the conflicting pressures of her numerous allegiances and had to be kept going on tranquilizers. In the second, she went to her workplace and rebelled:

> She shouts out: "I'm not a bloody THING!" . . . She calls out the workshop on strike. She leaves her husband and she sacks her lover. She joins women's lib. She leaves the Church of England.[114]

In the end, Thompson argued, a human being could not be reduced to abstract categories, no matter how intricate and subtle they were; out of the ongoing synthesis that each individual created among the structures that impinged on his or her life, a unique and ultimately unpredictable story arose. Above all, a human individual possessed the potential for taking the initiative and changing the structures; Thompson felt that, like the woman in his story, every human being shared in the double-sided possibility of either succumbing to society's complex pressures, or of rebelling and seeking to master them.

But how could a mere individual hope to prevail against the vast structures of contemporary society? Here, a second key concept came into play for Thompson: the intrinsic circularity or reflexivity of all social behavior. Since human beings were the stuff of which society was made, they changed themselves in the very process of transforming society; their role was simultaneously active and passive. Any action by an individual within a social context (insofar as it influenced or changed that social context) ultimately rebounded back upon that same individual's life and actions; for the existence of every individual was deeply conditioned by the social whole of which he or she was a part, and any changes in that social whole must in turn influence all of its constituent members. By changing social reality in however small a way, therefore, a single person could commensurately alter the manner in which other individuals perceived their environment and chose to act. These new perceptions could gradually add up, as increasing numbers of persons made them their own, and conveyed them (in turn) to still larger numbers. Over extended periods, what was collectively deemed possible or impossible, desirable or undesirable, might shift substantially as a result of ideas initiated by relatively few persons. Thus, an individual's impact might at first seem rather small and

insignificant, but, through the circular dynamic of human culture, it could ultimately "snowball" into major structural changes.

On the other hand, Thompson pointed out, this form of power also possessed
inherent limits; for the social context inevitably interfered with each individual's efforts to attain fully his or her own goals. Within the broader society,
where many persons' wills and exertions criss-crossed, conjoined, or canceled
each other out, the ultimate result was always a collective outcome that no
single individual had quite predicted or intended. Thompson referred to this
dual quality of social process as "the crucial ambivalence of our human presence in our own history, part-subjects, part-objects, the voluntary agents of our
own involuntary determinations." [115] And he quoted a famous passage from *The
Dream of John Ball* by William Morris to illustrate what he meant:

> I pondered all these things, and how men fight and lose the battle,
> and the thing they fought for comes about in spite of their defeat,
> and when it comes turns out not to be what they meant, and other
> men have to fight for what they meant under another name. [116]

It had been the work of Giambattista Vico that first alerted Thompson to this
aspect of historical process, in which human actions appeared simultaneously
as partly free and partly unfree; [117] and it became increasingly clear to him that
no metaphor (like "base and superstructure") could adequately express this
self-referential dialectic of cultural change. "The difficulty," he wrote at one
point, as he reflected over the possibility of a vegetation metaphor, "is not that
a tree cannot think but that, if it could think, its thinking could not change—
however imperceptibly—the soil in which it is rooted." [118]

Human agency, therefore, was like a form of play taking place within limits—limits whose evolution the players could consciously influence over time.
Each individual possessed a finite yet open-ended opportunity to contribute to
the shaping of culture. The ongoing collective result would be something different than any single individual had envisioned, yet each could participate to
some degree in determining the overall direction of social change. This was
the precious space of partial free agency that Thompson never ceased in his
writings to explore and to emphasize. In *The Making of the English Working
Class,* Thompson had tried to show that "class" was not something passive or
static, but the product of arduous cultural processes in which the moral courage
and practical initiative of real historical persons had played a central role. His
next work, *Whigs and Hunters* (1975), focused on the relation between law
and the common people in eighteenth-century England; its central concern
was, once again, to show that cultural factors could be more powerful in shaping society than most people normally believed.

In his research for *Whigs and Hunters,* Thompson had come to a startling
conclusion: the law, in eighteenth-century England, had served simultaneously

as an oppressive instrument of class rule *and* as a valuable constraint upon the naked exercise of power. Rulers and ruled had certainly stood at opposite ends of society; but they had also struggled within a common (or overlapping) medium of moral values and legal institutions that provided costs and benefits for both sides.

> Not only were the rulers (indeed, the ruling class as a whole) inhibited by their own rules of law against the exercise of direct unmediated force, . . . but they also believed enough in these rules, and in their accompanying ideological rhetoric, to allow, in certain limited areas, the law itself to be a genuine forum within which certain kinds of class conflict were fought out. There were even occasions (one recalls John Wilkes and several of the trials of the 1790s) when the Government itself retired from the courts defeated. . . .
>
> The rhetoric and the rules of a society are something a great deal more than sham. In the same moment they may modify, in profound ways, the behavior of the powerful, and mystify the powerless. They may disguise the true realities of power, but, at the same time, they may curb that power and check its intrusions.[119]

This was far from providing a sanguine vision of social conflict, in which the reconciliation of opposed interests lay within easy reach. Nevertheless, it proposed a conceptual framework in which two "enemy" groups were also subtly interdependent and could struggle to alter the mutual norms of tacit social consent that bound them together. In this picture, the domain of culture became a battleground in which crucial struggles could be fought out—struggles in which the dominance of one social group over others could be challenged, undermined, or even overthrown.[120]

Perhaps the most explicit formulation of Thompson's ideas on human agency, however, occurred not within a historical study but in his first published novel, *The Sykaos Papers* (1988).[121] In this rollicking and dryly ironic work of science fiction, Thompson described the confrontation between an extraterrestrial culture, Oitar, and the inhabitants of earth at some point near the year 2000. Oitarian civilization was like a human beehive: a highly ritualized society whose members serenely allowed the total regulation of their lives by a "sacred" central authority (a computer). The contrast with planet earth was a stark one; for on Oitar the effectiveness of collective agency in shaping history was nearly total, resulting in a social order where even innovation took place within carefully preprogrammed limits. On earth, however, the efficacy of collective decision making was so meagre that the resultant social order had reached the very brink of self-destruction. Somewhere in between these two extremes lay Thompson's "ideal" measure of free agency. Individuals needed enough leeway to allow for genuine and open variation; yet these individuals also required a capacity to regulate their own behavior so as to coordinate their collective actions. Precisely because human beings were "part-subjects, part-objects," they could never hope to attain complete control over events (as in Oitar), but they could reasonably aspire to make a partial impact on their society.

Thompson's historical theorizing was closely linked, of course, to his hopes for a peaceful and democratic "revolution." Still, he was as surprised as anyone else, near the end of 1979, when his ideas suddenly found a very tangible and practical application. He had been writing a series of articles for *New Society* on civil liberties and the "national-security state," when (as he later recollected it) he "turned on the wireless and heard the Government PR person telling us we were going to have cruise missiles. It all seemed to click."[122] The connection between the militarization of society and the decline of democratic values had long preoccupied him; and he had been conferring recently with Ken Coates of the Bertrand Russell Peace Foundation about the possibility of launching some kind of public manifesto or "Appeal." The announcement about cruise missiles thus provided an immediate focus for concerted action. Thompson's vision of historical agency, sharply focused after 1979 on the problems of war and peacemaking, was itself about to become an instrumental factor in the shaping of European politics.

1980–1989: Redefining Europe's Identity

The winter of 1979–80 marked a turning point in several key domains of international politics. After nearly a decade of somewhat stiff but significant cooperation, the superpowers entered a new phase of sharp hostility after the Soviet invasion of Afghanistan in December 1979. The SALT II treaty, which had set partial limits on the arms race, had been languishing in the U.S. Senate under heavy attack from American conservatives; it was now withdrawn by President Carter. Earlier in the fall, fanatical mobs in Tehran had taken fifty-three Americans hostage; the Iranians were seeking revenge for the long decades of close U.S. partnership with the Shah and his dreaded secret police, the SAVAK. Carter's hesitancy and tergiversation in confronting these foreign-policy challenges helped pave the way for his defeat in 1980 by Ronald Reagan, a presidential candidate far more straightforwardly committed to the building and the flexing of American muscle. In Britain, Margaret Thatcher's election victory in May 1979 had brought into power one of the few Europeans who could rival President Reagan in military toughness and uncompromising conservatism.

Amid these clamorous changes, a relatively unnoticed but nonetheless important decision was taken on December 12, 1979, at a gathering of the NATO countries' foreign ministers in Brussels. Late in 1983, it was announced, NATO would begin deploying two new types of U.S. nuclear missiles in Western Europe; if the Soviets wanted to forestall this deployment, they would have to enter serious negotiations on the reduction of their own newest missiles in Eastern Europe, the so-called SS-20s. The rationale behind this decision extended far back into the history of NATO.[123] Ever since its formation in 1949, the alliance had relied primarily on U.S. nuclear weapons to make up for the Soviet Union's geographical proximity and quantitative superiority in conventional weapons on the European continent. At the center of NATO's strategy lay the concept of "coupling"—that is, the unequivocal and automatic binding of U.S. military forces to the defense of Western Europe. The key to Europe's peace, as NATO officials saw it, lay in how the Soviets perceived the West's unity and willingness to fight. What deterred a Soviet attack (or Soviet political intimidation), they argued, was the prospect of an all-out war with the United States. As long as the risk of such an escalatory war remained credible, Western Europe would be safe.

The constant worry of NATO planners, accordingly, was how to sustain the credibility of that risk as the military strength of the Soviet bloc steadily increased after the 1950s. Would the United States really use its own strategic weapons to defend Europe, thereby risking a devastating counterattack against its own territory? What if Soviet forces were able to launch a blitz attack into Western Europe, overrunning West Germany and other parts of Northern Europe with purely conventional forces? Would the United States be willing to threaten a global nuclear holocaust to regain those territories, or might it not be forced by this military fait accompli to negotiate? The logic of these kinds of "worst-case" questions led inexorably to a NATO strategy that relied heavily on short-range (or "tactical") nuclear weapons. These might be carried by airplanes or missiles, or even fired from "nuclear howitzers" located in the middle of the hypothetical European battlefield. They would stop the advancing Soviet forces, giving NATO's political leaders the crucial time to bring in U.S. reinforcements and (hopefully) to negotiate a ceasefire.

One of the problems with this strategy was that the Soviets, too, began to build up impressive "short-range" nuclear arsenals of their own. By the early 1970s, they had stationed some seven hundred such missiles in various Eastern-bloc countries; and in 1977 they began to install a far more deadly model, the SS-20, at the rate of one per week. The SS-20 could carry three highly accurate warheads as far as five thousand kilometers. It, therefore, directly threatened all the Western European capitals, while none of NATO's U.S. missiles based in Europe could reach the USSR. Would this imbalance lead to a dangerous "decoupling" of American forces from Western Europe in the event of an East-West showdown? The NATO strategists who posed this question argued that the only way to restore balance was either to secure the removal of the SS-20s or to deploy a new "generation" of U.S. missiles in Europe. Their candidates for this job were the Pershing II, a ballistic missile that could strike Soviet targets from West Germany in less than fourteen minutes, and the cruise missile, a sophisticated device that could fly for thousands of kilometers just above the treetops, evading radar and thereby becoming practically impossible to intercept. Britain was slated to receive 160 of these cruise missiles—and it was this announcement that E. P. Thompson heard on the radio shortly before Christmas in 1979.

From its inception, the European Nuclear Disarmament campaign (END) was a collective undertaking, stretching out from England to seek the active collaboration of other Europeans from both blocs. The original idea for such a campaign had come from Ken Coates, a Socialist writer who headed the Bertrand Russell Peace Foundation in Nottingham. Coates had good connections with a broad spectrum of left-wing individuals and organizations throughout Britain and Europe, from the British Labour party to the Trotskyists, from Italian "Eurocommunists" to Scandinavian social democrats. Working together through January and February of 1980, he and Thompson began to recruit members for a British committee on European Nuclear Disarmament, and to contact like-minded persons throughout Europe for suggestions and pledges of support. Thompson drafted a vibrant appeal which was to form the platform of the new movement, and submitted it for editing to Coates and the five other British figures who agreed to help launch the campaign: Bruce Kent, a Catholic monsignor who had long been active in CND; Peggy Duff, who had organized CND in 1958 ("she was like having a battalion," Thompson observed);[124] Mary Kaldor, daughter of the economist Lord Kaldor and a prominent researcher and author on the arms race; Dan Smith, also a peace researcher and author; and Stuart Holland, a member of Parliament for the Labour party.

These "Magnificent Seven" (as they came to be called with affectionate irony among grass-roots activists, much to the discomfiture of the seven themselves) organized three small conferences in London during the spring of 1980. Their aim was to bring together representatives from peace organizations throughout Western Europe, creating a concerted strategy of protest and cross-cultural contacts for the coming year. In April, at a press conference in the House of Commons, the END Appeal was launched. "We are now in great danger," it stated.

> Generations have been born beneath the shadow of nuclear war, and have become habituated to the threat. . . . We do not wish to apportion guilt between the political and military leaders of East and West. Guilt lies squarely upon both parties. Both parties have adopted menacing postures and committed aggressive actions in different parts of the world.
>
> The remedy lies in our own hands. We must act together to free the entire territory of Europe, from Poland to Portugal, from nuclear weapons, air and submarine bases, and from all institutions engaged in research into or manufacture of nuclear weapons. . . .

> We must commence to act as if a united, neutral, and pacific Europe already exists. We must learn to be loyal, not to "East" or "West," but to each other. . . . We offer no advantage to either NATO or the Warsaw alliance. Our objectives must be to free Europe from confrontation, to enforce detente between the United States and the Soviet Union, and, ultimately, to dissolve both great power alliances.[125]

To Europeans who for decades had been hearing only the endless round of one-sided blame in the Cold War, with accusation and counteraccusation in mechanical pursuit of each other, this was indeed a new and startling tone. Signatures began trickling in from Eastern Europe, despite the risk of imprisonment such an act entailed; and from Western Europe, the signatures poured in by the thousands. The END committee began making plans for a pan-European convention of peace activists, and its members were soon engulfed by the sheer volume of correspondence, requests for public appearances, and organizational chores that filled their lives.

For Thompson, this problem became particularly acute, since he was rapidly singled out as the new movement's moral leader. One of Thompson's friends, the writer Mervyn Jones, later recollected his impressions after a peace march in 1980:

> As I walked with the Thompsons from Kirtlington to Upper Heyford, I was much intrigued to catch adoring glances and hear whispers of: "That's E. P. Thompson — look, it's E. P. Thompson." When Edward spoke in Trafalgar Square at the end of the London march, a man I knew—we recognized each other from what was now called the first wave of CND—said to me: "There's our new Bertrand Russell."
>
> Soon, with the aid of television, Edward was a national figure. He was, indeed, well cast as the prophet of protest and survival. His abundant hair was now a gleaming white, his lean face was lined, and he was visibly older than most of those who heard him. . . . On the platform, his speeches were impassioned but not studiously rehearsed; if he sometimes stumbled over his words, the impression of spontaneity and of burning sincerity was all the more convincing. It was no wonder that thousands of people gave him the same mingled admiration and affection that he had always evoked among his friends.[126]

This sudden popularity worried Thompson, however; for he wanted to avoid the excessive identification of the movement with leading personalities, and he hoped that peace activists would learn how to develop their own initiatives without relying on any central authority. "How do we broaden the opening," he asked his fellow committee members in August 1980, "so that END no longer can appear as the [Russell] Foundation's private movement, or, even worse, the private crusade of E. P. Thompson?"[127]

There were, nonetheless, two substantial reasons for Thompson's prominence within END—the first centering on his personality, the second resting on the originality of his ideas. A sketch of Thompson as an END activist would have to encompass a wide variety of contradictory character traits, for he could be pugnacious, irascible, or overly sensitive to real or perceived offenses; yet he seemed to inspire in the majority of his coworkers a sense of awe mingled with fiercely loyal affection.[128] As early as 1956, Thompson's friend John Saville had gently chided him for his prickly character:

> I think a typewriter must have a peculiar effect on you, because how you do rampage! Of the two long letters that you recently [have] written me, the first accused me of intellectual and moral arrogance and the second, a couple of days ago, of cultural philistinism. . . . You do need someone who is prepared to belch and be earthy when you soar on your higher flights and you do also need someone with the physique and the psychological armour plating of a sergeant major.[129]

Perhaps it was precisely the combination of Thompson's talents and apparent character flaws that endeared him to many of his readers, audiences, and coworkers: for he possessed an ability to express himself with a disarming directness, coming across in his writings and speeches as a real human being, whose foibles and insights both welled up together from a common, and very human, source. Other speakers might be just as sincere or morally committed as Thompson, but he possessed a rare talent for showing his ideas as they emerged from the full complexity of a struggling, groping, and also deeply *personal* experience. For instance, in a blistering review of a book by the right-wing British journalist, Chapman Pincher, who claimed as his own the heritage of the anti-Fascist struggle of World War II, Thompson suddenly approached his readers from the following unusual angle:

> It is difficult to explain how memories affect one in middle life. For months, the past stretches behind one as an inert record of events. Then, without forewarning, the past seems suddenly to open itself up inside one—with a more palpable emotional force than the vague present—in the gesture of a long-dead friend, or in the recall of some "spot of time" imbued with incommunicable significance. One is astonished to find oneself, while working in the garden or pottering about the kitchen, with tears on one's cheeks.
>
> I have found myself like this more than once since reading Mr. Pincher's book. I have no notion what the tears are about. They are

certainly not those of self-pity. There may be something in them of shame, that we should have let that world be degraded into this. There is also fury—that younger people, and among these some whom I most approve and admire, should have had this foul historical con passed upon them—should suppose that this is all that that generation was . . . Pincher's sort of people![130]

The historian Michael Howard once described his misgivings as he sought to rebut one of Thompson's critical salvos: "There was the alarm felt by anyone who suddenly finds himself matched against the polemical equivalent of Bjorn Borg on the Centre Court."[131] Nevertheless, Thompson's hold on his audiences cannot have stemmed from his polemical skills alone. Rather, the deeper source of his appeal arguably lay in his ability to speak with the directness of the passage above—as one human being to another, giving voice to a moment of personal and moral feeling.

Yet a sketch of Thompson in action would be incomplete without the element of his bitingly ironic humor. He could not resist interspersing his speeches and writings with irreverent barbs and asides that, once again, added a refreshingly human dimension to what was otherwise a "serious" scholarly exercise or political discussion. In the following "Elizabethan Diary," for instance (published in the magazine *Vole* in 1979), Thompson lampooned the capitalist rigors of the European Economic Community through the eyes of a fictional Worcester ancestor, "Squire Edwd Tomson," writing in 1593:

> But here's the Rubb. Fruit cannot go to Markett, not for Money nor even yett as Charitye for the Poor. Some say it be through a sort of Monopolisers in the Dealing Trade, wch wd keep all Price at its Customary Heighth as it is set in any Leen Yeer. And that these Dealers wd rather that the Poor Starve, the Fruits fall Rotted and Wormey, and the Husbandmen & their familys Toile & Swinke for no Reward—all so that their Proffits be not Sunke. . . .
>
> But Lawyer Grafter of Herefd who hath come but lately from the Innes of Court saith it is Otherwise & that it is (Save the Mark!) the Queens own Council wch is to blame, wch have made a Secret Treaty wth the French & the Low Countries & have thrown the Markett of the Cities wide to em, . . . & brings the Strangers Wares up all the Rivers of England. And the City Folk run after forrayn Facion & must have the Apples dresst in Papers like Ladyes Sweetmeetes & no Blemish on the Skinnes & all of a Size like Oysters in a Barrel, althow the Fruit be Nothing but Pith & Pulp & a Sort of Natureless Pap without neither Goodnesse nor Taste. So that the Sweete Juices of England, whose Coddlins & Pippins no Land cd ever Equal, are run into the Grownde like an Old Ox pissing in the Mudd.[132]

This same playful quality could also come out when Thompson was being interviewed on radio or television. One such encounter took place on American radio in 1981, with President Jimmy Carter's former press secretary, Jody Powell. Thompson had reiterated END's request for American and Soviet military forces to pack up their bags and return home from both sides of Europe—a request that evidently struck Powell as the height of ingratitude. Powell angrily responded with a story about General De Gaulle's break with NATO during the 1960s: as the story went, De Gaulle had summoned the American ambassador to the Elysée and asked him to have all American forces withdrawn from France by a certain date. The U.S. ambassador had allegedly responded, "I understand, General. But there is one thing I must tell my President. Are we also to remove all the graves of American servicemen killed in the liberation of France?" Powell apparently felt that by telling this story he had skewered Thompson as an ungrateful European neutralist. "But then," Thompson later recalled,

> as is the custom on American radio, there was a commercial break to advertise deodorants, cookies, and Kleenex tissues, with little bits of pop music, and I had time to think of an answer. When he came back on the air I told him that, however generous the act of liberation had been, it did not bring with it the right of perpetual occupation. And that, as it happened, I had myself taken part in the war of liberation in Italy and that there were many graves of my own comrades left behind in Italian soil. But that I did not for that reason wish to occupy Italy today. I preferred to live in Worcester in England.[133]

Of course, while these kinds of anecdotes provide some insight into the sources of Thompson's popular appeal, it is important to stress (as Thompson himself has repeatedly done) that the END campaign could not have resulted from a single person's efforts.[134] Such figures as Mary Kaldor, Bruce Kent, Ken Coates, or Mient-Jan Faber of the Dutch Inter-Church Peace Council arguably played equally crucial roles in shaping the campaign; nor could the "END idea" have gone far without the dedicated labor of hundreds of volunteers and grass-roots activists. Yet it remains true, nonetheless, that Thompson's position in the movement was unique, and that more than any other individual he came to embody the "public image" of END. He wrote dozens of articles for European and American newspapers, fired off constant "letters to the editor," and appeared often on British television, either in interviews or in news reports. He canvased the major British cities, giving speeches and holding meetings (an average of ten public appearances per month between 1980 and 1982); and he traveled abroad on speaking tours from California to Hungary, from Iceland to Greece, visiting fourteen countries in all.[135] In 1981, he found himself speaking on the same platform with Michael Foot (the leader of the Labour party) and

Olof Palme (soon afterward elected prime minister of Sweden); in February 1984, he engaged U.S. Secretary of Defense Caspar Weinberger in a televised debate at Oxford University.

At the same time, however, Thompson was acutely aware that his own public prominence might undermine the sense of democratic initiative within END. Since he participated closely in the daily work of running the campaign—attending committees and subcommittees, debating questions of tactics and strategy, and answering correspondence from around the world—he sensed a real danger that the organization might come to depend in an unhealthy way upon his presence and leadership. By most accounts, nevertheless, Thompson succeeded in averting such an outcome. In END meetings, according to a majority of his coworkers, he consistently strove to keep a low profile and to allow other participants an equal chance in determining the movement's policy.[136] "We have to watch ourselves," Thompson wrote to Mary Kaldor in 1981,

> and be a little more formal at putting things [through the END Committee] for formal decision; . . . it is more important that [the committee] should take decisions, and get on with things, than that it should do what we always like![137]

END activists generally agreed, however, that Thompson's opinions carried a special weight in collective deliberations. Some of them felt, moreover, that on specific occasions, when he took a strong and unequivocal stand on some issue of tactics or principle, they found it difficult to ignore or contravene his views. Still, the majority of Thompson's coworkers in END believed that his commitment to democratic procedure was a genuine and effective one; and they apparently bore him none of the resentment that was to prove disturbingly common among the coworkers of Danilo Dolci.[138]

The second—and arguably more important—reason for Thompson's prominence in END lay in the originality with which he articulated the campaign's goals and ideals. Demonstrations, marches, and the fear of missiles had long existed as potential foci of protest, but Thompson offered a genuinely new way of seeing the East-West rivalry—a vision of the Cold War as a historical process whose direction the European peoples could decisively influence.

END: Analysis and Strategy

The greatest strength of Thompson's position lay in the fact that he criticized both superpowers with equal vigor.[139] Many of his conservative critics in the West have argued that this was only a cynical maneuver on Thompson's part, designed to deflect the traditional accusation that the peace movement was "soft on communism" and guilty of "appeasement."[140] Such a line of argument, however, could not be sustained without grossly distorting Thompson's writings and public statements; for he had established himself as a prominent critic of the Soviet Union ever since 1956, and his disillusionment had become even sharper after the suppression of the Prague Spring in 1968. He had also consistently backed up his words with deeds: on several occasions during the 1970s, for instance, he had circulated petitions and given public speeches to protest the persecution of civil rights prisoners in the Soviet bloc.[141] Unless one was determined a priori to portray Thompson as a Communist stooge or a covert CIA agent (both of which accusations were publicly leveled against him by NATO and Soviet apologists), then it was nearly impossible to hear his speeches or read his articles without being struck by their rigorous even-handedness. Together with Dorothy Thompson, he directly took up this issue in an internal END letter circulated in 1980:

> The point is that [some figures on the Left] are trying to squash END policies down to a wholly anti-NATO stance, and to take out any anti-Soviet sting. . . . But if we had believed that the "fault" in the present build-up and war threat was entirely with one side in the great-power confrontation, then there would be no need for END. . . . If our protest movement is to reclaim its right to defend civil liberties and the right to dissent, then it must be prepared to speak out about Eastern Europe. . . .
>
> Since END proposes breaking down the strategy and ideology protecting both blocs, this "even-handedness" demands that the thrust against both NATO and the Warsaw Pact positions be steadily maintained. Our aim is the reassertion of a European tradition of a certain kind—or perhaps even the *creation* of such a tradition, the preservation of civilised values and of democratic process.[142]

Thompson did not believe, however, that the two superpowers were "equivalent" to each other, or that their roles in the arms race were necessarily the same. "I don't mean to argue for an *identity* of process in the United States and the Soviet Union," he told an audience in 1981,

> nor for a perfect symmetry of forms. There are major divergences, not only in political forms and controls, but also as between the steady expansionism of bureaucracy and the avarice of private capital. I mean to stress, rather, the *reciprocal* and inter-active character of the process. It is in the very nature of this Cold War show that there must be two adversaries: and each move by one must be matched by the other. This is the inner dynamic of the Cold War which determines that its military and security establishments are *self-reproducing.* Their missiles summon forth our missiles which summon forth their missiles in turn. NATO's hawks feed the hawks of the Warsaw bloc.[143]

This process, however, was not confined to the domain of military technology. It spilled over into politics, defining the agendas of statesmen according to preordained scripts that had been conceived long before. It distorted the economies of the superpowers, saddling the markets of the West and the bureaucracies of the East with a profound dependency upon their ever-expanding military sectors. Finally, it intruded into the collective psychology of the two societies, wrenching all impulses toward diversity or spontaneity into the conformist channels of a single binary opposition. "This threat of the Other," he wrote, "has been internalised within both Soviet and American culture, so that the very self-identity of many American and Soviet citizens is bound up with the ideological premises of the Cold War." [144]

Technology, ideology, economies, politics, popular culture—all these domains, Thompson argued, had become enmeshed in the self-reinforcing spiral of the Cold War. In his first article for the *New Left Review* since the early 1960s, entitled "Notes on Exterminism, the Last Stage of Civilization," he chided his fellow-socialists on two serious counts. On the one hand, he wrote, some of them still tended to cling dogmatically to the idea that all the world's ills stemmed from capitalist "imperialism," while explaining away Soviet aggressions as "defensive over-reactions" and ignoring such untidy phenomena as the Sino-Soviet split or Polish *Solidarność*. [145] On the other hand, their characteristic Marxist emphasis on economic factors led them to overlook the powerful irrational forces that fueled the Cold War at the levels of ideology, politics, and psychology. Returning to the intricate historical models he had explored in *The Poverty of Theory,* Thompson challenged the thinkers of the Left to consider a new concept, which he called "exterminism." This concept would reflect causal processes operating simultaneously on many "levels" of society; it would express the crucial importance of cultural factors as well as the roles played by technological and economic change; above all, it would seek to remain consistent with the apparent irrationality of the historical events it sought to explain. "[Exterminism] is a cumulative process," Thompson warned,

> crystallization in culture accelerating crystallization in the economy, and thence to politics, and thence back again once more. Security operations impinge upon politicians; job security in weapons industries impinges upon trade unions; expansion in military research, usually in the "public sector," generates bureaucratic pressures in Britain much the same as the bureaucratic thrust of the Soviet managers. . . .
>
> The outcome will be extermination, but this will not happen accidentally (even if the final trigger is "accidental") but as the direct consequence of prior acts of policy, of the accumulation and perfection of the means of extermination, and of the structuring of whole societies so that these are directed towards that end. [146]

Was there a way out of this increasingly complex and uncontrollable process? Thompson thought the answer was yes—but only if people acted quickly, before the historical tendencies had acquired an irreversible momentum.[147] Here he returned to the concept of "revolution" that he had espoused in 1960 (which was drawn in turn from his reflections on the making of nineteenth-century class-consciousness). "Exterminism," he wrote, "does generate its own internal contradictions. . . . As anxiety and dissatisfaction mount, there can be glimpsed . . . the possibility of a truly internationalist movement against the armourers of both blocs."[148] Just as the English workers in the early nineteenth century had rebelled against being turned into machine-like instruments of an exploitative social system, so the citizens of East and West might rebel today against the mindless social process that was carrying them collectively toward a thermonuclear war that no single individual wanted.

In concrete terms, Thompson argued, the way out lay in a vigorous reassertion of European autonomy. His understanding of this term, however, was precisely the opposite of Louise Weiss's. Whereas Weiss advocated the creation of a new pole of military power between the Americans and the Russians, Thompson envisioned a progressive withdrawal of military power from Europe, a demilitarization of the highly charged space between the blocs. The only way that such a process could succeed, he believed, was if people worked together from both sides to build new civil institutions and channels of communication, gradually replacing the structures of the Cold War with structures of cooperation, negotiation, and exchange. A resurgent *civil* society might steadily push back (from both sides) the rigid institutions of a *militarized* society.

Looking back over the history of the Cold War, Thompson noted the peculiar "double-bind" that had repeatedly paralyzed all those who tried to build bridges between East and West:

> Those who worked for freedom in the East were suspected or exposed as agents of Western imperialism. Those who worked for peace in the West were suspected or exposed as pro-Soviet "fellow travelers" or dupes of the Kremlin. In this way the rival ideologies of the Cold War disarmed those, on both sides, who might have put Europe back together. Any transcontinental movement for peace *and* freedom became impossible.[149]

It was precisely such a dual strategy, therefore, that END needed to embody. On the one hand, he argued, END activists had to push hard to establish contacts and regular channels of communication with like-minded persons across the Iron Curtain. They should uncompromisingly defend Eastern-bloc dissidents and human-rights activists, and they should also reach out to the less vocal sectors of the Eastern European population, forming bonds with religious and youth groups, trade unions, scientists, or professional organizations. At the same time, of course, END would seek to mobilize a powerful movement in Western Europe to stop the escalation of the arms race, bringing great pressure to bear on both superpowers to halt deployment and begin removing their European-based missiles.

Once these twin projects were underway, Thompson believed, they would strongly reinforce each other. A relaxation of international military tensions would remove the Soviet leadership's main excuse for its occupation of Eastern Europe; and any tangible steps toward liberalization in Eastern Europe would progressively mitigate the Western fears that provided NATO with its underlying rationale. Thompson remained unconvinced, moreover, by those who argued that the only way to achieve arms reductions was through bilateral agreements between the two superpowers. Such agreements, he contended, required precisely the kinds of endless negotiations and mutual posturing that had allowed the Cold War to continue, in an insidious way, throughout the SALT talks and détente of the 1970s. In a letter to an Eastern-bloc dissident written in 1984, he explained:

> I am not disowning those sections of the Western peace movement which called for a "unilateral" halt in Western deployment; on the contrary, I am convinced that only such unilateral initiatives will ever get a reciprocal process of disarmament going. Yet there must be a credible expectation that such a reciprocal process will ensue, and that measures of disarmament on one side will not simply be swallowed gratefully to enlarge the advantage of the other.[150]

The scaling-down of the Cold War, like the military build-up, would require an interactive process in which each side would respond successively to conciliatory initiatives from the other. It went without saying that any attempt by either side to gain disproportionate advantages from such a process would immediately sabotage the entire endeavor.

The idea of such a constructive cycle, in which the incentives of trust and mutual security replaced those of fear and threats, bore a striking resemblance to the disarmament plans of Leo Szilard. Where Thompson differed from Szilard, however, was in his emphasis on the European peoples as the key agents of a potential change of course. Thompson suspected that the two superpowers, as the "prime movers" in the Cold War, might go on indefinitely in their rigid minuet; but the Europeans had a direct and urgent interest in freeing themselves from the superpowers' embrace, for it was Europe that was physically divided by the Cold War, and Europe that lived under the most direct threat of a conflagration on its territory.

This was the broad vision that Thompson offered to his fellow Europeans, vigorously propounding it in hundreds of speeches, articles, and television appearances between 1980 and 1984. The word "vision" is deliberately chosen, for Thompson did not present a detailed blueprint of Europe's political and military future but concentrated, instead, on the more numinous idea of "setting history into motion once again." If only the glaciation of the Cold War began to melt and break apart, he told his audiences, then the Europeans could work out the details of their own future as specific issues arose. Judging from his favorable reception among extremely diverse groups throughout the Western half of the continent, this logic evidently exerted a powerful appeal.

END: Politics and Action

Scholarly experts on NATO widely concur that the early 1980s constituted an unprecedented crisis in the "Atlantic Community."[151] The broad chronology of this crisis was roughly shaped by NATO's timetable for installing its new missiles—reaching its peak in the fall of 1983, and then gradually subsiding after the deployment had proceeded as planned. Why did a major upwelling of popular protest occur at this particular historical moment? The reason probably lay in the peculiar conjunction of political and military events that occurred between 1979 and 1980: the announcement of NATO's new missile deployment, coupled with the Soviet invasion of Afghanistan; the collapse of the SALT II treaty, coupled with the boycott of the Winter Olympics in Moscow; the drastic sharpening of confrontational rhetoric from political leaders on both sides, signaling the irrevocable end of détente and the onset of a new spiral in the arms race.[152]

Early in 1980, at the same time as Thompson was preparing the END Appeal and launching (with Dan Smith) the best-selling pamphlet *Protest and Survive,* the West German Green party was officially formed. CND, at this time, had roughly five thousand regular members;[153] a peace demonstration in April at the U.S. airbase near Lakenheath, England, proudly claimed four hundred participants.[154] By the fall of the same year, however, the peace movement was already making major headlines. A CND rally in London brought fifty thousand demonstrators into Hyde Park;[155] and in West Germany, the one-sided Krefeld Appeal (which criticized only NATO's weapons) triggered an ongoing struggle within the West German peace movement between a minority of Soviet apologists and the more rigorously even-handed majority of the Green party.[156] Throughout 1981, the frequency and size of the antinuclear demonstrations steadily increased, culminating in the fall with marches by 150,000 persons in London and Rome, 120,000 in Brussels, 300,000 in Bonn, and a remarkable 400,000 in Amsterdam.[157] At the same time, the tactics of the peace activists were diversifying: they persuaded hundreds of cities and counties to declare themselves nuclear-free zones, pressed their churches to take a stand on the morality of nuclear weapons, and set up permanent "peace camps" outside projected missile bases (the most famous being the women's camp at Greenham Common).[158]

Evidently impressed by all the clamor, the leaders of both superpowers sought in their separate ways to win over the peace activists. In November 1981, President Brezhnev issued a solemn pledge that the Soviet Union would never launch a nuclear attack against a country that had banned nuclear weapons from its territory (he persisted, meanwhile, with the regular weekly deployment of SS-20 missiles in Eastern Europe).[159] Two weeks later, President Reagan launched a resounding "Zero Option," offering the Soviets a deal in which both sides would bring to zero their arsenals of medium-range European-based missiles. This was, it turned out, equally as manipulative and disingenuous as Brezhnev's offer of two weeks before. According to Strobe Talbott, the chief diplomatic correspondent for *Time* magazine:

> The U.S. was asking the Soviets to give up real weapons, already deployed at great expense, in return for the U.S.'s tearing up a piece of paper. . . . Administration officials privately conceded that the zero option was not intended to produce an agreement before NATO deployment began in late 1983. Rather, it was a gimmick—part of what Assistant Secretary of State Richard Burt . . . called "alliance management"—to make sure the nervous West Europeans kept to the self-imposed deadline. . . . Few strategic experts in the West expected—or, more important, wanted—NATO to be without any new missiles at all.[160]

Unswayed (for the most part) by these offers from the superpowers, the peace activists redoubled their efforts. While the huge demonstrations continued (reaching the figure of half a million marchers in New York City in June 1982), they held their first pan-European convention in Brussels early in July, with one thousand delegates attending.[161] These END conventions became annual events, held in succeeding years in West Berlin, Perugia, Amsterdam, Paris, and Coventry. By the fall of 1982, a Gallup poll in England showed 58 percent of the population opposed to the basing of American missiles.[162] Similar polls throughout Western Europe showed comparably high rates of opposition: West Germany, between 25 and 67 percent (depending on sources); Italy, between 40 and 54 percent; the Netherlands, between 51 and 68 percent; and even in France (where no missile deployment was scheduled) a surprisingly high 44 percent.[163] In England, meanwhile, the size of CND had swelled by 1,000 percent in just two years, with more than 50,000 members and 250,000 supporters in affiliated organizations.

Yet these very successes now called forth a particularly vigorous response from NATO's political leaders. Prime Minister Margaret Thatcher, buoyed by her victory over Argentina in the Falklands War (April–June 1982), announced early in 1983 that she would henceforth be turning her attention to the disarmers.[164] She ordered her new defense minister, Michael Heseltine, to devote himself full-time to a countercampaign against CND and END, and to use the considerable resources of the government's information services in bringing the case for nuclear weapons to the British public.[165] Heseltine was powerfully assisted by private right-wing organizations, such as the Coalition for Peace through Security, funded both from British sources and by more than $1 million in gifts from the conservative Heritage Foundation in the United States.[166] In March, President Reagan also went on the offensive, countering the American nuclear-freeze movement and the Catholic Bishops' recent condemnation of nuclear weapons with a characteristically ingenious *coup de théâtre:* the Strategic Defense Initiative (or "Star Wars"), a complex technological system that would allegedly render the United States invulnerable to nuclear attack.[167] This gigantic project, vigorously criticized by a majority of U.S. scientists, was eventually trimmed down and quietly prepared for integration into American offensive forces (a partial "shield" to make the "sword" more effective). Nevertheless, it also had its intended effect in 1983: stealing the thunder of the grassroots antinuclear movements by casting the president in the image of an ardent peacemaker.

The battle between the politicians and the peace activists reached its tumultuous climax in the fall of 1983. On October 22 and 23, some three to four million marchers demonstrated in the capitals of Western Europe—half a million in Rome, more than a million throughout West Germany, and 400,000 (roughly 4% of the total Dutch population) in Amsterdam.[168] In London's Hyde Park, E. P. Thompson and several other speakers addressed a crowd of 250,000 from a crane platform high in the air; and the following month, some thirty thousand women linked hands to form a circle around the cruise missile base at Greenham Common. Yet the deployment of the missiles proceeded on schedule, the first weapons becoming "operational" in Britain and West Germany on January 1, 1984. Despite the unprecedented popular turnout at the antinuclear rallies of the preceding fall, NATO's political leaders had been able to rely on the relative quiescence of their countries' overall populations—evidently wagering that the perceived "defeat" of the peace movement would lead to widespread demoralization and a subsequent decline in protests.

In this supposition they were partly right and partly wrong. The peace demonstrations swiftly faded in 1984 and never again reached the levels of earlier years; yet the peace movements themselves continued to organize, shifting now toward the more orthodox political strategy of lobbying among elected officials and taking their case directly to the voting citizenry. The relative success of this strategy (at least in England) was demonstrated by the continued growth of CND's membership, which doubled again by 1985.[169]

What had been the specific role of END within the broader "Euromissile" controversy of the early 1980s? Compared with the widespread impact of the "END vision," the actual size of END as an institution always remained relatively small. Early in 1980, the END Committee had decided not to compete with CND as a membership institution, but rather to focus on establishing a network of ties with other groups and organizations throughout Europe, East and West.[170] The structure of END remained fluid and loosely defined. It came to consist of a Coordinating Committee, composed of some fifteen to twenty-five persons; the central office staff in London (a paid full-time secretary, along with various volunteers); a number of stable committees specializing on such issues as contacts with Eastern-bloc countries, relations with the Labour party, overseeing END publications, or handling fund-raising and finances; and regional affiliated committees, such as West Yorkshire END. All these committees were staffed entirely by volunteers; they met at intervals of once or twice a month and reached decisions as far as possible by means of debate and consensual agreement. Where disagreements proved intractable, those in the minority were expected to go along with the ideas of the majority, but this usually did not pose much of a problem, since the END volunteers formed a fairly close-knit body of like-minded persons. Unlike the more broadly based membership of CND—which included middle-class leftists, religious groups, housewives, and a great many working-class individuals—the typical participants in END were highly educated and widely traveled intellectuals. Although they were uncomfortable with the "elite" image they tended to have among the broader peace movement, the fact remained that a disproportionately large number of them were graduates of Oxford or Cambridge.[171]

Like any volunteer organization, END was chronically in financial difficulty. Its funding came from END publications, from public events such as concerts and speeches, and from donations by individuals (roughly two thirds of them British, one third American).[172] A typical annual budget for END was between $100,000 and $150,000, which included rent for an office, salaries for staffers, publication costs (nearly half the total), and travel and fund-raising expenses.[173] The highest priority went to the production of the *END Journal,* a bimonthly publication edited by Mary Kaldor and reaching a circulation of three thousand readers.[174] Simultaneously an organ of analysis, activism, and self-critique for the European peace movements, the *END Journal* carried articles on wide-ranging military and political issues, offering particularly detailed coverage of events in the Eastern bloc.

The political work of END fell into three broad areas: relations within Britain, relations with other West European countries, and relations with the Soviet bloc. Perhaps the greatest challenge in all three of these areas lay in winning acceptance for the rigorously even-handed "END perspective"; and here the campaign ultimately proved most influential. In Britain, CND had long possessed an image—with some justification—of being harsher in judging the Americans than the Russians; but the election of Bruce Kent (one of END's cofounders) as general secretary of CND early in 1980 ensured a gradual transition toward a firmly nonaligned stance between East and West.[175] The British

Labour party, on the other hand, had been staunchly pro-NATO and pronuclear ever since Hugh Gaitskell's victory over the unilateralists in 1961. After Margaret Thatcher's election in 1979, however, many Labour politicians began to question the usefulness of a defense policy that amounted to a watered-down version of the Tory platform; and in the 1983 election campaign, the Labour leader Michael Foot faced a deep split within his party over nuclear weapons and relations with NATO. As one journalist commented shortly before the election: "For three days Mr. Michael Foot tried to clarify Labour's nuclear policy, but even the richness of the English language could not disguise the fact [that] a fundamental rift remained." [176] Mrs. Thatcher's landslide victory in June 1983 thus was attributed to two main causes: the "Falklands factor," which had boosted her approval ratings from 30 to 60 percent in a few short months; and the unreconciled differences within Labour. [177]

In the wake of this crushing defeat, the Labour party leaders decided to adopt a comprehensive defense policy based on the unequivocal renunciation of all nuclear weapons. At the national party conference in 1984 they announced their newly clarified ideas:

> We have laid down as our long-term objective the establishment of a new security system in Europe and the mutual and concurrent phasing out of NATO and the Warsaw Pact. . . . In the meantime, Labour believes in a realistic non-nuclear defence policy for Britain in NATO. . . . The significance of such reductions in nuclear arsenals and of a defensive deterrence policy depends on whether they can initiate a *political* process of reducing tensions between the blocs and allow for a political loosening within the blocs so as to make possible further steps towards disarmament and security. [178]

These lines, which might well have appeared in an END pamphlet, showed how far the influence of the "END perspective" had reached (Mary Kaldor herself had served as an advisor to the Labour party's National Executive Committee). By "defensive non-nuclear deterrence," the Labour party's leaders explained, they meant a defense policy that would no longer seek the capability for projecting military power deep into enemy territory. Instead, the British military, under a Labour government, would seek only to repel attacks against NATO territory, by relying on the latest electronic technologies, which had rendered conventional munitions particularly accurate and lethal. Such "smart" weapons, they argued, had themselves become sufficiently destructive to deter a potential aggressor, without having to rely on the more questionable "doomsday threat" of nuclear weapons. Finally, the Labour party expressed its hope that Britain's unilateral adoption of this "non-threatening defense posture" would not remain an isolated development, but might lead to a broader change along similar lines, both within the NATO alliance as a whole as well as within the Warsaw Pact. It was intended as a "first step" toward the denuclearization of Europe, East and West.[179]

In the long run, however, this perspective proved highly vulnerable as a political platform, for it was open to the claim by Mrs. Thatcher (publicly reinforced by American officials) that NATO could not survive without a united nuclear strategy. In the general election of 1987, therefore, defense policy became one of the pivotal issues. The British citizenry, faced with a choice that was presented in the extreme terms of "continuity" versus "risking the destruction of NATO," once again reelected Mrs. Thatcher by a wide margin.[180] END's ideas had advanced remarkably far, and then suffered an explicit political defeat.

Within the broader West-European framework, the most prominent allies of END were the West German Green party, the Italian Eurocommunists, the small French group CODENE, and the Dutch IKV (Inter-Church Peace Council).[181] CODENE, founded by the World War II Resistance leader Claude Bourdet, was perhaps the closest to END in ideological orientation—a non-Communist leftism with roots going back to the early postwar years. The Greens and the Eurocommunists were left-wing political parties, openly critical of both superpowers, but subject to greater pressures for caution and "moderation" due to their sensitive positions in German and Italian politics. The Dutch IKV, finally, had existed since 1966 as an umbrella organization for Christian pacifist groups in the Netherlands; in the late 1970s, under the leadership of Mient-Jan Faber, it had rapidly grown both in stature and in membership and had promoted a clearly nonaligned stance vis-à-vis the two blocs. One of the common beliefs uniting these rather disparate organizations was that demonstrations against Russian and American missiles should go hand in hand with the promotion of credible political alternatives for an autonomous and united Europe. Delegates from these organizations accordingly met in Rome late in 1981 to plan a pan-European convention for the following summer—a sort of grass-roots parliament for opponents of the Cold War. The first END convention duly took place in Brussels in July 1982.

These END conventions (held each summer during the following years, with one thousand to three thousand persons attending) represented the first time since World War II that large numbers of Europeans had met regularly together, independently from national or party organizations, to discuss the reunification of their continent. They were tumultuous affairs, touching on the most controversial political themes of the day—from global North-South relations to the "German Question," from the prospects of nonviolent civilian-based defense to the rechanneling of military industries along peaceful lines. Without a doubt, however, the thorniest problem of all (and the one that refused to go away, year after year) was the "East-West" division, the delicate task of defining a common stance vis-à-vis the other half of Europe.[182]

This problem arose in a very practical sense when it came to sending out invitations to "peace movements" from the Eastern bloc. Whom should one invite? Should END favor the official (Soviet-sponsored) peace committees of the Warsaw Pact governments, or the illegally organized and sorely persecuted peace activists who courageously pursued a nonaligned policy between East and West? END organizers adopted various expedients at successive conventions—from inviting only the unofficial groups, to inviting both the official and unofficial groups simultaneously; but the results were generally disappointing. At the first two conventions, only a few private individuals from Hungary and Rumania were able to attend;[183] and in December 1982 the chairman of the official Soviet Peace Committee, Yuri Zhukov, virulently denounced END in an open letter to the West European peace movements. The "evenhanded" stance of END, he charged, unjustly placed equal blame on both superpowers; it was "aimed at the disorientation, demobilization, and undermining of the antiwar movement and [was] called upon to conceal and justify an aggressive militarist policy of the USA and NATO."[184] This disheartening response from the Stalinist "Old Guard" (of which Zhukov was a classic exemplar) effectively blocked all efforts to render the END conventions a truly pan-European forum. Bitter clashes between official Soviet delegates and Western peace activists punctuated the third convention at Perugia in 1984,[185] and the Soviet representatives declared themselves particularly enraged by the following lines from a recent book by E. P. Thompson:

> I [am] a little vexed by the Simple Solomons who repeatedly assure us that, because the Soviet people suffered grievously forty years ago, their rulers could not possibly, in any circumstances, take an unpeaceful action today. . . . Those weeping Soviet grandmothers who still deck with flowers the graves of the last war have dry eyes for Afghanistan, as they had, in 1968, for Czechoslovakia.[186]

It was not until the sixth convention (Coventry, 1987) that the effects of *glasnost,* and the replacement of Zhukov by a more open-minded group of Soviet delegates, began to show possibilities for constructive exchanges at the official level.[187] Thus, the END conventions had proven disappointing as a framework for East-West communication; but they had provided a major institutional forum where Western Europeans could seriously raise issues that had been considered utterly marginal or "taboo" only a few years before. German reunification, disengagement from longstanding military alliances, alternative forms of military defense—all these themes now formed part of an ongoing dialogue among ordinary citizens from a dozen West-European nations.

Despite the blockages at the END conventions, however, Western peace activists increasingly succeeded in establishing contacts of a more personal and informal nature with independent groups in the East—and Thompson eventually came to regard this area of END's activities as his own primary focus. Before the 1980s, the principal channels of East-West communication had run either through the organs of the state, or through such international scholarly and scientific fora as the Pugwash conferences. In the late 1950s, Polish Foreign Minister Adam Rapacki had proposed various forms of nuclear-free zones for Central Europe; but Western leaders had rebuffed him, insisting that NATO's nuclear weapons provided the essential counterweight to Soviet forces in Eastern Europe. In the early 1970s, West German Chancellor Willy Brandt had launched a vigorous policy known as *Ostpolitik* (Eastern Politics), reassuring the Soviets that West Germany accepted the de facto division of the German-speaking peoples and securing a significant relaxation of tensions with the East German regime. This had helped pave the way for the signing of a major treaty at Helsinki in 1975, in which Western nations affirmed their acceptance of Europe's existing political divisions, in return for promises by Eastern-bloc nations to allow greater freedom of expression and travel for their own citizens. By the early 1980s, however, this "Helsinki process" had bogged down under growing recrimination from both sides.[188]

It was under these conditions that Thompson and other END activists began to grope about behind the Iron Curtain, seeking hands to shake on the "Other Side." The result was a great deal of frustration and misunderstanding, gradually giving way to a remarkable flow of convergent hopes and ideas. Perhaps the single greatest failure in communication—the primary "missed opportunity"—lay in the case of Polish *Solidarność*. This trade-union movement had been founded in August 1980, and had attained a membership of ten million persons at the time of its suppression under martial law in December 1981. One of the tacit conditions for its precarious existence was that it concentrated exclusively on Polish domestic problems, never openly questioning the international role of the Soviet Union. In private, however, many members of *Solidarność* regarded the Soviet Union as a historical enemy whose army was now occupying Poland by force; they regarded NATO, conversely, as a crucial bulwark against Russian hegemony and as a possible source of future emancipation.[189]

END activists (who enthusiastically supported *Solidarność*) accordingly found themselves in a very awkward position. When they contacted members of the Polish trade union, they discovered that the Poles generally distrusted the Western peace movements, perceiving them as mere tools of Soviet foreign policy—for this was the impression conveyed both by the official Polish media and by the U.S.-sponsored broadcasts of Radio Free Europe.[190] The "END perspective," which stressed European disengagement from both superpowers, struck many Poles as hopelessly naive, for they did not see how they could free themselves from Soviet domination without some measure of American help.

END activists were thus forced into a frustrating policy of muffled support for *Solidarność,* coupled with relative inactivity. They were acutely aware that an open endorsement by END might prove more dangerous than helpful to the Polish trade unionists; and they could not establish active links with them because of their vastly differing perceptions of the Cold War. The result was that these two mass movements against the status quo, East and West, ended up conducting their campaigns in nearly complete isolation from each other.[191]

One historian of *Solidarność,* Timothy Garton Ash, later criticized END for this relative inaction, setting forth his views in an "Open Letter to E. P. Thompson" published in the *Spectator* seven months after the declaration of martial law in Poland. Ash suggested that the only hope for the Poles would have lain in a "deal" between the blocs: Western banks would provide massive funding for Polish agriculture and industry, in exchange for the continued existence of *Solidarność* under stipulated conditions of free movement and self-organization.[192] Thompson in turn replied that the Soviet government would have regarded Ash's plan as a dangerous interference in East-bloc affairs, and hence would have rejected it. The only "deal" that might have saved *Solidarność,* Thompson countered, would have been some form of reduction of Western missiles, striking directly to the heart of the Cold War confrontation that had helped to render the life of *Solidarność* so precarious.[193]

In other parts of Eastern Europe, however, the "END perspective" proved far more appealing than it had in Poland. In Czechoslovakia, END activists found a crucial interlocutor in the dissident group known as "Charter 77" (co-founded by the future Czech president, Václav Havel); as early as the summer of 1980, Thompson had already traveled to Prague to meet with dissidents there, and had initiated an ongoing correspondence that was to lead toward steadily converging proposals and goals.[194] In East Germany, those most receptive to the ideas of END were members of the Protestant Church, with its long tradition of resistance to militarism;[195] while in Hungary, a group of approximately fifty students formed an autonomous organization called the "Peace Group for Dialogue," which worked closely with END activists in promoting a nonaligned perspective within the official Hungarian peace organizations.[196] Even in the Soviet Union, a still smaller group of independent-minded intellectuals created the "Group for the Establishment of Trust Between the USA and the USSR," seeking to provide an alternative voice to the heavy Stalinist tones of Yuri Zhukov and the official Soviet peace committee.[197] The histories and characters of these small movements were as varied as the national cultures in which they arose, but they shared certain common characteristics. All of them were persecuted (sometimes brutally) by the authorities of the state, and required a great deal of fortitude and self-sacrifice merely to exist and survive. All of them advocated the right for European citizens to exchange their ideas across national boundaries, without the tutelage of their governments. And all of them, finally, insisted on seeing the East-West rivalry in a more balanced and even-handed way, rejecting the one-sided judgments of NATO and Soviet apologists.

There could be no question of comparing these courageous individuals (who probably numbered no more than a few thousand in the entire Eastern bloc) with the vast popular movements of Western Europe. These small groups clearly understood that any opening toward reform would ultimately require at least the tolerance, if not the tacit support, of their own state hierarchies and of far-off elites in Moscow. What, then, did they hope to achieve, and why were they drawn toward the perspective of END?

Through forty years of experience—through the failed revolts of 1953, 1956, 1968, and 1980–81—they had gradually become convinced that NATO's missiles and armies could not protect them from Soviet power, but only provided an excuse for never-ending Soviet hegemony.[198] In 1982, therefore, after the suppression of *Solidarność* had demonstrated once again the real helplessness of the West as a source of liberation, these groups began to respond to the END Appeal, taking quite seriously its idea of European autonomy as a symmetrical goal for East and West. The END strategy of linking human rights with disarmament, backed up by millions of marchers in the West, began to seem more realistic than the vision of NATO somehow "rolling back" Soviet power through naked military pressure.

On January 25, 1982, two prominent East-German intellectuals, Robert Havemann and Rainer Eppelmann, launched the "Berlin Appeal," proclaiming that

> the whole of Europe must become a nuclear-weapons-free zone. . . . The victors of World War II must finally conclude peace treaties with both German states, as decided in the Potsdam Agreement of 1945. Thereafter, the former Allies should withdraw their occupation troops from Germany and agree on guarantees of non-intervention in the internal affairs of the two German states.[199]

This appeal was strongly approved in a letter from Czech Charter 77 in April 1982; and the Czech group initiated an "open correspondence" with E. P. Thompson and with the annual END conventions, culminating in the "Prague Appeal" of 1985:

> [We] propose that the NATO and the Warsaw Pact enter forthwith into negotiations on the dissolution of their military organizations, on the removal of all nuclear weapons either sited in or aimed at Europe, and on the withdrawal of US and Soviet troops from the territories of their European allies. . . . [We wish] to overcome the superpower bloc structure by way of an alliance of free and independent nations within a democratic and self-governing all-

> European community. . . . Perhaps this ideal sounds like a dream.
> However, we are convinced that it expresses the desire of a major-
> ity of Europeans.[200]

In Hungary, meanwhile, the Peace Group for Dialogue put forward its own
ideas for ending the Cold War, arguing that "the weakening of the two blocs
would make a decrease in the superpower domination of Europe possible."[201]
In 1984, the Hungarian writer George Konrad published his path-breaking
book *Antipolitics,* a comprehensive and soberly argued proposal for a political
solution to the division of Europe.[202]

The circulation of these ideas among relatively limited groups of citizens in
Eastern Europe did not in itself bring the Cold War much closer to an end.
Nevertheless, a significant shift had taken place. Only a few years earlier, *Solidarność* had remained caught between two rigid alternatives: either NATO
or the Soviet bloc. Now a third strategy—an "all-European" strategy—was
redefining the language and logic of East-bloc dissidence; and it would henceforth prove far more difficult for Party *apparatchiks* and opponents of reform
to proclaim the simple equation, "Dissidence = NATO subversion." In the end,
of course, the success of this strategy depended heavily on such factors as
President Gorbachev's reform movement and its reception among Warsaw Pact
elites. Yet Eastern-bloc reformers realized that their position would be greatly
strengthened if they could present their appeals for human rights, not in the
guise of anti-Sovietism but rather in the name of European autonomy, East
and West.

After 1985, as the two superpowers commenced the remarkable series of
interactive concessions and compromises that ended the Cold War, the spot-
light shifted back to the highest peaks of state power, where intensive negotiations led to the removal (after 1988) of those very SS-20, Pershing II, and
cruise missiles that the European grass-roots activists had so vehemently opposed several years before.[203] With the rapid progress of Gorbachev's reforms,
moreover, the initiative for further change passed to the citizens of the Eastern-
bloc countries. For Thompson, this meant an opportunity to resume some sem-
blance of a normal life and to catch his breath, since the frenzied pace of the
preceding years' peace demonstrations had also taken a serious toll on his
health. Slowly, he returned to the historical research that he had all but abandoned since 1979, turning his attention once again toward questions of class
and cultural identity in eighteenth-century Britain. He took up a long-term
research project on the thought of William Blake, began writing an account of
his father's friendship with the Indian poet Tagore, and devoted himself with
renewed vigor to the completion of his novel, *The Sykaos Papers.*

Thompson continued to work in END, of course; but the END office was
far less busy in the second half of the 1980s than it had been a few years before,

and he relied on younger members like Mary Kaldor to assume an increasingly prominent role. In 1990, finally, END's activists joined several dozen other European grass-roots groups in creating a broader East-West alliance, the Helsinki Citizens' Assembly. This international coordinating body, which had its central office in Prague, gave the peace activists and former East European dissidents a forum for working together toward their goals of promoting democracy "from below" and peacefully reintegrating East and West.[204]

Compared with the perspectives of Weiss and Szilard, Thompson's vision of an autonomous Europe arguably contained two important flaws. At the level of END's long-term strategy, he failed to answer crucial questions about safeguarding the peace in a Europe without superpowers. At a still deeper level, moreover, his search for a practical alternative to Machiavellian elitism led him to adopt an overly idealized image of the Europeans themselves.

The first of these weaknesses was perhaps most clearly spelled out in 1984 by a fellow writer on the Left—Diana Johnstone, a Paris-based correspondent for the magazine *In These Times*. Johnstone was broadly sympathetic to the goals of END, but in an article written shortly after the Perugia Convention of 1984 she raised some serious questions.[205] What if END and the Western peace movements succeeded in distancing Europe from the two superpowers, only to pave the way for the creation of a new Western European superpower? Was END serving as the unwitting ally of the West European Right? The logic behind Johnstone's questions was fairly straightforward. Ever since the Second World War, the alliance with America and the perception of a threat from the East had particularly favored the European political parties of the "moderate" center. Leftist ideas had been consistently held at bay through their association (real or perceived) with the Russians; while right-wing ideas, emphasizing nationalism and a neocolonial world role for the European powers, had been absorbed and "tamed" by the U.S.-dominated security system of NATO.

By seeking to pry Europe loose from the superpowers, and thereby upsetting this delicate Atlanticist balancing act, was Thompson functioning in effect as the best ally of Louise Weiss? Which way would a newly autonomous Europe go—toward Thompson's vision of demilitarization and open boundaries, or toward Weiss's vision of a Western "Eurobloc"? Thompson, Kaldor, and many other END activists were sharply aware of these questions, and they were not sanguine in answering them.[206] They only had to recall the vast popularity of the recent Falklands War to realize how easily the old atavisms of imperial glory and military prowess might gorge the consciousness of their fellow citizens.[207] Thompson had been a vocal member of the relatively small minority in Britain who strenuously opposed the Falklands War; the conflict had taught him, he later wrote, "of the disastrous inadequacy of the United Nations, the immense fragility of any attempt to establish an international rule of law; [it had demonstrated] how slender are the cultural and political defences against the surge of nationalism, when both politicians and the popular media license this atavism."[208]

For Thompson and others in END, however, these dangers constituted an unavoidable aspect of Europe's political future. "If you talk about European autonomy," Thompson told a meeting of the END Committee in 1984,

> the question isn't whether it's a nice thing or not—it is *actually happening*. . . . We have to see what shape this autonomy takes. It could easily be a beefed-up West Eurobloc, perhaps with its own nuclear weapons. It could be a very fearsome resurgence of Western militarism. And therefore the peace movement has from now on to assert its alternative shape to this. It cannot encourage this [alternative] shape unless it challenges the bloc division of Europe.[209]

Thompson was understandably reluctant to offer detailed predictions or "blueprints" of this "alternative shape," but he did, on various occasions, offer glimpses of the future that he envisioned. Here, his instincts as a historian obviously influenced him, for he looked back, somewhat paradoxically, to the prodigious upheaval of World War II for inspiration.[210]

He believed that a false choice had been imposed on the European peoples at the end of the Second World War—a Manichaean choice between Soviet-style Stalinism and full-fledged American-style capitalism. If the Europeans had been able to choose on their own, without the polarizing influence of the superpowers, he argued, then they might well have invented a "third way" between these two extremes, combining and resynthesizing the traditions of democracy and socialism.[211] The evidence for this historical interpretation, Thompson believed, lay in the tremendous strength of the European Left in 1945, a Left that embraced not just the Stalinist-oriented Communist parties but also the much broader spectrum of populist and parliamentary Socialist parties that sprang up from Italy to Czechoslovakia, from Greece to Scandinavia. Had it not been for the Cold War, he felt, these parties (along with the Christian and Liberal parties) might have worked out a democratic modus vivendi in authentic popular fronts and parliamentary arrangements throughout Europe, East and West.

Nevertheless, Thompson wrote in 1984 that "the lost causes of forty years ago have a way of returning as the necessary causes of today. This is the case with the 'third way'—the way for which the European peace movements are now searching."[212] What was necessary was "some 'historic compromise' between the hostile polities and ideologies of the adversary blocs."[213] Thompson did not see it as his place to specify or predict precisely what forms such a compromise might take within the distinct political cultures of the European nations. He was willing to wager, nonetheless, that "socialist democracy, in some sense, might be the vocabulary of change in both worlds."

> But it would have to be more sharply anti-statist and libertarian than anything in the dominant Communist or Social Democratic traditions. . . . It is likely also that . . . it will be informed by an alert ecological consciousness since the congruent struggles, East and West, will be founded upon the human ecological imperative.[214]

Thompson's right-wing critics were partly accurate, therefore, when they perceived his work in END as part of a struggle for a broader political cause. Yet they misunderstood his motives when they claimed that he was in effect trying to create "a united socialist Europe."[215] Thompson's ideals were more complex than this, for he remained acutely conscious of the immense diversity within the European continent; he envisioned an approaching phase of history in which the nation-state would begin to decline in importance, its functions gradually eroded "from below," at the local level, and "from above," at the supranational level:

> Some nation-states might begin to fragment somewhat; you might find the Baltic republics re-achieving autonomy, and a semi-autonomous situation in the Ukraine. You might find greater autonomy within the British Islands, in Scotland and Wales or similarly in other places. . . . One would hope to see what used to be called workers' control, smaller units of control; public industry being cooperative, or corporations municipally-owned. And that would underpin, perhaps, a growth in local and regional consciousness. But for larger economic, cultural and legal arrangements you would have bridging institutions—[institutions] more effective than the EEC but on that kind of all-European basis.[216]

What would keep the peace in this "open" Europe—a region in which the military dominance of the superpowers and the paralyzing fear of nuclear weapons had been removed? Thompson was well aware of the manifold national, religious, and ethnic conflicts that might arise within a newly autonomous continent; but he felt optimistic that the Europeans would be able to resolve these problems through peaceful means. "The small nations in Europe," he argued in 1986,

> have had a surfeit of war in the last century, and have also taken a big fright from the whole episode of the Cold War.
>   Short of the regeneration of some really bestial ideology like Nazism or Fascism . . . —which would come out of some particu-

lar trauma of failed European influence in the world and declining economic power—short of that, I don't see war as being on the immediate agenda.

But all things are possible, and in that sense one would have to develop international and perhaps all-European institutions. [There would be a need to] rebuild something better than the United Nations, so that the manifest emergence of an aggressor nation (which, with modern technology, could be quite a small nation) would be isolated at an early stage.[217]

Thompson never specified, in his speeches and writings, what concrete form he thought such institutions of "collective security" should take. Unlike Louise Weiss, who automatically assumed that force would continue to provide the ultimate arbiter of political relationships, and that most neighbors were by nature conniving and covetous, Thompson consistently downplayed the military aspects of a future society, stressing instead the need to develop "a culture solving its problems short of war."[218]

This arguably constituted a significant weakness in his thinking, for his failure to address the tangible problems of security and "policing" left his long-term vision rather sketchy and incomplete. What if a serious conflict emerged between two or more of Europe's peoples, such as Rumania and Hungary, or Poland and Germany—any of the countless pairs that had confronted each other with hostility and violence during Europe's long and bloody past? Who would arbitrate between them? Who would enforce the peace? These kinds of questions almost never arose in Thompson's writings; he appeared to pin his hopes (like Szilard and Aron) on a rather precarious notion that the memory of past violence, and the fear of a nuclear holocaust, would bring forth an unprecedented rationality and self-control among the peoples of Europe.[219] "It is quite possible that Europe will blow up before we succeed," he wrote in 1984 to a member of the Czech human-rights group, Charter 77:

> At every stage one or the other bloc will try to turn events to its own advantage. . . . To achieve our common objective will require an unprecedented maturity in those popular movements, West and East, which seek to pace and monitor the transition, and to limit episodes of "destabilization."[220]

It was precisely here that the second key weakness in Thompson's position became clear: his tendency to expect "unprecedented maturity" from the peoples of Europe, when in fact contemporary political developments on the continent gave no salient evidence that any far-reaching "maturation" had taken place.

This was, in effect, the central drawback of Thompson's antielitist and anti-Machiavellian stance. All too often, in both his historical and his political writings, Thompson tended to project an idealized image of the "common people," presenting most rulers and lawgivers as eternally arrogant, corrupt, or exploitative. In his fervent rejection of manipulative and authoritarian politics, he consistently implied that bigotry, aggression, and acquisitiveness were primarily the characteristics of the powerful; and that the "commoners"—if only they were given a chance—would create a world in which people were generally more peace-loving and decent to one another. Thus, for instance, he envisioned END as "a truly internationalist movement against the armourers of both blocs."[221] Yet it became difficult, if he placed too great a portion of the blame upon the "armourers," to grapple with the very real faults and flaws among the "common people"—to explain such phenomena as the bellicose enthusiasm of the British population during the Falklands conflict, or the tenacious adherence by many American and Soviet citizens to the self-righteous and militaristic forms of national identity so central to the Cold War. If Thompson imputed these warlike currents in popular culture exclusively to the propaganda of politicians and the mass media, then he was accepting in effect that the common people could be manipulated at will by their rulers. If, on the other hand, he stressed the historical capacity for popular culture to shape its own destiny, then he had to include within that culture many of the aggressive elements that had undoubtedly manifested themselves as active forces throughout history.

Did this underlying contradiction negate the value of Thompson's political activism? For someone like Louise Weiss, the answer would probably be a resounding "yes!" She would undoubtedly have argued that Thompson's idealism did more harm than good, because it demanded radical changes that could not possibly square with the political habits and capabilities of real Europeans. Someone like Szilard, on the other hand, might have pointed out that a more positive interpretation of Thompson's career was also possible. Szilard himself distrusted such unruly popular movements as CND, but his own willingness to embark on a campaign among American college students suggests that he appreciated the one great virtue of grass-roots activism: it built up potentially significant pressure on the politicians.

Seen from this perspective, Thompson's actions reveal a keen practical intent of their own. The essence of his strategy became very clear in a face-to-face discussion with the Swedish social-democratic leader Olof Palme, held before a large END gathering in London in 1981. Palme was widely known for the idealism and moral fervor that he brought into politics, but he warned the assembled activists that disarmament could only come about through an alliance between two very different kinds of political forces.

> PALME: If you want the bombs [to go] away someone has to negotiate them away. These two things are both indispensable: without the popular movement pressuring, hounding the politi-

cians, you won't get anywhere; but without politicians wanting in the end to tackle the matter, and sit down with their adversaries and try to get the negotiating done, you won't get anywhere either. . . . [Unless you respect this] dual role—the clearcut moral stand of the popular movement, and the necessity for [politicians] who do some of the practical work, . . . you won't achieve anything in this world. . . .

THOMPSON: What I think I've been saying, and what END has been saying, is that you start negotiations by action. . . . Let . . . [the Russians know] that a substantial section of the Western peace movement is asking . . . them to start reducing their SS-20s now, in advance of negotiations. We will pledge ourselves to negotiate by action in return.[222]

On one side lay the grass-roots movement—effervescent, ephemeral, strong in its moral convictions; on the other side, the political parties, built for stability and continuity upon a foundation of endless compromises. Thompson clearly saw his own role as that of "hounding the politicians," setting arduous long-range goals for his contemporaries, like moral beacons toward which they could turn for orientation. He had apparently wagered, like Leo Szilard, that the existing boundaries of the possible would not budge unless determined people like himself exerted steady pressure against the outer edges.

Despite the excessively idealistic elements in his vision, however, Thompson's anti-Machiavellian moralism proved highly efficacious in influencing contemporary politics. In 1989, the diplomatic correspondent for *Time* magazine, Strobe Talbott, offered an assessment of the superpowers' relations during the preceding decade. "Only under pressure from across the Atlantic," he concluded, "did the Reagan Administration enter talks with the Soviets on intermediate-range missiles."[223] President Reagan himself later confirmed, in his memoirs, that the Euromissile controversy of the early 1980s had played a major role in shaping his proposals to the Soviets.[224] Although this "pressure from across the Atlantic" certainly came from a far wider array of political forces than END, it would be hard to deny the impact of the huge antinuclear rallies, with their banners proclaiming "No to the Blocs!" This was a form of political pressure that Thompson helped to call forth and organize; and it was precisely his ardent moral stance that rendered him so compelling a figure for his audiences.

Historians will no doubt debate for decades over the causes of the "Revolutions of 1989." One line of argument will probably stress the forty years of NATO's "resoluteness" as the crucial factor. From this perspective, the peace movements of the early 1980s will appear as serious threats to the eventual Western "victory"; and activists like Thompson will be portrayed as naive (at best) and dangerous opponents of the massive Reaganite rearmament program that ultimately "forced" the Soviets to their knees.

It will remain impossible, of course, either to refute or to confirm this line of argument until *glasnost* (or some future variant) pries open the doors of Soviet archives; yet even with the limited information currently available, this interpretation of the Cold War's ending seems simplistic. A more plausible interpretation will have to take into account the pent-up pressures for reform that had been building up within the Soviet Union during the Brezhnev years, and that might well have forced significant changes on the Soviet system regardless of Western actions. Finally, of course, future historians will have to evaluate the unique role of Mikhail Gorbachev as the helmsman who, through a mixture of deliberate policies and startling improvisations, steered the Soviet bloc into a new era.

This kind of historical assessment will obviously have to wait until more information becomes available; yet one observation may already be made. Thompson and his fellow activists in END had begun to articulate the shape and spirit of the post–Cold War world exactly a decade before it came into being. "To our surprise," he wrote in 1990,

> our own words started to come back to us after 1985—from Moscow. It was Gorbachev who took our lines, who spoke of ridding Europe of nuclear weapons "from the Atlantic to the Urals," who proposed a practical agenda for the dissolution of both blocs, who advocated the withdrawal of Soviet and U.S. troops behind their own borders by the year 2000.[225]

The fact that these kinds of ideas had entered into circulation among millions of Western Europeans in the early 1980s may or may not have influenced Soviet elites as they put together their own "New Thinking." Clearly, however, the vast Euromissile controversy of 1980–83 had forced many politicians and citizens—in the West, if not in the East—to reconsider the idea of European autonomy in a new light.

Once associated primarily with De Gaulle's dreams of French grandeur, the notion of an independent Europe, like a chameleon, took on many new colors in the wake of the clamorous demonstrations against American and Soviet missiles. For the West European Left, "autonomy" offered new defense policies, like those of the British Labour party, sharply diverging from the East-West polarity that the conservatives had so long supported. For right-wingers like Louise Weiss, an independent Europe might once again discover its suppressed will-to-power, shaking off at last the humiliating "vassalage" of the Cold War years. Many American politicians, moreover, began in the 1980s to consider bringing home the troops stationed at great expense in Western Europe; if so many Europeans were taking a dim view of NATO, they reasoned, perhaps the time had come to let them take up (and pay for) their own defense. "Behind the 'troops-out' argument," wrote one *Washington Post* reporter in 1988, lay "a growing political consensus that range[d] from Zbigniew Brzezinski and Henry Kissinger to Jesse Jackson."[226]

Here, once again, the role of END proved substantial, for it had successfully shifted the theme of the peace rallies from a mere "No Nukes" to the much broader "European Autonomy and East-West Reconciliation." By politicizing the demands of the peace activists, focusing their attention beyond the warheads to the social and cultural division of Europe, the founders of END achieved an influence that survived well beyond the actual deployment of NATO's new missiles in 1984. By that point, although the demonstrations began to die down, the peace movements had already carried the idea of European autonomy into the headlines and held it there, in ferment, for three pivotal years.

When Thompson had rebelled against the state-centric system of Stalinism, he had founded his rebellion upon a rediscovery of the popular agencies at work in nineteenth-century England; and he had sought to recapture the impetus of that nineteenth-century awakening, in the New Left clubs of the early 1960s. Later on, when he rebelled against the state-centric system of the Cold War, he once again founded this rebellion upon a popular awakening: the rediscovery of a distinct European identity, with its own common traditions, underneath the rigid division imposed by the superpower blocs. Taken together, these efforts defined his enduring belief in forcing a social transformation through the agency of cultural change—a nonviolent revolution patiently pushed along by individuals who offered their contemporaries new ways of perceiving and mobilizing their own collective potential.

In one sense, these ideas were quixotic; yet they proved politically efficacious nonetheless. Although Thompson's vision of a peaceful and radically democratic Europe remains far from realization, he clearly succeeded in meeting his own criteria for "partial free agency" in history; for he deflected the political currents of his time a little closer to the direction he wanted, and he did so not through manipulation or coercion but through the power of persuasion, exercised at the grass roots. In this sense, therefore, his notion of "the power of culture"—and his rejection of Machiavellian thinking—stood vindicated, to a degree, through his own action.

Peace through Social Transformation: Danilo Dolci's Long-Range Experiments with Gandhian Nonviolence

If we are not naive, we will see clearly that the elimination of armaments is only possible insofar as a substitute for armed defense is developed—a substitute that is even stronger, more effective.

—Danilo Dolci, 1962[1]

In February 1952 a young architect named Danilo Dolci arrived from Northern Italy, with nothing but a small suitcase, in the dusty Sicilian fishing village of Trappeto. He had decided to leave everything behind him: a promising career in the industrial city of Milano, his family, his fiancée. He was twenty-eight years old, and he had experienced what he later described as a "calling of conscience."[2] For some set of reasons that never became fully clear to him, the orthodox trajectory of a middle-class life had gradually come to fill him with frustration and restlessness. What he wanted was to be useful, to give unconditionally of himself, to change the society around him. He had chosen Trappeto because it was the poorest, most dejected place he could think of—a tiny knot of square white houses on a cliff looking west over the broad curve of the Gulf of Castellamare.

Dolci had already lived there for two months as a youth, when his father had been station master at the minuscule train station whose architecture revealed, in its own provincial way, the monumental style typical of fascism. For a long time he had remembered only the violent beauty of the place, which he had tried to sketch in his notebooks: the brilliant blue of the sea water, the jagged ridges to the north where bandits made the roads unsafe, the cactus-covered hills to the south around the ancient Greek temple of Segesta. Now he was returning because he had also remembered the misery of the people who lived in this stark countryside, and he felt drawn to that misery by a still unclear sense of purpose.

Dolci's first impression of Trappeto in 1952 was no different than the image in his memory: dirt streets with open sewers, half-starved children in rags begging for a coin or a bit of food, swarms of black flies in the sweltering heat, houses slowly crumbling down upon the chickens, donkeys, and human beings who lived together inside them. Here he settled, rising at 3 A.M. with the fishermen, sharing their meager food, listening to their stories—and, very slowly, winning their confidence. They could not understand why on earth anyone would want to come and live like they did, but they were moved by his solicitude for them, and impressed when he bought a plot of land on a nearby hilltop, above the stench, and started a rudimentary infirmary.

Over the next few years, Dolci began to chart the broad shape and contours of the wretchedness that surrounded him. He enlisted the aid of intelligent local youths his own age, and began systematically to collect information on the Western Sicilian social structure: unemployment, number of people per household, lack of public hygiene, infant mortality rates, popular superstitions, banditry, illiteracy, emigration figures, child labor. Nobody interfered with this

seemingly innocuous project, but when Dolci had brought all the statistics together in a book, coupling them with vivid testimonials from the villagers and
peasants, it rocked the conscience of all Italy. *Banditi a Partinico* ("Bandits in
Partinico") was published in 1955 and widely circulated by a major southern
publishing house.[3] Focusing on the larger town of Partinico, near the village
of Trappeto, the book created a scandal for the politicians in Rome and brought
the name of Danilo Dolci into the front page of newspapers, where it would
remain (off and on) for two decades.

Not until later in his career, when Dolci was in his forties, did he begin to
make an explicit connection between the social pathologies he was discovering
in Sicily and the broader pathologies that he believed he could discern within
the international state-system. He became more and more intrigued by this
connection, and traveled widely to observe at firsthand the manifold social
forms that functioned in other parts of the world, from Asia and Africa to
the Americas. Gradually, the prevalent distinction between global North-South
relations (with their emphasis on "underdevelopment") and East-West relations (with their emphasis on military and ideological competition) began to
seem increasingly superficial and inadequate. Missiles and poverty, he suspected, were like two different branches of the same diseased tree, rooted in a
deeper set of social malignancies that permeated the four poles of the modern
world.

The causes of violence, for Dolci, lay in the basic attitudes of billions of
individual citizens, and in the kinds of choices that each of them separately
made in his or her daily life. "If threatened, I will threaten back"—this was a
good example of the attitudes to which Dolci referred: seemingly reasonable,
and even effective, in the small-scale context of the street corner or living
room. Yet when summed up and projected onto the vast scale of public power,
this basic (almost instinctual) mechanism of self-defense became embodied in
weapons systems and political ideologies of unimaginable destructive potential. It was not by chance that this had happened, nor was it simply a matter of
isolated decisions or of irresponsible leadership. What modern citizens were
witnessing were their own values and habits projected outward on a planetary
scale. Militarism, in this sense, constituted an integral part of the very fabric
of late twentieth-century society. The causes of the missiles did not merely lie
somewhere "out there"—in the narrow thinking of statesmen or in the elusive
mechanisms of the military-industrial complex. They also lay "in here"—in
the conditioned perceptions and tacit choices through which each individual
shaped his or her life.

This was, in one sense, a highly pessimistic assessment of human nature—
a perspective not dissimilar to the harsh vision of humanity espoused by Louise
Weiss. For both Dolci and Weiss, the phenomena of violence and domination
lay deeply rooted within the mental structures of every human being; both

these thinkers shared a profound skepticism about finding "solutions" to these problems at the level of diplomacy or politics. Yet Dolci diverged sharply from Weiss in his belief (or faith) that these deep mental structures might also be accessible and pliable; human beings, he felt, could perhaps be taught to think, perceive, and behave differently. By the mid-1950s, Dolci had concluded that the only practical solution lay in a radical form of reeducation for nonviolence. In his manifold Sicilian projects, he experimented with new methods of conflict resolution, community development, and pedagogy that might offer some promise, over many generations, of forming a fundamentally different society—a society in which cooperative habits and assumptions had edged aside the dominative patterns of the present day.

Dolci's vision of the future, therefore, lay at the opposite pole from Weiss's; yet it also differed markedly from those of Szilard and Thompson. Dolci believed that the construction of international peace had to begin at the "micro" level of each individual, in the reshaping of a thousand seemingly innocuous daily interactions. The word "peace" obsessed Dolci, but his career rarely focused on the "macro" level—the global military and political issues that preoccupied Szilard and Thompson. Instead, he concentrated on building a robust form of nonviolence within a small, strife-torn community, in the hope that a few successful experiments there might later inspire others to emulate his methods throughout the world.

1924–1952: Conformism and Rebellion

From an ethnic point of view, Dolci was only one quarter Italian. His mother, Meli Kontely, was of Slovenian and German origins; his father's parents were Italian and German. Dolci himself was born in 1924 in the village of Sesana, near Trieste, a village subsequently transferred from Italy to Yugoslavia by the territorial readjustments of the World War II armistice. One of Dolci's earliest memories was the sound of his mother's voice singing religious songs in her native Slavic dialect.[4]

Dolci was born two years after Mussolini's accession to power, but his youth was not strongly colored by the experiences of growing up under fascism. Like most other schoolchildren, he wore the black uniform of the *balilla* (the Fascist youth organization), and repeated the blustering slogans that he was taught in class: "Mussolini is always right," and "Better to live one day as a lion than 100 years as a sheep."[5] Yet these experiences did not make a deep impression on him. Unlike E. P. Thompson, whose family environment was highly charged with political polemics and idealistic causes, Dolci's family embodied the unquestioning conformism of the European *petite bourgeoisie*.[6] Dolci's father, Enrico Dolci, worked for the Italian railways; he acquiesced uncomplainingly, like most Italians, in the minimal requirements of life under the Fascist system—neither an enthusiast nor a dissident. Dolci's mother, for her part, took refuge in what her son later described as a "rather sentimental and superstitious religiosity" and did not concern herself with politics.[7]

The young Danilo, therefore, was left to follow his own inclinations, which were intensely oriented toward the love of nature and of books. "Already when I was eight years old," he told an interviewer in 1976,

> I had learned how to remove a top drawer above the bookshelves that my father kept locked, and to fish out the books at random. By the time I was ten, reading had become an irresistible need; and I discovered that I could obtain all the books I wanted from the library in Gallarate. In elementary school, my only pleasant memories are of rare excursions into the countryside. I started to read in class, at first by hiding the books in my lap, and then gradually ceasing even to hide it, disgusted by the clamor of the classroom.[8]

The older he grew, the more intense this need became—until, by age sixteen, he was getting up every morning at 4 A.M. and sitting close by the kitchen stove to pursue his reading while the rest of the family slept. He proceeded systematically, by category and chronological order: Euripides, Shakespeare (whose name he pronounced as if it were Italian), Goethe, Schiller, Ibsen, Tolstoy, Dostoyevsky; the Upanishads, the discourses of the Buddha, the Tao Te Ching, the Bhagavad-Gita, Confucius, the Bible; and the great philosophers, starting with Plato and Aristotle.[9] "Another principal joy," he recalled,

> was water: the cold stream where I swam after Easter, the river Ticino, Lake Maggiore, and other lakes that I came to know, seated at first on the handlebars of my father's bicycle; then on my own bicycle, with my father and his friends; and finally with friends of my own age. The boat, the reflections of the shore and mountains in the water, learning how to see underwater: these were essential discoveries for me in that period.[10]

Unlike Weiss, Szilard, and Thompson, whose lives had been deeply marked by the stridency and violence of European politics in the 1930s, Dolci remained completely aloof from this broader sphere of events. It would be inaccurate to describe him as a passive young man, for he could channel a prodigious amount of sharply focused energy into his own projects and reflections; yet these interests were always far removed from the social world that surrounded him. Even after the Italian declaration of war in 1940, which wrenched his attention toward politics, his reactions remained characteristically immature. He perceived clearly enough that the Fascist regime would call upon him when he came of age to leave aside his books and his countryside, compelling him to march out and kill other young men. The ubiquitous slogans and uniforms took on a dark new significance, but all he could think of doing was to vent his impotent disgust by walking furtively around town and tearing Fascist posters from the walls.[11]

In 1940, Dolci's father was transferred to Trappeto; the family stayed behind, in the North. Danilo's two brief visits with his father during the summers of 1940 and 1941 left him with vivid memories of the Sicilian peasants and fishermen he had met. Yet their misery, like the tribulations of the war and the rituals of fascism, still appeared to him as immutable "givens"—like features in the scenery or climate, beyond the grasp of human volition or action. It had not yet dawned on him that he could call these realities into question.[12] He plunged all the more vigorously into his readings, seeking an escape from the society whose violence repelled and confused him.

By 1943, however, as Mussolini's troops bogged down in Russia and suffered defeats in Northern Africa, it became clear even to the young Dolci that his hideaway in Plato's *Republic* could not last much longer. The Allied armies had landed in Sicily and were blasting their way north; he decided to evade his imminent draft call by fleeing south. What followed was a year of harried movements, with his life in continual danger. Yet this year's adventures also marked a turning point, for Dolci was brought down quite roughly from the ethereal world he had inhabited under the shelter of his family and placed in direct confrontation with the simple problems of survival. He fled, somewhat naively, by train—and was promptly arrested. After ten days' detention by the Gestapo in Genova, he was called up for interrogation. In the middle of questioning, one of the Nazi officials went into the adjoining office momentarily, leaving Dolci alone with a translator, who began to busy himself with paperwork. Dolci walked slowly out of the room, continued (as calmly as he could) down the hall past the guards, and eventually found his way out the front gate of the building—all without once being stopped or questioned. He never understood precisely how he had been able to do this; perhaps the very brazenness of the act made him seem like an Italian on ordinary business.[13]

Hitchhiking and walking, he made his way south through the Appennines, encountering other fugitives like himself as he went. Eventually, he found a stable hiding place in a remote village of the Gran Sasso, the barren mountains east of Rome. In exchange for Latin and Italian lessons for their children, the peasants gave him enough food to survive; and he shared their hardships, their stories, their toil. The idea of joining the anti-Fascist Resistance appealed to him, and he even procured a pistol for himself; but as he reflected on the violence he would have to commit, he found it hard to reconcile with the principles he had absorbed from all his readings.

> I got more precise information on the location of local Fascists and Nazis. I ruminated. What sense did it have to kill one or two Nazis

with my pistol? If anything, it would have made better sense to try to poison all of them throughout the region, in a well-organized plan. I thought a long time about this, by the shores of the nearby lake, amid the endless rasping of the frogs. Would this plan of mine really extirpate the seeds of the evil? After days and days, I began to see more clearly that the articulations of evil were far deeper, and that a solution could only be sought by going to the roots. Hence my decision: I picked up the pistol and threw it into the lake.[14]

The young man who returned to Northern Italy early in 1945 was therefore a very different person from the youth who had fled a year and a half before. On the surface, he was ready to begin the career that his father envisioned for him, going to university in Milan and studying to become an architect. Underneath, however, he had begun to ask himself uncomfortable questions. He had seen for himself how the peasants lived in squalor throughout the rural areas of Central Italy, yet now he was supposed to learn the techniques for building large and impressive houses for the wealthy. He went to church with his family every week, and yet he faced open derision when he talked about building a new society that would truly reflect the spirit of the Gospel. The political parties of the newly formed Italian Republic furiously competed with each other in preparation for their first major electoral contest coming up in 1948; yet everywhere, beneath the rhetoric of democracy and renewal, he perceived a systemic entrenchment of corruption, nepotism, and moral compromises. As a young architect, for instance, he learned that he would have to give and receive bribes in exchange for contracts and favors.[15] "The real danger," he recalled

> lay in being forced to give up those things which I had intuited as essential in my life. All around me I saw people of value who were practically selling themselves, or selling the substantial part of their daily life, in the hope of "saving themselves" in the bits of time that were left over. Wasn't this to let oneself slip into schizophrenia, into suicide? Deeply troubled, I understood that I would have to choose whether or not to live a life that persuaded me.[16]

Dolci wrestled with this choice over several years, until 1949. He continued to attend university, passing his exams one after another, and supporting himself by giving private lessons on the side. He wrote two technical works, *The Science of Construction* and *The Theory of Reinforced Concrete*.[17] In 1948 he became engaged to an art student named Alice, whose father owned a small construction company. Together they read poetry and took long walks, discussing their ideals and their future family.[18] In 1949 Dolci bought an apartment in Milan, making the monthly installment payments out of the growing income that he earned as an architectural consultant. His father and mother were immensely pleased and proud of him.

Yet Dolci was in fact becoming increasingly restless. In 1948 he had met a remarkable man named Don Zeno Saltini, an eccentric priest who had founded a Christian community and orphanage in the countryside south of Milan. Dolci had gone to visit this community, called Nomadelfia—or the place of "fraternal law," as Don Zeno had baptized it. Both Don Zeno and Nomadelfia struck Dolci as embodiments of the very coherence and integrity that he found so sadly lacking in his own daily life. With growing enthusiasm, he appealed to Alice to come and see Nomadelfia with him and to consider the possibility of settling there. "She responded as if overcome by panic," he later recalled.

> She refused even to go there a single time. But, I asked myself, did this mean that all the things on which we had reflected together, and dreamed together as a necessary ideal—all this was nothing but a froth of words?[19]

In the fall of 1949, Dolci made his decision, braving the outrage and dismay of all those whom he was leaving behind—Alice and her family, his own family, his colleagues at the university. "After days and days as if in a fever," he recalled, "finally the rupture came, and I went to Nomadelfia. The time had come to strip away an intellectualism which might have trapped me and, who knows, even appeased me."[20]

Nomadelfia had been founded only four years before, when Don Zeno had unceremoniously occupied an abandoned Nazi concentration camp among the fields of Emilia, near the town of Fossoli. During the war, several hundred Jews had died in this camp; Don Zeno and his followers broke down the walls and set up dovecots in the watchtowers. Their aim was to establish a Christian haven for children who had been orphaned by the war; by the time Dolci arrived in 1949, Nomadelfia was a bustling community with fourteen hundred children and some sixty volunteer "mothers and fathers" to take care of them.[21]

Don Zeno's personality appealed immensely to Dolci. He was a gruffly passionate man of fifty, with a visceral dislike of all large organizations, from the Fascist state (which had imprisoned him for his opposition) to the present Republic, from the bureaucratic charity organizations to his own Catholic hierarchy. Despite this iconoclastic nature, however, he was also a moral traditionalist and an ardent believer in God, family, and work. "Just by being near him," Dolci later recalled, "one developed a greater sense of moral clarity."[22]

Don Zeno soon took notice of Dolci as well, for the young man plunged, with the earnest and methodical absorption that was his dominant trait, into the work and spirit of Nomadelfia. He chose as his first job the cleaning of toilets and the emptying of cesspools, so that the illiterate volunteers would not feel humiliated by his higher education.[23] Then he helped them build roads and till the communal fields, rising before dawn and collapsing on his cot late at night, totally spent. He loved the children who were everywhere with their noise and games, and he was drunk with the feeling that his life had been given over to others. When the Italian government sent him official forms to complete in 1950 for his compulsory military service, he filled them out in clear terms:

PATERNITY: God
NUMBER OF BROTHERS: About a billion
NUMBER OF SISTERS: ditto
PROFESSION: I'm learning to be consumed.[24]

Dolci still considered himself a Catholic, although his sense of religion was becoming increasingly mystical and ecumenical. The discourses of the Buddha returned with particular insistence to his mind as he observed the interactions of his fellows at Nomadelfia, or took long nocturnal walks in the Emilia countryside.[25] In a poem he wrote:

Blue-white, far off in the night
Even the stars have a soul of fire.
The name by which I am called
is not my own.
No name is enough for me.
This body that quickly congeals
is not my own.
As yet unborn
I have flowed forth forever
Even as I die.[26]

Dolci immersed himself in the spirit of Nomadelfia for two years. As he and Don Zeno became increasingly close, members of the community speculated that Dolci might someday become Don Zeno's successor. In actuality, however, the differences between their two kinds of moral vision were gradually leading toward a parting of ways. Dolci disapproved of the fact that Nomadelfia was open only to Catholics and tried (unsuccessfully) to prod Don Zeno toward a broader conception of their work. He asked himself, with growing frustration, how the ideals of Nomadelfia might make an impact on social problems of the outside world; yet he found Don Zeno obstinately unreceptive to these kinds of questions. For Don Zeno, the problem presented itself in utterly concrete terms: saving these children from the streets, building a coherent community founded on Christian love. As he later explained to an interviewer: "We're not a closed shop—we're closed only to non-Catholics. With Danilo his idea was you could form a community even with different religions. It was a case of seeing and not seeing."[27] For Dolci, this Catholic microcosm seemed excessively limited. "Those two years of experience," he later recalled, had cleansed me and reduced me to essentials. . . . I understood that Nomadelfia could only grow at a certain rhythm, if it was to maintain its inherent qualities; yet I felt as though it were an island, a warm nest: . . . What about the rest of the world?

The figures of the peasants and fishermen of Trappeto, whom I had met years before, kept returning to me, like a call. It wasn't a difficult choice. More than a choice, it was like answering a call. . . . I left for Trappeto toward the end of January, 1952.[28]

1952–1958: The Challenge of Underdevelopment

Sicilian society, at the time of Dolci's arrival in Trappeto, was a striking hybrid of ancient and modern cultural forms, heavily burdened by its convulsed history at the geographical crossroads between Europe, Africa, and the Middle East. The roots of Sicily's underdevelopment probably lay in the recurrent waves of foreign domination that had affected the island since pre-Christian times.[29] After roughly a thousand years of Phoenician, Greek, and Roman colonization, Sicily was successively held (for centuries at a time) by Ostrogoths, Moslems, and Normans, followed by German and French dynasties, and by six centuries of Spanish rule (1282–1860). The social patterns established under this succession of invasions rested on collusion between indigenous landed elites and foreign rulers in extracting a maximum of economic output from the Sicilian peasantry. The Romans and Spaniards particularly distinguished themselves as rapacious conquerors, imposing heavy taxes, tightly integrating Sicilian wheat exports into a larger Mediterranean market, and establishing highly specialized forms of cultivation based on forced labor.[30] Sicily retained the basic characteristics of a semifeudal economy long after other European regions had witnessed the birth of commerce and of an entrepreneurial middle class. Huge landholdings or latifundia persisted into the nineteenth and even twentieth centuries, owned by noble families and a few *grands bourgeois* who left the administration of their vast territories to trusted subordinates. The large majority of Sicilian peasants, who worked on these agricultural lands, were either landless laborers or individuals who owned a few scattered plots of land—barely enough to scratch out a day-to-day living.

It was under these conditions that the distinctive form of power relations known as "clientelism" was able to flourish. One scholar has described this relationship as essentially a "lopsided friendship" in which one person is dominant and controls access to essential resources or privileges, while a second, subordinate person provides services and loyalty in exchange for protection.[31] Local Sicilian notables, well-connected with the foreign owners of the land and the bureaucracies of foreign governors, obtained protection and favors for their peasant followers; the peasants, bound by a strictly personal and direct relationship with their patron, gratefully gave their labor in return. Clientelism had pervaded Sicilian society for centuries, but it was not exclusive to Sicily or Italy; it also occurred, with local variations and peculiarities, in Latin America, India, and certain Asian countries.[32] Political scientists have also discerned more "modern," or less strictly personalized, variants of this form of power in the United States—for instance, in the corrupt political machines that came to dominate certain cities within the last century, of which New York's Tammany Hall was perhaps the most notorious.[33]

The mafia was first born in the nineteenth century (after the abolition of serfdom in 1812), as a means of enforcing this highly unequal form of reciprocity and of preventing the newly emancipated peasantry from developing a sense of cohesion or internal self-organization.[34] The original *mafiosi* were the local "managers" and hired guns of the large landowners, collecting rents from starving tenants and sharecroppers and keeping them in a state of continuous intimidation. "There is no contradiction," writes the political scientist Luigi Graziano,

> between the violence which permeates Sicilian clientelism and the accentuated paternalism which characterizes it. Simply, when the power differential is so great and the client is socially isolated, a highly affective relationship is the best strategy to soften the terms of an unequal exchange. Such deference can become, with the process of time, a cultural compensatory mechanism which preserved this very inequality of reciprocity.[35]

The unification of Italy in 1860 raised hopes among progressive Sicilians that reasonable reforms might at least be forthcoming; but they were bitterly disappointed. The national parliament that met in Rome after 1870 imposed new and heavy taxes on the southern population, while removing the tariff barriers that had provided marginal local artisans and a fledgling textile industry with protection from foreign competition. This produced a rapid deterioration of the southern economy. Those southerners who could vote—and it was not until 1913 that Italy introduced universal male suffrage—tended to follow the old clientelistic patterns. Where once the patron-client relationship had bound together local notables with their peasant followers, now the old system was adapted to meet the needs of modern electoral politics. The new patron became the local senator, or mayor, or city councillor, and the new clients became the voting citizens of an allegedly modern state. In order to get a building permit or a tax exemption—or, perhaps, a comfortable job for one's nephew, or a favorable judgment in a trial—one relied on one's personal connections with a local official. At election time, however, that official (or his political party) received back in loyal votes what he had doled out in favors and patronage. In this way, the substance of paternalism reappeared, skillfully cloaked, within the external trappings of democracy.[36]

Southern politicians, moreover, quickly learned after 1860 how to strike a fundamental bargain with the central government in Rome: Rome would not tamper with the entrenched privilege of the southern ruling class; and the southern elites, in return, would provide the ruling parties in Rome with large numbers of guaranteed votes (through their patron-client bonds). This unhealthy symbiosis became especially important in the late nineteenth and early twentieth centuries, as new left-wing political parties in the industrial North increasingly challenged the established parties of the Liberal republic. The southern masses, illiterate and disunited, provided a crucial counterweight to the Socialist and Communist workers of the North.

With the advent of fascism in 1922, this North-South trade-off reemerged in a new form. Mussolini's ultimate success, during the years in which he consolidated his regime, hinged crucially on the support of southern politicians with their huge and docile constituencies; he therefore allowed the Fascist party in the South to become solidly rooted in the old networks of clientelistic power, "buying" the support of the South with the same kind of state patronage that had worked so well for his Liberal predecessors. It is interesting, however, that the *Duce* also recognized in the mafia a form of parallel government that challenged the monopoly of violence exercised by his own state. Thus, while tolerating the high-level institutions of political clientelism, he moved vigorously against the lower-level *mafiosi,* installing a special prefect in 1925 to crush the most notorious exponents of organized crime.[37]

The long-term effect of these North-South political bargains was that Southern Italy actually became poorer and more backward between the time of Garibaldi and World War II. Southern Italians were forced to flee their native region by the millions to look for new possibilities in the factories of Milan and Turin, or as day laborers and menial workers in Northern Europe, or as part of the new immigrant class in countries like the United States, Canada, and Argentina.

After the war, the new Italian Republic made a concerted effort to address the "Southern Question" (Questione Meridionale). Unfortunately, it proved difficult to break the habits and patterns ingrained over centuries; for the postwar ruling party, the Christian Democrats, proved particularly vulnerable to infiltration by the corrupt networks of clientelism.[38] In 1950, the government in Rome set up the Cassa Per il Mezzogiorno, or "Southern Fund," disbursing the equivalent of hundreds of millions of dollars each year to aid industrialization in the South. Time after time, however, the funds mysteriously disappeared, or ended up in the hands of private construction firms that made huge profits by charging far more than market value for their work.[39] In several instances, gigantic steel mills or chemical plants were built, only to fall into disrepair and close down a few years later—becoming notorious "Cathedrals in the Desert" whose vast decaying structures constituted the most tangible emblems of the Southern Question. After twenty-five years of massive investments by the Southern Fund, investments amounting to billions of dollars, southern society was certainly showing signs of a broader prosperity. Infant mortality, for instance, had declined dramatically by the mid-1970s.[40] But the structural gap between North and South remained essentially as broad as ever; and total employment in the South in 1975 was actually lower than it had been in 1951.[41]

Meanwhile, the mafia, having suffered during the Fascist period only at its lower echelons, rapidly returned to prominence in Sicilian life. Within a few years after World War II, mafia connections were widely believed to extend all the way up to the ministerial level in the central government in Rome.[42] Mafia bosses oversaw a highly diversified array of activities, from extortion and racketeering to the intimidation of trade unionists and the murder of troublesome political activists. They controlled specific sectors of the legal economy, such as the construction industry; and, especially in the 1970s, they moved aggressively into international drug trafficking.[43] Periodically, the Italian state made brave attempts to attack the power of the mafia, but this was a difficult proposition, since the roots of mafia power lay in the same clientelistic system that permeated Southern Italian politics. It was almost like asking the left hand to investigate and punish the misdeeds of the right hand—when both belonged to the same body.

Not surprisingly, Sicilian clientelism possessed its own concomitant code of values and customs.[44] At the heart of this cultural code lay a hierarchical and deferential view of social order, coupled with an extremely fatalistic attitude toward the agencies of social change. A fierce loyalty and bonding within small networks of individuals or families went together with a profound diffidence toward the public sphere, the state, or the idea of "common weal."[45] Sicilians placed a high premium on cleverness and cunning (or *furberia*), but only valued self-sacrifice if it benefited the intimate group defined by family ties or patronage.[46] These three nodal points of Sicilian culture (deference, fatalism, and small-group bonding) constituted a self-reinforcing world view, a coherent set of Hobbesian perceptions that continually perpetuated itself through the Hobbesian social reality that it helped to generate.

It was into this complex nexus of cultural, economic, and political relationships that Danilo Dolci plunged early in 1952. He had no knowledge of the Sicilian dialect, no money, nor even a very clear idea of what he wanted to accomplish. "Upon arriving in Trappeto," he later recalled,

> I looked around me. There were no real roads, no sewers, there were no newspapers, not a pharmacy, not a telephone. No bathrooms. The desperate misery was not for any single person; the whole mass of people was submerged within it.

I had a tent, which I pitched near the village; and I started working alongside the fishermen and peasants, day after day. During the
rest breaks, I kept asking, "Can this be changed? How can all this
be changed? Where can we begin to seek a change?"[47]

Gradually, it became clear to Dolci that two problems preoccupied these
men more than anything else: the lack of jobs, and the well-founded fear that
their families would suffer if they were incapacitated. According to official
statistics, 26.9 percent of Sicily's population in 1953 was "totally destitute,"
while 20.2 percent was "semi-destitute."[48] The officially claimed unemployment level for Southern Italy in 1951 was about 10 percent; yet this figure
grossly underestimated the real scarcity of jobs in a region where, according
to one scholar, "large numbers of persons in precarious employment . . . characterized by instability of jobs and pay, [were] recorded among the employed."[49] One of Dolci's coworkers, in a subsequent study of local underem-
ployment in 1957, estimated that even those agricultural workers who qualified
as "employed" spent roughly half of their annual workdays in idleness for lack
of labor opportunities.[50]

At frequent intervals throughout the year, therefore, many of these men were
reduced to walking the countryside searching for frogs and snails to sell in the
markets of Palermo; or to combing the railroad lines for pieces of unburned
coal fallen from passing steam engines; or, worst of all, into desperate acts of
theft (a chicken, a bunch of grapes) which led inexorably toward the abyss of
banditry and imprisonment.[51] The fishermen complained that large trawlers
were coming in from Palermo and using illegal nets to catch *neonata*, the
newly hatched fingerlings that fetched a high price on the black market; local
fishermen, as a result, had all but lost their livelihood, for the number of fully
grown fish had rapidly declined. No number of complaints or petitions to the
police had made the slightest difference; the trawlers flagrantly continued, in
open daylight, to break the law.[52]

Dolci decided to concentrate his efforts on a single project that would bring
immediate results: building an infirmary and hospice in which orphans and the
children of imprisoned bandits could receive a decent upbringing. He traveled
briefly to Milan to borrow money from a former professor, then returned to
Trappeto and bought a plot of land on a hilltop overlooking the village and the
sea. There, among the olive trees, he traced out the shape of a small L-shaped
building. When the unemployed men in the village asked him to hire them, he
explained that he simply had no money left, but that if more money could later
be found, he would pay them then. Soon eighty villagers were hard at work,
carving a road up the hillside and laying the foundations. Within two months,
the new infirmary was finished; Dolci called it Borgo di Dio (Hamlet of God).[53]

The basic problem with the idea of the Borgo, however, quickly made itself apparent. Parents eagerly brought their children in from Trappeto and the neighboring countryside, and before long Dolci had sixty of them on his hands, half-starved, half-savage. Two of the widows from the village moved up to the Borgo to assist him; and local authorities—the Christian Democratic mayor, the poor-relief officers in Palermo—provided emergency funds to keep the center functioning. Yet when Dolci looked around him, he realized that creating the Borgo had been like throwing a thimbleful of water onto a raging fire. The villagers had indeed seen that concrete changes were possible, with a little initiative; but the structural poverty of the local society remained untouched, producing its regular quotient of desperation and hungry mouths to feed.

Dolci then hit upon a notion that was to remain central in his work throughout the following decades: he called it *autoanalisi popolare,* or "popular self-analysis."[54] The idea developed from the dozens of conversations in which he had engaged the local people, conversations that revealed to him not only their widespread ignorance and superstition but also a shrewd, pragmatic intelligence. Gradually winning the confidence of the villagers, he persuaded them to come together in groups of twenty or so, sitting in a circle, to discuss their problems. Proceeding clockwise around the circle, he asked each person to contribute some comment or opinion; and in this way, the women and old people (who would otherwise have remained silent) began to break through their timidity and speak for themselves. "Repeating this process again and again," he later explained,

> we were actually generating a mentality of research around us. . . .
> Some, from what they told me and from what I was able to observe, changed quite a lot; they were helped by this kind of introspection to become different persons.
>
> All this was not simple: it cost considerable sweat and anxiety, it was like giving birth. In Trappeto, to speak with the people about their poverty, about their superstitions, became each time an extremely painful experience. On the other hand, if we didn't discuss a problem, how could we succeed in resolving it?[55]

Out of this arduous procedure, "from among a whole trash-pile of useless things and false problems," the idea of irrigation began to take shape.[56]

Each year, for six months, the Sicilian summer brought with it a period of acute drought that rendered agriculture impossible; just as regularly, at the onset of the dry season, the parish priest led a procession of chanting villagers, with holy images and full regalia, "ad petendam pluviam" (to pray for rain). Meanwhile, nearby, the river Jato flowed throughout the summer months, spilling millions of cubic meters of fresh water into the sea. Dolci calculated that a 40-horsepower pump could irrigate 750 acres of dry land, quadrupling the local agricultural output.[57] Yet when he brought these figures to the regional authorities, they showed little interest. "The monstrous reality," he later recalled, "was that instead of stepping in to create jobs for the poor, the State's main role consisted in imprisoning them."[58]

In October, nine months after Dolci's arrival, a child died of starvation in Trappeto. Dolci was called at the last minute to the mother's side; she had not eaten for days, and her baby was unconscious. Her husband was in prison for having stolen lemons. Dolci rushed to the pharmacy in the neighboring town of Balestrate to buy milk, but he returned too late. He called a meeting of his closest friends among the fishermen and peasants. "Together," he later recalled, "we took a simple, clear decision. One by one, we would fast until the village had been pulled out of this desperate situation. I would start, and if I died, the others would go on."[59] He wrote to an old friend from Milan, Franco Alasia, who immediately traveled down by train to assist him. Then he drafted a terse letter to the regional authorities, asking for emergency funds to launch an irrigation project. "Rather than see another child die of hunger," Dolci stated, "I would rather die myself. As from today I will not eat another mouthful until the money required to employ the neediest and help the most urgent cases has arrived."[60]

Dolci had only heard vague reports of the nonviolent methods adopted by Gandhi in India and did not read Gandhi's autobiography until two years later. The idea of fasting, he later explained, had not developed out of mystical readings or reflections but out of a very direct and practical set of intuitions:

> We had to demonstrate that the forces of the State were the real outlaws here, showing clearly that the villagers wanted above all to work, to participate in life, to give their own contribution to development. For these people, who knew what hunger meant, the thought that one of them was [deliberately] refusing food had a precise significance.[61]

Dolci's fast lasted for eight days. He chose as his location the same tiny cot in which the child had died a few days earlier and lay there, receiving continuous visits from the alarmed villagers. Two of the illiterate fishermen, Paolino Russo and Toni Alia, later dictated their impressions to one of Dolci's coworkers:

> The whole village, frightened by this thing that he was doing, because he wanted to die before other little ones starved, day by day came to see him, in the house with its little bed of straw, and he didn't want to eat.
> The villagers begged him to eat, because they didn't want "that for us you would die," but he still continued not to want to eat. And he stayed calm and happy as when he had been eating.[62]

Since it had not occurred to Dolci to inform the press in Palermo about his fast, only the villagers and the handful of friends and officials to whom he had sent letters knew what he was undertaking. After five days, a representative of the Sicilian regional government and a high-ranking member of the Christian Democratic party drove to Trappeto to urge him to desist; but they could offer little in the way of concrete assurances.

"If somebody doesn't die, nothing will happen," Dolci told them.[63]

They drove away, promising to do what they could. On the seventh night of the fast, Dolci's pulse suddenly turned very weak, and his right leg and arm became half-paralyzed. The villagers called a doctor, who declared that Dolci could not survive much longer: his heart was giving out. At daybreak, armed with a written statement from the doctor, Dolci's friend Franco drove to Palermo on a motorcycle to plead with the regional officials. Later that day, a carload of notables arrived in Trappeto—a monsignor, two Christian Democrats, a baroness, and the personal envoy of the Sicilian regional president—with tangible promises. As the fishermen later recollected,

> they told Danilo that they would help the old and young who were in extreme want to stop living in the street (which they never did), and that they were giving a million and a half *lire* [about $3,000] right away and would take care of all the costs for irrigation (and this they did do).[64]

Dolci consulted with the villagers, who declared themselves abundantly satisfied (and relieved) by this unexpected offer from the authorities; and he ended his fast that afternoon.

This, therefore, was Dolci's first success. The authorities, no doubt, had thought that this eccentric young man would be fully satisfied by the improvements they were promising for Trappeto; they could not have known that his fast would only mark the beginning of a steadily broadening campaign. In successive years, Dolci's relations with Sicily's rulers would become far more tense, as he began to challenge the economic and political system in which their power was rooted. Yet he succeeded, through an unusually deft sense of timing and of symbolism, in avoiding the open confrontation that almost invariably characterized these kinds of power struggles. Although he did not fully articulate his ideas until much later, he understood early on, in a more intuitive and concrete way, the same principle that was to strike E. P. Thompson in his research on the eighteenth century: the rhetoric of the rulers could itself become a powerful tool of social change. By pressing the ruling classes to fulfill the social promises embedded within their own ideology of governance, one could extract significant concessions while operating *within* the value system of the rulers themselves. This had been a principle that Gandhi had applied with great efficacy in India, relentlessly exposing the contradictions between the British liberal ideology and the gross relations of force and inequality upon which colonialism rested. In a similar way, Dolci would now challenge the

Italian government to fulfill—at least in minimal terms—the social contract embodied in the Constitution of the postwar republic.

Dolci's work in the 1950s fell into three broad categories: analyzing the Sicilian social system, publicizing the horrors that it produced, and organizing long-term forces of reform. These three tasks were closely linked; for without a clear understanding of the dimensions and nature of the region's social problems, he could not make precise demands on the political authorities; and without public support, he would remain weak and isolated. Effectiveness required that statistics, public indignation, and new forms of popular self-organization be brought together into a single coordinated force.

Between 1953 and 1955 Dolci took his first tentative steps in this direction, concentrating on the region of Trappeto and the larger nearby town of Partinico. He published two books on the local social system: *Act Quickly (and Well) Because Here They Are Dying* (1954), and *Bandits in Partinico* (1955).[65] The first of these was a brief, "spontaneous outpouring" (in Dolci's words)—an urgent appeal for help based on graphic descriptions of the squalor around Trappeto.[66] Although this first book was not of sufficient analytical or literary caliber to become famous, it brought Dolci what he most urgently needed: a steady influx of volunteers and private donations from Northern Italy. In 1952 his efforts at Borgo di Dio and his fast had come to the attention of Aldo Capitini, a widely respected theorist of nonviolence and a survivor of Mussolini's prisons. Capitini publicized Dolci's projects among progressive political circles in Florence, Turin, and Milan, introducing him to such prominent writers as Carlo Levi, Elio Vittorini, and Ignazio Silone (all of whom immediately began to send money and to drum up support for his work). After 1953, therefore, Dolci could generally count on the assistance of four or five young volunteers, some of whom stayed as little as two months, others for years at a time. Invariably, he directed them to join in his systematic pursuit of information, interviewing the peasants and compiling statistics in a methodical grass-roots variety of sociological analysis.

In the spring of 1953 Dolci decided to marry one of the two widows who had come to assist him at the Borgo, a woman in her thirties named Vincenzina Mangano, who already had five children. This decision, he later explained,

> left many people perplexed. Vincenzina, in her commitment [to the children], deeply moved me. I decided I wouldn't marry a young princess: I would marry her. My father, who had understood my motivations, politely objected: "And what if you happen to fall in love with someone someday?" This seemed unlikely to me. I had made my decision in the little cemetery near Trappeto, standing before the grave of [the child who had died of starvation]. I knew I was taking a difficult step, but I considered it the right thing to do from a Christian point of view.[67]

Dolci adopted Vincenzina's children, the oldest of whom was fifteen; and within the year, he and Vincenzina had a child of their own.

By 1955, the face of Trappeto had changed considerably. Sewers had been installed, the Borgo was functioning efficiently, and the new irrigation system had produced not only a surge of the village economy but (more importantly, from Dolci's point of view) a self-sustaining irrigation cooperative run by the peasants themselves. Dolci accordingly decided, much to the consternation of the Trappeto villagers, to broaden the scope of his projects, transferring his base to the nearby town of Partinico. In June 1955, he and his new family moved into a fetid two-room house in the most wretched quarter of Partinico, a quarter appropriately called Spine Sante (Holy Thorns). Not surprisingly, the move to Partinico deeply displeased Vincenzina, who had seen her life transformed in the space of a few years, as if by a miracle. She loved the Borgo, the clear air, the view of the sea; yet she quietly followed her new husband with the resignation that ancient tradition imposed upon Sicilian women.[68]

The town of Partinico, where Dolci was to base his work during the coming decades, had a particularly sinister reputation in Western Sicily. It was a notorious mafia town, without the harsh picturesqueness of other mafia strongholds like Montelepre or Corleone. Surrounded on two sides by barren mountains with spectacular jagged outcroppings, it sprawled out on the plain below, a flat mass of dirty-white houses cut in two by a single straight street, the *Corso*. On the plain beyond, solitary peasants tilled the arid land with their mules; about five miles farther, too distant to see except from the nearby mountain, lay Trappeto and the sweeping blue curve of the Gulf of Castellamare. Under the Spanish Bourbons, Partinico had briefly flourished as a center of wine production, but now its economy was utterly stagnant—a textbook example of the Southern Question at its worst.

Once again, just as he had done in Trappeto, Dolci spent his first months in Partinico asking questions. He and his small group of volunteers began organizing the same forms of *autoanalisi popolari* that had produced the irrigation cooperative in Trappeto; and, gradually, the idea of building a major dam on the river Jato began to emerge. In December 1955, he published *Banditi a Partinico,* a book whose unique combination of hard statistics and heart-wrenching interviews with local men and women quickly gained an international audience. "After I was arrested," said one of the "banditi" accused of stealing,

> they put the mask on me twice. Each time for about ten minutes. The mask sucked in salt water from the bucket and then my head was pulled back so that all the water went down my throat. One's stomach swells up as if one was pregnant. I was beaten on my bare back and legs, and all over my bare body. On the *cassetta* [a wooden box-like instrument] they twist your genitals. . . . It's not

[that] the guards do these things without the knowledge of their superiors; they are done in the presence of their superiors, who write down what you say and draw up the evidence.[69]

Naturally, this kind of testimonial did not endear Dolci to the local authorities; yet they found that it was too late to stop him. Early in January 1956, he formulated a plan for a new nonviolent campaign to dramatize his work; and this time, following the advice of Capitini and others, he ensured that all of Italy would be watching.[70]

For two weeks in January, Dolci traveled throughout Northern Italy, stopping in each of the major cities to hold meetings and to announce that he was about to launch a nonviolent protest in Sicily. On January 13, he appeared in a live interview from Turin on the state-owned television network, denouncing the collapse of effective government in the southern half of the nation and promising a peaceful campaign of popular action. (Two days later, the men who had aired Dolci's interview were summarily fired on orders from Rome.)[71] Returning to Partinico, Dolci wrote a detailed letter to the police, explaining what he planned to do. On January 30 (a date deliberately chosen to commemorate the eighth anniversary of Gandhi's death), he and a thousand of the poorest residents of Partinico would fast for a day; then, having prepared themselves together in the spirit of nonviolent action, they would march up to one of the caved-in public roads that ran across the hillside above Partinico and set about repairing it. In doing this, he explained, they would be deliberately exercising their fundamental right to work, which the neglect and corruption of Sicily's government was in effect denying them. It was the Italian Constitution itself, he wrote, that clearly stated (in Article IV): "The Republic recognizes the right of all citizens to work and ensures the conditions necessary to make this right effective."[72] In this nation where the highly politicized trade unions regularly paralyzed public life with their massive strikes, these Sicilian workers were engaging in a day of voluntary, unpaid labor: a *sciopero alla rovescia* (or strike-in-reverse).

The police responded by barring any public gathering in Partinico on January 30. They called in hundreds of reinforcements from Palermo, clogging the roads with their convoys of army trucks before dawn on the first day of the protest. When peasants came in from the countryside to join the fast, they found that police roadblocks were holding the entire region under siege. The thousand fasting men then fanned out into the fields, reassembling a few hours later on the beach below Trappeto to continue their vigil. Newspaper reporters rushed to and fro, interviewing the peasants and the acutely irritated police officers.

Three days later, when Dolci and his fellow protesters converged on the old road above Partinico, preparing to carry out their strike-in-reverse, the police once again appeared in force, bracing for a riot. The chief inspector from Palermo ordered the peasants to go home, but they silently continued their work on the road. At this point, several dozen officers surrounded Dolci and six of the peasants' main leaders, declaring them under arrest. Dolci and the others sat down on the ground. The officers, under the intense gaze of the silent workers and the arrayed legions of police, lifted Dolci up and carried him off to their vans. He was handcuffed and taken to the *Ucciardone,* the notorious stone fortress in Palermo which had served as a prison since the time of the Spaniards.

The effect could not have been closer to what Dolci intended. During the following two months, the photograph of this large, serene man with chains around his wrists churned through the Italian mass media, raising difficult questions for politicians, journalists, and ordinary citizens. "It was as if the whole country had been punched in the eye," wrote one commentator in the magazine *Il Ponte.*[73] In the Italian Parliament, Dolci's arrest became the focus of a heated debate which lasted throughout the month of February. Politicians on the Left and Center-Left described his work as "the high and solemn expression of the age-long sufferings of our people," while the Christian Democratic undersecretary of the interior questioned Dolci's motives and insisted that he was doing nothing but "trampling on the laws" and "getting people to hope for miracles."[74]

At first, the majority of Italy's newspapers went along with the tendentious press release furnished by the Palermo police: Dolci was a "noted agitator," he had been arrested for organizing "an insidious (but abortive) demonstration," and "public order had been restored."[75] He was defended only by the left-wing press and by his prominent intellectual supporters, from the filmmakers Federico Fellini and Vittorio De Sica to the artists Renato Guttuso and Corrado Cagli, from writers like Carlo Levi and Alberto Moravia to scientists like Maria Sacchetti-Fermi.[76] Gradually, however, as journalists began reading *Banditi a Partinico* and traveling down to Palermo to speak with Dolci, the tide began to turn. A reporter for the major Milan daily *Corriere della Sera* observed on February 5:

> Those who have read Dolci's latest book; those who discover the methods by which he pursues what he considers to be essential actions of human solidarity; those who listen to Dolci's friends, certainly fail to recognize in him [the "noted agitator"] portrayed by the police.[77]

By the end of February, the debate had shifted away from Dolci himself, moving toward the more general questions that he had been trying to raise. "Italy may indeed be lovely," wrote a columnist in the popular magazine *L'Europeo,* "but in Partinico, the quarter of Spine Sante is an immense cesspool."[78]

Dolci's trial, which took place late in March, thus became known as "Article Four on Trial"—an allusion to the clause on the right to work in the Italian Constitution. The eminent Florentine lawyer Piero Calamandrei traveled to Palermo to defend Dolci and his associates free of charge, delivering a widely publicized oration on March 30 in which he argued that Dolci was in fact defending the true spirit of the Republic and of the laws. The Palermo judges, who had been inclining toward a sentence of five years' imprisonment,[79] were, therefore, compelled by the weight of an aroused public opinion to reach a compromise solution: they found Dolci and his friends guilty of a minor charge, sentenced them to pay a substantial fine, and pronounced them free to go.

When Dolci emerged from the *Ucciardone* in April 1956, he discovered that he had become internationally famous. "Dolci vs. *Far Niente* [Doing Nothing]," ran the headline of a highly favorable article in *Time* magazine.[80] A writer in Jean-Paul Sartre's review *Les Temps Modernes* described him as "a Christian Gandhi among the 'bandits' of Sicily."[81] Much to the embarrassment of the Italian government, he had turned Partinico into a concrete symbol of the tension between individual initiative and the cumbersome machinery of the modern state. "Dolci," wrote a French journalist,

> refuses to wait until conservatives become illuminated reformers, or until a revolution takes place on the Left. He believes that, even if a revolution were to occur, there would always be a need for individuals who *personally* took the initiative among their fellow human beings—operating outside the political parties and trade unions.[82]

Dolci had not been out of jail two weeks when he plunged into a new phase of activity which was to last a year and a half. Leaving his family behind in Partinico, he moved into the worst slums of Palermo, known as Cortile Cascino, and set about with a team of twenty-three assistants to conduct the research for a third book. From the level of the rural village, to that of the midsized town, he was now seeking to complete his analysis by surveying Sicily's capital city and its suburbs.[83] The febrile intensity of his work was such that he completed this urban research in a mere eight months. In December 1956, *Inchiesta a Palermo* ("Report from Palermo") was published; it combined technical analysis and heartrending stories with a skill that promptly earned him Italy's highest literary award, the Viareggio Prize (shared in 1957 by such figures as Italo Calvino and Pier Paolo Pasolini).[84]

Dolci's particular talent lay in the way he was able to place a human face on the dry statistics of extreme poverty.[85] He interviewed ragpickers, stevedores, street cleaners, shoemakers, hawkers of vegetables, frog hunters, thieves, beggars, prostitutes, purveyors of spells and magic—the legions of wretched individuals who inhabited the dank alleyways between Palermo's Byzantine Cathedral and the Baroque Palace of Justice. While meticulously cataloguing the fact that families of seven, ten, or thirteen persons lived in single rooms without windows or toilets (they relieved themselves along the railroad tracks), Dolci also recorded their dreams, anger, and illusions:

[A frog hunter:]

When you've sliced the head off a frog, its eyes seem to go on watching you, just the way the eyes in a painting seem to follow you. When all the heads are cut off, it's like a real massacre. . . . The rich people that keep all their land and money for themselves, and never give us a thought, and let us starve to death—they ought to dream at night about a basket full of heads—not frogs' heads, but the heads of all the men and women they've killed—yes, they ought to dream about all those eyes in all those faces just watching and watching them.

[A sixty-year-old woman who cleaned fish:]

Most people vote DC [Christian Democrat] because if they vote DC they're voting for our Lord.

[A fruit hawker:]

Just before the elections some priests came around to teach the kids their catechism. We cleaned up the courtyard as much as we could, cleared away the slop and stamped the earth down flat. After they gave the children two or three lessons, they brought a projector along and started showing a movie all about the Madonna and the saints. But in spite of what we'd done the priests couldn't stand the filth, and the kids were too much for them—they wouldn't sit still and pay attention—so they packed up the film in the middle, and off they went with the kids shouting dirty words at them: "You give us a pain in the ass, you shits! You only come here when there's an election! Screw you!"

[A jailed shepherd:]

I understand much more about cows and sheep and goats than I do about Christians. . . . My animals, they've showed much more love for me than Christians have. Some of them always stayed close to me. I had a kid and a lamb that used to follow me wherever I went. If I had a little bit of bread, I used to share it with them. They got so tame they'd even eat pasta and tomato sauce . . . I hardly ever saw my father—he was either away in the army or away in prison, and when they let him out he wasn't allowed to leave the village. My mother and my brothers love me, but nobody, not even God himself, has ever cared about me as much as that kid and that lamb did.

[A "bandit":]

My wife was cooking some pasta for our supper when a little girl came in. "Donna Titidda," she said, "Mamma says when you've finished cooking the pasta, can she have the water you boiled it in, please?" My wife nodded like she didn't even hear her, but the thing struck me as being so strange that, just out of curiosity, I asked the kid why her mother wanted it. She told me they hadn't had anything to eat for three days. "Mamma has been trying to nurse the baby, but her milk has dried up. She thought maybe if she drank the pasta water, the milk would come back." . . . [My wife and I] both had tears in our eyes. As soon as the kid had gone, we set the table and sat down to our supper. . . . "Franco," [my wife said] "I'm not hungry, would you mind if I gave my share to the kids?" "I'm not hungry either," I said, "We'll take them over the whole works." That night, it was the third night of our honeymoon, we went to bed on an empty stomach. But it was worth it, knowing that for just one night we were able to give those kids a meal.[86]

In June 1957, just after *Report from Palermo* had won the Viareggio Prize, the Rome chief of police declared the book "pornographic" and had it banned. He claimed that certain passages from the testimonials of a prostitute and a pickpocket were unnecessarily explicit in their description of sexual acts.[87] Dolci was summoned before a magistrate in Rome and sentenced to two months' imprisonment. Once again, Italian intellectuals rallied to his side and prestigious lawyers offered to defend him for free. Dolci appealed his case, and the judgment against him was overturned the following year—much to the displeasure of the Vatican, which issued a formal statement of its disapproval.[88]

Indeed, the Catholic Church had become one of Dolci's most persistent critics. Like the Catholic hierarchy in Spain, the Sicilian clergy had for centuries provided a crucial bulwark against social change, steadfastly defending the privileges of the powerful and preaching deference and other-worldly rewards to the peasants.[89] Dolci's work clearly threatened this ancient power structure; and as early as 1954 the village priest in Trappeto had begun warning his parishioners to shun this "Communist sympathizer."[90] This label was highly misleading, for Dolci had not only refused to join any political party but had made a special point of avoiding all political entanglements—precisely so as to preclude such accusations of partisanship. While there could be no question that Dolci's allegiances and sympathies leaned sharply toward the left of the political spectrum, his greatest allegiance was to a personal, and highly eclectic, pantheon of historical figures. Lenin and Marx did have a place within this pantheon because they had championed the cause of the earth's wretched masses; but Dolci vehemently rejected the Marxist-Leninist notion of violent revolution led by a "vanguard elite." The greatest revolutionaries, in his view, were those religious figures, scientists, and artistic pioneers who had changed the world through the power of their insight or moral example: Bach, Einstein, Gandhi, Kant, Buddha, Martin Luther King, and (perhaps most of all) Saint Francis of Assisi. "Often," Dolci was to write in a 1968 essay,

> those of us who seek change tend to admire violent revolutionary forces, not because those forces offer the only possible avenue of change, . . . but because they are the only ones that have the courage to exist at all.
>
> But whoever thinks that violence represents the highest form of struggle, the ultimate way to resolve conflicts, is still relying on a very limited vision of humankind. Those who have had real revolutionary experience know that if you want to change a situation, you must appeal to a moral level that lies beyond the material level and above the reigning worldview; . . . in this way, your action becomes revolutionary in an even deeper sense, because it helps generate a new culture, new capabilities and instincts within people—in short, a new human nature. Personally, I am convinced that peace can only come through nonviolent revolutionary action . . . ; for violence, even when it is directed toward generous goals, still contains within itself the seed of death.[91]

Not surprisingly, the officials of the Catholic Church remained uninterested by these nuances in Dolci's thought; they perceived him (accurately) as an implacable enemy of that long-established social hierarchy in which their powerful institutions had flourished. Thus, the Church's hostility continued to grow, reaching a peak in 1964, when Sicily's Cardinal Ernesto Ruffini issued a pastoral letter denouncing Dolci as one of the three deadly plagues afflicting the island (the other two were the mafia and the critical novel by Giuseppe Tomasi di Lampedusa, *The Leopard*). Dolci never directly responded to these kinds of attacks, preferring to avoid any open confrontation. By the late 1960s, moreover, the influence of liberalizing tendencies within the Church made its way into Sicily, and the clergy's opposition to Dolci gradually diminished.

Throughout the spring and summer of 1957, Dolci continued to divide his time between Partinico and the slums of Palermo. He established a regular correspondence with Giulio Pastore, the head of the Cassa Per il Mezzogiorno (or "Southern Fund"); for Dolci had discovered that Pastore was a Christian Democrat who earnestly wanted to do all he could for the southern poor.[92] The *Cassa* was funding the construction of highways and transportation infrastructures throughout Southern Italy, and Dolci hoped that these state-supported measures could be coordinated with the work of local activists like himself— creating, if possible, "an integrated effort that brought together planning 'from above' and initiatives 'from below.'"[93] In November 1957 he organized a three-day conference in Palermo, bringing together experts from all over Italy to discuss "a new political strategy for full employment."[94] In order to publicize this conference, he and his friend Franco Alasia fasted for thirteen days in one of the subhuman hovels of *Cortile Cascino,* where an infant had been gnawed to death by rats the preceding summer.

On January 1, 1958, Dolci read in the newspapers that he had just been awarded the Soviet Union's Lenin Peace Prize, which carried a cash award of $27,000. Only the preceding year, Italy's Socialist leader Pietro Nenni had turned down the same prize, with explicit references to the events in Budapest of 1956. Dolci, however, decided to accept the prize, announcing his intention of founding a new center to combat the chronic unemployment in Sicily. Within days, he faced a huge outcry, both in the Italian press and among his numerous friends and supporters.[95] The substance of the accusations against him was that he had allowed himself to be used by the Soviets; for by funding his work, they were now established as his respectable "collaborators." According to his critics, Dolci had allowed his priceless stance of political neutrality to be co-opted for the sake of dirty money from the world's leading totalitarian state.

On January 8, for instance, Dolci received an urgent letter from his friend Ignazio Silone (author of the novel *Bread and Wine,* and an advocate of a European "Third Way" between the two blocs in the Cold War). The tone of Silone's letter made clear its author's deep affection for Dolci, but its message was also bitterly clear. Dolci had badly fooled himself, Silone wrote, if he thought the awarding of the Lenin Prize meant that Khrushchev and the Soviet leaders were acknowledging any validity in Dolci's nonviolent methods. Dolci should have recognized that fallacy clearly enough in the whole functioning of the Soviet system. He should never have accepted the prize; but if he insisted on accepting it, then he should at least have stated frankly that he was taking tainted money because it was a large sum that made a big difference in a worthy cause. And Silone concluded:

> In any spiritual vocation, the most dangerous temptation may be that of effectiveness. Do you remember the argument of the Grand Inquisitor? Can't you see the sorry state to which the Catholic Church has fallen? The great difficulty is remaining faithful to one's own intuition of what is right, without giving up one's effectiveness.[96]

Dolci defended his actions on January 16 in a lengthy statement to the press. Even if there was a possibility of ulterior motives behind the act of generosity, he argued, the only way to break out of the endless cycle of distrust and aggression was to begin—first on one side then on the other—to take a genuinely peaceful gesture at face value and to act upon it as such. "Reality is complex," he wrote, and human beings have sought through the ages to understand it and simplify it. They have produced syntheses which they have called, for example, Christianity, Liberalism, Gandhism, Socialism. Each group, in its own time, manages to grasp a fragment of the truth. This is why it is essential for us to remain open to each other, so that we can share in the values conquered by others. Reality will be more perfectly discovered, and the truth realized, insofar as diverse groups learn how to coexist and, without losing their integrity, work together. . . .

Peace will not come suddenly one fine day, by a sort of magic between the two [Cold War] blocs. . . . The beginning of peace lies in knowing when to accept a reasonable proposal from the "Other Side" because it is a good thing—to regard it as a bridge being built, rather than as a Trojan Horse.[97]

Which "neutralist" position was the more far-seeing one—Silone's or Dolci's? Obviously, the question did not admit a pat answer. Silone based his position on a deep distrust of both superpowers, and on the desire to remain free from all forms of their interference. Dolci emphasized the fact that the influence of the superpowers constituted an inevitable aspect of European politics; it was better, he believed, to respond selectively to their policies, resisting them when they played their aggressive "Cold War game," cooperating with them when their actions seemed unobjectionable and constructive. This line of argument satisfied some of Dolci's supporters, like Capitini; it left others, like Silone, profoundly uneasy.[98] Undaunted, Dolci quickly began making plans to put the money from the Lenin prize to full use.

1958–1971: Broadening the Front

During the decade that followed, Dolci's projects advanced along three distinct gradients. In the foreground lay his activities as a local community organizer. At a broader level, he became increasingly absorbed by Italian national politics, especially by the links between mafia power and the state. Finally, he also began organizing international opposition to militarism, probing questions of peace and security among states. The interpenetration of these three concerns—the impossibility of truly solving problems at one level in separation from the others—became one of the central themes in his thought.

"One thing that has repeatedly amazed me," he told an international conference in New Delhi in 1962,

is to hear peace activists saying, at meetings like this one: "We didn't come here to discuss problems of a social or economic nature, but rather to confront the menace of nuclear weapons." . . . Can there be a genuine peace as long as the world is filled with hunger, poverty, ignorance, exploitation, unemployment, and all manner of structural obstacles to the full fruition of life?[99]

For Dolci, the phenomenon of war was directly linked to the more general problems of domination and resistance. It represented a continuation, on a larger scale, of power struggles that were already occurring in peacetime within each nation, and within each local community. The word "prepotente" recurred throughout his writings—an Italian term that denoted the arrogance of the powerful in their dealings with the humble and weak. He observed the way the two superpowers treated ostensibly "allied" governments like Hungary or South Vietnam. Were there not striking similarities, he asked, between those international relationships and the way the Italian state treated its weak and disunited citizens in Southern Italy? Naturally, one could point to important differences, both in scale and in style, but Dolci believed the similarities were also worth examining: the regular predominance of the larger "partner" in decision making, the dependency of the small on the large. How, he asked, could these dominative power relations be changed? What alternative shape of power might take their place?

Since he was primarily concerned with awakening a desire for change among the poor and the illiterate, Dolci considered it essential to express these problems with the greatest possible concreteness and simplicity. Accordingly, he based his conception of peace on the tension between two opposed forms of social order, which he called "the old structures" (in the sense that they needed to be analyzed, opposed, and discarded) and "the new structures" (which still had to be clearly identified, invented, built up, and solidified).[100] Out of several *autoanalisi popolari* which he organized in Partinico and Trappeto during the mid-1960s, the following rough oppositions emerged:

The old politician	*The new politician*
1. commands	1. coordinates
2. centralizes	2. evokes the participation of individuals and groups
3. operates in secret	3. communicates
4. is rhetorical	4. is simple, essential
5. is corrupt, corrupting	5. is an educator
6. is violent	6. is nonviolent
7. gets on the winning side	7. gets on the side of the weakest and the lowest
8. changes opportunistically, seeking immediate advantages	8. tries to interpret reality in order to generate long-term changes
9. intervenes with negative sanctions; creates repetition, blockages	9. intervenes so as to elicit innovation

| 10. uses technology and information to impose his own will on others | 10. uses technology and information to bring out the best in others |
| 11. develops warlike traits | 11. develops the traits of a builder[101] |

For Dolci, the "old structures" seemed to underlie much of international politics, just as they permeated power relations in a national polity like Italy or a local community like Partinico. Working for peace, therefore, meant building the foundations for "new structures" at all three of these levels. "What we need to promote," he told his New Delhi audience in 1962,

> is a form of "action from below," through which a given population can become conscious of its own problems. Even the smallest local endeavor, if it is carried out with precision and good faith, can give people a taste of what it means to act together along a common front—and this is directly related to the subject of peace.
>
> It is not enough to put ourselves in the hands of leaders and "summits," whether they are political, religious, or cultural. . . . We need a new kind of community planning, born out of the people themselves—first at the local level, then at the regional level, then gradually on a larger scale, among entire peoples. This is what Aldo Capitini calls "nonviolent federalism from below." [102]

Like Leo Szilard, Dolci remained wary of the grandiose rhetoric used by some advocates of world government. In his opinion (as in Szilard's), what counted were the actual relations of power between local and large-scale institutions, not the theorizing of a well-intentioned intellectual. Dolci differed sharply from Szilard, however, in his prescriptions for change; for he believed that the lopsided power relations between "superpowers" and lesser nations could never be put to constructive use. Szilard had advocated a cooperative relationship between the superpowers in "managing" world affairs; but in Dolci's opinion, the intrinsic inequality of such an arrangement could only bring more suffering and violence in the long run. For him, therefore, the highest priority lay in awakening and organizing the forces of the grass roots, so as to counterbalance the antidemocratic tendencies of an increasingly centralized and top-heavy international order. "We need to make the transition," he wrote, "from an authoritarian and fragmented world to a pluricentric and coordinated world." [103] Dolci's efforts to realize this three-tiered conception of peace—local, regional/national, and international—were to occupy him throughout the turbulent decade of the 1960s.

In May 1958, Dolci had founded in Partinico his Centro Studi e Iniziative ("Center for Research and Initiatives"), which continued to function as his base of operations through the 1990s. Within five years, the Centro Studi had developed into a bustling institution with 60 staff members working in five towns of Western Sicily: 10 social workers, 3 agricultural technicians, 26 teachers, 1 doctor and 2 nurses, 2 field researchers, and 16 persons working in administration and general research. Ten of Dolci's coworkers were foreign volunteers: Swiss, German, Swedish, English, and American. In a brochure produced in 1963, Dolci explained that

> the work of the *Centro Studi* is by no means an attempt to usurp or replace the functions of the government agencies—indeed, it seeks to stimulate the government to take an ever greater role. Its goal is to fill the gap between the government and the people, between the planners and "the planned"—to mitigate the dehumanizing elements of economic planning, and to insure that human values are not left by the wayside in the process of development.[104]

Dolci's rationale in this aspect of his work was closely linked to the failure of the massive land-reform program the Italian government had undertaken in 1950 (simultaneously with the creation of the Cassa Per il Mezzogiorno). During the 1950s, the government had bought most of Southern Italy's uncultivated *latifundia*, then subdivided them into parcels and sold them (on long-term loans) to landless peasants; yet this ambitious restructuring had failed to create the society of independent farmers that its proponents intended. Although 113,000 peasant families acquired land, they represented only 1 percent of the rural population.[105] Those fortunate ones who established their own farms, moreover, tended to rely on ancient and inefficient traditions of cultivation, which further diminished the already low yield of the soil. Worst of all, perhaps, the land reform established a perverse form of bureaucratic clientelism among the peasantry. According to one team of scholars who studied the phenomenon,

> peasants joined [government-run cooperatives] in order to qualify for land allotments, credit, and other services, but their participation was strictly nominal. In effect, a cooperative consisted of several bureaucrats of the land reform agency and a roster of members. Being included in the roster was a matter of political patronage; loyalty to the government party was the "quid pro quo."[106]

This form of social order, in which a congeries of isolated families was lumped together in a bureaucratic and top-heavy organization imposed from outside, represented precisely the opposite of the healthy community that Dolci envisioned. The five centers that he created after 1958, therefore, sought to foster an ethic of self-sufficiency and mutual assistance among the peasants—an attitude of collective initiative that would be "cooperative" in more than mere name. In each of the villages around Partinico where the Centro Studi established a branch, Dolci usually assigned an agricultural technician and a social worker to serve side by side. The agricultural technician taught the peasant farmers how to use manure and other fertilizers (they had previously burned manure, as an age-old tradition); introduced them to the use of pest-control chemicals; and showed them how to rotate crops and make use of more productive seed strains. Having won the confidence of the farmers, sometimes by planting spectacularly productive demonstration plots, the agricultural expert organized meetings in which the peasants could begin to articulate their own grievances or aspirations. Frequently (as in the case of irrigation, for instance), they realized that only their collective voice would stand a chance of bringing about what they wanted; and they began to organize themselves in groups ranging from a wine-producing cooperative with ten or twenty members to an irrigation consortium with several hundred members.[107] Alongside these efforts by the agricultural experts, the social workers from the Centro Studi focused on problems of education, for which the villagers showed a passionate interest. In most of the branch centers, they organized special classes for the illiterate and a series of *doposcuole* (or extracurricular courses) for young children. In the village of Roccamena, with the help of local youths, they established a reading room with eight hundred books and launched a highly popular "local history project."[108]

A typical day for Dolci, as he worked in his Centro Studi, would begin at 3:30 A.M.—a habit he had kept up, with clockwork regularity, since his early days in Trappeto, when he had risen early to toil alongside the village fishermen. By the time most other Sicilians were beginning their day, Dolci had already spent several hours working on his own writing projects and correspondence. Then, as the early daylight broadened, he would make his way to the Centro Studi, stopping along the way to buy several newspapers, both local and national, for he considered it essential to avoid the isolation that could easily engulf a grass-roots organizer like himself. The Centro's offices in Partinico occupied the ground floor of a dilapidated building dating back to nineteenth-century baronial times; its whitewashed walls were clean but cracked, its cavernous rooms cluttered with worn-out furniture, stacks of books, copying machines, boxes of leaflets, and all the paraphernalia of an activist organization. The American writer Jerre Mangione described his first impressions after visiting the center one winter day in 1965:

> We returned to [Dolci's] office where staff members, representing the study centers in western Sicily under Danilo's jurisdiction, were gathering around a long conference table. I noticed for the first time what a barn of a room it was, with walls at least fourteen feet tall. The one opposite Danilo's desk bore a series of posters dominated by three headlines: "The Dam is prosperity," "The Dam is Progress," "The Dam is the Future." The wall nearest to the desk displayed large photographs of Einstein, Gandhi, and Lenin, ar-

ranged below each other in that descending order. The hugeness of the room accentuated its dampness and cold; the only heat came from a small circular contraption fueled by butane gas. As we sat around the conference table studying the agenda Franco [Alasia] had given each of us, I saw small clouds of vapor issuing from the mouths of the assembled.[109]

The Centro's pace of events could vary tremendously from one week to another, going from the steady routine of daily organizing and planning to the frenzied activity that preceded a public demonstration or a nonviolent campaign. On quiet days, Dolci would usually have several meetings to attend, as he followed the progress of the center's endeavors on several fronts simultaneously. After a quick break for lunch and a one-hour afternoon nap (also a matter of clockwork regularity), he might meet with foreign visitors, sometimes taking them personally on a tour of the most squalid sections of Spine Sante, or, in a different vein, telephoning his wife and children at home and inviting them to meet him at the beach for an impromptu swim in the Gulf of Castellamare. Then back to work at the Centro, where Dolci usually remained until at least 7 P.M. Going back home for dinner (which he usually helped his wife to prepare), he might spend the rest of the evening with visitors, playing Schubert and Mozart on an ancient but still serviceable piano, and intensely discussing the Centro's latest challenges and activities.

Dolci saw no barrier between his personal life and his work: he apparently considered every waking moment, whether devoted to "leisure" or more formally to the projects of the Centro, a precious opportunity for advancing his long-term goals. His coworkers learned not to be too surprised if a casual bit of conversation, exchanged in haste while Dolci was driving down the dusty streets of Partinico, might appear a few months later in one of his books, meticulously encompassed within an intricate web of theoretical ideas. In everyday interactions, whether with his family, visitors, or coworkers, Dolci maintained the same calm, earnest, pensive presence. Although he could be jovial on occasion, if things seemed to be going well with a particular project or enterprise, he almost never indulged in wisecracks or jokes. The obverse of this was also true: Dolci rarely gave signs of discouragement, no matter how grim the circumstances might appear. He could lose his temper, however, and berate his coworkers with a biting sharpness if he felt they had somehow failed in their duties; but he maintained a careful control in his dealings with the Centro's opponents or with public officials, speaking to them frankly but courteously.[110]

The Centro Studi had no fixed schedule, nor could it. Although Dolci and his coworkers painstakingly planned and organized their long-term projects, they also had to accommodate the often unpredictable crises and obstacles that inherently characterized their activism—and this made for an exhilarating, as well as exasperating, climate of work. One British writer, James McNeish, gave the following description of life in the Centro and in Partinico during the early 1960s:

> It was a strange world. You worked too long and ate too little, . . . [you] had no privacy, worked to no discipline, save what you imposed yourself, you had no criteria because the conditions were new and apart from Dolci's figures, which were accurate but limited, no statistics worth counting on. . . . You swore often, drank too much heavy wine and were comforted by the thought that if you fell seriously ill the nearest good hospital was in Rome. [In Partinico] you witnessed more quarrels, heard more screams, saw more mawkishness in a week than you had known in a lifetime. . . . Sometimes you found yourself believing, along with Gandhi, that it was the reformer and not society who was anxious for the reforms. Gradually you found yourself becoming involved in a love-hate relationship with the place, and knew that when you left there would be deep nostalgia for this curious organization and these smelly streets. You wondered how in hell you had become embroiled in what was really a pacifist outfit, and then you remembered that behind it all was the inspiration of this plodding, moon-faced man who had such an unshakeable belief in the basic goodness of human beings. You supposed that that was what kept him going. He neither smoked nor swore, and seldom drank, and worked harder than any three of you together. You waited for him to crack but he never did. He seemed to grow younger with the days.[111]

Dolci had initially founded his five centers with the money from the Lenin prize, but this provided funds for only a single year of operations. In 1958 and 1959, he was invited by philanthropic groups throughout Northern Europe to travel abroad and speak about his work, and it was in this way that the idea came to him of creating a loosely structured international partnership for development. "What we would like," he told one gathering in Switzerland in 1960,

> is that every city in the highly-developed areas should send some of the more level-headed and mature of their young people to work in the underdeveloped areas for at least two or three years. . . . We hope to find those who (either by teaching themselves or by showing us where teachers are to be found, or in any other way) will help us to set up a training school for workers in the underdeveloped areas.[112]

Not surprisingly, Dolci's firsthand accounts of his projects in Sicily elicited an enthusiastic and generous response from his audiences. By the end of 1960, active support groups were functioning in France, Switzerland, England, Belgium, West Germany, and Sweden, providing a regular flow of donations and volunteers for the Centro Studi. These foreign committees, soon afterward joined by a group in the United States, were to become Dolci's primary source of financial backing in the decades to come.

By 1961, therefore, Dolci's work had shifted from what was essentially a single man's campaign to a much broader, collective effort. This process of institutionalization proved only partially successful, however; for Dolci refused to relinquish the freedom of movement that he had enjoyed before the creation of the Centro Studi. On several occasions during the following decades, large groups of his coworkers split off from their association with him, complaining that he was not a "team player" and that he insisted on pursuing only those specific courses of action that matched his own ideas and principles. It was true, of course, that he had established the five branches of the Centro Studi as semiautonomous institutions with their own independent staff and sources of funding. Still, many of Dolci's coworkers came away with the feeling that despite the rhetoric of "coordination" and "consultation," the major policy decisions were usually, in the words of one participant, "either Danilo's ideas, or in line with Danilo's ideas, or else quietly pushed to the wayside."[113] Although plenty of volunteers usually arrived to take the place of those who had left, these kinds of internal conflicts seriously undermined the continuity of the Centro's projects and demoralized those who stayed on. To Dolci himself, however, they seemed an inevitable aspect of the collective work he was undertaking; for while he could not expect his coworkers to follow blindly in his footsteps, he also felt it unfair for them to expect that he would pursue all their manifold (and sometimes contradictory) plans of action.[114]

This was to become one of the central paradoxes of Dolci's career. On the one hand, he was fascinated by the theory of cooperative work, and devoted much of his attention during the following years to the study of how individuals and groups could make collective decisions in an authentically democratic way. On the other hand, many of those who came to work with him described him as a monumentally stubborn and willful individual, whose personality seemed far better suited to the solitary role of catalyst and innovator than to that of administering a relatively large institution. Dolci was of course sharply aware of his coworkers' criticisms, but he possessed an uncanny ability to suppress that awareness, or to explain away the negative comments, while continuing doggedly and placidly on his own way. One of his closest coworkers, Eduard Watjen, gave the following perceptive assessment in 1965:

> Danilo is incapable of the kind of relationship that you and I consider friendship. He is a man in love with his ideas on how to help people; it is a blind love that often excludes the feelings of individuals. He literally stops listening if someone is saying something that it contrary to what he is thinking.[115]

This personal failing as a "team player," however, did not necessarily invalidate Dolci's subsequent theorizing about participatory democracy; for, as one of his disaffected ex-colleagues observed, "the value of Rousseau's *Emile,* as a theory of education, is not necessarily diminished by the fact that Rousseau himself was incapable of applying it to his own children."[116] Dolci's theories would have to be judged on their own merits; his actions, for their part, were to prove far more effective when he operated either alone or in concert with a small group of loyal followers. By the early 1970s, the scope of the Centro's operations had shrunk (appropriately, perhaps) to offices in Trappeto and Partinico, staffed by five to ten coworkers who were willing to adapt themselves to Dolci's often unpredictable lead.

The Dam, the Mafia, and the Italian State

In April 1960, Dolci convened his second major conference on poverty in Sicily, situating it in Palma di Montechiaro, the town that the novelist Tomasi di Lampedusa had rendered famous in *The Leopard.* Dolci had been working closely with Silvio Pampiglione, a professor of parasitology from the University of Rome, who had prepared a searing document on the disastrous conditions of public hygiene among the town's twenty thousand inhabitants; and he further broadened Pampiglione's indictment by publishing his fifth book of oral history and sociological research, *Spreco* ("Waste"), just as the conference was opening.[117] By this point in his career, Dolci's name was sufficiently well-known to draw an impressive array of participants to converge on this squalid Sicilian town. The group included internationally recognized scholars like René Dumont and Julian Huxley; writers like Carlo Levi, Leonardo Sciascia, and Elio Vittorini; and high-ranking Italian politicians (from both Left and Right).[118] Yet the conference was the last of its kind that Dolci organized; for despite the fact that it attracted international attention to the problems of Southern Italy, he was reluctantly forced to conclude, as the months went by, that it had produced very little in the way of tangible results.[119] "If we wanted a form of change that came 'from below' and not 'from above,'" he later explained,

> then it was essential for the local people to see concretely what kinds of change they themselves could bring about; it was necessary for them to comprehend their own latent power. So we needed to produce a shock in their experience—an event that would tear them away from their fatalism and self-doubt. . . . I gradually realized that the building of a major dam could provide precisely the point of leverage that we needed.[120]

As early as 1955, when he had first begun conducting *autoanalisi popolari* among the townsfolk of Partinico, Dolci had become convinced that a dam on the Jato river could produce a drastic transformation of the local economy. He had initiated a lengthy correspondence with regional officials, who had eventually agreed (in 1956) to conduct a technical survey of the Jato basin. In 1957, the completed survey had indicated that the Jato was indeed a suitable site for a dam. While absorbed with his work in Palermo, Dolci had continued to press the *Cassa* in Rome to proceed with construction; and in 1959 he had been delighted to receive word that the official "green light" had finally come through. Late in 1959, the Sicilian regional government issued a public call for bids on the Jato project. Mysteriously, not a single construction company made a bid.

By 1960, it became clear to Dolci that the dam project was being obstructed by hidden interests—and he suspected (rightly, it turned out) that the Jato dam had run afoul of the mafia. Up to this point in his career, Dolci had never directly challenged this shadowy organization. He had denounced its negative impact on social progress, charting the precise number and location of annual mafia murders; but he had not openly sought to organize peasants *against* the mafia, nor had his projects directly clashed with mafia interests. Now, however, he had inadvertently embarked on a path that placed him in open confrontation with a local branch of this complex criminal network.

The mafia, according to scholars working from the perspective of the 1980s, was undergoing in these years a major transition from its traditional rural base to a more sophisticated set of operations founded on urban construction and smuggling.[121] Where once the *mafiosi* had concentrated on extortion, kidnapping, and cattle rustling, now they were moving increasingly into cities like Palermo, where they could reap huge profits in land speculation, public construction projects, and the control of wholesale commerce. Their typical victim in the 1950s had been either the isolated peasant who refused to respond to extortion threats, or else the rural trade-union organizer, like Salvatore Carnevale, whose activities threatened the monopoly of power held by local bosses. Carnevale had become a famous folk hero among the Sicilian poor after being gunned down in 1955, both because of the brazen fearlessness with which he had challenged the mafia, and because his story symbolized the obscure fate of dozens of young peasant activists like him who had been systematically murdered since 1945.[122] During the 1960s, however, rural violence sharply declined, as the locus of mafia activity shifted into the coastal cities. Especially in Palermo (where the stakes had become particularly high), rival mafia clans began to engage in open warfare, killing each other with a fratricidal ruthlessness that would have been inconceivable only a decade before.

The persons who opposed the Jato dam were probably connected with what was known as "the water-mafia"—a typical expression of the older, rural power structures of the 1950s. These were individuals who controlled access to existing springs and irrigation conduits, and who realized that a large public dam would ruin their lucrative business. In a more diffuse sense, they also formed part of a broader group of *mafiosi* who feared that any major transformation of the region's economy would threaten their control over the peasants.[123] Only a few years before, they had successfully blocked the construction of a dam above the nearby town of Corleone;[124] and they were evidently well-connected enough to ensure that no Sicilian construction company would place a bid to build the Jato dam.

Suspecting that this was the case, Dolci began writing regular letters to Giulio Pastore, head of the *Cassa* in Rome, urging him to take direct control over the Jato project and to extend the bidding process to the nationwide level. Early in 1960, accordingly, a large Roman firm made a successful bid of $25 million, and government representatives began the arduous procedure of buying the private lands that would eventually be flooded.

The *mafiosi* of Partinico retaliated on two fronts. Between 1961 and 1962, they formed an organization supposedly designed to protect the peasants who were selling their land to the government; this "committee," openly orchestrated by Partinico's alleged mafia boss, Gaspare Centineo, stalled the land-acquisition process by setting absurdly high prices.[125] In addition, the mafia sent threatening letters to the technicians from Rome who were drawing up blueprints for the dam. In August 1961, they burned down the house of a Socialist leader who had been actively promoting the dam among the residents of Partinico.[126] By the summer of 1962, these kinds of tactics had amply demonstrated their efficacy: the Jato project had ground to a complete halt, and two officials of the land reform agency quietly informed Dolci that the dam might never be built.[127] On the evening of July 26, he and Franco Alasia arranged a direct meeting with Gaspare Centineo, in an effort to resume negotiations and to find out what kind of price the "peasants' committee" might be willing to accept for their land. Centineo told Dolci: "For us, this land is priceless. . . . Anyone who tries to get their hands on it had better watch out."[128]

A week later, Dolci launched a major nonviolent campaign. On August 7, he sent a letter to the *Cassa* in Rome announcing that in September he would undertake another fast—the first since 1957.[129] Throughout the month of August, the sixty members of the Centro Studi and its branch offices suspended all their other projects and concentrated on rousing the population of Partinico. They designed colorful posters and splayed them on the walls of the town; they wrote abroad to their support committees, asking them to send telegrams and letters of solidarity to public officials from the local to the national level; and they organized dozens of meetings among the people of Partinico, so that they could discuss and evaluate the idea of the dam for themselves.[130] Perhaps most important, Dolci's coworkers confronted the local civic and political organizations one by one, publicly challenging them to declare whether they wanted the dam or not, and "whether they wanted mafia water or democratic water."[131]

By August 28, city officials had formed a "Working Committee for the Dam," headed by the Christian Democratic mayor of Partinico and supported by the trade unions and all the major political parties, from the Communists to the neo-Fascist MSI.[132] "In this way," Dolci later explained, "we left the *mafiosi* out in the open. The alignment of forces was reversed."[133]

On September 7, Dolci began his fast, lying on a cot in one of the wretched houses of Spine Sante. Two days later, a throng of five thousand persons (roughly a fifth of the town's population) marched through the streets of Partinico, gathering in the main square to hear a speech by the regional secretary for agriculture.[134] Press coverage was overwhelmingly favorable, with the exception of one right-wing newspaper in Rome, *Il Popolo:* "This Danilo Dolci who fasts—or pretends to (who in fact checks on him night and day?)—is flanked by national and international communism. . . . The dam will be delayed just the same."[135] On September 14, the Sicilian regional president, the prefect, and the mayor of Partinico traveled to Rome to meet with officials of the *Cassa;* Dolci began suffering from acidosis but refused to allow sugar to be mixed into his drinking water.[136] On September 16, the ninth day of the fast, the *Cassa* issued a public statement promising that it would directly oversee the acquisition of lands and guaranteeing that actual construction would begin within five months. Dolci immediately wrote to Pastore to thank him, and ended his fast.

The deeper impact of this nonviolent campaign only became visible with the passing of time. At the most obvious level, it resulted in the speedy construction of the dam: the first heavy equipment began excavating at the site, as promised, in February 1963; five hundred local men labored in three continuous shifts, round the clock, for the next five years; and the dam was completed in 1968. By the early 1970s, more than 7,000 hectares (17,500 acres) were being irrigated. Most of these lands belonged to small-scale, independent farmers who were thus able to shift their primary crops from wheat (which had required little water) to the more lucrative and labor-intensive cultivation of fruit and vegetables for export to the North. This expansion of agriculture, estimated by Dolci's technicians as a net increase of 3,200 jobs, immediately stimulated a concomitant growth in services and commerce, thereby raising the quality of life not just for farmers but for broad segments of the local population.[137] Perhaps the most tangible sign of the new prosperity in the 1970s was the widespread return of emigrants from Northern Europe, eager to settle once again in Partinico now that work was available.[138] Of course, this local economic transformation was inseparable from the broader growth that Southern Italy had experienced in the three decades after World War II. Nevertheless, the crucial role played by the Jato dam in regenerating the local economy was obvious to the region's inhabitants; and when the city of Palermo attempted, in the mid-1980s, to divert large amounts of water from the Jato reservoir for its own consumption, the entire countryside around Partinico erupted in spontaneous (and effective) protest.[139]

Not only had the land itself been transformed from an arid plain into an expanse of green vineyards and flowering orchards, but the people of Partinico had changed significantly as well. One of the workers who helped build the dam (a man named Serra) later described how the process of organizing against the mafia, in order to get construction started, had paved the way for other forms of self-organization that eventually followed. "At first there was nothing," he explained to Dolci in 1965: "The workers went to their jobs on the dam like sheep. No one in Partinico really knew what a workers' organization was." Gradually, during the spring of 1963, Serra and twenty of his fellow dam workers banded together to form a workers' committee.

> We went and informed the chief engineer of our decision. He told us it wasn't really necessary, because the workers would be treated well and the company would meet all its commitments. But he said if we really wanted to proceed we were free to do so.

By December 1963, the committee of dam workers had grown to 108 members, with regularly elected officers, and had affiliated itself with local trade unions. Early in 1964 it organized a brief and successful strike, because the company had reneged on its contractual obligation to reimburse workers if they used their own tools. But most important of all, for Serra and his associates, was the sense of dignity that went along with self-government.

> On May 1, 1964, we held an important *festa* in the valley where the lake was going to be. There was music, singers; those of us in the workers' committee brought fifty liters of wine—the best wine from Partinico—so that the fellows from other parts of Italy could taste it. We danced, there were about fifteen hundred of us. And then we had the satisfaction of taking our families to visit the work site and the tunnels. We had asked the directors for permission to do this, and they said yes, as long as we took the responsibility on ourselves. All our wives and children got to see the work we're doing.
>
> Being organized is like a *caramella* [candy], it's a taste you develop, and your mouth gets used to it, the sweetness of being respected.[140]

Later, when the first water from the dam started to flow in 1971, a similar process of "organization from below" took place. The eight hundred peasants whose farms were going to be irrigated immediately formed a cooperative, the "Jato Irrigation Consortium," which oversaw the distribution of water and periodically elected its own governing body. The peasants knew all too well that if they allowed the regional government to administer irrigation, it might soon be in mafia hands once again.[141]

For Dolci, in 1962, this first confrontation with the mafia over the Jato dam seemed to require further investigation. He had read the path-breaking (and courageous) book on the symbiosis between *mafiosi* and politicians recently published by Michele Pantaleone, and he felt that it was necessary to pursue this link still further, focusing sharply on a few specific individuals so as to compile documentation that was as detailed and explicit as possible.[142] Earlier in the year, the Italian Parliament (after years of categorical denials that the mafia existed at all) had finally created an official commission to inquire into alleged mafia activities. Dolci decided to prepare a report for this commission on the leading local *mafiosi* and their political connections.

The two most important politicians from the Partinico region in the 1960s were Calogero Volpe and Bernardo Mattarella. Both had climbed to national prominence through the ranks of the Christian Democratic party, the former becoming a member of Parliament in Rome, the latter holding major ministerial positions (transportation, foreign trade, agriculture) in various Christian Democratic administrations during the 1950s and 1960s. Both were widely rumored to be associated with the mafia.

Throughout 1963 and 1964, Dolci and his friend Franco Alasia quietly gathered information about these two politicians (while continuing their regular work with the Centro Studi). They interviewed dozens of persons, from the city of Palermo to Mattarella's hometown of Castellamare del Golfo, putting together an increasingly clear picture of the mutual support between local gangsters and these two influential men. As the evidence accumulated, they began asking their witnesses to take the momentous step of formalizing their statements in a signed deposition. Their names, Dolci and Alasia assured them, would be known only to the members of the Parliamentary Anti-Mafia Commission. Would they be willing to risk their lives by breaking the age-old code of silence (*omertà*) that had protected the mafia since its early days? To the surprise of Dolci and Alasia, a substantial number of the witnesses made up their minds to go along with this request.[143] As one of them, Vito Ferrante, was to explain in an ensuing trial:

> I am a humble clerk, I live in a small centre, Castellamare del Golfo, which is still dominated by *omertà* and fear. So I know what I'm up against, I know what I risk in making these declarations; but I mean to testify, because I am one of the people who believes in a better world.[144]

On September 22, 1965, Dolci and Alasia held a press conference in Rome. They presented extracts from fifty of the depositions they had received (withholding the witnesses' names, of course), and announced that this dossier was being submitted to the Anti-Mafia Commission the same day. Dozens of eye-witnesses, Dolci told the Italian and foreign newspapermen, were testifying that they had seen Volpe and Mattarella meeting regularly and ostentatiously with the leading *mafiosi* of the Western Sicilian region. These witnesses gave the names of all those involved and provided the exact location and time of each meeting. In addition, they described in detail how the *mafiosi* procured votes for these two politicians, both through intimidation and through the distribution of gifts.[145]

By making his accusations in this open and highly publicized manner, Dolci had effectively protected himself and his witnesses from mafia retaliation; for if any of them were killed, it would now make Mattarella and Volpe look more guilty than ever. Even if a precise link between the two politicians and the murder of a witness were never established, the resulting suspicion would destroy their political careers. "In certain situations," Dolci later explained,

> the most certain way to defend oneself is to attack in public. I myself had only recently had a narrow escape, one morning at 4 a.m., as I was walking to the *Centro* with Franco for an early start on the day's work. Franco saw a shotgun pointed at me from a passing car, and pushed me against a wall, jumping between me and the gun.[146]

A few days after the press conference (which received broad coverage both in Italy and abroad), Mattarella and Volpe sued Dolci for libel. A trial date was set for March 1966.

During the week of January 10–16, 1966, Dolci organized a series of public meetings in Mattarella's hometown of Castellamare—meetings in which the town's citizens might openly discuss the subject of the mafia for the first time, thereby helping to undermine the still powerful code of *omertà*. In a leaflet distributed by the Centro Studi to publicize this antimafia campaign, he wrote:

> Government politicians—not all, of course, and certainly not the better ones—[have been] entrusting the responsibilities of Minister and Under-Secretary to men of the mafia, maintaining them in office even after the Anti-Mafia Commission has initiated serious proceedings against them. The mafia flourishes—the time has come to state this quite plainly—not only in Parliament but actually in the Italian Government.[147]

The police chiefs of Castellamare and Palermo promptly brought charges against Dolci, accusing him of "vilifying the institutions of the State." They added these charges to those already pending before the Tribunal in Rome.[148]

Undeterred, Dolci proceeded with the public meetings, which drew ever-larger crowds as the days went by and evoked passionate exchanges among the local citizens:

FIRST GENTLEMAN: I can state that in Castellamare I don't know any *mafiosi* at all. Either we're all *mafiosi*, or there aren't any.

SECOND GENTLEMAN (ironical): How can you, of all people, say that? (Laughter and applause) You of all people, knowing what you know, in public, for all these people to hear—*you* come here and say that in Castellamare either we're all scoundrels or else there aren't any scoundrels! What about when they shot at you that time, what were they? Honest men? (Confusion, shouting) . . .

THIRD GENTLEMAN: I've been digging the earth all my life— up till this very day I've always worked on the land, digging the earth, and everybody in Castellamare knows me. I've never studied, but I know from my own experience that there's a difference between crime and mafia. Crime means the ordinary type of thief—and may I say that crime is a lot less evil than the mafia, and the mafia as it exists in Castellamare is much more serious than ordinary crime. . . .

FOURTH GENTLEMAN: It's fear that makes us hold back. We're afraid of the harm they could do to us and our families.[149]

Two weeks later, in Rome, Italian Prime Minister Aldo Moro reshuffled his Cabinet, removing Bernardo Mattarella from his position as minister of foreign trade and excluding him from the new Cabinet.[150] "It is for me an occasion for the deepest regret," Moro wrote to Mattarella, "that I have had to forego your collaboration." And he added his wish that his Sicilian colleague might "one day again assume a position of governmental responsibility."[151]

On March 15, the trial began. Dolci was defended (once again) by lawyers who volunteered their services free of charge. Mattarella and Volpe, for their part, had chosen two lawyers whose careers were in themselves revealing. One of them, Girolamo Bellavista, had been the lawyer of Don Calò Vizzini, the acknowledged "Boss of bosses" within the Sicilian mafia between 1943 and 1954.[152] The other lawyer, Giovanni Leone, had a more distinguished career: in 1955, he had successfully defended the individuals accused of murdering the popular trade unionist Salvatore Carnevale; in 1963, after rising to the highest echelons of the Christian Democratic party, he had served as prime minister of Italy during a four-month round of interparty negotiations. (Later, in 1971, he was to be elected president of Italy; and in 1978, he became the first Italian president to resign under duress, after facing charges of fiscal fraud, illicit trafficking in the construction industry, and complicity in receiving kickbacks from the Lockheed Corporation.)[153]

The trial proceeded with dispatch. Throughout March, April, and May, Mattarella and Volpe brought forward character witnesses who vouched for their longstanding opposition to the mafia. In June, the court heard the testimony of Vito Ferrante, one of the few of Dolci's witnesses who was willing to confirm his deposition in public. The court then adjourned for the summer, and Dolci used this precious interval of time to muster a new group of witnesses who would be willing to testify openly, as Ferrante had done. The new witnesses included Don Giacomo Caiozzo, the eighty-one-year-old priest of Castellamare, and several others who were ready to present evidence linking Mattarella directly to the notorious Sicilian bandit Salvatore Giuliano.[154] This raised the stakes considerably in the trial, for the alleged collusion between certain mysterious political figures and Giuliano in suppressing the postwar peasants' movement had been a subject of intense controversy since the late 1940s.[155]

When the trial reopened in the fall, the lawyers for Mattarella and Volpe predictably opposed any introduction of new witnesses on Dolci's behalf. The public prosecutor, too, "opposed any evidence concerning the dealings Mattarella had with Giuliano and his associates"; he asked the court to reject Dolci's new dossier of evidence on the grounds that "the documents . . . are not those concerning which the [libel suit] was brought."[156] On December 9, without giving any explanation, the presiding judge rejected the introduction of Dolci's key witnesses. At this point, Dolci and Alasia decided that the trial was a travesty, and they sent a letter to the Court in January announcing that under these circumstances they would no longer even attempt to defend themselves. The remainder of the trial, therefore, took place with Dolci and Alasia absent from the courtroom. They were duly found guilty in June 1967 and sentenced to two years' imprisonment, along with heavy fines.[157]

"We appealed, of course," Dolci later recalled. "One part of the comedy was over."[158] The final act of the "comedy" took place after ten more years of intermittent judicial wrangling. Both Mattarella and Volpe eventually retired; Volpe died in 1976. One year later, in February 1977, an appeals court in Rome concluded its reexamination of the evidence and declared Dolci innocent of libel. "Volpe was a *mafioso*," ran the headlines in the newspapers; the case of Mattarella was still pending.[159] "At least," commented Dolci in his characteristically laconic manner, "the facts have now been officially recognized."[160]

Why did the mafia not kill Dolci, when it routinely eliminated so many others who crossed its path? The answer probably lies in a combination of several factors. Unlike the typical mafia targets of the 1950s and early 1960s, Dolci was not an isolated peasant but an internationally renowned figure whose murder would inevitably have triggered an extensive investigation. Unlike activists like Salvatore Carnevale, he did not allow his enemies to remain anonymous; instead, he made his accusations publicly, so that the identities of those who would want him killed would be obvious to all. Finally, he carefully avoided any confrontation with the purely criminal factions of the mafia, whose leaders would almost certainly have ordered him killed, regardless of his fame; instead, he focused on the political protectors of the mafia, who (once they had been publicly accused) were forced to fight back through legal channels in order to preserve their legitimacy as government officials. By maintaining this delicate balance between the potential benefits to the mafia of having him silenced, and the potential costs that his murder would incur, Dolci was able to bring about an unprecedented public airing of the connections between mafia and politics within the Italian government.

During the following decades, the mafia continued to flourish in Sicily, openly challenging the authority of the Italian state. The bold murders in 1982 (and again in 1992) of high-level antimafia investigators and magistrates, and the clamorous "maxi-trial" of several hundred *mafiosi* that began in the mid-1980s, gave evidence of a continuing stand-off between these two foci of power in Southern Italy. Dolci's denunciation of Mattarella and Volpe in the 1960s certainly had not "solved" the problem of the mafia; rather, it had called attention to this problem, in new and particularly graphic terms. To those who had sought to deny the extent of mafia infiltration into the structures of the Italian state, Dolci had responded with irrefutable evidence. To those who feared that opposing the mafia was too dangerous a task for private citizens, he and his fellow witnesses had clearly demonstrated the potential strength of organized, public action. In this sense, his skirmish with the mafia constituted a significant episode in the ongoing struggle that has plagued the Italian republic since World War II—the struggle between the rule of law and the reign of patronage, corruption, and *omertà*.[161]

The International Horizon

As far back as the 1950s, Aldo Capitini had sought to bring out the implicit link between Dolci's nonviolent pressures for social change and the broader movement to oppose militarism and to legitimize conscientious objection in Italy.[162] Dolci's direct interest in international politics, however, was first stimulated by a series of travels he undertook after 1961, visiting the United States, the Soviet Union, Africa, and Latin America in several successive summers.[163] Since he had become famous as a nonviolent campaigner, he was also invited with growing frequency to participate in international conferences of peace activists—from New Delhi and Moscow in 1962 to the Bertrand Russell Tribunal in 1966. As he reflected on his travels, and debated directly with longstanding pacifists like Martin Niemöller and A. J. Muste, his own ideas became steadily more general and global in scope.[164]

Dolci was quite explicit in pointing out the forms of international domination that he thought peace activists should oppose. He did not spare either side in the Cold War, nor did he exonerate the Europeans themselves from seeking to perpetuate their own forms of international hegemony. In his travel writings, he argued that the effect of American domination over Puerto Rico (for instance) was equally as stifling, in its own way, as Soviet hegemony over East Germany—just as the period of French domination over Senegal had produced its own profound legacy of distortions within the indigenous society.[165] As he compared what he saw with his own experiences in Sicily, he noted that the common denominator was often the same: a social system imposed from alien and far-away centers of power had done violence to local culture. The result had been widespread mentalities of apathy or dependency among the subordinate peoples. In Puerto Rico, he observed that despite the luxuriant vegetation of the region's natural environment, nearly all the agricultural products on sale in the local markets were imported from abroad—"onions, potatoes, tomatoes, lettuce, rice, even coffee."[166] In a rural town in Senegal, he observed that the local women were selling their silver tribal jewelry in order to buy plastic trinkets imported from Europe.[167] Countries like East Germany and Czechoslovakia became exemplars, in his mind, of a form of international clientelism:

> If we substitute the leader of the superpower for the local political leader, and similarly substitute the leaders of the satellite states for each member of the local clientelistic group, what we seem to have is a variant of clientelism on the international scale.[168]

Dolci maintained a highly skeptical attitude toward the ideological rhetoric of the Cold War, because his travels in the United States and the Soviet Union had convinced him that both these societies were founded on social dogmas that remained one-sided and fragmentary. The United States, he felt, had developed strong qualities of creativity and self-motivation at the level of the individual, yet remained immature at the level of collective, long-term planning.[169] The Soviet Union, for its part, had embarked on a valuable experiment in social planning, yet had foundered on a rigid form of centralization that stifled the initiative of the grass roots.[170] In 1963, he was given the opportunity to address this ideological issue before an East-West conference of peace activists in Norway, and he was deeply intrigued by the response he received:

> I explained my idea that a social transformation had to be sought on three levels simultaneously: that of the individual or local group, that of the regional group, and that of the larger structures, national or international.
>
> As I spoke, I noticed that delegates from the Eastern bloc seemed profoundly sceptical when I mentioned the need to elicit a greater sense of initiative and participation from among individual persons and local groups. Their response became progressively more positive, however, as I talked about regional organizations. When I got to the level of large-scale structures and the need for coordination and planning, they beamed.
>
> All the while, the exact opposite was happening among many of the western delegates: they were radiant when I emphasized the level of the individual, but became visibly troubled as I approached the level of large structures and long-term planning. . . .

It was a perfect example of an ideological filter—the symmetrical blind spots created by two opposed ideological traditions.[171]

Among these three levels in Dolci's conception of peace, it was clearly the international level that remained farthest from his own tangible experiences in Sicily. Compared to his innovations in local community building, his ideas about alternative structures of international politics remained rather vague and rudimentary; nor did he, like E. P. Thompson, carry his struggle directly to the military bases and politicians. Nevertheless, Dolci's principled opposition to militarism took several concrete forms in the 1960s.

During the first part of the decade, he sought to create direct links between his own Centro Studi and a wide network of antiwar organizations abroad. In 1962, he joined War Resisters International, the pacifist organization founded in Britain shortly after the First World War; he was promptly elected vice-chairman and participated actively in meetings and consultations throughout the following years. During the summer of 1962 he entered into correspondence with Bertrand Russell, who requested that Dolci fly to England to participate in an important sit-in by the Campaign for Nuclear Disarmament (CND). Dolci replied that the projected date for the sit-in (September 9) coincided exactly with his own scheduled fast for the Jato dam; but he added:

> Since, during September, we shall be busy here devoting all our energies to a nonviolent pressure drive, I thought it would be appropriate to coordinate our two dates, thus showing explicitly the reciprocal bond of solidarity existing between the two actions. . . .
> I am convinced that the cruelty and twisted views that you speak of in your letter exist objectively among people of great responsibility and among others as well (even if, as I think, these people are not in themselves cruel or twisted but, for the most part, closed and primitive, being limited culturally and morally). I also enclose some notes drawn up recently to clarify the connection between our work and the drive for peace.[172]

Russell immediately wrote back with an enthusiastic public statement to be released in Partinico:

> I wish to offer my most earnest support for [Danilo Dolci's] fast, and for the mass action of reclamation in Partinico. It is by such actions that the conscience of the world may be awakened, and it is in the same manner that we who are preoccupied with the struggle against nuclear war hope to alert mankind to our common danger. The cause is one cause; human dignity and human survival, human responsibility and the exercise of conscience.[173]

This exchange eventually led to a further strengthening of bonds in 1963, as Dolci became one of the founding sponsors of the Bertrand Russell Peace

Foundation. In the fall of 1963, when the Centro Studi launched a campaign for a second dam on the river Bruca near the village of Roccamena, CND sent down a representative, Peter Moule, to participate directly.

After a hiatus of several years (during which Dolci was concentrating his energy on Mattarella and Volpe), Russell again wrote to Dolci early in the summer of 1966. Dolci's name had received fresh international exposure the preceding year, when a committee of Swedish parliamentarians had formally proposed him as a candidate for the 1965 Nobel Peace Prize (the prize went to UNICEF instead).[174] Russell needed figures of Dolci's stature to sit on a War Crimes Tribunal he was organizing, a Tribunal in which the U.S. government would stand accused of unprovoked aggression and attempted genocide in Vietnam. Dolci, who had felt growing outrage at the escalating violence of the Vietnam War, agreed to participate.

During the summer and fall of 1966, however, Dolci began hearing reports about the Tribunal which puzzled and worried him. Russell had spoken initially of assembling a balanced and impartial group of prominent intellectuals, yet the eventual list of participants included only such well-known leftist figures as Jean-Paul Sartre, Simone de Beauvoir, and Isaac Deutscher.[175] To make matters worse, Russell's zealous aide, Ralph Schoenman, began making statements to the press in the name of the Tribunal, pronouncing what sounded like a "guilty" verdict before the Tribunal had even convened.[176] Dolci complained about this to Russell in August and October, emphasizing that he would withdraw from the endeavor unless a more even-handed approach were taken; and Russell responded reassuringly each time.[177] On November 13, Dolci flew to London for a consultative meeting with Russell and the other Tribunal members. "I was not satisfied by what I found," he later recalled.

> The issue, as I saw it, was not whether the U.S. war in Vietnam was a just or unjust war: I knew it was unjust. The real issue was to obtain a dossier of evidence—documents so clear and precise, so undeniably authentic—that they could be placed before the public and judged on their own merits. In this way, all those persons who had not yet confronted the war as a moral issue would be able to make up their own minds. . . .
>
> But the Tribunal seemed to have no clear purpose. At the London meeting, I remember, I was sitting next to Sartre. He proposed that the Tribunal focus on whether or not U.S. actions were violating basic principles of warfare like those set forth in the . . . [Hague and Geneva Conventions]. I could see the intelligence of this kind of proposal—especially given the vagueness and one-sidedness of what had already been said to the press. But it nonetheless remained unacceptable to me, because I couldn't agree that a war should be fought according to the "rules of the game." It meant, in effect, that war is legitimate as long as it respects the

"rights" of the wounded, of noncombatants, and so on. This was not enough for me.[178]

As tactfully as he could, Dolci withdrew from the Russell Tribunal, promising to take up the cause in his own way after his return to Italy. The Tribunal went on with its plans, issuing a strong condemnation of U.S. policy the following spring.

Dolci kept his promise. During the spring and summer of 1967 he and his coworkers at the Centro Studi contacted dozens of pacifist, religious, and left-wing organizations throughout Italy, sounding out their willingness to undertake a nationwide protest against the Vietnam War. Since the response was generally favorable, he convened a meeting of Italian peace activists in Milan early in October, proposing a 1,000-kilometer peace march for the following month. On November 4, accordingly, two separate columns of marchers (mostly university students) left Milan and Naples, singing songs and waving banners, and headed toward Rome.[179] Their numbers varied between several hundred and several thousand, depending on the areas they traversed; and their goal, as stated in the leaflets they handed out, was the following:

> To ask the Italian Government to dissociate itself completely from its current position of support for U.S. policy in Vietnam; to help pave the way for peace negotiations along the lines stipulated at the Geneva Conference of 1954; . . . to promote a new international politics, beyond the system of military blocs.[180]

On November 29, the two columns converged in Rome, their numbers swelling to the tens of thousands.[181] They gathered in front of the Italian Parliament, then marched to the American Embassy, where Dolci was permitted to pass through the dense ranks of riot troops to deliver a letter for President Johnson—a letter, according to the *New York Times,* which was "an emotional, personal appeal, [calling] for the immediate end to the bombing of North Vietnam."[182] The demonstrators then moved on to the nearby Piazza della Repubblica, where they heard speeches by students who had participated in the long trek. As one contemporary left-wing magazine commented:

> It was a new experience in the history of a democratic Italy: the experience of youths coming together, above and beyond the divisions of religious faith and party politics, to challenge the rigid modes of thinking that still permeate so much of Italian society.[183]

1971–1989: Pedagogy for Self-Rule

Dolci's absorption with international politics by no means implied an abandonment of his work in Sicily. In January 1968, a major earthquake struck the Belice valley in Western Sicily, leaving thousands homeless; the Centro Studi played a major role in channeling aid to the afflicted and in publicizing the corruption and inefficiency that hampered the government's relief efforts.[184] Two years later (in March 1970), when many of the homeless had still not received the slightest assistance from official sources, Dolci set up a powerful radio transmitter in Partinico, broadcasting the complaints of the Belice refugees throughout Southern Italy. This action constituted a direct challenge to the government's monopoly over all public broadcasting and was, therefore, forcibly interrupted by the police. Nevertheless, Dolci had effectively made his point, for the ensuing legal battle shamed the regional agencies into assuming direct responsibility for earthquake relief. It also contributed, as a side effect, to the nationwide legalization of private radio stations in 1976.[185]

In Trappeto, meanwhile, near the site of the old Borgo di Dio of 1952, the Centro Studi had secured funds from foreign donations to begin building a new Borgo—a modern conference center, equipped with a full-scale auditorium and accommodations for sixty persons. This project eventually became one of Dolci's major and tangible failures (though he himself was reluctant to regard it as such). The initial idea for the new Borgo had grown out of the "community development" efforts fostered by the five branches of the Centro Studi during the early 1960s; its intended function was summed up by its cumbersome name, "Center for the Training of Cadres for Organic Regional Planning." In Dolci's vision, it would become an important focal point for the revitalization of civic culture in Western Sicily—a stable school for local administrators and planners, staffed by a revolving group of Italian and foreign experts. Construction of an impressive quadrangle of buildings, overlooking the sea, had commenced in 1968; and three years later, after an expense of roughly $200,000, the new Borgo had been nearly completed.

By the early 1970s, however, the Centro Studi had itself changed significantly. It had shrunk to a more homogeneous set of ten to twelve persons, grouped around Dolci in Partinico; and its activities had steadily broadened in scope, encompassing projects of a national or international bearing as well as the local challenge of community development. The original purpose of the training center was therefore becoming somewhat anachronistic during the very period of its physical completion; for the training of regional planners no longer occupied the same central position in Dolci's work that it had a decade before. Thus, although he organized several dozen successful seminars on regional planning at the new Borgo during the 1970s, the building failed to become the nucleus of a self-sustaining educational institution. Instead, it was used to house periodic conferences on various subjects organized by Dolci and his coworkers, and for concerts and cultural events held by the people of Trappeto and Partinico. By the mid-1980s, the maintenance costs and mortgage payments were becoming a heavy burden on the finances of the Centro Studi; Dolci eventually decided to make the best of a difficult situation by selling the

Borgo (at cost) to the town of Trappeto. It was an outcome far short of Dolci's earlier hopes, but at least the debts of the Centro Studi had been paid off, and Trappeto had acquired its own modern community center.[186]

The early 1970s marked a crucial turning point in Dolci's career, a shift equally as profound as those that had occurred in 1952 (with his arrival in Trappeto) and 1958 (with the founding of the Centro Studi). Between 1969 and 1972, Dolci began making plans to build an experimental elementary school near Partinico; he commenced (somewhat gingerly) to write poetry again, after two decades of writing political prose and "giving voice to the illiterate"; and finally, he shifted his primary theoretical inquiries from the areas of social science and politics to those of pedagogy and philosophy. "I felt a need," he later explained, "to dig deeper than before, to look more directly at how our culture is formed."[187]

The causes of this reorientation were closely related to the turbulent events of Italian public life that came in the wake of 1968. In the economic sphere, Italy had risen with astounding rapidity from the status of a prostrate and war-ravaged nation in 1945 to that of a major industrial power by the mid-1960s.[188] In the political sphere, too, Italy had experienced two decades of relative quiet and stability.[189] During the late 1960s, however, this stability rapidly weakened. Sociologists and historians have pointed to many possible causes for the up-heavals surrounding the year 1968—from the disappointed expectations of a generation accustomed to ever-growing prosperity, to the frustrations of a "managed" society in which all significant political innovation was stifled or co-opted into the status quo.[190] Whatever the deeper causes, the fact remained that the broad social consensus of the first two postwar decades dramatically disintegrated. Starting in 1967, and culminating in the "Hot Autumn" of 1969, Italian workers began defying their own trade unions, organizing wildcat strikes that increasingly paralyzed the country's economy and public life. Universities erupted in an ongoing series of protests and demonstrations that continued far longer and more persistently in Italy than in France or West Germany. Political extremism of both Left and Right began to acquire an unprecedented weight, as new groups and factions formed; and the first of a harrowing series of terrorist incidents took place in Milan's Piazza Fontana late in 1969—the planting of a powerful bomb by neo-Fascists, killing sixteen and injuring ninety.[191]

For Dolci, these events posed a new and urgent set of questions. Italy had undeniably joined the foremost ranks of the industrialized nations: Was this necessarily a good thing? Where would this form of "progress" lead? Dolci was thus embarking on what might be called a "second-generation" development project. Moving beyond his earlier concerns with economic and social backwardness, he now began to focus his attention on the "advanced" industrial societies themselves. "In 1970 I looked around me," he later recalled, and saw the Jato dam rising up in its final stages. . . . I was aware that the income of the average local family was similarly going up, and that it would rise even faster once irrigation began. I saw the first of the emigrants making their hesitant return.

How to ensure that this new prosperity would not simply reinforce a conception of life based on the commercial models propounded on TV? How to develop a form of local culture that was solid in itself, while remaining open to the cultures of the world? . . .

I felt, more strongly than ever, a need to work within a broader scale of time. There is a Chinese proverb that says, "He who looks ten years into the future, plants trees; he who looks a hundred years into the future, plants human beings."[192]

The meaning of the word "realism" had undergone a subtle shift for Dolci, as his projects developed from the 1950s to the 1970s. Initially, like his mentor Don Zeno, Dolci had focused on making an immediate and tangible impact on the lives of those who were suffering around him. As the years went by, however, he had felt increasing frustration with these kinds of efforts, for they came to strike him as part of an endless cycle, like applying bandages to a chronically recurring wound. It was here that he began to think in truly long-range terms. "Realism," in this new sense, meant penetrating to the underlying causes of the malady rather than concentrating on the symptoms. These "causes," as he interpreted them, lay in the social habits and mental patterns associated with domination; only the very young, he believed, possessed sufficient flexibility to break the vicious cycle.

Perhaps his central hypothesis here was that wars do not occur because millions of "normal" people suddenly wax aggressive and try to conquer each other. Instead, Dolci suspected that wars were only the final consummation of social patterns widely accepted as "normal" in peacetime. Children play with guns, he observed, and adults point missiles at each other. Children grow up in families whose structure is often rigidly hierarchical, and adults establish elaborate systems of social stratification based on power, prestige, and wealth. Children are taught in school according to fixed and preordained curricula, and the vast majority of adults submits unquestioningly to a predigested view of reality concocted by the mass media. Can it be, Dolci asked himself, that these generational symmetries are only a coincidence? Or is it not the case that industrial society—both East and West—is shaping itself, replicating itself, in a way that profoundly contradicts the avowed social and ethical values of most modern individuals? While cherishing peace, equality, and freedom, he asked, are we not systematically enshrining violence, hierarchy, and uncritical conformism among our own children?[193]

Starting in the early 1970s, therefore, Dolci embarked on a totally new project—an experimental school devoted to the principle of thoroughgoing non-violence. He began by organizing a series of meetings with parents from Partinico, probing and questioning them about the kind of school they would want to create.[194] Since the most common request was for a school situated in the open countryside, he eventually bought a piece of land outside Partinico, on a hillside overlooking the sea. "From up there," he explained, "the children could observe the changing seasons in the valley below. Most of all, they could watch the works of irrigation transforming the fields, and become aware that the world can be changed."[195] Philanthropic groups in Sweden and West Germany donated money for the land and for the initial phase of construction; the school building itself was designed by two architects from Milan who volunteered their services. By the fall of 1975 an imposing, ultramodern structure had emerged amid the rocky foothills near Partinico; Dolci gave it the name of Mirto, adopting the peasants' traditional name for the surrounding valley. The school had a brook flowing through its courtyard, a series of broad, interconnected rooms with huge windows, and a stone amphitheater where the children could put on plays for the people of Partinico. On the plain below, the water from the Jato dam had produced a curving swath of green—the new citrus groves that Dolci had dreamed of seeing since the 1950s.

Although instruction formally began in 1975, with several groups of five- and six-year-olds, the school faced a continuous series of difficulties and obstructions. The only road to Mirto passed over an ancient bridge, which had fallen into acute disrepair; Dolci was forced to haggle, plead, and eventually to mount a nonviolent campaign before the regional public works office finally rebuilt the road nine years later.[196] An equally frustrating process of bureaucratic wrangling ensued at the level of the national state, as Dolci struggled to have Mirto accorded the status of a state-sponsored "experimental school." Five such schools already existed elsewhere in Italy, and Dolci had received assurances from government officials that they would quickly include Mirto within this innovative network. Yet it was not until 1983 that the Italian government at last began to subsidize the school; the Centro Studi was forced to suspend instruction several times because it lacked funds for teachers' salaries.[197]

Despite these obstacles, however, Dolci ultimately succeeded in developing Mirto into a stable center where he could bring his ideas on pedagogy and nonviolence toward a creative synthesis. His approach was largely empirical, but it resulted (over several years) in a set of practices that might have struck a professional pedagogist as a unique hybrid of the ideas of Maria Montessori and Paulo Freire. Like Montessori, Dolci sought to develop the creativity, inquisitiveness, and independent individuality of the child; yet he placed a far greater emphasis than Montessori on the building of social skills and group relationships.[198] Like Freire, he aimed at awakening a sense of collective initiative, of social potentials waiting to be realized, among his students; unlike Freire, he chose to work with schoolchildren rather than illiterate peasants, cultivating among them a taste for democratic decision making that might later come to fruition in the political habits of young adults.[199]

At the beginning of each school year, the five- and six-year-olds who were enrolled at Mirto came to school—at the insistence of Dolci and his fellow teachers—with a parent who had made plans to spend the entire day there. In this way, during the first seven to ten days of classes, the children were able to get accustomed to their new environment without the trauma frequently associated with an abrupt separation from the home. Dolci's idea here was that children should attend school on the basis of interest and desire rather than compulsion; and the same principle applied to the process of learning. Each morning, after the children had arrived, they assembled in small groups around low, circular tables. A teacher, too, sat at each table, and discussion began: one by one, proceeding clockwise as in an *autoanalisi popolare,* they were asked to propose what the activities of the day should be. According to one of the teachers who worked for several years at Mirto, Renata Zwick-Rubino, this process usually started off fairly awkwardly at the beginning of the year, but became second-nature to the children within a few months.[200] After each child had expressed his or her hopes for the day, the teacher (who also proposed various games and projects along with the rest) moderated a conversation in which the children decided upon a plan of activities. If a child had proposed something clearly inappropriate (like a walk along the creek when it was raining), the teacher suggested that it be postponed until a better opportunity arose. If one group of children disagreed with the preferences expressed by the majority, they were encouraged to pursue their own endeavor separately (as long as this was compatible with the activities of the others).

Dolci wanted Mirto's teachers to watch out for two principal dangers in this procedure. On the one hand, he wanted to avoid what had happened in certain progressive schools where, in the name of "anti-authoritarianism," teaching had degenerated into a shapeless anarchy.[201] On the other hand, he noted,

> there was a risk that the decision-making process would become like a superficial rite, especially if the teacher was not genuinely open and alert to the ideas of the children. It was also perfectly natural for the little ones to get tired of doing something which they themselves had chosen.[202]

The key, however, lay in the innate curiosity of the children themselves. After they had repeatedly experienced the fact that the adults took their proposals seriously, noted Zwick-Rubino, they often planned ahead for the following day, discussing their ideas excitedly with their classmates. Dolci's eventual goal was to expand Mirto until it could harbor children from ages five through fourteen.

At each level, he believed, the substance of democratic participation could be broadened and deepened, building on the habits and skills learned at an earlier age. His work was continually slowed down, however, by the practical and financial difficulties of launching this innovative institution; and by the late 1980s Mirto's classes were still limited to five teachers working with two groups of five- and six-year-olds.

How was it possible, within this framework, to cover the preestablished curriculum of the "Three R's" that all state schools were required to follow? Each morning, the teachers sought to frame their own proposals in such a way as to channel the curiosity of the children toward some project or theme that explicitly combined "pedagogy" and enjoyment. Dolci frequently cited examples of such projects in his own pedagogical writings:

> In New York I met a young teacher, Jim Bruni, who studied the pedagogy of mathematics. . . . He was working with a group of eight-year-old boys who were completely bored by math and by school in general. So he asked them, one day, what they would most like to be doing. After some debate, they all agreed that they loved cars. Each day, after that, Jim took the kids down to a busy intersection where they could watch the cars going by. And he asked them to note the colors of the cars, the different models, license-plates, engine sizes—each of them keeping track in a little notebook. Gradually, with his guidance, they started organizing all this information, compiling statistics and making diagrams. In the end, they were even learning how to carry out simple calculations of probability. Working with the basic interests of the children, the adult had taken on a precise role—neither that of a dictator, nor that of someone who hands over his entire responsibility to the kids.

> .   .   .   .

> In a seminar with young teenagers from Partinico, someone had proposed a rather odd project: examining how many different types of silence exist. The young coordinator suggested we each spend half an hour alone in the countryside, reflecting and taking notes—which we all did, myself included.

> When we got back to our round table, one boy began: "There's the silence of midnight, when a *mafioso* prepares to attack some poor fellow." Then a young girl: "There's also the silence of a mother who is giving milk to her baby for the first time.". . . And another girl, turning red in the face: "There's the silence of two people in love." And so on, one after another. Then one boy stood up and said that in his view, silence didn't exist. An intense discussion followed, in which the boy tried to demonstrate the truth of what he had said: "When we're alone in the countryside at night

and we think it's silent, it's not true. Because we hear the wind going through the trees and each one makes a different sound."

In the end, we all agreed: there is no such thing as silence. What exists (or doesn't exist) is the capacity to listen. I left the room afterwards, with my notebook in my pocket, reflecting about what would have transpired if I had held a "lesson."[203]

Dolci observed that during their two years at Mirto, the sophistication of the children's proposals rapidly increased. As they grew older, they spontaneously began to ask about reading and writing skills, which would allow them to write letters to their friends and give them access to new books. "What we noticed," he wrote, "is that children who are deeply interested in a project, motivated from within, can learn more in two years' time than they would otherwise learn in ten."[204]

Another pivotal aspect of Dolci's pedagogy lay in working closely with the children's families. Teachers from Mirto considered it part of their job to pay regular visits to each child's home, starting even before the first day of school and continuing at intervals of one or two months throughout the year. In this way, they could understand more concretely what a child's particular strengths and weaknesses might be, and also involve the parents directly in the learning process that had begun at school. Many parents were profoundly disconcerted, at first, when their children began asking for a different kind of decision making in the home; it was up to Mirto's teachers to explain what the school was trying to accomplish and to enlist the parents' help in reinforcing this new scale of values and ideals. The school, Dolci explained to an interviewer in 1977,

> is becoming like a lever operating on family relationships as well; it represents another way of pushing aside the old structure of social, economic, and political power. Our work is not only aimed at helping the children to mature, but at reaching through them to their families, influencing their mentality, creating and promoting new democratic fronts.[205]

Dolci regarded his tangible projects at Mirto as intimately related to his poetry and philosophical writings. Starting in the early 1970s, he began to write short poems and aphorisms which he used as the points of departure for group discussions at the Centro Studi and for cultural seminars at the new Borgo. He returned increasingly to the mystical perception of human life that had animated his years at Nomadelfia, but it was now a mysticism deeply informed by metaphors derived from biology and ecological science:

> As creatures, we can all develop boundless roots that connect us with the whole world. Our eyes, ears, and skin can emit roots and umbilical cords.

> In the dark we might see a distant light and perceive, amid the infinite rays given off, one point of emanation. Every body, every creature, can be a core of such radiance.
>
> The midwife pushes gently, sets free.
>
> If we crush the shell, we risk damaging the seed. But if the shell—an almond, a pine nut, a metropolis, an empire—threatens to suffocate the seed, we must somehow make the shell wither and disintegrate to let the seed press forth.[206]

At the heart of these aphorisms lay a vision of the world as a single "creature of creatures," an organic unity more complex than any particular living organism. Dolci rejected the age-old analogy of the "body politic" with a head (government), hands (workers), and so on. What constituted the world organism, instead, was the active presence of infinite interconnections and relationships that were not always visible to the naked eye, or to superficial scrutiny.[207] "Medical science," he wrote in 1985,

> studies diseases, alterations of wholeness. From the cell to the biosphere, the health of an organism depends on how specific adaptations are coordinated and linked. The citizens of today's earth must clearly articulate—from the local region to the entire planet—how the connections and contradictions occur: violence, fear, production, exploitation, weary boredom, economies, politics, the emergent ecological consciousness and remorse of the species, education, the feeling of emptiness, creativity, hallucinogens, hope, the threat of thermonuclear extermination.[208]

Just as he had done in the 1960s, so in the seventies and eighties Dolci sought to order these positive and negative tendencies into two opposed sets—the "old" and the "new" worlds—each of them comprising a social whole of its own, with its characteristic rules and internal connections. Neither of these two visions corresponded exactly to contemporary reality: rather, they represented two alternative paths, two possible directions of evolution, between which human beings must choose.

The first vision was a nightmarish one, which Dolci concisely evoked in one of his aphorisms: "In my mind I hear a lugubrious noise: the metallic din of a million hens, their beaks tick-ticking on tin feeders in the orderly rows of an industrial chicken-farm."[209] This was Dolci's image of civilization as it might become. The huge scale of contemporary social units, he argued, was incompatible with genuine democracy; for how could authentic consultation and mutual compromise take place among individuals living thousands of miles apart, in separate environments that presented utterly different difficulties and opportunities? How could social relations help but be abstract and dehumanizing within the vast political entities of modern society? In one of his poems he wrote:

> I detest you, New York
> not because you are a City
>   (and yet, in the rust-colored debris
>   amid the opaque shining of rigid,
>   humorless leaves—
>   intense seeds are sprouting)
> but because you think you are a City.[210]

Dolci was not hostile to technology, but he deeply opposed many of the uses to which it was put in "advanced" societies. Too many of his contemporaries, he believed, uncritically accepted television and computers as tools that automatically rendered communication more efficient; he therefore devoted an entire book to this subject, analyzing the manifold distinctions between transmitting (an essentially one-directional process) and communicating (a far more complex and mysterious process of give-and-take).[211]

This concept of reciprocity became central to Dolci's thought; and he devoted much of his writings in the 1980s to exploring the often subtle ways in which this precious two-way relationship might be either undermined or strengthened. He focused not only on "public" actions but also interrogated the more intimate domain of relationships within a family. At what point, for instance, did a father who was speaking to his child really begin to *listen* to what the younger person was trying to express? What did it take to see a flower in one's garden as if one were noticing it for the first time? One of his favorite examples, which he used in the manner of a Zen *koan* to elicit discussion at public seminars, was the following:

> A mother and her five-year-old son are together on the terrace. She is reading a book, while he plays with his toy truck several meters away. Every so often, she looks up from her book, at her child. The child senses the mother's glance as he plays; he looks up, then returns to his game. Who is affecting whom? Is there not a sort of umbilical cord between them—in which something infinitely precious travels both ways?[212]

In Dolci's view, this mutual openness between two persons could be translated, with appropriate changes, into the broader framework of public life. By contrast, the conventional roles of "the leader," "the teacher," "the expert"—all these rested on exactly the opposite type of relationship, in which one individual initiated and steered the interaction while others docilely submitted or followed. "What does it mean to speak of 'mass society?'" he wrote.

> If we look attentively, we see that the idea of "the masses" is essential to any large society where domination persists. In order for the few to dominate, it is necessary for all the other people to be reduced to a "mass"—passive, undifferentiated. . . .

Schools that operate like assembly-lines; spectacularly idiotic TV shows to lure the foolish (their value measured by the number of spectators); consumer products to satisfy artificial needs; the habit of valuing only those things that sell the most; and above all, treating all these tendencies as if they were natural, unavoidable—these are the means by which "the masses" are produced. Any political regime that does not explicitly oppose this process is complicitous in it.[213]

Uncritical conformism, absurd consumerism, absence of leisure and silence—these were all interconnected elements, for Dolci, of a social order in which democratic decision making could only become increasingly difficult. Modern "mass society," in his view, was perversely based on the stultification of individuals rather than the cultivation of their autonomous and creative participation. In his writings, he did not explicitly mention the collective critique that had been articulated since the early decades of the century by the theorists of the Frankfurt School—Max Horkheimer, Theodor Adorno, Walter Benjamin, Leo Lowenthal, and later Herbert Marcuse. Nevertheless, Dolci's work clearly expressed (albeit in less systematic fashion) the same anxiety over the opaque and impersonal instrumentalities of social control that appeared to be taking shape during the twentieth century.[214] He persistently denounced the unidirectional quality of power relations in this emerging civilization—a culture in which an individual's choices could be increasingly preprogrammed and inculcated from external centers of control.

In the Communist world, he noted, the repression of free thought was a blatantly violent affair; but in the West, the processes of control tended to be more subtle and insidious, relying on the channeling of "free choice" through a combination of highly structured education, material inducements, and the blandishments of the mass media.[215] Politicians who spent huge sums on promotion and advertising to create a "sellable" image of themselves; scientists who peddled their knowledge to large corporations and the military, heedless of the products they created; teachers who unabashedly described their job as "shaping the young according to the demands of society"; generations of youths mesmerized by video games; popular television shows equating "success" with money, sex, or luxury items; movies depicting "power" as the ability to bend others to one's own will—all these images haunted Dolci as he read about them or witnessed them in his travels. They could only be understood, he felt, as symptoms of an oppressive social order taking shape on both sides of the Iron Curtain: a society in which the individual citizen was increasingly cut off from the order of nature and from the shaping of his or her own life.[216]

Like E. P. Thompson, moreover, Dolci made an explicit connection between the development of this manipulative social order and the phenomenon of militarism; he would have agreed intensely with Thompson's statement: "We are becoming *the kind of society* that goes to war."[217] Militarism, for Dolci, represented the extreme form of unidirectional relationship—a means of "resolving" conflicts not by disciplined and democratic decision making but by the same forms of coercion that a tyrant or a *mafioso* would use. The "military solution," in other words, merely constituted the harshest, most naked expression of a broader conception of power based on domination.[218] Wherever possible, those who conceived of power in this way would seek to manipulate the behavior of others without resorting to physical violence; when this kind of manipulation failed, they would cross the threshold into the realm of guns and missiles. "Someday, perhaps even in a few decades," Dolci told an interviewer in 1977,

> atomic weapons may become accessible even to small groups of private citizens—this is the prediction made recently by some of the world's leading physicists. I do not know whether human beings will ultimately decide to survive or to commit collective suicide, but I do know this: if they decide to survive, they will be forced to invent a new culture, a new morality, a new social order—and these will have to rest on the foundation of nonviolence. The seeds of that nonviolent future exist today, but we are still at the early stages: an entire developmental process lies ahead.[219]

How could one create valid alternatives to militarism, if the vast majority of human beings accepted dominative relationships as "normal"? Dolci's answer was that these one-way relationships had somehow to be unmasked, to lose their widespread legitimacy in the conscience of ordinary citizens. It was here that Mirto acquired its broader connection to the quest for international peace. Mirto, for Dolci, represented a concrete attempt to instill the instinct for self-rule among a new generation of children. Sitting at their round tables, the youngsters in his school might gradually learn how to listen to each other, how to compromise, how to coordinate their wishes and their collective decision making. They would learn to think of one-way relationships as a form of unacceptable violence; and as they grew up, Dolci hoped, they might begin creating that authentic, two-directional system of power that had so far eluded humankind. Eventually, if each generation of students made incremental steps away from the "old" worldview, changing its patterns of behavior accordingly, a slightly different social reality would confront each incoming generation—becoming in its turn the starting point for still more arduous changes. This was the logic behind Dolci's long-range vision, aimed at a gradual transformation of the age-old "givens" of politics. The question of whether such a strategy could plausibly be called "realistic" will constitute a central theme in the concluding chapter of this study.

***

In May 1986, at the historic "maxi-trial" in Palermo where hundreds of *mafiosi* were being brought to justice, a peculiar development occurred.[220] Two of the most ferocious mafia bosses, Michele Greco and Luciano Liggio, who had terrorized the city of Palermo and the town of Corleone at the time of Dolci's campaign for the Jato dam, decided that they had had enough of the maximum-security conditions in the *Ucciardone* prison. They complained that they were not being allowed to see their families and that this isolation constituted a "cruel and unusual" form of punishment. When the judicial authorities refused to give in, the two "godfathers" (now in their late fifties) adopted a radical technique: they fasted. Within a few days, hundreds of *mafiosi* in different cell blocks had joined the hunger strike, creating a situation of "highest emergency" throughout the prison. Eventually, the warders compromised, allowing occasional visits by relatives to the redoubtable inmates of the *Ucciardone*.

Did Liggio and Greco learn this effective technique from the example set by Dolci? If so, had they acquired a tentative respect for Dolci's ethic of "nonviolent power"—or were they merely subsuming his tactics within the ancient mentality of *furberia*, or self-interested cunning? What sort of impact did Dolci's multifarious campaigns make on his fellow Sicilians and on the international movements for peace?

At the heart of Dolci's career lay an unresolved tension between the willful individualism of his personality and the social or collective nature of his aims. Occasionally, it was true, Dolci did form alliances with various groups, such as the trade unions—but, as one union leader in Trappeto, Orazio de Guilmi, explained, "Dolci's alliances tended to be a somewhat one-way affair. When he was organizing a march or a demonstration, he called upon us; but we almost never got him to participate directly in our union struggles."[221] This was, of course, due to Dolci's ironclad policy of remaining "above the political fray"; for in Italy's highly politicized atmosphere, where almost every social organization was perceived as "belonging" to one party or another, he had to tread cautiously in declaring his solidarities. Nonetheless, it was characteristic of Dolci's whole modus operandi: rather than sacrifice his freedom of action by joining any single group or movement, he invariably preferred to act alone, as an individual.

The price that he paid for this freedom was considerable. In the early 1960s, at the culmination of the Jato dam campaign, he had amassed a truly powerful base of local and international support. Many of Dolci's followers pleaded with him to forge this vast wave of sympathy into some form of coherent political agency—be it a party, or a movement, or perhaps something entirely new. Dolci's deep distrust of institutionalized political groupings led him to refuse, at one point even overriding a majority of his coworkers, who promptly walked out on him.

Not surprisingly, therefore, Dolci's insistence on remaining independent from any institutional ties forced him to rely on his own personal image as the main promotional tool of his work. Having started out as a "man with a cause," he identified himself increasingly with that cause until the two became virtually inseparable. This led to a personalization of his major projects that left them sadly dependent upon his own driving presence. When he moved on to new projects, the old ones tended to languish; when this led to bitter schisms in the ranks of his followers, he tended to remain aloof, allowing continuous hemorrhages of supporters and volunteers. The reasons for these periodic schisms were different in each case; but the common element was usually Dolci's unbudgeable insistence on following his own conscience and taking his own decisions, no matter what the cost.

This represents the central paradox of Dolci's career. He was sufficiently committed to the ideal of grass-roots democracy to risk his life over many years in an unrelenting campaign against clientelism, yet he himself proved incapable of allowing the Centro Studi to operate in a fully democratic way. Later, in the 1970s and 1980s, his poems and pedagogical experiments explored the subtlest nuances of group interaction and collective decision making; yet he himself remained essentially a solitary figure, pursuing his ideas with the same single-minded perseverance that had marked his earlier years in the Borgo di Dio. Did this underlying contradiction negate the value of Dolci's work? Most of his ex-colleagues—even the most bitterly disaffected among them—hastened to answer this question with an emphatic "No."

For many, like the sociologist Alberto L'Abate (who had worked alongside Dolci in the 1950s), Dolci never succeeded in becoming a "builder" and "founder" of self-sustaining institutions, as he had hoped; yet he played a significant role in postwar Italian history nonetheless. Dolci, according to L'Abate, acted as a catalyst, becoming a rallying point for an entire generation of idealistic young activists, and providing a crucial focus for the development of an "alternative politics" in Italy.[222] Another of Dolci's coworkers, Pino Lombardo, expressed it this way:

> To me, the important question is not, "Why did so many of his coworkers leave Danilo?" but "What are they doing now?" If you track down those people, I think you'll find that they have merely changed the trench in which they carry on the struggle, but they are all still fighting along the same broad front. And in that sense working with Danilo has probably helped them all, immeasurably.[223]

Still another of Dolci's coworkers, Franco LaGennusa, while sharply critical of his leadership style, nonetheless regarded his own encounter with Dolci in 1969 as a turning point in his life.[224] Hired at age nineteen as a construction worker to help build the new Borgo, LaGennusa had hardly been able to read and write. His exposure to Dolci, and to the people surrounding him, had led LaGennusa to pursue a frantic effort of self-education, leading eventually to a staff position in the Centro Studi and finally to a leadership role in the Jato Irrigation Consortium. Among the dozens of Dolci's former coworkers whose testimonials contributed to the present study, one finds social workers, peace activists, city planners, creators of libraries for the poor, trade union organizers, political activists, advocates of conscientious objection, or theorists of nonviolence.[225] These figures, active throughout Italy (and in other countries as well), arguably constituted an important aspect of Dolci's legacy; for they had shaped their own aspirations and convictions partly through their work with the Centro Studi.

During the 1970s, the Italian government fulfilled a promise it had made three decades before (in the final draft of the Republic's Constitution): it handed down substantial functions of governance, such as the administration of health-care and welfare benefits, to Italy's nineteen regional assemblies. This devolution of power was certainly not a direct result of Dolci's campaigns, but it constituted a key element in the philosophy of decentralization that Dolci had helped to promote since the late 1950s. In a similar way, the rise of important fringe movements like the Italian Radical party in the 1970s was not directly linked to Dolci's activities in Sicily; yet the clamorous campaigns of the Radicals, carried out with hunger strikes and popular referenda, closely echoed ideas that Dolci had promoted two decades before: conscientious objection to the draft, denunciation of political corruption, and the protection of the environment. It would be implausible to maintain that Dolci's nationally publicized efforts, carried out year after year, had not contributed substantially to the definition of this new political climate.

The building of the Jato dam did not revolutionize the southern economy, but it proved to all Italians—especially the southerners themselves—that conditions in Southern Italy could be rapidly changed by concerted action from below. Dolci's open denunciation of mafia figures in politics did not undo the mafia, but it was one of the very first breaches in that sacrosanct "wall of silence" that has been slowly crumbling ever since. Four out of the five development centers that Dolci established in 1958 are now defunct; but those centers challenged Sicily's regional government to take up their pathbreaking work, demonstrably raising the standards (and popular expectations) of public administration wherever they operated. Finally, the school at Mirto has not yet fully established itself as a successful enterprise, but it is pioneering a new kind of education based on a two-directional conception of power.

In all these cases, the most important achievement may not have lain in the immediate results of Dolci's projects (though these results were often substantial in themselves). Rather, the real achievement may have lain in the leavening of public consciousness, the broadening of possibilities, that they created. It was to this intangible contribution that the writer Carlo Levi pointed when he wrote an open letter to the people of Partinico in September 1962, at the climax of the Jato dam campaign: "Your action today has the power of an example, not just for Partinico, but for Sicily and Italy. It shows us a path that is the only path for modern democracy and for liberty."[226] As a renowned authority on the Southern Question, Levi was well-placed to savor the ironic inversion implicit here, in which the wretched "bandits" of Partinico could offer moral and civic leadership to the prosperous society of the North. Under Dolci's prodding, these illiterate peasants were demonstrating that social problems widely accepted as "normal"—or unavoidable—were in fact wide open to human agency.

CONCLUSION
The Limits of the Possible:
Three Core Debates

Order is not sufficient. What is required is something much more complex. It is order entering upon novelty; so that the massiveness of order does not degenerate into mere repetition; and so that the novelty is always reflected upon a background of system.

—Alfred North Whitehead, *Process and Reality* (1929)[1]

In this book, we have traced the careers of four persons—Weiss, Szilard, Thompson, Dolci—who challenged the old tradition of *Realpolitik,* questioning it and probing it for weak spots. Would international politics always have to remain a competitive struggle for power? Louise Weiss concluded (after two decades of resistance) that the answer was an unequivocal "Yes." The others demurred, and devoted their lives to undermining this competitive conception of politics, seeking to replace it with varying degrees and styles of cooperation.

In the twentieth century, an early instance of this reassessment of *Realpolitik* had already occurred well before World War I, with the Hague disarmament conferences of 1899 and 1907.[2] Then came the absurd slaughter of 1914–18, which forcefully concentrated the minds of many Europeans and Americans upon the question, "Why war?" For the first time in history, organized peace movements became a mass phenomenon, especially in Britain and the United States, but in other countries as well.[3] These idealists of the interwar years, of whom Louise Weiss provides a sober and level-headed example, placed great hopes in the institutionalization of the desire for peace through the League of Nations and its associated agencies. Surely, they reasoned, humankind was not condemned to another orgy of senseless killing; war could be averted by rational compromise and a greater willingness to experiment with international mediation and communication. This hope proved all too vain, and for persons like Weiss the resulting disillusionment led to a particularly strong embrace, after 1945, of time-worn *Realpolitik.*

Over this new generation, however, loomed a new peril—a peril that, in the eyes of some, changed everything. Leo Szilard, E. P. Thompson, and Danilo Dolci were by no means alone in regarding the mushroom cloud as the harbinger of a qualitatively distinct era in human history—an epoch in which the diverse tribes and groupings of human beings would either learn how to get along with each other, creating a stable peace, or else lurch spastically toward eventual self-destruction. The technology of killing had become so refined and effective as to threaten the entire biosphere. Some self-avowed "realists," like Arnold Toynbee, Hans Morgenthau, and even Winston Churchill, shared many of the fears expressed by relative "idealists" like Szilard, Thompson, and Dolci; and they, too, voiced ardent hopes that some sort of international cooperation, some dimension of compromise and rational control, might come into play.[4] But how? Through what kinds of changes? To what extent would this pugnacious species, with its long record of brutality, prove capable of altering its own ingrained habits?

These are the questions that have lain at the heart of the present study. Thoughtful people, to be sure, have been asking such questions for millennia; but these fears and concerns seem to have arisen with particular urgency in the early twentieth century, and it is plausible to argue that this sense of urgency has steadily increased and accelerated as the decades have gone by—most notably after 1945.[5] In this sense, what we have been charting in this book might be described as the first tentative gropings toward a new awareness among the earth's peoples, a new set of ground rules dictated by the fear of military technology itself.

From competition to cooperation—what were the limits of the possible? In the discussion that follows, I will sum up three essential "debates" or controversies that have been at issue here, recurring implicitly throughout the foregoing chapters. The first of these revolved around the future of government on a global scale—the appropriate size and structure of political institutions, and the need for force as a final arbiter among them. In a broad sense, this theme pitted Weiss and Szilard against Thompson and Dolci (although Szilard's and Thompson's positions tended to shade away from the extremes of Weiss and Dolci). A second recurring tension centered on the human capacity for change—the relative fluidity or rigidity of human character traits and social habits. Here, Weiss stood alone against the more hopeful and optimistic visions of Szilard, Thompson, and Dolci. A final implicit dispute focused on the idea of power itself—the two rival conceptions that underlay these activists' writings and struggles. In this area, once again, the *Realpolitik* of Weiss's later years cut against the basic political assumptions of the other three figures.

Let me begin, however, with a brief digression about the role of utopian hope in the career of the Czech playwright and statesman Václav Havel. Throughout the sixties, seventies, and eighties, Havel was a sharp thorn in the side of the Stalinist Czech regime. He criticized the government, circulated petitions, organized opposition groups, and refused to be intimidated, even by repeated prison sentences and other, subtler forms of harassment. In 1986, shortly after he had been released from one of his longer stays in jail, Havel was asked by an interviewer to describe how he saw the world situation. Gorbachev had only been in power one year. Totalitarianism in Eastern Europe showed no signs of changing.

The interviewer asked Havel: "Do you see a grain of hope anywhere in the 1980s?"

Havel replied:

> I should probably say first that the kind of hope I often think about (especially in situations that are particularly hopeless, such as prison) I understand above all as a state of mind, not a state of the world. . . . Hope, in this deep and powerful sense, is not the same as joy that things are going well, or willingness to invest in enterprises that are obviously headed for early success, but, rather, an ability to work for something because it is good, not just because it stands a chance to succeed. The more unpropitious the situation in which we demonstrate hope, the deeper that hope is. Hope is definitely not the same thing as optimism. It is not the conviction that something will turn out well, but the certainty that something makes sense, regardless of how it turns out.[6]

Three and a half years later, on New Year's Day 1990, Havel was still using the same "idealistic" language, but he was addressing his fellow citizens as the newly elected president of a free country.

> Thomas Masaryk founded his politics on morality. . . . Let us teach both ourselves and others that politics does not have to be the art of the possible, especially if this means the art of speculating, calculating, intrigues, secret agreements, and pragmatic maneuvering, but that it also can be the art of making both ourselves and the world better.[7]

This is not the place to retrace those remarkable events that led Havel, in the space of a few short months in 1989, from his status as a persecuted intellectual to the Hradčany Castle above Prague. Nevertheless, the story is worth a few moments' reflection.

Even in the most sober of history books, the revolutions of 1989 sound almost like a fairy tale. The great foreign empire began to give signs of loosening its stranglehold. Eastern Europeans gingerly came out into the streets—and the police beat them back. Then more people came out into the streets, and more people, and more people; and these hundreds of thousands of common citizens simply said that they had had enough.

And the rulers, in some cases, resigned. In other cases, they tried to put up a fight, but their own security forces refused to obey. Only in Rumania, the worst of the hardline Stalinist states, was there substantial violence; but even there, it was all over relatively quickly.

In retrospect, one of the most striking aspects of this "Springtime of Nations" is that no one would ever have dared to predict that such a thing could happen. It is a simple fact that the events of 1989 utterly confounded the majority of professional observers of contemporary politics: scholars, journalists, politicians, diplomats. Virtually everyone (including Havel himself!) was taken off guard. It was as if history was suddenly rebelling against humanity's accepted ideas of what power is all about.

What does this story tell us about tough-minded *Realpolitik* and its accuracy as a conception of politics? In one sense, of course, it proves nothing at all; for one could reasonably argue that the revolutions of 1989 merely constituted a rare exception. Earlier in the same year, after all, a similar exercise of idealistic "people power" in Beijing's Tiananmen Square had met with a very different fate. Nevertheless, the events of 1989—precisely because they are so hard to explain—add a certain sharpness to the basic questions underlying this book. What is realistic, and what is utopian? When all the experts of the world are caught completely off guard by one of the most far-reaching political transformations of a century, it is time to loosen one's grip on such words as "obviously" and "of course."

The Future of Government on a Global Scale

Louise Weiss and Leo Szilard assumed that the basic institutions of government—hinging upon the centralized, bureaucratic state—would remain roughly constant as the world evolved into an increasingly unified political arena. The units of administration would probably grow larger, but the structure of state power would continue to lie at the heart of world politics. The key question for these two activists, accordingly, was how to foster peace among such vast and powerful units—with Weiss inclined toward an explicit notion of international hierarchy, and Szilard emphasizing more the roles played by tolerance and rational compromise. Although Szilard would certainly have disapproved of Weiss's authoritarian temperament, the solutions that he proposed were similar to hers in their essentially elitist and statist character. It is true that he disliked the large bureaucracies of modern states and sought to circumvent their cumbersome machinery through direct international contacts, but he reserved this special role for a select group of individuals like himself. Just as the scientists had done in "The Voice of the Dolphins," this self-appointed elite of "global managers" would work paternalistically behind the scenes, using the power of state institutions to protect humankind from its own primitive habits.

E. P. Thompson and Danilo Dolci took a different tack. Whereas Szilard and

Weiss had taken for granted the historical tendency toward larger and larger units of power, Thompson and Dolci called this tendency into question. From the tribe to the feudal fiefdom, from the regional principality to the nation-state to the emerging structures of multinational blocs, the direction of social evolution over the past ten thousand years appeared to point toward ever-larger forms of government and of cultural identity. Thompson and Dolci did not deny that this trend existed, but they rejected the idea that such huge aggregates of human beings could be compatible with the principles of democratic rule. As long as the institutions of governance kept growing indiscriminately in size, comprising state-structures of ever-increasing complexity and power, the values of pluralism and popular self-determination would be more and more deeply threatened.

Here, then, were two very different conceptions of social order and political power. Weiss and Szilard both conceived of peace as an extension (with modifications) of existing state-centric systems of politics, whereas Thompson and Dolci concluded that peace would require radically new political forms, both "below" and "above" the traditional bureaucratic state. Which of these two fundamental visions was more realistic—the scenario of big, centralized, hierarchical blocs, or the scenario of small, decentralized, and egalitarian structures? The former (which I will call the "bloc" model) possessed two distinct advantages over the latter (which I will call the "grass-roots" model).[8] At the level of domestic politics, the "bloc" model took into account the requirements of bureaucracy, whereas the other did not. At the level of foreign or external relations, the "bloc" model at least addressed the problem of military force, whereas the "grass-roots" paradigm failed to do so convincingly.

Let us begin with domestic politics. Unlike Weiss and Szilard, who believed that growing populations would probably mean growing bureaucracies, Thompson and Dolci rejected this hierarchical form of government as inherently prone to corruption and authoritarianism. Their egalitarian visions were strikingly similar: at the local level, workers organizing their own cooperatives, municipalities overseeing their own affairs, groups of citizens actively making the decisions that affected their lives; while at the regional and international levels these smaller groupings would rely on loose federative institutions to coordinate their actions. Yet both Thompson and Dolci appear to have ignored certain key implications of this "grass-roots" model. In their ideal world, would not an average citizen be forced to spend several hours of each day sitting on a wide range of committees? Who would coordinate the vast panoply of local, regional, and international meetings that would be required to keep this "non-violent federalism" functioning? What would distinguish this intricate network of self-governing councils from any other immense bureaucracy? And finally: What would prevent this "citizens' democracy" from lapsing back into all the classic games of power mongering that characterized contemporary governments? These kinds of questions never found a clear answer in the writings of Thompson and Dolci. In the end, their vision presupposed a society in which two crucial changes had *already* occurred: it would have to be much smaller in scale and simpler in structure than contemporary society; and it would hinge upon an unprecedented maturity and civic-mindedness among the common citizens who would ultimately be responsible for making it work on a day-to-day basis.

Therefore, if "realism" meant taking society and human beings "as they are" and basing one's extrapolations on existing trends, Weiss and Szilard clearly possessed an advantage in this aspect of their thought. Although they did not provide solutions to the problems of bureaucracy, their "bloc" model at least took into account the basic logistical and administrative requirements of politics in a mass society. Thompson and Dolci, in this sense, could not be called realists, because their visions ultimately presupposed the existence of a different, or transformed, humanity.

At the level of foreign or external relations, moreover, another weakness afflicted the "grass-roots" model. Supposing "nonviolent federalism" became a reality, would the multiple layers of self-governing councils unite, at the top, to form a single world government? If they did not do so, then what international institution would act as a global arbiter in case serious conflicts emerged among two or more grass-roots groups? And if they did form a world government, then what would prevent that government from becoming a tyrannical enforcer of its own rules and principles? Here, Thompson and Dolci faced some of the same difficult questions that had apparently puzzled Szilard. How to create an effective global arbiter, possessing sufficient clout to enforce its decisions on all peoples, without simultaneously creating a potential Frankenstein? Only Louise Weiss, among the four figures in this study, provided a fully consistent answer to this fundamental question: she rejected the idea of a single global authority and assumed that each power bloc would ultimately fend for itself. Szilard, in his desire to reduce the role of military force, at least designated a locus of arbitration (the United Nations); but he shied away from vesting decisive military power in any single body and hence failed to provide a credible answer to the problem of enforcement. Thompson and Dolci, however, hardly broached this subject at all. Although Thompson was more open than Dolci to the notion of "collective military security," he remained evasive on the vital issues of final arbitration and the ultimate power to compel compliance. Both these thinkers apparently assumed that future grass-roots groups would find ways to compromise on every serious conflict, or to cooperate successfully in enforcing majority decisions upon renegades—but this assumption, once again, seemed hard to reconcile with the quarrelsome and violent humanity of historical fact.

Nevertheless, these important flaws in the "grass-roots" model should not obscure the equally important flaws of the "bloc" model; nor do they invalidate the penetrating critique that Thompson and Dolci leveled against it. What kind of world lay ahead, they asked, if large, monolithic bloc-structures truly represented the "wave of the future"? In Weiss's estimation, the monolithic organization of the dictatorships generated political strength, while the pluralism of the democracies represented a relative weakness; for monolithic power was decisive and streamlined, whereas pluralism was hesitant, divided, and cumbersome. One had but to compare Hitler's Germany with Blum's France to see the sources of Weiss's conviction. Thompson and Dolci, however, believed that in the long run the exact opposite was the case: pluralism and diversity became signs of health, while monolithic power reflected a society in decay. They observed that monolithic societies, with their centralized governments and hierarchical authority, proved highly inflexible over long periods of time. Pluralistic societies, on the other hand, were continually in a ferment of self-renovation; their competing political groups and diverse sources of authority rendered them far more dynamic and creative. For Thompson and Dolci, therefore, the principle of pluralism exerted two different kinds of attraction. First, it represented a moral choice in favor of protecting human rights and the self-determination of the individual; and second, it represented a rejection of the stagnancy and maladaptive rigidity that characterized monolithic power—a practical choice in favor of social forms that throve on change.

Both Thompson and Dolci, in this sense, shared a common nightmare—a fear that contemporary civilization was becoming similar in too many respects to the one George Orwell had depicted in his novel, *Nineteen Eighty-Four.* In that novel, written with remarkable prescience in 1949, three superpowers dominate the earth: Eurasia, Oceania, and Eastasia.[9] Perpetually battling with each other, yet never going over the brink into all-out war, these three megastates have frozen their conflicts into an ongoing condition of military tension that becomes "business as usual"—a peculiar form of militarized peace. At the same time, since these three societies are continuously mobilized on a war-footing, they become virtual garrison states, in which the actions and inner thoughts of every single individual must be tightly controlled by an omnipresent Central Government. "War is Peace," state the party slogans on walls throughout the cities of the modern world; and "Freedom is Slavery." The perpetual fear of the Enemy reinforces the internal regimentation of society; and the xenophobic hatred inculcated in each of society's members reinforces the ever-present state of foreign hostilities. International politics and domestic politics have fused into a self-perpetuating order of "perfect" repression.

It was precisely such a society that Dolci and Thompson saw looming over the horizon, not just in the Eastern bloc but possibly in the West as well—a society in which the individual and the state stood at increasingly polarized opposites, without the benefit of intermediary institutions; a world of huge political units, huge economic units, and rigid, impersonal bureaucracies; a civilization in which local cultures were increasingly reduced to a homogeneous "mass culture" controlled and shaped by centralized media industries and educational systems; an era in which the allegiance of "the masses" to the state—the internal bonding of an otherwise disaggregated society—could only be secured by inculcating a xenophobic fear of the "Other" (whether that "Other" was defined by ideology, religion, or race). Like Orwell, moreover, they did not feel that the "free West" was much safer from these pernicious currents than the blatantly oppressive society in the east.[10]

The crucial link here, of course, was the link with fascism; for both Dolci and Thompson perceived ominous continuities between fascist society and Cold War society. Neither of them feared an explicit resurgence of Fascist styles of government in Europe; their argument, rather, was that the Cold War era perpetuated many of the antidemocratic and militaristic habits that had flourished under fascism. They believed that the anti-Fascist struggle of World War II had been only partially successful—defeating and discrediting only the most obvious aspects of the Fascist system, while remaining dangerously vulnerable to other, more insidious tendencies. "We must frankly acknowledge," wrote Dolci in 1972,

> that Fascism was not a fortuitous accident which rained down like a thunderstorm upon the Italian people, but a manifestation of a profound malady and immaturity.
> The spirit of Fascism lives on, in forms of leadership that rely on outright repression or on conniving strategies of manipulation, and in the attitudes of cowed and servile opportunism that characterize a significant part of the Italian population.[11]

Thompson, for his part, decried the incipient authoritarianism of governments that increasingly defined their raison d'être in terms of "national security:"

> It is normal in times of war for states to acquire emergency powers. What distinguishes the Cold War is that the hypothesis of "emergency" is built into the daily routines of the peacetime state. This supplies, for the authority of the peacetime state, what the hypothesis of Satan supplied for the medieval church.[12]

For Thompson and Dolci, therefore, the repressive social forces manifested in the Cold War might very plausibly extend far beyond the specific historical circumstances of the bipolar era. It was true, of course, that the postwar U.S.-Soviet rivalry had taken a particularly harsh and tenacious form, because it rested on the superimposed dualisms of geopolitics and ideology. Yet the mere ending of this dualistic era would not necessarily constitute a victory for their ideals of peace. As in Orwell's *Nineteen Eighty-Four,* it was possible to envision tripolar (or even multipolar) configurations of power in which militarism, xenophobia, and authoritarianism would interact in a spiral of reciprocal aggravation. A Western European superpower, a Chinese or Japanese superpower, a nuclear-armed Islamic confederation—the advent of these kinds of military and ideological units would certainly bring an end to the bipolar geopolitics of the "Cold War"; yet such an outcome would constitute the exact opposite of the kind of world that Thompson and Dolci had sought to foster.

Seen from this perspective, these two men were arguably engaging in a qualitatively different kind of endeavor from that of Weiss and Szilard. Their deepest aim was not merely to avert large-scale war but also to prevent the emergence of a particular type of society—a society that, even in "peacetime," would be inherently oriented toward war. Throughout their writings, both these thinkers repeatedly emphasized the all-pervasiveness of the "military phenomenon" within the contemporary world. This was particularly true for Dolci, but it deeply characterized the thought of Thompson as well. Instead of seeing militarism as a cancer growing on an otherwise healthy body—a condition or ailment that was separable from the way contemporary society functioned—they saw it as an integral part of the very tissue of that society. Hence their practical strategy of linking peace to local politics as well as international relations: they conceived of war as a larger-scale manifestation of the same dominative power relations that often characterized conflicts *within* nations. Militarism, they believed, represented only the crudest form of dominative logic in action. Like the tip of an iceberg, it was merely the most blatant expression of coercive and manipulative forms of behavior that permeated the whole range of human interactions—from the workplace to local politics to the international level.

In one sense, therefore, Thompson and Dolci offered a far more pessimistic diagnosis than one that neatly ascribed the causes of militarism to the actions of specific statesmen or the aggressions of particular nations. For if the missiles of the Cold War truly had their deepest roots in diffuse social and economic relationships, in the attitudes and habits of common citizens, then only a full-scale social transformation would suffice to get rid of them. On the other hand, this pessimistic analysis also had a positive side. Precisely because the phenomena of international violence were so broadly rooted, the potential for initiating change lay close at hand. The power to influence military realities did not merely lie in the hands of politicians, diplomats, and generals but also in the countless unobtrusive choices made daily by innumerable individuals. Most of Thompson's and Dolci's projects, from the 1950s on, can best be understood in this light: as efforts to instill the taste for cooperative self-rule, as apprenticeships for a more active and constructive citizenship. If growing numbers of people took part in reinvigorating (or reinventing) these elemental democratic processes, they reasoned, then an Orwellian future might still be avoided.

In conclusion, therefore, it seems fair to say that both the "bloc" model and the "grass-roots" model contain within themselves a combination of promising and problematic elements. Thus, the rift between them should not be construed as a contest between two competing visions, one of which is likely to triumph in the future over the other. Instead, it would seem more fruitful to regard these two models as reflecting a very real and fundamental tension between two levels of world politics: the level of interstate relations, and the level beyond the state, where nongovernmental actors ranging from private individuals to multinational corporations carry out their transactions. Scholars and political thinkers have long pointed out the qualitative difference between these two layers of activity; it is a difference that has grown more rapidly than ever since the Second World War, with the spread of technologies that render direct contacts among citizens and private organizations on separate continents a normal matter of everyday life.[13]

For the foreseeable future, the sovereign state as a political institution shows few signs of withering away; and political theorists as diverse as Jean Bethke Elshtain and Hedley Bull have put forth convincing arguments that this is not necessarily a bad thing. "So long as the international community consists of sovereign states," writes Elshtain,

> war remains a possibility. . . . [But] what is the alternative? Continuous eruption of murderous local conflicts, whether tribal, familial, ethnic, or religious wars that were enormously destructive and repressive prior to the formation of states? The state is the guarantee of internal order. It has eliminated much of that conflict.[14]

On the other hand, it appears equally valid to argue that the sovereign state is finding its functions in world politics eroded simultaneously from "above" and "below," and that this slow process may be increasing rather than diminishing in momentum.[15] Below the nation-state, the past four decades have witnessed an unprecedented burgeoning of nongovernmental organizations—from advocacy groups for human rights to religious societies, from professional associations to ecological lobbies—effectively communicating with each other and building themselves into truly global networks; in a similar vein, international economic competition has prompted a rapid expansion of multinational business corporations, whose activities have now come to define a new sphere of interests and endeavors quite separate from those of any single state. Meanwhile, "above" the nation-state, formal and institutionalized cooperation among governments, as in the European Community or the North American Free Trade Area, has slowly but steadily grown since 1945.

Thus, we are left with the unavoidable task of steering between Scylla and Charybdis. The continued existence of nation-states poses serious dangers, not the least of which are war and bureaucratic ossification; but such states also offer the advantage of providing a well-established source of order amid the welter of competing groups in world politics. The experience of post–Cold War Yugoslavia wrenchingly demonstrates the painful truth that "smaller" is not necessarily more beautiful. On the other hand, the erosion of the nation-state's functions from "above" and "below" appears to be a fundamental fact of twentieth-century history; it is a process that seems inextricably entwined with the growth of new technologies for communication and transportation, and it appears likely to continue, regardless of the hopes and fears that humans attach to it.

Thinkers like Szilard have maintained that "the military question"—and hence the question of human survival—will never be definitively resolved until the power to coerce is vested exclusively in a single global authority. Szilard tried to "disguise" this assumption by proposing multiple police forces operating under U.N. auspices, but he could not disguise the circular logic at the heart of this notion:

> 1. Only a central military authority with a monopoly on the use of force can keep the squabbling nations at peace.
> 2. Therefore, the squabbling nations must agree to create such a body and abide by its decisions.

The flaw in this logic remains an irreparable one: if the world's nations are truly divided and squabbling, it seems very unlikely that they would agree to come together and constitute such a higher body in the first place.

Scholars and political observers have closely watched the struggle for supra-national integration in Western Europe since its inception in the late 1940s, for it seemed to offer an excellent test case for the gradual transfer of sovereignty from nation-states to a higher federal authority.[16] Thinking along these lines, some scholars have argued that a future world government might operate *alongside* existing nation-states, just as today's European Community continues to function alongside France, Germany, Britain, and other such well-established national units.[17] The Norwegian political theorist Johan Galtung has even gone one step farther, speculating that a global parliament may some-day emerge, analogous to the European Parliament with its direct popular suf-frage but with citizens voting as members of a far wider array of units: at the local, national, and world levels, but also as voting members of nonterritorial agencies (such as Amnesty International, the Nonaligned Movement, or OPEC).[18]

These kinds of speculations, however, while thought-provoking and im-portant, cannot conceal the fact that Western Europe actually provides a rather limited test case for thinking about world government. As one compares the relatively small and homogeneous territory of the Western European nations with the vast complexity, cultural diversity, and economic disparities of the global arena, one rapidly perceives the limitations of federal solutions at the planetary level. This cautionary note becomes especially important, moreover, when one considers the constant bickering and obstacles that the Western Europeans themselves continue to face in their search for unity. Although the European Community may offer ingenious innovations in the machinery of supranational government, the cooperative functions exercised by the United Nations, and by other such global agencies, seem likely for the foreseeable future to remain more limited in scope and piecemeal in nature.[19]

Seen from this perspective, both the "bloc" model and the "grass-roots" model offer useful elements for thinking about government on a global scale. Perhaps the most fruitful concept to adopt here is that of the *hybrid:* the notion that powerful nation-states and increasingly powerful nonstate actors coexist in today's world and are likely to continue to do so, perhaps indefinitely. Thus, the possibility of creating a world government is not likely to confront humankind as an "either-or" decision but rather as an incremental, evolutionary process in which subtle gradations of change are brought about by one generation after another. Perhaps certain regulatory functions, such as overseeing the use of ozone-destructive chemicals, will increasingly come to be exercised by international bodies; perhaps diplomatic agreements among sovereign states will suffice to ensure that certain categories of weapons (such as biological agents) are banned, subject to inspection, by all the great powers. If these kinds of cooperation grow in scope as time goes by, then the erosion of national sovereignty would be taking place, not in any grand unified ceremony but in more unobtrusive and fragmentary ways. This line of speculation, according to some thinkers, leads toward the conclusion that a federal world government may never become necessary; for if a sufficient degree of voluntary cooperation can be achieved, both among territorial states and among growing numbers of nonstate organizations, then the creation of a formal and centralized governing body would prove redundant.[20] All that would be required, under these relatively favorable conditions, would be a limited central authority for orchestrating the cooperative efforts undertaken, on an ad hoc basis, by a wide variety of state and nonstate actors. Such an agency could presumably take up judicial and policing functions, on a similarly ad hoc basis, if and when its members could reach a consensus in authorizing it to do so.

These are only a few of the tantalizing possibilities lying implicit in the tension between the "bloc" model and the "grass-roots" model. But here, inevitably, we confront the second fundamental debate that has recurred throughout the foregoing chapters: Is it reasonable to expect human beings to make such far-reaching and constructive changes?

The Human Capacity for Change

Questions about "human nature" tend to cut deeply into the domains of psychology, anthropology, and sociobiology, as well as philosophy and religion. Some scholars have argued that the ability of the human species to adapt rapidly to changing environments has earned it a special place within the animal kingdom; others have called into question this notion of humankind's uniqueness, emphasizing instead the commonalities between our species and others. This is not the place to attempt a review of such an immense array of age-old controversies.[21] I will concentrate, rather, on the specific level of human behavior that has provided the focus of this study—the level of politics (broadly conceived).

Louise Weiss tended to place her major emphasis on the inertia and inflexibility of human social evolution. It was useless, in her view, to call for a moral transformation of world politics; for in moments of international tension and conflict, the temptation to revert to that ancient arbiter, the use of force, would inevitably prevail. This did not mean, however, that Weiss considered her fellow Europeans incapable of making radical political changes. On the contrary, she believed that the fear of domination by Russians, Americans, or Asians would eventually arouse her European contemporaries, forcing them to lay aside their internecine squabbles. High-sounding moral principles would, of course, play their part, she believed; but the real motivation for forming a new superpower would not flow from such idealistic wellsprings. If the Germans and the French, the British and the Italians, ever came together in a single state, their action would ultimately stem from the millennial struggle for greater power, the ruthless logic of competition that had lain at the core of all politics since the time of the Melians and Athenians.

It was precisely this emphasis on force, according to thinkers like Szilard, Thompson, and Dolci, that had been rendered obsolete by nuclear weapons. Moralists of previous eras—like Immanuel Kant, for instance, in his essay on "Perpetual Peace"—had argued that the resolution of conflicts by means of physical violence debased human beings to the level of mere animals; it was through reason alone that conflict-resolution would attain its own peculiarly human dimension.[22] Now, for the first time in history, the "ought" of the moralists no longer stood alone; it was reinforced by the grim logic of collective survival. For these three thinkers, the crucial question posed by the barbarous wars of the twentieth century was the following: Would human beings be able to adapt quickly enough to the requirements of a new system of politics—a system in which conflicts were resolved without violence or the threat of violence?

Szilard, Thompson, and Dolci were painfully aware of how far this picture lay from contemporary reality. Yet they pointed with anguish to the lack of plausible alternatives other than "muddling through" in a world of increasingly fearsome armaments. It is significant that these three men, so drastically different from each other, should all have worked their way toward the same, seemingly inescapable conclusion: if humankind wanted to survive, then it had to bring forth a new sense of its own collective identity. The ancient distinctions between "us" and "them," "domestic" and "external," had to give way to a more fluid perception of boundaries, based on a new mentality that could not help but elicit scoffs from a hard-bitten Machiavellian. Trusting a potential enemy, tolerance for opposed ideas, compromise between conflicting interests—these values, with their rather sanctimonious Sunday-school ring, had to become the guideposts for a new generation. Szilard, Thompson, and Dolci were not pious-minded types. Yet they saw no alternative to the extension of civic responsibility far beyond its existing confines. "Collective security" would not work until each citizen's sense of "us" had outgrown its contemporary limits—until individuals in one continent were willing to commit a substantial portion of their own resources and talents in order to meet the needs of other individuals, total strangers on another continent.

"Very nice," Louise Weiss would probably have commented, "but impossible." These same noble ideals, she believed, had underpinned the League of Nations—the miserable institution that had already begun to show its impotence even before Hitler and the other dictators of the 1930s crushed it under their steel-toed boots. Then the second great experiment had come, the United Nations; its widely touted mechanisms of collective security had been paralyzed for four decades by the underlying competition between its two preeminent members. These were the unfortunate realities of world politics, in Weiss's view. Human groups never "coexisted" as equals within a neutral medium; they invariably struggled to dominate each other, and achieved a precarious "coexistence" only when their capabilities for domination happened to reach a temporary equilibrium. To expect anything else was not only futile but dangerous.

Szilard, Thompson, and Dolci did not deny these harsh realities, but they differed from Weiss on one crucial point: the word "invariably." Human beings, they insisted, were made of a more pliable material than thinkers like Weiss believed. Although Szilard's vision of social change was quite different from Thompson's and Dolci's, he shared with these two radical intellectuals a sense of political order as something that could be gradually reinvented. In particular, these three thinkers pointed to two main factors that might become powerful levers of change: the role of culture, or collectively held values and expectations, in shaping social reality; and the immense background of existing cooperative practices.

The first of these factors—the power of shifting ideas—was eloquently described during World War II by the French historian Marc Bloch, writing from Nazi-occupied France on the lost opportunities of the 1930s:

> But of what is the general mind composed if not of a multitude of individual minds which continually act and react upon one another? For a man to form a clear idea of the needs of society and to make an effort to spread his views is to introduce a grain of leaven into the general mentality.[23]

Bloch's metaphor of "leavening" rested on a notion of society as an ongoing cultural creation. The "general mentality" to which he referred was not something clear-cut and definable, but it comprised the sum total of interacting expectations and values that operated within the minds of society's members at any given time. By introducing new ideas and models of behavior into this circulating medium of culture, a single individual could exert a potentially appreciable influence on the shaping of the future. This was exactly the premise underlying Václav Havel's "power of the powerless" in totalitarian Czechoslovakia, and it represented the central element in the long-term strategies of Szilard, Thompson, and Dolci as well. "As a social historian," Thompson wrote in 1981,

> I have often offered the view that symbolism is a profoundly important constituent of historical process. . . . A contest for "face" may, in its outcome, confirm or call in question the authority of the rulers. The rituals of State, the public execution, the popular demonstration—all carry symbolic force; they may consolidate the assured hegemony of the rulers or they may bring it into disrepute with numbers and ridicule. Symbolism is not a mere colour added to the facts of power: it is an element of societal power in its own right.[24]

Like Václav Havel, Szilard, Thompson, and Dolci believed that an individual who took a strong moral stand on some issue of public moment was accomplishing far more than merely bearing witness to his or her own personal convictions. A moral stand was at the same time an act of potentially influential "symbolism," reverberating outward among the expectations and values of other persons like a ripple across a pond. Far from constituting a powerless act, this deliberate assertion of new possibilities had a chance of subtly altering the collective perceptions on which tomorrow's social order would be based.

The underlying logic here was that of the self-fulfilling prophecy. As with a run on a bank, or an economic recession, what mattered most was the public's *perception* of the direction events would probably take. Even the healthiest bank could be destroyed, if enough people came to believe its future was shaky; for with each uneasy client who canceled an account, the bank's status truly became more and more precarious. In a similar way, what was "realistic" also depended on which kinds of events and behaviors were widely deemed likely or unlikely at any given moment. By showing that something new or radically different was attainable, one acted like the first client who publicly withdrew his or her funds from the bank; other individuals would henceforth become more willing to participate in similar experiments—which might in turn produce still more encouraging results to convince still broader numbers of people. As more people joined in, the nature of the *real* situation shifted. Just as a cumulative change in perceptions had tangibly altered the status of the bank, so the "givens" of politics also could be gradually transformed. What had once been politically unthinkable was now in the process of becoming feasible, normal, commonplace—for the point of departure itself had concretely changed.

These thinkers were not so much calling for a "revolution," therefore, as for a gradual (but urgent!) erosion of old habits and expectations. The real revolution, they argued, would have to take place within the mind of each individual. Such a goal could not help but seem utopian at the outset; but as growing numbers of persons broadened their perceptions of what was possible, this would in itself shift the boundary between "reality" and "utopia."

It follows that most of the projects pursued by these three men had a dual nature. On the one hand, they aimed at making tangible advances in the contemporary world of politics—staving off a superpower confrontation, arousing public opinion against militarism, improving the lot of the poor and illiterate. On the other hand, they aimed at prefiguring, through their own example, the values and functioning of a different form of society. Szilard's contacts with Khrushchev, the END conventions promoted by Thompson, Dolci's Centro Studi and school—these were meant to provide contemporary citizens with tangible evidence that radically cooperative undertakings could indeed prove effective, even within the difficult context of today's world.

Here, the second key element in their strategy came to the fore: the vast reservoir of existing cooperative practices. It was Dolci who gave perhaps the clearest articulation of this idea, during an interview in 1977. "Journalists and intellectuals," he explained,

> have had the impression that I was trying to parachute nonviolence into a highly violent region: this was absolutely false. What I felt was that, deep within this population which had been crushed and exploited for millennia, it was only necessary to uncover the values of nonviolence where they already existed: the woman, the fisherman, the artisan. Violence was indeed the tool of those 20 or 30 individuals in each zone, of whom the newspapers wrote; but this did not mean that all of Sicily was violent.[25]

Dolci's optimistic conviction here was explicitly shared by Szilard and Thompson. They felt that a transition to a more fully cooperative society did not require the invention, *ex nihilo,* of entirely new modes of thinking and behaving. On the contrary, the moral framework of cooperative values already pervaded innumerable peaceful and constructive interactions in daily life. Although the news media typically concentrated their attention on clamorous and violent conflicts, the vast majority of human deeds was either nonconflictual or downright cooperative in nature. Already, in contemporary society, citizens often trusted relative strangers, took responsibility for the welfare of the needy, and compromised with opposed interests. The goal, in this sense, was to accentuate these very real and tangible cooperative practices, extending them into new areas of politics—and to undermine wherever possible the old habits founded on fear and punishment.

Louise Weiss would no doubt have argued that such a goal was unattainable—particularly at the level of nation-states or entire peoples. In defense of Szilard, Thompson, and Dolci, however, one could point out that history provided significant examples of precisely this kind of transition from hostile competition into cooperation. The research of the economist Kenneth Boulding has perhaps proved the most sophisticated and instructive in this area. In an important series of lectures given in 1977, Boulding pointed to such cases as the mutually accommodating separation of Norway from Sweden in 1905, or the emergence of a sturdy peace between France and Germany since 1945, as instances of a gradual pacification process that deserved further study. These were both cases, he argued, in which a clear potential for conflict had existed; yet they had been shaped by underlying expectations and perceptions that rendered a violent solution unnecessary.[26] Cooperation and compromise had come to seem more "realistic" than mutual antagonism.

At the heart of Boulding's concept of pacification lay the notion of "taboo structures." A few centuries ago, he noted, most Europeans considered slavery and torture perfectly acceptable and normal. Yet as time went by, these practices were gradually pushed beyond the threshold of legitimate behavior—they became "taboo." In a similar way, he argued, the violent resolution of conflicts was only considered acceptable in contemporary society under fairly specific conditions. Most people condemned violence as a solution among citizens or organizations *within* the same nation (those citizens who contravened this principle became criminals, and were themselves subject to state-sanctioned coercion). On the other hand, most people considered violence acceptable as a last resort *among* entire nations or peoples. The goal of a peace activist, therefore, was to find ways to extend society's taboo on violence, broadening the range of conflicts for which compromise and arbitration would be considered "the only solution." As in the case of France and Germany, Boulding pointed out, this process did not necessarily entail the creation of a supranational state; it could also rest on voluntary accommodation and compliance, pursued by two independent parties simply because the rewards of cooperative conflict-resolution greatly outweighed those of violence. Thus, war between France and Germany, while still very much a physical possibility, had gradually become a "taboo" idea in the minds of a majority of French and German citizens; a strong bias had emerged in favor of finding creative ways to resolve their conflicts by conciliatory means. For Boulding, this case offered a compelling insight into the possibilities for pacification in the broader arena of world politics. Like Szilard, Thompson, and Dolci, he argued that the threshold of legitimate violence was not fixed or static; it could gradually shift, either downward or upward, depending on the prevailing intentions and expectations of the world's peoples.

To be sure, a skeptic like Weiss could easily juxtapose the case of postwar France and Germany with vivid counterexamples in which amicable neighbors had slid down the long incline from peace into full-scale war. She could also object that successful cases of nonviolent conflict-resolution had rested on particular military, political, and economic circumstances that could not always be guaranteed to obtain. Yet this kind of objection only reinforced the logic pursued by Szilard, Thompson, and Dolci: if appropriate conditions for nonviolent conflict-resolution could and did exist, then why not try to cultivate them as extensively as possible? Certainly, there were real limits on what was attainable at any given historical moment; but the transition into a more peaceful or more warlike future was a matter of human choice. Human beings, they felt, were not condemned to endless struggles for domination and fearful self-defense; these were merely the attributes of a historical era in which the culture of cooperation had not yet attained its full potential.

Was this position "realistic?" Not in the conventional sense—for it placed its greatest emphasis upon the hidden possibilities lying latent in the human species; it wagered on something that did not yet exist (and might never exist). Nevertheless, it was not "utopian" in the conventional sense, either; for it did not invent a magical world of its own, an imaginary time and place in which serious conflicts no longer plagued human life. Instead, Szilard, Thompson, and Dolci built their strategies around the actual characteristics of contemporary citizens; they threw themselves into the practical problems of their society, obstinately seeking out the areas of sharpest conflict and most intractable controversy. Thus, these three men might plausibly be described as "utopian realists"—for they sought to establish a creative tension between the tangible conditions of the present, with all its limitations, and an alternative future. They were realistic because they sought tools of change that ordinary human beings, with all their flaws and shortcomings, could wield with a reasonable chance of success; they were utopian because they rebelled against the "givens" of contemporary politics, seeking to revise the basic ground rules that had governed society for several thousand years. They were realistic, in other words, because they pinned their hopes on tangible cooperative qualities that were observable within real people in contemporary history; they were utopian because they wagered that these positive factors might steadily outstrip the equally real and ubiquitous factors of aggression and domination.

Two Conceptions of Power

As we stand back from the foregoing discussion, attempting to reach a final assessment, it is tempting to seek a "middle road" between the two extremes of Louise Weiss and Danilo Dolci. In this closing section, I will therefore try to show why the notion of such a "middle road" can be misleading. My point of departure is a lucid and subtly argued essay by the historian Michael Howard, an essay entitled "Ethics and Power in International Policy." Howard, who would probably describe himself as a "moderate realist," *appears* to offer exactly the sort of compromise solution that weds the best elements of Weiss's and Dolci's worldviews. In fact, I will argue, the issues at stake are more resistant to compromise than they appear on the surface.

In his essay, Howard points out the quandaries that face any head of state in reconciling the often contradictory imperatives of moral rectitude and political effectiveness. "Political activity," he writes,

> takes place in a two-dimensional field—a field which can be defined by the two coordinates of ethics and power. The ethical coordinate (which we may appropriately conceive as vertical) indicates the purposes which should govern political action: the achievement of a harmonious society of mankind in which conflicts can be peacefully resolved and a community of cultures peacefully coexist within which every individual can find fulfillment. The horizontal coordinate measures the capacity of each actor to impose his will on his environment, whether by economic, military, or psychological pressures. Movement along this coordinate, the increase or decrease in coercive capability, has *as such* no dimension of morality, any more than does any elevation of moral standards necessarily involve an increase in one's power to implement them.
>
> Effective political action needs to take constant account of both dimensions. To concern oneself with ethical values to the total exclusion of any practical activity in the dimension of power is to abdicate responsibility for shaping the course of affairs. To accumulate coercive power without concern for its ethical ends is the course of the gangster. . . . Thus political action, whether in the international or any other sphere of activity, needs to be *diagonal.*[27]

Howard's position here is appealing because it remains sensitive to the moral imperatives typically stressed by activists like Dolci, while still cleaving closely to the harsh realities of power politics underscored by Weiss. Thus, he concludes,

> in pursuing his diagonal course, the statesman is like a pilot reading a compass bearing from which he must not diverge in either direction if he is to achieve his goal. . . . [He] needs to grow in moral awareness and responsibility as he grows in power.[28]

Does this represent a "middle position" between the extremes of Weiss and Dolci? In one sense, it clearly does. Weiss tended to stress the role of naked force more brashly than Howard, and she placed far less importance on the mitigating role of ethical considerations in international politics. On the spectrum ranging from Weiss to Szilard to Thompson to Dolci, therefore, Howard would probably fall somewhere between Weiss and Szilard.

In another sense, however, this comparative exercise is misleading; for at the core of Howard's schema lies an underlying assumption that ethics and power are not only separable but *in principle* opposed to each other. "Too rigorous a concern for moral absolutes," he writes, "may reduce or destroy [the statesman's] capacity for effective action."[29] The more stringently ethical one's actions, the less likely they are to be effective in politics; insofar as one wants to be truly powerful, one must proportionately renounce the demands of moral rigor.

This was precisely the kind of assumption that Szilard, Thompson, and Dolci sought to challenge—Szilard perhaps less radically than the other two, but still with great vigor and consistency. Political actors, these three men believed, did not face an unavoidable trade-off between the principles of morality and effectiveness—between impotent idealism and a tough-minded focus on "getting results." Rather, they faced a broad array of choices between many different *ways* of getting results—some of them ethically preferable to others.

The distinction here is an important one, worth elucidating in some detail. For Howard, power meant "the capacity of each actor to impose his will on his environment, whether by economic, military, or psychological pressures." Efficacy was synonymous with "coercive capability," or (in simple words) getting one's own way.[30] The role of ethics, in Howard's schema, was to complement this purely coercive capability by softening and mitigating its harsher tendencies, and by bringing into consideration the needs of a broader community. For thinkers like Szilard, Thompson, and Dolci, on the other hand, this way of thinking about power seemed insufficiently nuanced. In their view, the word "power" could also have a broader meaning than merely "coercive capability"; effectiveness did not presuppose a single actor imposing his or her will on others. Instead, it could also include such connotations as the capacity of two or more actors operating in concert to shape their common environment.

Here, perhaps, lay the deepest common conviction that bound together Szilard, Thompson, and Dolci. At some point in the twentieth century, they felt, the notion of power as "the ability to impose one's own will" had become dangerously obsolete. In a world of nuclear weapons, economic interdependence, and urgent ecological pressures, the perspective of the unitary actor pursuing its own advantage had become an anachronism. All three of these men believed that another meaning of power had to gain sway in the minds of the world's peoples, a meaning derived from the needs of all the participants and attuned to bringing forth viable compromises among them. The obsolete conception of power had aimed at enhancing the independent capabilities of a single actor. The alternative meaning, on the other hand, stemmed from a conviction that in the twentieth century this very notion of "independent capabilities" had become illusory. A war, an economic recession, a default on national debts, a nuclear meltdown, a breakdown of the atmosphere's ozone layer— these phenomena no longer took place within the traditional boundaries of territorial sovereignty and national security. They flowed across borders like the invisible currents of wind, forcing even the strongest nations to take them seriously into account. Thus, with the world's peoples becoming, to an increasing degree, mutually *dependent* and *vulnerable,* the exercise of power would have to aim at solutions that left no single actor radically dissatisfied. "We shall not have peace," Szilard wrote in 1949, "until we create a structure in which cooperation will be secured by incentives rather than precariously enforced by fear of punishment."[31]

Two distinct meanings of power lay implicit here, which I will label "coercive politics" and "cooperative politics." The former focused primarily on the interests of a single actor; its goal was to further the specific aims of that actor, regardless of how this might affect the interests of others. The second form of power came from a broader perspective: its goal was to reconcile the conflicting or overlapping interests of a plurality of actors, achieving a successful compromise among them, so that all could accept the final result. Thus, "cooperative politics" represented all those interactions in which one party secured the voluntary compliance of another party, through such means as persuasion, compromise, bargaining, or the influence of a moral example. "Coercive politics" comprised all those interactions in which human beings secured the nonvoluntary compliance of other persons or groups, through such means as physical force, threats, deceit, or manipulation.[32]

In the contemporary world, both of these types of power were likely to coexist in countless mixtures and variations. Even Gandhi himself, according to his biographers, engaged in subtle (and not-so-subtle!) forms of manipulation and coercive pressure; even Hitler relied on complex networks of cooperation and voluntary compliance. Both of these forms of power found their ultimate test in those situations when severe conflicts of interest or of ideology seemed to leave no option but violence as the ultimate arbiter. In coercive politics, however, violence represented the final threshold in an escalating array of actions that aimed primarily at subordination and compulsion. In cooperative politics, violence represented the failure of an equally broad array of actions aimed at reaching reconciliation in a manner acceptable to all sides.[33]

Both types of power, finally, could be used to pursue either moral or immoral ends. Thus, violence could serve in protecting the weak from unprovoked attack, just as cooperation could serve as the internal instrument for coordinating one group's vicious act of betrayal or aggression against another. Nevertheless, most societies have understandably placed a high intrinsic value on cooperative politics, regarding it in most cases as a morally preferable form of power to coercive politics.

The contrast here is not a mere theoretical quibble; it represents a dispute between two fundamentally divergent ways of thinking about the future. Although Howard makes it clear in his essay that he hopes the ethical component in politics will grow larger in the future, his conceptual framework actually leaves no room for such a constructive development. In his schema, the most plausible pathway for action remains the diagonal line, halfway between "ethics" and "power," whether ten years or one hundred years from today; any deviation from that line will inevitably constitute a proportionate loss either of efficacy or of moral rigor. Since the only way to achieve efficacy is through "coercive capability," the ratio between "coercive capability" and ethical action must always remain roughly the same. Violence and the threat of violence, as crucial components of this concept of power, must continue to play approximately the same role in tomorrow's society as they always have done in the past.

On the other hand, if one adopts the alternative framework, in which at least two *kinds* of power confront the political actor, then the range of possibilities for the future becomes much wider. An increase in cooperative or noncoercive forms of action would not necessarily imply a loss of effectiveness. As with Kenneth Boulding's example of postwar France and Germany, one can envision situations in which formerly antagonistic peoples have come to regard coercive forms of conflict-resolution as unacceptable, "taboo." These two peoples continue to engage in a wide variety of transactions, effectively shaping their common social environment, yet they carry out these transactions according to an ethos of mutual accommodation rather than one of domination by one actor over the other. Over time, if such a cooperative ethos indeed became more generalized, the range of violent solutions in international politics might be gradually narrowed. Although the possibility of violence would always exist, the probability of people resorting to it would have diminished significantly. Thus, in this framework, coherent political forms that evolve toward diminishing levels of coercion become at least conceivable.

One simple way of picturing such a transition is through the metaphor of a piano keyboard, in which the left edge represents the extreme of coercive politics, while the right edge represents the extreme of cooperative politics. At any given time, the range of human interactions is likely to encompass a specific spectrum of keys and notes, corresponding to a specific constellation of power relations among different individuals and peoples. The goal of a peace activist, in this sense, would be to persuade as many people as possible to choose forms of power along the right side of the keyboard, gradually shifting the "center of balance" from the left toward the right, from coercion to cooperation. Although the option of coercion would always remain open, the frequency of cases in which people resorted to it would then steadily decrease. To be sure, even if this optimistic picture became a reality, renegade cases of aggression or violence would presumably still have to be countered with the tools of coercion; but this would take place as part of a broader cooperative effort among a wide coalition of actors seeking to restore the prevailing environment of cooperative conflict-resolution.

From the perspective of Louise Weiss and *Realpolitik,* of course, the great weakness of cooperative politics lay precisely in the fact that it requires *two* or more actors to work reasonably together, if it is to succeed. But what if one's neighbors refuse to go along? What about cheaters, freeloaders, and those who are unwilling to bear their fair share of the burdens that cooperation imposes? What about aggressive and militant ideologies, ethnic or religious hatreds, or that elemental historical factor, expansionist greed? The answers given by Szilard, Thompson, and Dolci to these kinds of objections were strikingly similar. Now that virtually all the earth's peoples were bound increasingly by ties of mutual dependence and vulnerability, a new awareness had to take root among them: cooperation did not represent a matter of choice but rather of sheer survival. If such an awareness failed to spread, then disastrous military conflicts would probably become harder and harder to avoid. But if this new mentality *did* begin to gain sway, then the likelihood of finding strongly motivated partners for cooperation would grow proportionately. If the stakes came to be perceived by growing numbers of national governments as very high, then the incentive to compromise and work with others as a team would also increase. Under such conditions, the exercise of cooperative politics might begin to register important successes; a group that adopted a belligerent and unyielding stance in a conflict would be far more likely than in the past to find itself rapidly isolated, and to face a strong coalition of opponents, all conjoined in pressuring it to compromise. According to the political scientist Ernst B. Haas, this kind of "learning" has already begun to occur among many nations—although it still has a long way to go:

> A sequence of episodes involving conflict and its abatement through the United Nations can be expected to make [national] actors aware of the fact that they are subject to constraints other than their relative weakness vis-à-vis their opponents. Such constraints include the need to justify themselves when attacked in a United Nations forum, to be threatened with boycotts or ostracism, to be made the subject of peacekeeping against their will. The constraints also include the recognition that persistence in unilateral behavior can result in eventual isolation and even defeat. . . .
>
> In the language of the game theory, the players in the security game must be conscious about the advantage of collaborating, instead of defecting. . . . We must recall that learnt cooperative behavior is not a selfless act: it depends upon being rewarded.[34]

Szilard, Thompson, and Dolci were by no means sanguine about the likelihood of achieving such a self-reinforcing learning process among the world's nations; but they believed that nuclear weapons, and the fear they created, had changed the odds dramatically—perhaps enough to give cooperative politics a chance.[35]

Such are the indirect, but momentous, consequences of how one thinks about power. If, as Howard argues, power can only mean "the ability to coerce," then one must draw conclusions similar to Louise Weiss's: violence will inevitably play a key role in all future international relations. If, on the other hand, one believes that an alternative type of power exists that can be equally effective, then the goal of gradually reducing international violence remains at least possible. If cooperative politics can have its own efficacy, *separately* from coercive politics, then one form of power could incrementally displace the other.

Seen from this perspective, the "middle road" between the extremes of Weiss and Dolci would not involve an indefinite trade-off between coercion and ethics, but rather an acute awareness that two *kinds* of political efficacy are open to human beings. A stance of cautious hope, its maxim might be: "Remember Hitler, but don't forget Gandhi either." Statesmen following this middle road would take constant account of the widespread coercive forces active in contemporary society, while placing equally constant pressure on the outer edge of innovative cooperation.

In concrete practice, these leaders would most probably continue to rely on military forces controlled by their own sovereign governments, but they might also undertake to strengthen as much as possible such coordinating bodies as the United Nations. They would vigorously promote collective forms of international arbitration and decision making, and hand over the role of military enforcement to U.N.-controlled armies whenever possible.[36] In the words of the historian Stanley Hoffmann,

> We need a statecraft that stresses long-term collective gains rather than short or long-term national advantages; that accepts the need for a large measure of institutionalization in international affairs, and for important commitments of resources to common enterprises; that shows great restraint in its use of means; and that goes, in its ends, far beyond the [current] realm of interstate relations.[37]

The result of such innovative statecraft would not necessarily have to be the centralized global superstate that Thompson and Dolci feared; nor would it necessarily bear much resemblance to Szilard's vision of spheres of influence. Yet the existence of such a reinvigorated United Nations, performing growing numbers of functions alongside existing governments, could in time greatly accentuate the credibility of cooperative conflict-resolution. It would be a far cry from Dolci's vision of nonviolent grass-roots democracy, yet it would be equally far from Weiss's world of bristling blocs, armed to the teeth and glaring at each other in mutual defiance. Whether such a reenergized international body could eventually go farther, assuming exclusive authority over all military and perhaps ecological matters, would be for another generation to decide; but that generation would presumably have been able to witness—and experience directly—how far such a global agency could be trusted. This "middle road," therefore, would start out quite pragmatically with existing institutions and habits, but would seek to prod them, in incremental steps, toward an ever-greater reliance on cooperative politics.

To be fair to Dolci (and Thompson), moreover, it is important to add that this "middle road" would also need to go beyond the state-centric forms of change we have just discussed. Without discounting the central role to be played by states and statesmen, another dimension of change could prove equally crucial: private citizens, grass-roots groups, business associations, religious organizations, and professional societies could all play a significant part in pushing the world's nations toward greater cooperation. These initiatives "from below" could take countless forms, but their common aim would be to promote the mentality and the habits of cooperative politics among the world's peoples themselves—not just among their formal institutions of government.[38] Isolated examples of such grass-roots initiatives almost inevitably end up sounding rather quaint, appearing almost "microscopic" compared to the magnitude of the earth's problems—as in the following item from a *Newsweek* article on the African famine of 1984:

> In the Northwest territories of Canada, two Eskimo villages raised $7,000 for Ethiopian relief.[39]

Yet such an action—Eskimos coming to the aid of Ethiopians—also contains the promise of considerable power. A thin lifeline thrown from one continent to another, it links the small and local with the very large and abstract, and makes real something that had only existed before as potential: a bond of solidarity. To the extent that human beings shape their own history, it is partly through such "microscopic" choices and commitments, laid in against daunting odds, that they do so at all; for a particular act may appear minuscule and frail in its impact, but when it recurs over innumerable instances, the result of similar choices made by other individuals, it can acquire potency on a scale that affects the entire world.

Is the pursuit of such a "middle road" any different, in practice, from what many earnest politicians and common citizens have always regarded as their civic duty? Probably not. Yet the contribution of the "utopian realists" remains important nonetheless, because it counteracts the insidious tendency to settle for less, to acquiesce in the tantalizing habit of coercive action. By affirming cooperative politics as a viable alternative, a coherent form of power in its own right, the "utopian realists" were prying open the door for a different future.

Perhaps their greatest contribution, therefore, lay precisely in this: they pioneered and put into practice a set of ideas that had long tended to be dismissed as fanciful, and they did so in a way that proved hard to ignore—by turning those ideas into concrete reality. Many of their experiments were failures, or only partial successes; but they also won some impressive victories for their ideal of cooperation, victories that broadened the imagination of their contemporaries. Szilard's exchanges with Khrushchev, his Council for a Livable World, the White House/Kremlin hotline—all these endeavors challenged the prevailing superpower diplomacy, urging Americans and Russians to adopt a logic of cooperative self-interest, based on a core of vital needs shared in common. Thompson, through the mass rallies and annual conventions of END, showed that millions of Europeans adamantly rejected the confrontational stance of figures like Reagan, Thatcher, and Brezhnev; these millions put strong and effective pressure on their political leaders to stop portraying the Cold War as an immutable "given," and to act vigorously in seeking accommodation between the two sides. Dolci, finally, aimed toward the most distant horizon of all three. The Jato dam provided a looming testimonial to the power of organized nonviolent action, even against so ruthless an opponent as the Italian mafia. His school at Mirto put a new set of power relations into daily practice, both between students and teachers, and among the students themselves—a form of decision making that placed its main emphasis on finding creative pathways for teamwork and compromise. Thus, although the tradition of competitive *Realpolitik* certainly remained alive and well as the Cold War era came to an end, these three men had also opened up practical alternatives to *Realpolitik,* from the highest pinnacles of diplomacy to the raw immediacy of the grass roots. Their efforts, carried on tenaciously over decades, set new standards and expectations for the resolution of conflicts in the future. It was a limited achievement, but a substantial one.

Louise Weiss, in thinking about peace, stressed the recurring patterns of aggression and domination in history; Szilard, Thompson and Dolci stressed the human capacity for adaptation to meet new needs. The tension between these two positions could not be definitively resolved, for they each emphasized essential aspects of historical process: continuity and innovation. The drawback of the more radical position was that it required taking risks, exploring new and untried forms of social order that might or might not succeed. The drawback of the conservative position, on the other hand, lay in its tendency to reinforce existing patterns of behavior, replicating the inheritance of the past and diminishing the possibilities for new patterns to emerge.

This tension also had a positive side, however, for it implied that human endeavors possessed a cumulative quality, so that each individual's efforts, and each generation's achievements, might contribute to the building of something partially new. "If humanity wants peace, where does it need to start?" a journalist asked Danilo Dolci in 1977. "Let me tell you about something I have learned," Dolci replied.

> In the 1700s, the city of Venice possessed no fewer than 27 print shops devoted exclusively to producing musical scores; the population didn't merely listen to music, it *made* music. It was the same with architecture. Venice was not just built by architects with a capital "A," but by each family working in close collaboration with designers and construction workers, determined to render each house a work of art. The city grew in this kind of climate, each house, each piazza, one by one. In this way, over the years, a creative population was able to build the Venice that we see today, a collective masterpiece.
>
> The Venetians' achievement consisted in setting high standards, and then painstakingly putting the pieces into place, one by one. We, too, must proceed in a similar way if we want to bring forth a new culture for our own terrestrial city: each of us doing our part, piece by piece.[40]

A "new culture" for the terrestrial city: What shape would this collective creation take? Here was the great question that these four careers left open, for the coming generations to answer through their actions.

NOTES

Introduction

1. Interviews with Danilo Dolci, Partinico, Italy (May–June, 1986).

2. Kenneth Waltz, *Theory of International Politics* (New York: McGraw-Hill, 1979), 117.

3. The tension between "realism" and ethics in foreign policy has been the subject of many scholarly studies and analyses. See for instance Terry Nardin and David R. Mapel, eds., *Traditions of International Ethics* (Cambridge: Cambridge University Press, 1992); Joel H. Rosenthal, *Righteous Realists: Political Realism, Responsible Power, and American Culture in the Nuclear Age* (Baton Rouge: Louisiana State University Press, 1991); Michael J. Smith, *Realist Thought from Weber to Kissinger* (Baton Rouge: Louisiana State University Press, 1986); Gerard Elfstrom, *Ethics for a Shrinking World* (New York: St. Martin's, 1990); Louise Henkin et al., *Right vs. Might: International Law and the Use of Force* (New York: Council on Foreign Relations, 1991); Stanley Hoffman, *Duties beyond Borders: On the Limits and Possibilities of Ethical International Relations* (Syracuse: Syracuse University Press, 1981); Dorothy V. Jones, *Code of Peace: Ethics and Security in the World of the Warlord States* (Chicago: University of Chicago Press, 1991); Kenneth Kipnis and Diana T. Meyers, eds., *Political Realism and International Morality: Ethics in the Nuclear Age* (Boulder, Colo.: Westview, 1987); Mary Maxwell, *Morality among Nations: An Evolutionary View* (Albany, N.Y.: State University of New York Press, 1990); Kenneth W. Thompson, *Morality and Foreign Policy* (Baton Rouge: Louisiana State University Press, 1980); Daniel Warner, *An Ethic of Responsibility in International Relations* (Boulder, Colo.: L. Rienner, 1991); Martin Wight, *Power Politics,* ed. Hedley Bull and Carsten Holbraad (Leicester: Leicester University Press, 1978).

4. Leo Szilard, "Letter to Stalin" (December 1947), in Helen S. Hawkins et al., eds., *Toward a Livable World* (Cambridge, Mass.: MIT Press, 1987), 28–29.

5. Albert Wohlstetter, "The Delicate Balance of Terror," *Foreign Affairs* 37, no. 2 (January 1959).

6. E. P. Thompson, "Will 1983 End in Darkness for Europe?" *Sanity* (December 1983).

7. Interviews with Danilo Dolci, Partinico, Italy (May–June, 1986).

8. E. P. Thompson, "Mr. Attlee and the Gadarene Swine," in *The Heavy Dancers* (London: Merlin Press, 1985), 245.

9. Interview with Basil Davidson, North Wootton, England (November 26, 1986).

Chapter One

1. Louise Weiss, "Tempête sur l'Occident," *Mémoires d'une Européenne, 1945–1975*, vol. 6 (Paris: Albin Michel, 1975), 123 (hereafter *Mémoires*, vol. 6).

2. Louise Weiss, *Le Fer Rouge*, no. 7 (June 20, 1957): 2, 6. Weiss Papers, Bibliothèque Nationale (Paris), Département des Manuscrits, Don 84-06, Carton 8.

3. Louise Weiss, "Une petite fille du siècle," *Mémoires d'une Européenne, 1893–1919*, vol. 1 (Paris: Payot, 1968), 60ff. (hereafter *Mémoires*, vol. 1).

4. "Renaissance Woman," *Time* (January 28, 1980) (European ed.).

5. See Tom Kemp, *Economic Forces in French History* (London: Dennis Dobson, 1971), chap. 9; Eugen Weber, *France, fin de siècle* (Cambridge, Mass.: Belknap Press, 1986); Jean-Marie Mayeur et al., *Histoire du peuple français: Cent ans d'esprit républicain*, vol. 5 (Paris: Nouvelle Librairie de France, 1965), chaps. 1–8.

6. See Theodore Zeldin, *France, 1848–1945: Ambition, Love, and Politics*, vol. 1 (Oxford: Clarendon Press, 1973), 343ff.; and Louise A. Tilly and Joan W. Scott, *Women, Work, and Family* (New York: Holt, Rinehart, and Winston, 1978), 150ff.

7. Louise Weiss, *Mémoires*, vol. 1, 47.

8. Ibid., 162.

9. Ibid., 291.

10. Ibid., 292.

11. Ibid., 121.

12. Ibid., chaps. 20, 22.

13. Louise Weiss, "Trotsky parle," *L'Europe Nouvelle*, no. 51 (December 17, 1921): 1620.

14. Louise Weiss, "Ce que dit Tchitchérine," *L'Europe Nouvelle*, no. 51 (December 17, 1921): 1627.

15. Louise Weiss, "Le tsar famine," *L'Europe Nouvelle*, no. 51 (December 17, 1921): 1648 (emphasis in original).

16. See Martin Ceadel, *Pacifism in Britain, 1914–1945* (Oxford: Clarendon Press, 1980); Louise Weiss, "Combats pour l'Europe," *Mémoires d'une Européenne, 1919–1934*, vol. 2 (Paris: Albin Michel, 1979), 213 (hereafter *Mémoires*, vol. 2).

17. See for instance A. P. Thornton, *The Imperial Idea and Its Enemies* (New York: St. Martin's Press, 1985); and Paul C. Sorum, *Intellectuals and Decolonization in France* (Chapel Hill: University of North Carolina Press, 1977).

18. For an excellent discussion of the League of Nations and of the obstacles faced by its creators, see Dorothy V. Jones, *Code of Peace: Ethics and Security in the World of the Warlord States* (Chicago: University of Chicago Press, 1989).

19. Louise Weiss, "Notre bilan," *L'Europe Nouvelle* 6, no. 52 (December 29, 1923): 1654.

20. Louise Weiss, "Entre le Traité de Versailles et le Pacte," *L'Europe Nouvelle* 8, no. 399 (October 10, 1925): 1338–39.

21. Louise Weiss, "Du Traité de Versailles au Pacte Kellogg," *L'Europe Nouvelle* 11, no. 550 (August 25, 1928): 1142–43.

22. Louise Weiss, "1925, L'année de Locarno," *L'Europe Nouvelle*, 8, no. 410 (December 26, 1925): 1723.

23. Conférences de l'Ecole de la Paix: Sommaire. Weiss Papers, Bibliothèque Nationale (Paris): Département des Manuscrits: *Nouvelles Acquisitions Françaises* (hereafter Weiss Papers, *NAF*), vol. 17815, 10–16.

24. Louise Weiss, "Auditeurs de l'Ecole de la Paix," Weiss Papers, *NAF*, vol. 17817, 5ff.

25. Ibid., 247.

26. Ibid., 241–42.

27. Louise Weiss, *Mémoires,* vol. 2, 335.

28. Ibid., 286.

29. Ibid., 214–15.

30. Ibid., 330–31.

31. Ibid., 330.

32. Louise Weiss, "Combats pour les femmes," *Mémoires d'une Européenne, 1934–39,* vol. 3 (Paris: Payot, 1970), 16 (hereafter *Mémoires,* vol. 3).

33. Ibid., 19.

34. Ibid., 36.

35. Weiss blamed this pervasive inequality partly on the electoral fears of political parties in the moderate Center and Center-Left (the Radicals, Moderates, and Socialists). These politicians, she argued, continued to mouth a vague rhetoric of universal suffrage and democracy, while adamantly blocking all serious attempts to accord women the vote. They feared that most women would vote according to the instructions of priests, thereby vastly reinforcing the parties of the Right and destroying the fragile electoral balance on which the Third Republic rested. See ibid., 26.

36. With the passing of years, Weiss became increasingly convinced that women could behave even more aggressively, in moments of dire threat, than men. At the outbreak of the Second World War, she was particularly moved to witness the fervor with which women sought to volunteer for military action against the Nazis. "The most touching ones," she wrote, "were the solitary women, widows of the past war." Ibid., 207.

37. Ibid., 36.

38. Ibid., 59ff.

39. Ibid., 87.

40. Ibid., 120.

41. Ibid., 233ff.

42. Louise Weiss, "Le sacrifice du Chevalier," *Mémoires d'une Européenne, 3 Séptembre 1939–9 Juin 1940,* vol. 4 (Paris: Albin Michel, 1971), 13 (hereafter *Mémoires,* vol. 4).

43. Ibid., 266.

44. See Robert O. Paxton, *Vichy France: Old Guard and New Order, 1940–1944* (New York: Columbia University Press, 1972).

45. Louise Weiss, "La Résurrection du Chevalier," *Mémoires d'une Européenne, Juin 1940–Août 1944,* vol. 5 (Paris: Albin Michel, 1974), appendix 1, 433 (hereafter *Mémoires,* vol. 5).

46. Ibid, 262ff.

47. Ibid., 354–55. Two excellent accounts of the French Resistance, by direct participants, are Henri Noguères et al., *Histoire de la Résistance en France, de 1940 à 1945,* 5 vols. (Paris: Robert Laffont, 1981); and Claude Bourdet, *L'aventure incertaine: De la résistance à la restauration* (Paris: Stock, 1975).

48. Louise Weiss, *Mémoires,* vol. 5, 357ff.

49. Ibid., 413.

50. See M. Adereth, *The French Communist Party: A Critical History, 1920–1984* (Manchester: Manchester University Press, 1984), 132ff.; and B. D. Graham, *The French Socialists and Tripartisme, 1944–1947* (Toronto: University of Toronto Press, 1965), 17ff.

51. Louise Weiss, *Mémoires,* vol. 6, 510.

52. Louise Weiss, "Elections municipales, 8 Mai 1945," personal notes. Weiss Papers, *NAF,* vol. 17800, 139.

53. These included *L'Aurore, Parisien-Libéré, France-Illustration,* and *Paris-Match.*

54. Interviews with Georges Bourdelon, March 1987.

55. Louise Weiss, "Remarques sur la co-existence des civilisations primitives et de la civilisation occidentale," speech before the Académie des Sciences Morales et Politiques, Paris (February 22, 1954); printed in *Revue des Travaux de l'Académie des Sciences Morales et Politiques* (premier sémestre, 1954): 83–93.

56. See Raymond Betts, *Assimilation and Association in French Colonial Theory, 1890–1914* (New York: Columbia University Press, 1961); and Raoul Girardet, *L'idée coloniale en France de 1871 à 1962* (Paris: La Table Ronde, 1972).

57. See Raymond Betts, *Assimilation and Association.*

58. For a systematic study of this mystificatory device in the work of several French social thinkers, see Susanna Barrows, *Distorting Mirrors: Visions of the Crowd in Late-Nineteenth-Century France* (New Haven: Yale University Press, 1981). For an analysis focusing specifically on the moral and cultural ideologies of colonialism, see Edward Said, *Orientalism* (New York: Pantheon, 1978).

59. Louise Weiss, "Remarques sur la co-existence des civilisations primitives et de la civilisation occidentale."

60. Louise Weiss, "Le retournement des morts à Madagascar" (1961), and "Allah aux Comores" (1961), documentary films. Original prints in Archives du Film, Bois D'Arcy, France.

61. Louise Weiss, "Extrait du discours au déjeuner de la presse Anglo-Américaine" (February 1950). Weiss Papers, *NAF,* vol. 17803, 90–97.

62. Louise Weiss, personal notes (1950). Weiss Papers, *NAF,* vol. 17803, 150–51.

63. Claude Bourdet, *L'Afrique du Nord et nous* (Paris: Burin-Martinsart, 1973), 25.

64. Raymond Betts, *Tricouleur: The French Overseas Empire* (New York: Gordon & Cremonesi, 1978), 81.

65. Ibid., 80.

66. Ibid., 83.

67. Ibid., 86ff.

68. See Maurice Agulhon and André Nouschi, *La France de 1940 à nos jours* (Paris: Nathan, 1984), 160ff.

69. See Louise Weiss, *Mémoires,* vol. 6, 184ff., 202–6, 333ff.

70. Ibid., 455.

71. See *Sondages: Revue Française de l'opinion publique,* no. 3 (1956): 32; and no. 2 (1957): 49.

72. The enduring image of a "humanist empire" for the French Left is analyzed in detail in Paul C. Sorum, *Intellectuals and Decolonization in France* (Chapel Hill: University of North Carolina Press, 1977). See also the criticism of this tendency in Claude Bourdet, *L'aventure incertaine: De la résistance à la restauration* (Paris: Stock, 1975), 443ff.

73. Raymond Betts, *Tricouleur,* 143.

74. Agulhon and Nouschi, 142.

75. Walter LaFeber, *America, Russia, and the Cold War, 1945–1984* (New York: Alfred A. Knopf, 1985), 161.

76. Agulhon and Nouschi, 151.

77. Claude Bourdet, *L'aventure incertaine,* 444ff.; Raymond Betts, *Tricouleur,* 136–38.

78. The one notable exception, of course, was U.S. assistance to France in its attempt to recolonize Indochina from 1945 through 1954. The United States made this exception because the threat posed by Ho Chi Minh's Communist affiliations took precedence over the traditional U.S. abhorrence for colonial rule.

79. Louise Weiss, *Le Fer Rouge,* no. 7 (June 20, 1957): 2,6. Weiss Papers, Bibliothèque Nationale (Paris), Département des Manuscrits, Don 84-06, Carton 8.

80. Louise Weiss, *Mémoires,* vol. 6, 215.

81. Louise Weiss, "L'Europe se fera en Afrique," *Dépêche Marocaine de Tanger* (January 7, 1952). Weiss Papers, *NAF,* vol. 17802, 1–3; see also *Mémoires,* vol. 5, 214ff.

82. Louise Weiss, *Mémoires,* vol. 6, 516.

83. In 1954, on a tour through Central America, she held up the civil war in Guatemala as a classic example of this contradiction:

> The conflict between Guatemalan rebels and government forces exposes the basic problem of American neocolonialism. What is at stake is the expropriation of the United Fruit Company: the transfer of commercial sovereignty from American capitalism (paternalistic but foreign) to the hands of the local government. This government does not know how to manage the huge company, . . . with its complex ties to the global economy; but its act of expropriation is the expression of a jealous rage on the part of the local populations. . . .
>
> Today [the Americans] must recognize that certain formulas of [direct] French tutelage brought about far more significant and lasting results than their own disguised protectorates. (Louise Weiss, "Bananes, Chewing-Gum, et Perroquets," unpublished article (1954). Weiss Papers, *NAF,* vol. 17804, 80–88)

84. Louise Weiss, "Le barrage des treize tombeaux," documentary film (1958). Original print in Archives du Film, Bois D'Arcy, France.

85. Louise Weiss, *Le Fer Rouge,* no. 12 (October 31, 1957): 3. Weiss Papers, Don 84-06, Carton 8.

86. Louis Weiss, *Mémoires,* vol. 6, 507–08.

87. Ibid., 505–06.

88. From 1966 to 1970, Weiss worked part-time with Gaston Bouthoul, a scholar whom she had known since the 1950s who was a sociologist specializing in the statistical analysis of war. Weiss assisted Bouthoul as the editor of a periodical journal, *Guerres et Paix* ("Wars and Peace"), funded by the French Ministry of Defense. She and Bouthoul acrimoniously ended their collaboration in 1970, after he refused to credit Weiss as a joint author of his scholarly publications. See Gaston Bouthoul and René Carrère, *Le défi de la guerre* (Paris: Presses Universitaires de France, 1976), 171ff; and Louis Weiss, *Mémoires,* vol. 6, 73.

89. Weiss's correspondence with such individuals as the president of the French Senate and the French ambassador to Sweden, spanning the years from 1970 to 1980, are contained in Weiss Papers, Don 84-06, Carton 6.

90. Interviews with a close friend of Louise Weiss, Andrée Martin-Pannetier, Paris (February–March 1987).

91. Ibid.

92. Louise Weiss, *Mémoires,* vol. 6, 16.

93. An exhaustive record of Weiss's travels during the late 1970s is in Weiss Papers, Don 84-06, Carton 5.

94. Edouard Herriot, "La naissance de l'union Européenne," speech before the Ecole de la Paix (November 12, 1931). Weiss Papers, *NAF,* vol. 17817, 23ff.

95. Walter Lipgens, *A History of European Integration, 1945–1947,* vol. 1, trans. P. S. Falla and A. J. Ryder (Oxford: Clarendon Press, 1982), 36.

96. For a detailed account of the early decades of European integration, see Richard Mayne, *The Recovery of Europe* (New York: Harper & Row, 1970). See also F. Roy Willis, *Italy Chooses Europe* (New York: Oxford University Press, 1971), 286ff.; Alain Greilsammer, *Les mouvements fédéralistes en France de 1945 à 1974* (Paris: Presses D'Europe, 1975); Hans A. Schmidt, *The Path to European Union* (Westport, Conn.: Greenwood Press, 1981); Russell B. Capelle, *The MRP and French Foreign Policy* (New York: Praeger, 1963), esp. 52ff.; and Office for Official Publications of the European Communities, *Steps to European Unity* (Luxembourg, 1985), 79.

97. Daniel Lerner and Raymond Aron, *France Defeats EDC* (New York: Praeger, 1957), 162.

98. Louise Weiss, "Allocution de la doyenne d'age," *Débats du Parlement Européen* (Séance du Mardi, 17 Juillet, 1979): 6.

99. Louise Weiss to Carl Carstens (president of West Germany) (November 5, 1980). Weiss Papers, Don 84-06, Carton 7.

100. Louise Weiss, speech before the French Senate (October 27, 1978). Weiss Papers, Don 84-06, Carton 4.

101. See for instance the survey of these critical reviews in Stanley Hoffmann, *Decline or Renewal? France since the 1930s* (New York: Viking, 1974), 63ff., 283ff. See also H. Stuart Hughes, "A French Form of Fascism," in F. Roy Willis, ed., *DeGaulle: Anachronism, Realist, or Prophet?* (New York: Holt, Rinehart, & Winston, 1967), 40ff.; and Claude Bourdet, *L'aventure incertaine,* 422–26.

102. See Stanley Hoffmann, *Decline or Renewal;* Alfred Grosser, *French Foreign Policy under De Gaulle* (Boston: Little, Brown, 1967); and Edward A. Kolodziej,

French International Policy under De Gaulle and Pompidou (Ithaca: Cornell University Press, 1974).

103. Even the French Resistance leader Claude Bourdet, whose political sympathies lay with the non-Communist Left, and who did not spare the mainstream politicians of postwar France from harsh criticisms, nevertheless strongly defended the manner in which De Gaulle managed to extricate France from the Algerian quagmire:

> De Gaulle had at least one major positive quality: his pragmatism, his ability to perform an about-face and to head in a new direction when faced with an insurmountable obstacle. It is this quality, I think, that best explains De Gaulle's often contradictory maneuvering in his Algerian policy. He was not a cynical Machiavellian, deliberately deceiving both sides in the dispute—as he has been accused of being, both by his enemies, and, surprisingly, also by some of his closest friends. (Claude Bourdet, *L'Afrique du Nord et nous,* 43.)

104. Stanley Hoffmann, *Decline or Renewal,* 32; Kolodziej.

105. Louise Weiss, "Discours à Bonn" (November 20, 1980). Weiss Papers, Don 84-06, Carton 5.

106. See for instance Louise Weiss, *Lettre à un embryon* (Paris: Julliard, 1973), 99–101.

107. Louise Weiss, *Mémoires,* vol. 6, 14 (see also 72ff. and 510). Weiss's only extended discussion of nuclear catastrophe (three pages long) occurs in another work, *Lettre à un embryon.* Here, once again, her main focus is not on the danger of nuclear war, or on how to mitigate it, but rather on how the *fear* of nuclear war has in effect paralyzed the Great Powers from flexing their military muscle as much as they would like. See Louise Weiss, *Lettre à un embryon,* 99–101.

108. See Louise Weiss, *Lettre à un embryon,* 99–101.

109. See for instance Louise Weiss, "Discours à Bonn."

110. Louise Weiss, "Note sur la sécurité Européenne," draft proposal (October 14, 1981). Weiss Papers, Don 84-06, Carton 4bis.

111. Louise Weiss, personal memorandum (July 7, 1976). Weiss Papers, Don 84-06, Carton 2.

112. Not surprisingly, Weiss's proposal was rejected by the Parliament. Louise Weiss, "Proposition de résolution presentée par Louise Weiss sur la faim dans le monde" (September 15, 1980), Doc. 1-383-80. Weiss Papers, Don 84-06, Carton 4bis.

113. Louise Weiss, *Dépêche Marocaine de Tanger* (January–February, 1952): 1 (emphasis in original). Weiss Papers, *NAF,* vol. 17802, p. 1.

114. Louise Weiss, *Mémoires,* vol. 6, 508.

115. Louise Weiss, *Le Fer Rouge,* no. 4 (May 9, 1957): 2.

116. Louise Weiss, *Lettre à un embryon,* 43ff.

117. Louise Weiss, *Mémoires,* vol. 6, 76.

118. Louise Weiss, "Qui sont les victimes?" *Le Figaro* (June 4, 1981).

119. The conversation took place on April 16, 1953. Vincent Auriol, *Journal du Septennat, 1947–1954,* vol. 7 (Paris: Armand Colin, 1971), 120–21.

120. Louise Weiss, *Mémoires,* vol. 6, 515, 508.

121. Weiss vigorously defended South Africa, for example, from its anti-*apartheid* detractors. She argued that it was against European interests to weaken this bastion of anticommunism and crucial foothold of "white civilization" in Africa. Her correspondence on this subject is contained in Weiss Papers, Don 84-06, Carton 5.

122. Hans Morgenthau, *Politics among Nations,* 3d ed. (New York: Alfred A. Knopf, 1961), 337.

123. See Jean Klein, "Le débat en France sur la défense de l'Europe," *Stratégique* (quatrième trimestre, 1984): 8–14.

124. Ibid., 24ff.

125. Edouard Balladur, *Le Figaro* (June 26, 1980): 1, 4.

126. Jean-Pierre Chevènement, "Intervention au colloque 'L'Europe face aux empires,'" unpublished manuscript, Strasbourg (January 19, 1987), 12, 13, 17 (emphasis in original).

127. At times, moreover, Weiss's views also were echoed by the increasingly popular and vocal politicians on the extreme Right of the French political spectrum. Weiss had no connections with these politicians, but her picture of a resurgent Europe sometimes came remarkably close to theirs. Consider for instance the following excerpt from a 1985 pamphlet by Jean-Marc Brissaud, the secretary-general of the European Parliament's extreme-right-wing grouping, and a prominent member of Jean-Marie Le Pen's National Front:

> Europe—a united and independent Europe capable of defending itself—must understand that its future and its expansion lie toward the south. Eurafrica [*sic*] must become the master-word of tomorrow. The European states allowed their first chance to go by when they lost their colonial empires; . . . they must not miss this second opportunity. . . . In the hour of the great empires—America on one side, Soviet Russia on the other; in the hour of the rising political power of China and economic power of Japan; in the hour of the renewal of Islam and the danger of demographic invasion; Europe, only Europe possesses the scale required to meet the economic, technological, political, and military challenges of the 21st century. (Jean-Marc Brissaud, *Eléments pour une nouvelle politique étrangère* [Pau: Front National, Université d'Eté, September 1985], 38, 43; interview with Jean-Marc Brissaud, Paris [April 15, 1987])

128. The nation-by-nation figures were as follows:

	France (%)	Great Britain (%)	Italy (%)	West Germany (%)
Keep NATO as is	26	41	19	54
European Common Defense	35	23	38	19
Return to National Defense	20	26	31	25
No Opinion	20	10	12	2

Source: Carlos de Sa Rego, "Le parapluie de l'Oncle Sam a perdu ses charmes," *Libération* (February 16, 1987).

129. Nicole Zand, "La mort de Louise Weiss," *Le Monde* (May 28, 1983): 1, 9.

130. Interview with Pierre Pflimlin, Strasbourg (April 25, 1986).

131. See Diana Johnstone, *The Politics of Euromissiles* (London: Verso, 1984), chap. 3.

132. Lance Morrow, *Time* (January 14, 1980): 18–19 (European ed.).

133. Thucydides, *The Peloponnesian War,* vol. 2, book 5, trans. Benjamin Jowett (Oxford: Clarendon Press, 1900), 169.

Chapter Two

1. Leo Szilard, "Draft of a Proposal for a New Organization Called 'Der Bund,'" in Spencer R. Weart and Gertrud Weiss Szilard, eds., *Leo Szilard: His Version of the Facts*, vol. 2 of the Collected Works of Leo Szilard (Cambridge, Mass.: MIT Press, 1978), 23 (hereafter *His Version of the Facts*).

2. Leo Szilard, "Letter to President Roosevelt" (March 25, 1945), *His Version of the Facts*, 205ff.

3. Since Szilard's lifetime up to 1945 has been amply documented elsewhere, I will limit myself here to a brief sketch. See Richard Rhodes, *The Making of the Atomic Bomb* (New York: Simon & Schuster, 1986); Gertrud Weiss Szilard and Spencer Weart, eds., *Leo Szilard: His Version of the Facts* (Cambridge: MIT Press, 1978); and the biography by William Lanouette and Bela Silard (Leo Szilard's brother), *Genius in the Shadows* (New York: Scribner's, 1993). See also on Szilard's postwar activities Barton J. Bernstein, "Introduction," in Helen S. Hawkins, G. Allen Greb, and Gertrud W. Szilard, eds., *Toward a Livable World: Leo Szilard and the Crusade for Nuclear Arms Control*, vol. 3 of the Collected Works of Leo Szilard (Cambridge, Mass.: MIT Press, 1987), xvii–lxxiv (hereafter *Toward a Livable World*).

4. Bela Silard, in Helen Weiss and Alain Jehlen, "Rough Assembly Script [April 19, 1989]," WGBH program on Leo Szilard, 4. Courtesy of Helen Weiss and Alain Jehlen.

5. Leo Szilard, "Recollections," in *His Version of the Facts*, 3.

6. Ibid.

7. Ibid., 4.

8. Leo Szilard, "Are We on the Road to War?" *Bulletin of the Atomic Scientists* 18, no. 24 (April 1962).

9. Leo Szilard, "Recollections," 9–11.

10. Ibid., 16.

11. Ibid., 13.

12. Ibid.

13. Ibid.

14. Ibid., 17.

15. Ibid., 17n.23.

16. Ibid., 13 (emphasis in original).

17. Ibid., 21.

18. Szilard to F. A. Lindemann (January 13, 1939), in *His Version of the Facts*, 50–52.

19. Leo Szilard, "Recollections," 55.

20. Quoted in Martin J. Sherwin, *A World Destroyed* (New York: Vintage, 1977), 27.

21. See *His Version of the Facts*, 164ff.

22. Leo Szilard, "Reminiscences," in Gertrud Weiss Szilard and Katherine Winsor, eds., *Perspectives in American History* (1968), 2, 128.

23. General Leslie Groves, the military director of the Manhattan Project and an anti-Semite, developed a particular hatred of Szilard, and even sought authorization from the secretary of war, Henry Stimson, to have Szilard thrown in prison until the war was over. Stimson refused. See *His Version of the Facts*, chaps. 5 and 6; Richard Rhodes,

esp. 502–10; and Barton J. Bernstein, "Introduction," in *Toward a Livable World,* xxxii–xxxiii.

24. See Manhattan Engineer District Records, Record Group 77, National Archives: File 201 (Szilard); cited in Barton J. Bernstein, "Introduction," in *Toward a Livable World,* xxxiii.

25. A year later, the question of rockets was taken up in Senate hearings by Vannevar Bush, one of the Manhattan Project's administrators. Asked by a senator "whether it would be possible to build ballistic missiles that would fly across the Atlantic, or a distance of 3,500 or 4,000 miles," Bush responded that a 2,500-mile range rocket was conceivable; "But 3,000 miles? . . . I think we can leave that out of our thinking." U.S. Congress, Senate, *Atomic Energy, Hearings before the Special Committee on Atomic Energy,* 79th Cong., 1st sess., pursuant to S. Res. 179 (1945–46); cited in *His Version of the Facts,* 228–29; Leo Szilard, "Atomic Bombs and the Postwar Position of the United States in the World," memorandum for President Roosevelt, in *His Version of the Facts,* 196ff.; and "Letter to President Roosevelt" (accompanied by cover letter from Albert Einstein) (March 25, 1945); *His Version of the Facts,* 205ff.

26. James F. Byrnes, *All in One Lifetime* (New York: Harper & Row, 1954), 284.

27. Leo Szilard, "Reminiscences," 128.

28. Ibid., 128.

29. Leo Szilard, "Draft of a Proposal for a New Organization Called 'Der Bund,'" in *His Version of the Facts,* 24–25.

30. H. G. Wells, *The Open Conspiracy: Blue Prints for a World Revolution* (London: V. Gollancz, 1929).

31. See H. G. Wells, "The Open Conspiracy," in W. Warren Wagar, ed., *H. G. Wells: Journalism and Prophecy, 1893–1946* (Boston: Houghton Mifflin, 1964), 406; and Leo Szilard, "Draft of a Proposal for a New Organization Called 'Der Bund,'" 25.

32. Leo Szilard, "Draft of a Proposal for a New Organization Called 'Der Bund,'" 24, 27, 28.

33. Ibid., 25, 29.

34. For detailed discussions of the broader German currents of elitist political thought that provided the context for Szilard's ideas, see Walter Struve, *Elites against Democracy: Leadership Ideals in Bourgeois Political Thought in Germany, 1890–1933* (Princeton: Princeton University Press, 1973), esp. 186–215; George L. Mosse, *The Crisis of German Ideology* (New York: Grosset & Dunlap, 1964), esp. 171–217.

35. Leo Szilard, "Draft of a Proposal for a New Organization called 'Der Bund,'" 24.

36. Robert Oppenheimer, "Speech before the Association of Los Alamos Scientists" (November 1945), in Alice K. Smith and Charles Weiner, eds., *Robert Oppenheimer: Letters and Recollections* (Boston: Harvard University Press, 1980), 317.

37. Leo Szilard, "Can We Avert an Arms Race by an Inspection System?" in Dexter Masters and Katherine Way, eds., *One World or None* (New York: McGraw Hill, 1946), 61.

38. Leo Szilard, "Calling for a Crusade," *Bulletin of the Atomic Scientists* 3, no. 102 (April–May 1947).

39. Leo Szilard, in *His Version of the Facts,* vi.

40. Spencer R. Weart and Gertrud Weiss Szilard, "Preface," *His Version of the Facts,* xviii.

41. Alice K. Smith, "The Elusive Dr. Szilard," *Harper's* (August 1960): 85.

42. Ibid., 77. I am paraphrasing two sentences here from the vivid description provided by Alice K. Smith.

43. Dennis Gabor, "Leo Szilard," *Bulletin of the Atomic Scientists* 39, no. 52 (September 1973).

44. Leo Szilard, "Security Risk," *Bulletin of the Atomic Scientists* 10, no. 384 (December 1954).

45. Leo Szilard, "Reminiscences," 128.

46. Alice K. Smith, 84.

47. Edward Shils, "Leo Szilard: A Memoir," *Encounter* 23, no. 6 (December 1964): 37, 41.

48. Alice K. Smith, 84.

49. Ibid., 77.

50. Shils, 35. This description is a composite taken from two parts of Shils's article.

51. Alice K. Smith, 81.

52. Leo Szilard, "Talk Given at University of Colorado Medical School" (November 11, 1950), Szilard Papers.

53. Ibid.

54. Ibid.

55. Robert Oppenheimer, "Physics in the Contemporary World," Lecture at MIT (November 5, 1947), in *Technology Review* (February 1948).

56. Leo Szilard, "Recollections," 5.

57. Louis Wirth, "Preface," in Karl Mannheim, *Ideology and Utopia* (New York: Harcourt, Brace & World, 1936), xxiv.

58. Leo Szilard, "Notes to Thucydides' History of the Peloponnesian War" (September 20, 1949), in *Toward a Livable World*, 41.

59. Leo Szilard, "Shall We Face the Facts?" *Bulletin of the Atomic Scientists* 5, no. 269 (October 1949).

60. Leo Szilard, "Draft of a Statement about Edward Teller" (August 23, 1963), in *Toward a Livable World*, 405.

61. See George F. Kennan, "Resumé of World Situation," Policy Planning Staff memorandum 13, in Thomas H. Etzold and John Lewis Gaddis, eds., *Containment: Documents on American Policy and Strategy, 1945–1950* (New York: Columbia University Press, 1978), 92–93, 97.

62. Adam B. Ulam, *Expansion and Coexistence: Soviet Foreign Policy, 1917–1973* (New York: Praeger, 1974), 398ff.

63. See for instance Robert Griffith and Athan Theoharis, eds., *The Specter: Original Essays on the Cold War and the Origins of McCarthyism* (New York: New Viewpoints, 1974).

64. Edward Shils, 38.

65. Szilard to René Spitz (March 29, 1963), Szilard Papers; cited in Barton Bernstein, "Introduction," *Toward a Livable World*, lxiii.

66. Leo Szilard, "Disarmament and the Problem of Peace," *Bulletin of the Atomic Scientists* 11 (October 1955): 297–307

67. Leo Szilard, *The Voice of the Dolphins and Other Stories* (New York: Simon & Schuster, 1961; repr., Stanford, Calif.: Stanford University Press, 1992).

68. Leo Szilard, "Disarmament and the Problem of Peace," 304.

69. Ibid., p. 283.

70. Leo Szilard, *The Voice of the Dolphins*, 68–69.

71. Leo Szilard, "Disarmament and the Problem of Peace," 301.

72. Edward Shils, 36.

73. For a fine account of Szilard's prominent role in the early atomic scientists' movement, see Alice K. Smith, *A Peril and a Hope* (Chicago: University of Chicago Press, 1965).

74. Szilard to Einstein (March 27, 1950), Szilard Papers.

75. See for instance "United States Objectives and Programs for National security: NSC-68" (April 14, 1950), in Etzold and Gaddis, 386–87.

76. Walter LaFeber, 178. See also Robert Griffith and Athan Theoharis, eds., *The Specter.*

77. It is interesting that Szilard extended this silence to his private papers as well, avoiding any reference to what must have been for him an acutely painful and harrowing episode. It is possible, however, that Szilard did write down his reactions in 1956, but subsequently destroyed any such documents in the fear that they might fall into the wrong hands and undermine his precious public stance of neutrality.

78. Joseph Rotblat, *Pugwash: The First Ten Years* (London: Heinemann, 1967), 22.

79. Albert Wohlstetter, "The Delicate Balance of Terror," *Foreign Affairs* 37, no. 2 (January 1959).

80. Leo Szilard, "How to Live with the Bomb and Survive—the Possibility of a Pax Russo-Americana in the Long-Range Rocket Stage of the So-Called Atomic Stalemate," *Bulletin of the Atomic Scientists* 16 (February 1960): 59–73.

81. See Jerome Kahan, *Security in the Nuclear Age* (Washington, D.C.: Brookings Institution, 1975), for a summary of prevailing views among defense experts of the late 1950s and early 1960s.

82. For an elaboration of these views, see Leo Szilard, "To Stop or Not to Stop," *Bulletin of the Atomic Scientists* 16 (March 1960): 82–84, 108; " 'Minimal Deterrent' vs. Saturation Parity," *Bulletin of the Atomic Scientists* 20 (March 1964): 6–12; and "The 'Sting of the Bee' in Saturation Parity," *Bulletin of the Atomic Scientists* 21 (March 1965): 8–13.

83. Louis P. Bloomfield, Walter C. Clemens, Jr., Franklyn Griffiths, *Khrushchev and the Arms Race: Soviet Interests in Arms Control and Disarmament, 1954–1964* (Cambridge: MIT Press, 1966), 138ff.

84. Roy Medvedev, *Khrushchev,* trans. Brian Pearce (Oxford: Basil Blackwell, 1982), 151ff.; see also Nikita S. Khrushchev, *Khrushchev in New York* (New York: Crosscurrents Press, 1960).

85. Nixon called Kennedy "naive and inexperienced" and "the spokesman of national disparagement," while the GOP chairman Thruston Morton said Kennedy and other Democrats "were guilty of sheer desertion of American patriotism." Kennedy lashed back that "personal attacks and insults will not halt the spread of communism. . . . This is no time to say that we can outtalk or outshout Mr. Khrushchev. I want to outdo him—out-produce him." *Time* (October 3, 1960): 17.

86. Nikita S. Khrushchev, *Khrushchev Remembers,* trans. Strobe Talbott (Boston: Little, Brown, 1974), 468.

87. Roy Medvedev, 154.

88. *Time* (October 3, 1960), 12; *Time* (October 10, 1960), 28 ff.

89. Leo Szilard, "Conversation with K," *Toward a Livable World,* 279.

90. Leo Szilard, "Conversation with K," 285.

91. Ibid., 285.

92. Ibid., 284.

93. Szilard wrote to President Eisenhower a week later, reporting his proposal and the Soviet leader's response—but the White House–Kremlin "hotline" was not installed until three years afterward, when the Cuban missile crisis had brought the two superpowers to the very edge of war. Szilard to Eisenhower (October 13, 1960), *Toward a Livable World,* 288.

94. Dulles, quoted in Walter LaFeber, *America, Russia, and the Cold War,* 205.

95. Leo Szilard, "Conversation with K," 286.

96. Ibid., 286.

97. Ibid., 282.

98. Ibid., 283.

99. Ibid., 283.

100. Leo Szilard, "Can We Get Off the Road to War?" (manuscript for speech, May 3, 1962), in *Toward a Livable World,* 287n.2.

101. Szilard to Khrushchev (October 9, 1962), in *Toward a Livable World,* 300.

102. W. K. H. Panofsky to Szilard (February 20, 1963), Szilard Papers.

103. Szilard to Panofsky (February 22, 1963), Szilard Papers.

104. Ibid.

105. Khrushchev to Szilard (November 4, 1962), in *Toward a Livable World,* 305.

106. Ibid., 306.

107. Leo Szilard, "Letter to President Kennedy with Copies of a Memorandum to Members of the National Academy and of a Proposed Petition" (May 10, 1961), in *Toward a Livable World,* 341.

108. Ibid., 345.

109. McGeorge Bundy to Michael Bess (May 13, 1982).

110. John F. Kennedy to Hudson Hoagland (June 15, 1963), Szilard Papers.

111. Szilard to Khrushchev (July 15, 1963), in *Toward a Livable World,* 321–22.

112. "Soviet Reply to Letter of July 15, 1963," in *Toward a Livable World,* 328.

113. Szilard to McNamara (February 10, 1964); cited in Helen S. Hawkins, G. Allen Greb, and Gertrud Weiss Szilard, "Notes to Section V," *Toward a Livable World,* 261.

114. Leo Szilard, "The Council and the Lobby," in *Toward a Livable World,* 463.

115. Jerome Kahan, *Security in the Nuclear Age,* 85, 111. For a thoughtful insider's view, see McGeorge Bundy, *Danger and Survival* (New York: Random House, 1988).

116. Ulam, 675ff.

117. Leo Szilard, "Comment to the Editors [of the *Bulletin of the Atomic Scientists*]" (November 13, 1947), in *Toward a Livable World,* 32.

118. Dwight D. Eisenhower, "Farewell Radio and Television Address to the American People" (January 17, 1961), in Robert L. Branyan and Lawrence H. Larsen, eds., *The Eisenhower Administration, 1953–1961: A Documentary History,* vol. 2 (New York: Random House, 1971), 1375.

119. Leo Szilard, "Are We on the Road to War?" *Bulletin of the Atomic Scientists* 18 (April 1962): 29 (emphasis in original).

120. Leo Szilard, "Responses to Date" (February 24, 1962), in *Toward a Livable World,* 450.

121. Jack Mabley, "Mabley's Report: Atom Expert's Plan to Avert All-Out War," *Chicago's American* (February 1962).

122. Leo Szilard, "Are We on the Road to War?" *Bulletin of the Atomic Scientists* 18 (April 1962): 30.

123. Leo Szilard, "Letter (Progress Report) to Council Members" (March 25, 1963), in *Toward a Livable World,* 480.

124. Leo Szilard, "Draft of a Letter to the Secretary of State" (September 8, 1950), in *Toward a Livable World,* 103.

125. See Hans J. Morgenthau, *Politics among Nations,* chap. 1.

126. Hans J. Morgenthau, "On Negotiating with the Russians," *Bulletin of the Atomic Scientists* 6 (May 1950): 143.

127. Ten years later, in a letter to Szilard, Morgenthau made it clear that the admiration between the two men was reciprocal: "May I say on this occasion," Morgenthau wrote, "how deeply I admire what you have been doing recently. I very much hope that you will be able to continue doing it for a very long time to come." Morgenthau to Szilard (September 21, 1960), Szilard Papers.

Arnold Toynbee, "Lecture at Columbia University" (1948), cited in Morgenthau, "On Negotiating with the Russians," 148.

128. Leo Szilard, "Shall We Face the Facts?" *Bulletin of the Atomic Scientists* 5 (October 1949): 270.

129. Ibid., 271.

130. Raymond Aron, "The Atomic Bomb and Europe," *Bulletin of the Atomic Scientists* 6 (April 1950): 110–14, 125–26.

131. Ibid., 114, 125.

132. Leo Szilard, "Shall We Face the Facts?" 269.

133. Raymond Aron, "The Atomic Bomb and Europe," 114.

134. Leo Szilard, "The Voice of the Dolphins," 25–26. (For the sake of consistency, tenses of verbs in this quotation have been changed.)

135. Rae Goodell, *The Visible Scientists* (Boston: Little, Brown, 1975), 39–40.

136. See Leo Szilard, "How to Live with the Bomb and Survive," 59–73; "The Mined Cities," *Bulletin of the Atomic Scientists* 17 (December 1961): 407–12; and "The Voice of the Dolphins."

137. Leo Szilard, "The Voice of the Dolphins," 33.

138. Norman Cousins, "Foreword," *Toward a Livable World,* xii–xiii.

139. Shils, 37.

140. Nicholas and Robert Halasz, "Leo Szilard: The Reluctant Father of the Atomic Bomb," *New Hungarian Quarterly* (1974): 172–73.

141. Leo Szilard, "Excerpt from a Television Interview with Mike Wallace," in *Toward a Livable World,* 337.

142. Leo Szilard, "The Diary of Dr. Davis," *Bulletin of the Atomic Scientists* 6 (February 1950): 51.

143. Leo Szilard, "The Physicist Invades Politics," *Saturday Review of Literature* 30 (May 3, 1947): 7.

144. Shils, 41.

145. Leo Szilard, "Excerpt from a Television Interview with Mike Wallace," 340.

146. Szilard to Alfred W. Painter (August 11, 1945), in *His Version of the Facts,* 230.

Chapter Three

1. E. P. Thompson, "Deterrence and Addiction," in *Beyond the Cold War* (New York: Pantheon, 1982), 23 (emphasis in original) (hereafter *Beyond the Cold War*).

2. E. P. Thompson, "The Liberation of Perugia," in *The Heavy Dancers* (London: Merlin Press, 1985), 195, 196, 194 (hereafter *The Heavy Dancers*).

3. "Interview with E. P. Thompson," *Radical History Review* 3, no. 4 (Fall 1976): 10–11.

4. Interview with E. P. Thompson, Worcester, England (November 10, 1986).

5. E. P. Thompson and T. J. Thompson, eds., *There Is a Spirit in Europe: A Memoir of Frank Thompson* (London: Gollancz, 1947), 11.

6. E. P. Thompson, "The Nehru Tradition," in *Writing by Candlelight* (London: Merlin Press, 1980), 138 (hereafter *Writing by Candlelight*).

7. Ibid.

8. E. P. Thompson, *There Is a Spirit in Europe,* 12–13.

9. Interviews with E. P. Thompson, Worcester, England (August 5 and November 10, 1986).

10. "Interview with E. P. Thompson," 21–22; "The Poverty of Theory, or An Orrery of Errors," in E. P. Thompson, *The Poverty of Theory and Other Essays* (New York: Monthly Review Press, 1978), 84ff. (hereafter *Poverty of Theory*).

11. "Interview with E. P. Thompson," 11.

12. Ibid., 11.

13. *There Is a Spirit in Europe,* 20.

14. See for instance "Overture to Cassino" (1944), "Casola Valsenio: The Cat" (1945), and "Drava Bridge" (1945), in *The Heavy Dancers,* 203–37.

15. E. P. Thompson, "The Liberation of Perugia," in *The Heavy Dancers,* 188 (grammatical errors in original letters).

16. E. P. Thompson, ed., *The Railway: An Adventure in Construction* (London: British-Yugoslav Association, 1948).

17. E. P. Thompson, "Omladinska Pruga," in *The Railway,* 10.

18. Ibid., 20.

19. Ibid.

20. Ibid., 30.

21. Ibid., 1.

22. Ibid., 30.

23. Ibid., 19.

24. E. P. Thompson, "An Open Letter to Leszek Kolakowski," in *The Poverty of Theory,* 370.

25. See Gordon Wright, *The Ordeal of Total War* (New York: Harper and Row, 1968), 246–47.

26. Alan Sked and Chris Cook, *Postwar Britain* (Brighton: Harvester Press, 1979), 27–28.

27. "Interview with E. P. Thompson," *Radical History Review,* 12.

28. The term is Thompson's. As the historian Eric Hobsbawm was later to write: "For those [Communists] not already in academic posts before the Cold War blacklisting began in the late Spring of 1948, the chances of university teaching were to be virtually zero for the next ten years." Eric Hobsbawm, "The Historians' Group of the Communist Party," in Maurice Cornforth, ed., *Rebels and Their Causes* (London: Lawrence and Wishart, 1978), 25.

29. For a perceptive analysis of the impact of poetry and literature upon Thompson's writing and thinking, see Henry Abelove, "Review Essay on 'The Poverty of Theory,'" in *History and Theory* 21, no. 1 (1982): 132–42.

30. Interviews with E. P. Thompson, Worcester, England (August 5 and November 10, 1986).

31. Ibid.

32. Ibid.

33. Editorial, *The Yorkshire Voice of Peace* 2, no. 1 (1953): 1.

34. The broader tradition of British Marxist historiography has been the subject of a study by Harvey J. Kaye: *The British Marxist Historians* (Cambridge: Polity Press, 1984). Kaye argues persuasively that the British Marxist historians formed a coherent theoretical "school" with considerable continuity over time; and he provides a substantial assessment of Thompson's contribution to that school.

35. Eric Hobsbawm, "The Historians' Group of the Communist Party," 25–26.

36. "Interview with E. P. Thompson," *Radical History Review,* 12–13.

37. E. P. Thompson, *William Morris: Romantic to Revolutionary* (London: Lawrence & Wishart, 1955), 795, 760.

38. E. P. Thompson, *William Morris: Romantic to Revolutionary* (New York: Pantheon, 1976), 810.

39. E. P. Thompson, *William Morris* (1955), 282.

40. Ibid., 893.

41. Ibid., 411.

42. Ibid.

43. "William Morris: Romantic to Revolutionary," anonymous review, *Times Literary Supplement* (July 15, 1955): 391.

44. See for instance Edmund Penning-Rowsell, "The Remodeling of Morris," *Times Literary Supplement* (August 11, 1978): 913–14; and Peter Stansky, "The Protean Victorian," *New York Times Book Review* (May 15, 1977): 7, 48.

45. E. P. Thompson, *William Morris* (1976), 810.

46. Adam Ulam, *Expansion and Coexistence,* 574ff.

47. "The Khrushchev Speech, the PCF, and the PCI: Two Interviews with Jean Pronteau, Maurice Kriegel-Valrimont, and Rossana Rossanda," in John Saville and Ralph Miliband, eds., *Socialist Register 1976* (London: Merlin Press, 1976), 59.

48. See John Saville, "The Twentieth Congress and the British Communist Party," in *Socialist Register 1976,* 2–6.

49. Interviews with E. P. Thompson, Worcester, England (August 5 and November 10, 1986).

50. *Reasoner,* no. 1 (July 1956).

51. John Saville, "The Twentieth Congress and the British Communist Party," 8.

52. Ibid., 10.

53. Interviews with E. P. Thompson, Worcester, England (August 5 and November 10, 1986).

54. See John Saville, 14.

55. E. P. Thompson and John Saville, "Editorial," and E. P. Thompson, "Through the Smoke of Budapest," *Reasoner,* no. 3 (November 4, 1956): 1ff.

56. Ibid.

57. Margot Heinemann, "1956 and the Communist Party," in John Saville and Ralph Miliband, eds., *Socialist Register 1976,* 50.

58. E. P. Thompson, *The Making of the English Working Class* (New York: Vintage, 1963, 1966). For discussions of the book's impact on subsequent social history, see Bryan D. Palmer, *The Making of E. P. Thompson* (Toronto: New Hogtown Press, 1981), 65ff.; and Harvey J. Kaye, *The British Marxist Historians,* 172ff.

59. For a perceptive account of Thompson's career that stresses the unity between his historical research and his political activism, see Bryan D. Palmer, *The Making of E. P. Thompson.*

60. See especially E. P. Thompson, "Revolution," *New Left Review* 3 (May–June 1960): 3–9; and "Revolution Again," *New Left Review* 6 (November–December 1960): 18–31. But see also "Socialist Humanism," *New Reasoner* (Summer 1957); "Agency and Choice," *New Reasoner* (Summer 1958), and "The New Left," *New Reasoner* (Summer 1959). For a retrospective look at this period, see "The Peculiarities of the English" (1965) and "An Open Letter to Leszek Kolakowski" (1973), both reprinted in *The Poverty of Theory.*

61. E. P. Thompson, "Revolution Again," 24.

62. Ibid.

63. E. P. Thompson, "Socialist Humanism," 131.

64. Ibid., 132–33.

65. Ibid., 133.

66. Ibid., 112.

67. E. P. Thompson, "Revolution," 7.

68. Ibid., p. 7 (emphasis in original).

69. See the summary of these criticisms in E. P. Thompson, "Agency and Choice," 6.

70. See the essays and correspondence published in response to Thompson's article, "Revolution," in *New Left Review* 4 and 5 (July–August and September–October 1960).

71. E. P. Thompson, "Revolution Again," 31 (emphasis in original).

72. E. P. Thompson, "The New Left," 7.

73. See for instance "The New Left," 17; and "Socialist Humanism," 138.

74. "Revolution Again," 31.

75. See Peggy Duff, *Left, Left, Left* (London: Allison & Busby, 1971), 118ff.; and Richard Taylor and Colin Pritchard, *The Protest Makers* (Oxford: Pergamon, 1980), 4–8.

76. Richard Taylor and Colin Pritchard, 5.

77. See Peggy Duff, 118ff.

78. For an early sociological study of the Campaign's supporters, see Frank Parkin, *Middle Class Radicalism* (Manchester: Manchester University Press, 1968).

79. According to E. P. Thompson and John Saville, historians of this period have tended to underestimate the significance for both the New Left and CND of the seven thousand ex-Communists who had been "left homeless," as it were, by the events of 1956. Although some went into the Labour Left and others moved into Trotskyist groups, this still had not provided a sufficient alternative. CND, however, with its loose structure and broad moral goals, provided the perfect focus for their energies. Interviews with E. P. Thompson, Worcester, England (August 5 and November 10, 1986); and interview with John Saville, Hull, England (November 19, 1986).

80. Interviews with E. P. Thompson, Worcester, England (August 5 and November 10, 1986); see also Peggy Duff, 127.

81. E. P. Thompson, "Revolution," 9.

82. Ibid.

83. Peggy Duff, 130–31.

84. If CND protestors had known, as subsequent research was to demonstrate, just *how* close to armed conflict the superpowers had come during the Cuban crisis, it is possible that they would have been stimulated to renew their campaign with greater vigor than ever. As it was, however, "the major influence of [the Cuban crisis] on the protestors . . . was to demonstrate the fundamental irrelevance of the Movement (at least in the immediate context) and indeed of Britain generally, to the life-and-death decisions . . . of the two superpowers." Taylor and Pritchard, 12.

85. See Peggy Duff; Taylor and Pritchard, 52ff. and 106ff.; and John Minnion and Philip Bolsover, eds., *The CND Story* (London: Allison & Busby, 1983), 56ff.

86. "Notes for Readers," *New Left Review* 12 (November–December 1961): inside front cover.

87. For a sampling of these views see Perry Anderson, "The Left in the Fifties," *New Left Review* 29 (January–February 1965): 3ff.; E. P. Thompson, "The Peculiarities of the English," in John Saville and Ralph Miliband, eds., *Socialist Register 1965* (reprinted in *The Poverty of Theory*); David Widgery, *The Left in Britain* (Harmondsworth: Peregrine Books, 1976); Ken Coates, "How Not to Reappraise the New Left," in John Saville and Ralph Miliband, eds., *Socialist Register 1976*, 111ff.

88. E. P. Thompson, "Revolution," 22.

89. Perry Anderson, *Arguments within English Marxism* (London: New Left Books, 1980), 137.

90. E. P. Thompson, unpublished manuscript, 1962 (emphasis in original).

91. Interviews with E. P. Thompson, Worcester, England (August 5 and November 10, 1986).

92. Ibid.

93. E. P. Thompson, "The Peculiarities of the English"; and Perry Anderson, "Socialism and Pseudo-Empiricism," *New Left Review* 35 (January–February 1966): 2–42.

94. Perry Anderson, *Arguments within English Marxism*.

95. Interviews with E. P. Thompson, Worcester, England (August 5 and November 10, 1986).

96. "E. P. Thompson: Recovering the Libertarian Tradition," interview, *The Leveller* 22 (January 1979): 21. This tenacious adherence to the political label of "Communist"

was arguably due more to a sense of loyalty and tradition than to any substantive correspondence with contemporary ideological alignments. Unlike the vast majority of the world's self-proclaimed Communists in the late twentieth century, Thompson rejected the primacy of economic causes in historical process and expressed a marked antipathy to the ideas of violent revolution, dictatorship of the proletariat, leading role of the party, and so on. To an outsider, therefore, his political position might justifiably appear closer to the label of "social democracy" than to that of "Communism"—although in reality his appeal for direct popular self-government placed him equally far from the state-centric traditions of both. For a discussion of Thompson's views on apostasy, see his "Open Letter to Leszek Kolakowski," reprinted in *The Poverty of Theory*.

97. "Our first application to join the Labour Party was turned down by a high-level screening committee, which interviewed us and demanded that we say if we were Marxists or not. The Halifax Labour Party protested against our rejection and eventually admitted us." E. P. Thompson to Michael Bess (April 2, 1989).

98. "E. P. Thompson: Recovering the Libertarian Tradition," 22.

99. Raymond Williams, ed., *May Day Manifesto* (Harmondsworth: Penguin, 1968), 147–48.

100. Interviews with E. P. Thompson, Worcester, England (August 5 and November 10, 1986).

101. "Interview with E. P. Thompson," *Radical History Review*, 9; interviews with E. P. Thompson, Worcester, England (August 5 and November 10, 1986).

102. Interview with E. P. Thompson, Worcester, England (November 10, 1986).

103. Ibid.

104. See E. P. Thompson, ed., *Warwick University Ltd.* (Harmondsworth: Penguin, 1970), chap. 6.

105. Ibid., chap. 7. This argument was in fact inconsistent with the liberal principles that Thompson sought to defend. Later in the decade, he would bitterly oppose any attempt by the State to use illegally obtained information in prosecuting criminal suspects; yet in this case he was willing to use the illegally obtained documents from the university files to launch an investigation of its administrators. Thompson had been placed in a classic dilemma on the evening of February 11, in which he was forced to violate some aspect of his own liberal values either by taking action or by remaining silent. It is arguable that his choice to proceed with the publication of the documents represented a basic error of judgment—for it contradicted the underlying principles that Thompson would passionately defend throughout the following years.

106. Ibid., 151–52.

107. Many of these articles were subsequently gathered into a single volume, *Writing by Candlelight*.

108. E. P. Thompson, "A State of Blackmail," in *Writing by Candlelight*, 133.

109. Mervyn Jones, *Chances* (London: Verso, 1987), 283.

110. In the 1950s, he had attacked the rudimentary version of this model put forth by Stalinists; and in a two-hundred-page essay written in 1977, "The Poverty of Theory," he attacked the more sophisticated variant of the same model proposed by the French Marxist philosopher Louis Althusser. As Thompson saw it, Althusser had done nothing to mitigate the dangerous reductionism of the Stalinist metaphysic; he had merely substituted a fancy form of machinery for the crude mechanism of the earlier

model. Where the Stalinist had posited a blunt linear relation between economic cause and cultural effect, Althusser had proposed an epicyclic model that Thompson likened to an orrery—a machine used by astronomers to illustrate the complex movements of the solar system. If one turned the handle, the moons began to revolve in tiny circles around their planets, which themselves revolved in larger circles around the unmoving Sun. In precisely the same way, Thompson argued, Althusser's view of history assigned small circles of "relative autonomy" to cultural factors like religion, politics, and the arts; and all these lesser spheres were governed "in the last instance" by economic causal processes, located at the unmoving center of the machine. See for instance Louis Althusser, *For Marx* (Vintage Books, 1970); and *Reading Capital* (New Left Books, 1970).

111. E. P. Thompson, "Socialist Humanism" (1957), quoted in "The Peculiarities of the English" (1965), reprinted in *The Poverty of Theory,* 292–93.

112. See E. P. Thompson, *The Poverty of Theory,* 150–52.

113. Ibid.

114. Ibid.

115. Ibid., 88.

116. William Morris, *The Dream of John Ball* (1886), quoted in *The Poverty of Theory,* 88.

117. See *The Poverty of Theory,* 84ff.

118. E. P. Thompson, "The Peculiarities of the English," 289.

119. E. P. Thompson, *Whigs and Hunters,* 265.

120. For an excellent discussion of this aspect of Thompson's work, see Suzanne Desan, "Crowds, Community, and Ritual in the Work of E. P. Thompson and Natalie Davis," in Lynn Hunt, ed., *The New Cultural History* (Berkeley: University of California Press, 1989), 60ff. "In interpreting the relationship between patricians and plebeians as emerging classes in early modern England," Desan writes, "Thompson subtly reformulates the Gramscian model. He thinks that Gramsci overestimated the capacity of the elites to impose 'cultural hegemony' on the masses and underestimated the resilient ability of the lower classes to limit and reformulate these cultural impositions."

121. E. P. Thompson, *The Sykaos Papers* (London: Bloomsbury, 1988).

122. Interview with E. P. Thompson, Worcester, England (November 10, 1986).

123. For a sampling of the vast literature on NATO and its military/political strategies, see Jerome Kahan, *Security in the Nuclear Age* (Washington: Brookings Institution, 1975); Robert Art and Kenneth Waltz, eds., *The Use of Force,* 2d ed. (Lanham: University Press of America, 1983); Thomas Schelling, *Arms and Influence* (New Haven: Yale University Press, 1967); Wallace Thies, *The Atlantic Alliance, Nuclear Weapons, and European Attitudes* (Berkeley: Institute of International Studies, 1983); Alva Myrdal, et al., *Dynamics of European Nuclear Disarmament* (Nottingham: Spokesman, 1981); and Diana Johnstone, *The Politics of Euromissiles* (London: Verso, 1984).

124. Interview with E. P. Thompson, Worcester, England (November 10, 1986).

125. "Appeal for European Nuclear Disarmament" (April 28, 1980), reprinted in E. P. Thompson and Dan Smith, eds., *Protest and Survive* (Harmondsworth: Penguin, 1980), 224–25 (hereafter *Protest and Survive*).

126. Mervyn Jones, *Chances,* 285.

127. Dorothy and Edward Thompson, "END—Retrospect and Next Steps" (August

18, 1980), unpublished letter; in private papers of Mary Kaldor on END, Brighton, England (hereafter "Kaldor Papers").

128. Interviews with END activists, London (1986).

129. John Saville to E. P. Thompson (November 29, 1956), reprinted in *Socialist Register 1976,* 18–19.

130. E. P. Thompson, "A State of Blackmail" (1978), *Writing by Candlelight,* 113–33.

131. Michael Howard, "Surviving a Protest," in *The Causes of Wars and Other Essays* (Cambridge, Mass.: Harvard University Press, 1983), 118.

132. E. P. Thompson, "An Elizabethan Diary," *Writing by Candlelight,* 91–92.

133. E. P. Thompson, "The Normalization of Europe," in Ferenc Köszegi and E. P. Thompson, *The New Hungarian Peace Movement* (London: END and Merlin Press, 1982), 51.

134. See for instance E. P. Thompson, *Double Exposure* (London: Merlin Press, 1985), viii (hereafter *Double Exposure*); Thompson made the same point several times in private interviews.

135. Interviews with E. P. Thompson, Worcester, England (August 5 and November 10, 1986).

136. Interviews with END activists, London (1986).

137. E. P. Thompson to Mary Kaldor (October 12, 1981), Kaldor Papers.

138. Interviews with END activists, London (1986).

139. Thompson articulated his ideas on the Cold War in a steady series of speeches, pamphlets, articles, and books that poured forth from his pen starting in 1980: "Protest and Survive" (April 1980), in *Protest and Survive;* "Notes on Exterminism, the Last Stage of Civilization" (May 1980), *New Left Review,* no. 121 (May–June 1980); *Beyond the Cold War* (New York: Pantheon, 1982), a collection of his speeches and articles from 1981); New Left Review, ed., *Exterminism and Cold War* (London: New Left Books, 1982 (hereafter *Exterminism*), a collection of essays by Socialist writers responding to Thompson's "Notes on Exterminism"; *The Heavy Dancers* (London: Merlin Press, 1985), a broad compilation of Thompson's writings on peace and war since 1945, with particular emphasis on the period between 1982 and 1985; *Double Exposure* (London: Merlin Press, 1985), a response to Thompson's critics, East and West; *Star Wars* (New York: Pantheon, 1985), a collection of essays edited by Thompson on the American "Strategic Defense Initiative"; *Mad Dogs* (London: Pluto Press, 1986), a group of essays edited by Thompson on the U.S. raids against Libya in 1986; and *Prospectus for a Habitable Planet* (Harmondsworth: Penguin, 1987), coedited with Dan Smith, a survey of the peace movement seven years after the launching of END.

140. See for instance Paul Mercer, "The Thompson Technique," in *Peace of the Dead: The Truth behind the Nuclear Disarmers* (London: Policy Research Publications, 1986), 321ff.; Scott McConnell, "The 'Neutralism' of E. P. Thompson," *Commentary* (April 1983): 31; and Thomas M. Cynkin, "The British Antinuclear Movement," in James E. Dougherty and Robert L. Pfaltzgraff, Jr., eds., *Shattering Europe's Defense Consensus* (McLean, Va: Pergamon-Brassey's, 1985), 41ff.

141. See E. P. Thompson, *Double Exposure,* 14–15; and "Letter to Václav Racek," in *Beyond the Cold War,* 86.

142. Dorothy and Edward Thompson, "END—Retrospect and Next Steps," 10.

143. E. P. Thompson, "Beyond the Cold War," lecture delivered at Worcester Guild Hall (November 26, 1981); *Beyond the Cold War,* 169 (emphasis in original). Thompson had been commissioned to give this lecture on television, but the BBC abruptly canceled its "invitation" at the last moment.

144. Ibid., 171.

145. See E. P. Thompson, "Notes on Exterminism, the Last Stage of Civilization," 2–3, 17–20; and also "Europe: The Weak Link in the Cold War," esp. 330–45, in *Exterminism.*

146. E. P. Thompson, "Notes on Exterminism," 24, 22.

147. In 1982, Thompson's friend Raymond Williams criticized the "Exterminism" article for its promotion of a potentially deterministic and excessively pessimistic interpretation of the Cold War. Thompson subsequently accepted this criticism, agreeing with Williams that any tendency toward mechanistic or deterministic metaphors would be both inaccurate and counterproductive. See Raymond Williams, "The Politics of Nuclear Disarmament," in *Exterminism,* 67–68; and Thompson's reply in the same volume, 330.

148. Ibid., 24.

149. E. P. Thompson, *Beyond the Cold War,* 160.

150. E. P. Thompson, "Letter to Jaroslav Sabata" (March 1984), in *The Heavy Dancers,* 178.

151. See for instance Nigel Young, *The Contemporary European Anti-Nuclear Movement: Experiments in the Mobilization of Public Power* (Oslo: International Peace Research Institute, 1983), 1–10; Ralf Dahrendorf and Theodore C. Sorensen, *A Widening Atlantic? Domestic Change and Foreign Policy* (New York: Council on Foreign Relations, 1986); Gregory Flynn and Hans Rattinger, eds., *The Public and Atlantic Defense* (London: Rowman & Allanheld, 1985), 1–9. For a partially dissenting view, arguing that the period between 1980 and 1984 had possessed numerous precedents among the stresses and strains of NATO's history, see Wallace J. Thies, *The Atlantic Alliance, Nuclear Weapons, and European Attitudes.*

152. See for instance Nigel Young; Diana Johnstone; and Clive Rose, *Campaigns against Western Defence* (London: Macmillan, 1985).

153. Ian Bradley, "Many Turn to CND as Nuclear Fear Increases," *Times* (April 24, 1980).

154. Ian Boyne, "400 March in Missile Protest," *Daily Telegraph* (April 8, 1980).

155. John Witherow, "50,000 Rally against the Bomb," *Times* (October 27, 1980).

156. Even a frankly pro-NATO scholar, Clive Rose, has conceded that the Green party "based its defence policy on the immediate dissolution of NATO and the Warsaw Pact, rejection of the NATO Double-Track decision, unilateral German disarmament, withdrawal of all foreign forces from Germany and the creation of a European nuclear-free zone. It has also called for the dismantling of Soviet intermediate-range missiles and condemned Soviet policies in Afghanistan and Poland." Clive Rose, 171–72.

157. Catherine Steven and Peter Dobbie, "150,000 in CND Rally," *Sunday Telegraph* (October 25, 1981); "Anti-Nuclear Marchers Challenge Reagan's Strategy," *Financial Times* (October 26, 1981); Clive Rose, 165.

158. For an excellent account of the ideals that motivated the women at the Greenham

Common peace camp, and of their daily life, see Barbara Harford and Sarah Hopkins, *Greenham Common: Women at the Wire* (London: Women's Press, 1984).

159. Michael Farr, "Brezhnev Offers Non-Nuclear War Pact for Europe," *Daily Telegraph* (November 2, 1981).

160. Strobe Talbott, "The Road to Zero," *Time* (December 14, 1987): 20. Talbott's article also brings out the subsequent ironies in the history of the "zero option." Although it had been deliberately designed to be so one-sided as to prove totally unacceptable to the Soviets, it later provided the nucleus for the successful U.S.-Soviet INF (Intermediate-Range Nuclear Force) treaty of 1987. By 1987, of course, much had changed: the far more flexible Mikhail Gorbachev had come to power in the Soviet Union, and roughly two hundred American missiles had been stationed in Europe. The final treaty required the United States to remove a total of 436 warheads, as compared with 1,575 for the Soviet Union.

161. John Lambert, ed., "Talking Peace: The Inside Story of the European Nuclear Disarmament Conventions," *Agenor 97* (June–July 1986): 5.

162. David Fairhall and Martyn Halsall, "Majority Opposes Trident Missiles in Poll," *Guardian* (November 16, 1982). While the title of the article mentions only Trident missiles, the text gives figures for opposition to cruise missiles as well.

163. Gregory Flynn and Hans Rattinger, eds., *The Public and Atlantic Defense* (London: Rowman & Allanheld, 1985), 89, 134, 192, 256.

164. George Jones, "Thatcher Goes onto Attack," *Sunday Telegraph* (January 2, 1983).

165. Richard Norton-Taylor, "Strategic Tory Attack on the Nuclear Disarmers," *Guardian* (February 14, 1983).

166. "Heritage Group Is Said to Aid European Right," *San Francisco Chronicle* (May 29, 1987): 19.

167. See John A. Jungerman, *The Strategic Defense Initiative: A Primer and Critique* (La Jolla, Calif.: Institute on Global Conflict and Cooperation, 1988).

168. Jane Dibblin, "An Outpouring of Protest—Peaceful and Determined," *END Journal* 7 (December 1983–January 1984): 10–11; and Clive Rose, 157ff.

169. Seumas Milne, "CND's Successor Story," *Guardian* (May 17, 1985).

170. For its first year of existence, END was harbored within the institutional framework of the Russell Foundation at Nottingham; but in January 1981, the Committee voted to establish a London office, with Peggy Duff as organizing secretary. A tacit division of labor developed between these two END centers, with Nottingham focusing especially on the organization of conventions, while the London office became the "official" home of END as a political movement. This division proved to be a fruitful one, but it also reflected ongoing tensions, particularly between Coates and Thompson, over issues of tactics and daily procedures. Despite their disagreements, however, Coates and Thompson continued to play key roles side-by-side in many of END's activities.

171. These generalizations are based on observations of END's functioning in 1986, and on interviews with END and CND activists.

172. Interviews with E. P. Thompson, Worcester, England (Aug. 5 and Nov. 10, 1986).

173. "END—Proposed Budget for 1986"; and Dorothy Thompson, "Memo to All

Members of the Coordinating Committee From the Treasurer" (December[?], 1983); both in Kaldor Papers.

174. This journal, born in 1983, was the third regular publication created by END. The others were the *Bulletin of Work in Progress* and *END Papers,* both published by the Russell Foundation in Nottingham.

175. Paul Anderson, "The Peace Movement, END, and Political Parties," unpublished ms. (1985), Kaldor Papers; also see Nigel Young, 6.

176. Ian Mather, "Missile Split Hurts Labour," *Observer* (May 29, 1983).

177. Ian Aitken, "Labour Totters on Brink Over Nuclear Policy," *Guardian* May 25, 1983): 1; David Blake, "The Anatomy of a Conservative Landslide," *Times* (June 11, 1983). See also Peter Jenkins, *Mrs. Thatcher's Revolution: The Ending of the Socialist Era* (Cambridge, Mass.: Harvard University Press, 1988).

178. Labour Party National Executive Committee, *Defence and Security for Britain* (Manchester: Labour Party, 1984), 3, 12 (emphasis in original).

179. Ibid.

180. Although the "defense question" was considered by most voters to be less important than the domestic platforms offered by Labour and the Tories, it ranked as one of the most decisive factors in determining the Conservative majority. See David McKie, "Tory Lead Cut But Polls Back Firm Majority," *Guardian* (June 11, 1987): 1; Peter Kellner, "Labour's Future: Decline or Democratic Revolution," *New Statesman* (June 19, 1987): 11.

181. See Diana Johnstone, *The Politics of Euromissiles,* 54ff., 136ff., 168–71; Jolyon Howorth, *France: The Politics of Peace* (London: Merlin Press/END, 1984); Alva Myrdal, et al., 122–41; and Clive Rose, 156ff.

182. Mary Kaldor, "Report on the Berlin Convention" (July 31, 1982); Fiona Weir, "Perugia: Third END Convention" (August 1984); Mary Kaldor, "Liaison Committee Report" (November 9, 1984); Mient-Jan Faber, "A Few Lessons from the [Amsterdam] Convention" (1985); all in Kaldor Papers.

183. John Lambert, ed., "Talking Peace," 17ff.

184. The "Zhukov letter" is reprinted in Ken Coates, *The Most Dangerous Decade,* 117ff.

185. Henry Kamm, "Soviet Peace Group Is Jeered at Disarmament Parley," *New York Times* (July 20, 1984): 5.

186. E. P. Thompson, *Double Exposure,* 106.

187. Paul Anderson, "Responding to Soviet Peace Proposals Highlights Different Views in END," *Tribune* (July 24, 1987); Jonathan Steele, "Won, with Two Zeroes: The Mood among the European Disarmers at Coventry," *Guardian* (July 20, 1987).

188. See Vojtech Mastny, *Helsinki, Human Rights, and European Security* (Durham, N.C.: Duke University Press, 1986); and Adam B. Ulam, *Dangerous Relations: The Soviet Union in World Politics, 1970–1982* (New York: Oxford University Press, 1983).

189. See Timothy Garton Ash, *The Polish Revolution* (New York: Charles Scribner's Sons, 1983); and Lawrence Weschler, *Solidarity* (New York: Simon & Schuster, 1982).

190. See E. P. Thompson, *Double Exposure,* 118ff.

191. For a detailed explanation of the difficulties inherent in "building bridges" between Western peace activists and Eastern-bloc dissidents, see the brilliant essay by

Václav Havel, "An Anatomy of Reticence" (1985), in Jan Vladislav, ed., *Václav Havel: Living in Truth* (London: Faber, 1987), 164ff.

192. See Timothy Garton Ash, "An Open Letter to E. P. Thompson," *Spectator* (August 21, 1982); see also Ash's more detailed views in *The Polish Revolution*, 324ff.

193. See E. P. Thompson, "The Polish Debate," *Spectator*, October 30, 1982 (reprinted in *The Heavy Dancers*); and *Double Exposure*, 132.

194. See for instance the remarkable evolution in perspectives reflected in Thompson's correspondence with the Czech dissidents Václav Racek (1981) and Jaroslav Sabata (1984). E. P. Thompson, *Beyond the Cold War*, 81ff; and *The Heavy Dancers*, 169ff. See also Jan Kavan and Zdena Tomin, eds., *Voices from Prague: Documents on Czechoslovakia and the Peace Movement* (London: Palach Press/END, 1983).

195. See John Sandford, *The Sword and the Ploughshare: Autonomous Peace Initiatives in East Germany* (London: Merlin Press/END, 1983).

196. See Ferenc Köszegi and E. P. Thompson, eds., *The New Hungarian Peace Movement* (London: Merlin Press/END, 1983); and Hugh Baldwin, ed., *Documents on the Peace Movement in Hungary* (London: END Hungary Working Group, 1986).

197. See Danielle Artman, ed., *The Moscow Trust Group* (London: END/UK-USSR Trustbuilders/SOK, 1986).

198. See Václav Havel, "The Anatomy of Reticence"; George Konrad, *Antipolitics*, trans. Richard E. Allen (New York: Quartet Books, 1984), esp. 1–11, 50ff; Jiri Háyek, "Charter 77 and the Present Peace Movement," in Kavan and Tomin, eds., 37ff.; Jaroslav Sabata, "Letter to E. P. Thompson," in Kavan and Tomin, eds., 52ff.; Robert Havemann and Rainer Eppelmann, "The Berlin Appeal—Make Peace without Weapons," in Sandford, 95–96.

199. Robert Havemann and Rainer Eppelmann, "The Berlin Appeal—Make Peace without Weapons," 95.

200. Charter 77, "Prague Appeal," *END Journal* 15 (April–May 1985): 34.

201. Hugh Baldwin, ed., *Documents on the Peace Movement in Hungary* (London: END Hungary Working Group, 1986), 15.

202. George Konrad, *Antipolitics* (New York: Quartet Books, 1984).

203. See Strobe Talbott, "The Road to Zero," *Time* (December 14, 1987): 18ff.

204. For more details on the Helsinki Citizens' Assembly (named after the important human rights accord signed in Helsinki in 1975), see Mary Kaldor, ed., *Europe from Below: An East-West Dialogue* (London: Verso, 1991).

205. Diana Johnstone, "Has the European Peace Movement Reached a Dead END?" *In These Times* (August 22, 1984); see also Thompson's response, "Diana Johnstone Has END Wrong," *In These Times* (November 7–13, 1984); and Johnstone's rebuttal, "Point Slid Past Thompson," *In These Times* (November 7–13, 1984).

206. See for instance Mike Gapes, "European Defence—Enhanced Security or a New Arms Race?" *END Journal* 10 (June–July 1984): 10–12; Paul Anderson, Stephen Brown, Jos Gallagher, Ian Leveson, "Eurobomb—an Idea Whose Time Has Come?" *END Journal* 26 (February–March 1987): 9–11, 23; and Richard Falk and Mary Kaldor, "Introduction," in Kaldor and Falk, eds., *Dealignment* (New York: Basil Blackwell/UNU, 1987), 7ff.

207. See E. P. Thompson, "The War of Thatcher's Face," *London Times* (April 29,

1982), reprinted in E. P. Thompson, *Beyond the Cold War* (New York: Pantheon, 1982), 189ff.

208. E. P. Thompson, "A Preface in Sackcloth," *Beyond the Cold War,* ix. See also the lengthy discussion of the Falklands War in *The Heavy Dancers,* 61–105.

209. "Transcription of Tape Recordings of END Discussion at a Meeting in Hampstead Friends Meeting House" (March 17, 1984), Tape One, 29; in Kaldor Papers (emphasis in original).

210. See for instance E. P. Thompson, "The Liberation of Perugia," in *The Heavy Dancers,* 199–200.

211. See for instance E. P. Thompson, "Mr. Attlee and the Gadarene Swine" (1984), in *The Heavy Dancers,* 245.

212. Ibid.

213. E. P. Thompson, "The Liberation of Perugia," 195.

214. E. P. Thompson, "Europe: The Weak Link in the Cold War," *Exterminism,* p. 347.

215. See for instance Thomas M. Cynkin, "The British Antinuclear Movement," 44.

216. Interview with E. P. Thompson, Worcester, England (November 10, 1986).

217. Ibid.

218. Ibid.

219. For a critical discussion along these lines, see Michael Howard, *The Causes of Wars* (Cambridge, Mass.: Harvard University Press, 1983), 116ff.

220. E. P. Thompson, "The Two Sides of Yalta," 181.

221. E. P. Thompson, "Exterminism," 24.

222. "Meeting between Olof Palme, Edward Thompson, and Michael Foot (Chair: Mary Kaldor) Held at the Caxton Hall on 2 September, 1981," typewritten transcript, 24; in Kaldor Papers.

223. Strobe Talbott, "Back in Business," *Time* (June 12, 1989): 34.

224. "My proposal of the zero-zero option," Reagan wrote, "sprang out of the realities of nuclear politics in Western Europe. . . . Whipped up by Soviet propagandists, thousands of Europeans were taking to the streets and protesting the plans to base additional nuclear weapons in Europe, arguing that their presence would cause future nuclear wars to be confined to Europe. . . . Helmut Kohl . . . told me during a White House visit that the propaganda offensive was becoming highly sophisticated and effective in convincing Europeans that the United States was a bloodthirsty, militaristic nation. This view of America shocked me: We were the most moral and generous people on earth, . . . and now we were being cast—effectively, Kohl said—as villains. It was clear we'd have to do a better job of conveying to the world our sense of morality and our commitment to the creation of a peaceful, nuclear-free world. After considerable discussion with the cabinet and our arms control experts, I decided to propose the zero-zero plan." Ronald Reagan, *An American Life* (New York: Simon & Schuster, 1990), 295–96; see also 552–59, 590–91.

225. E. P. Thompson, "History Turns on a New Hinge," *Nation* (January 29, 1990), 118.

226. James Adams, "Memo to NATO: Shape Up before America Ships Out," *Washington Post* (May 15, 1988): 1,B.

Chapter Four

1. Danilo Dolci, "Schema della relazione per il Congresso per la Pace di New Delhi" (June 16–18, 1962) (Partinico: Centro Studi e Iniziative, 1962), cicl. 218, 2–6; in Archival Files of the Centro Studi e Iniziative, Partinico, Italy (hereafter Archives, Centro Studi).

2. Interviews with Danilo Dolci, Partinico, Italy (May–June 1986).

3. Danilo Dolci, *Banditi a Partinico* (Bari: Laterza, 1955).

4. For two personalized accounts of Dolci's early career, written during the 1960s, see James McNeish, *Fire under the Ashes* (London: Hodder & Stoughton, 1965); and Jerre Mangione, *A Passion for Sicilians: The World around Danilo Dolci* (New York: William Morrow, 1968).

5. McNeish, 22.

6. Giacinto Spagnoletti, ed., *Conversazioni con Danilo Dolci* (Milano: Mondadori, 1977 (hereafter *Conversazioni con Danilo Dolci*), 17ff.

7. Ibid., 15.

8. Ibid., 16.

9. *Conversazioni con Danilo Dolci,* 19; Danilo Dolci, "Ciò che ho imparato," in *Esperienze e riflessioni* (Bari: Laterza, 1974 (hereafter *Esperienze e riflessioni*), 198.

10. *Conversazioni con Danilo Dolci,* 16–17.

11. Ibid., 22.

12. Interviews with Danilo Dolci, Partinico, Italy (May–June, 1986).

13. Ibid.; see also *Conversazioni con Danilo Dolci,* 22–23.

14. *Conversazioni con Danilo Dolci,* 23–24.

15. Interviews with Danilo Dolci, Partinico, Italy (May–June, 1986); *Conversazioni con Danilo Dolci,* 25, 33.

16. *Conversazioni con Danilo Dolci,* 23.

17. McNeish, 29.

18. *Conversazioni con Danilo Dolci,* 33.

19. Ibid., 34.

20. Ibid.

21. McNeish, 32ff.

22. *Conversazioni con Danilo Dolci,* 35.

23. Ibid., 34.

24. Dolci attended a military training camp in 1951, but he worked out an arrangement with his officers by which he was allowed to spend nearly half of his time continuing the work at Nomadelfia. McNeish, 36.

25. Interviews with Danilo Dolci, Partinico, Italy (May–June, 1986).

26. Biancoazzurre lontane nella notte
    pur le stelle hanno un'anima di fuoco.
    Il nome che mi chiama non è il mio,
    non mi basta alcun nome.
    Questo corpo che presto s'aggruma
    non è il mio—
        non ancora nato
    sgorgo da sempre
          mentre muoio.

Danilo Dolci, "La Luce Chiama" (1949–50), in *Creatura di creature* (Venice: Corbo e Fiore, 1983), 4.

27. McNeish, 39. The fact that the site of Nomadelfia had formerly been used for the murder and persecution of Jews apparently did not strike Don Zeno as sufficient reason to open his institution to children of all faiths.

28. *Conversazioni con Danilo Dolci*, 38.

29. For a concise overview of Sicily's history, see M. I. Finley, Denis Mack Smith, and Christopher Duggan, *A History of Sicily* (London: Chatto & Windus, 1986).

30. For a detailed analysis of this process, carried out within a framework similar to Immanuel Wallerstein's concept of a "capitalist world-system," see Jane and Peter Schneider, *Culture and Political Economy in Western Sicily* (New York: Academic Press, 1976).

31. See Judith Chubb, *Patronage, Power, and Poverty in Southern Italy* (Cambridge: Cambridge University Press, 1982), 4.

32. See Steffen W. Schmidt, Laura Guasti, Carl H. Landé, and James C. Scott, eds., *Friends, Followers, and Factions: A Reader in Political Clientelism* (Berkeley: University of California Press, 1977), 361.

33. See for instance Edward C. Banfield and James Q. Wilson, *City Politics* (Cambridge, Mass.: Harvard University Press and MIT Press, 1963), 115ff.

34. See Giuseppe Alongi, *La maffia* (Palermo: Sellerio, 1977 [1886]; Anton Blok, *The Mafia of a Sicilian Village, 1860–1960* (New York: Harper & Row, 1974); and Filippo Sabetti, *Political Authority in a Sicilian Village* (New Brunswick, N.J.: Rutgers University Press, 1984).

35. Luigi Graziano, "Patron-Client Relationships in Southern Italy," in Steffen W. Schmidt et al., eds., *Friends, Followers, and Factions: A Reader in Political Clientelism,* 363.

36. For an excellent discussion of the political transformation of patronage in Southern Italy after 1860, see Judith Chubb, chap. 3. See also Sidney Tarrow, *Peasant Communism in Southern Italy* (New Haven: Yale University Press, 1967); and *Between Center and Periphery* (New Haven: Yale University Press, 1977).

37. See Judith Chubb, 24ff.; and M. I. Finley et al., *A History of Sicily,* 207–17.

38. See Pino Arlacchi, *La mafia imprenditrice* (Bologna: Il Mulino, 1983), 109–129.

39. See Judith Chubb, esp. 88–159, 219–21.

40. Between 1951 and 1975, private *per capita* consumption in Southern Italy increased by 287% (compared to a 257% increase in the Center-North); gross internal product grew by 267% (compared with 255% in the Center-North); infant mortality declined from 82 per 1,000 births to 24 per 1,000 births (compared with a decline from 51 per 1,000 to 17 per 1,000 in the Center-North). Gisèle Podbielski, *Twenty-Five Years of Special Action for the Development of Southern Italy* (Rome: Giuffré, 1978), 105–22.

41. In 1975, the gross internal product of Southern Italy still represented roughly 25% of the national total—the same as in 1951. Illiteracy in the south had been cut from 24% of the adult population in 1951 to 10% in 1975, but it still lagged far behind the figure of 2.5% for 1975 in the Center-North. Between 1951 and 1975, almost four and a half million persons (the equivalent of the total population of Sicily in 1953) chose to emigrate from Southern Italy. During these twenty-five years, writes Gisèle Podbielski, "labour market conditions worsened in the South in relation to those in the

rest of the country. . . . Over the whole period southern employment fell by 693,000 units compared to an increase of 407,000 units in the Centre-North." Podbielski, 105ff., 111.

42. See Michele Pantaleone, *Mafia e politica* (Torino: Einaudi, 1962); and Roberto Scarpinato, ed., *Mafia, partiti, e pubblica amministrazione* (Napoli: Jovene, 1985).

43. See Pino Arlacchi; and Mario Centorrino and Emanuele Sgroi, eds., *Economia e potere mafioso in Sicilia* (Milano: Giuffrè, 1984).

44. See Schneider and Schneider, 81–112, 227–38; Sabetti.

45. For an early descriptive study of these cultural norms in the Southern region of Lucania, see Edward C. Banfield, *The Moral Basis of a Backward Society* (New York: Free Press, 1958). Banfield's analysis is limited, however, by its tendency to underemphasize the role played by historical and socioeconomic factors (poverty, unemployment, foreign exploitation) in the shaping of Southern cultural codes.

46. For a study that construes these aspects of Sicilian culture as a rational response to millennia of oppression by outsiders, see Filippo Sabetti.

47. *Conversazioni con Danilo Dolci*, 39.

48. Danilo Dolci, *Report from Palermo*, trans. P. D. Cummings (New York: Orion Press, 1959 [1956]), xix.

49. Gisèle Podbielski, 34.

50. See Danilo Dolci, *Spreco: documenti e inchieste su alcuni aspetti dello spreco nella Sicilia occidentale* (Torino: Einaudi, 1960), 307–23. See also Danilo Dolci, ed., *Una politica per la piena occupazione* (Torino: Einaudi, 1958).

51. See the oral histories reported in Danilo Dolci, *Sicilian Lives*, trans. Justin Vitiello (New York: Pantheon, 1981 [1963]). See also *Spreco*.

52. Danilo Dolci, "Diario di un'anno (1954)," in *Esperienze e riflessioni*, 3–58.

53. See *Conversazioni con Danilo Dolci*, 39ff.; and McNeish, 50ff.

54. Interviews with Danilo Dolci, Partinico, Italy (May–June, 1986).

55. *Conversazioni con Danilo Dolci*, 53.

56. Ibid., 54–55.

57. McNeish, 54.

58. *Conversazioni con Danilo Dolci*, 59.

59. Ibid., 42.

60. Danilo Dolci, "Letter to All My Friends" (Trappeto, October 14, 1952), reprinted in Danilo Dolci, *Outlaws*, trans. R. Munroe (New York: Orion Press, 1961), 55.

61. *Conversazioni con Danilo Dolci*, 58–59.

62. Paolino Russo and Toni Alia, *Due pescatori raccontano la storia di Borgo di Dio* (January 15, 1954); excerpts reprinted in *Conversazioni con Danilo Dolci*, 164.

63. Ibid.

64. Ibid., 166.

65. Danilo Dolci, *Fare presto (e bene) perché si muore* ("La Nuova Italia," 1953); *Banditi a Partinico*.

66. Interviews with Danilo Dolci, Partinico, Italy (May–June, 1986).

67. *Conversazioni con Danilo Dolci*, 51.

68. For an excellent account of women's daily life in Southern Italy during these years, see Anne Cornelisen, *Women of the Shadows* (New York: Vintage, 1976).

69. Danilo Dolci, *Outlaws*, 208.

70. The account that follows is derived from Danilo Dolci, "Lo Sciopero alla Rovescia," in *Esperienze e riflessioni*, 61–81; and from *Conversazioni con Danilo Dolci*, 61–69.

71. See *Conversazioni con Danilo Dolci*, 62–63.

72. Quoted in Danilo Dolci, *Outlaws*, 216.

73. Lamberto Borghi, quoted in Giovanni Lombardi, "Il Caso Dolci Visto Attraverso la Stampa," *Scuola e Città* (March 31, 1958): 101. Lombardi surveyed twenty-one newspapers and four magazines from February through March 1956, assessing responses to "the case of Dolci."

74. P. Bini, ed., *Il Mezzogiorno nel parlamento repubblicano, 1948–1972*, vol. 4, book 1 (Milano: Giuffré, 1978), 259, 278–79.

75. Giovanni Lombardi, 98–99.

76. Mario Farinella, "Hanno Arrestato Danilo Dolci," *L'Ora* (Palermo), (February 3, 1956): 1.

77. Giovanni Russo, in *Corriere della Sera* (February 5, 1956); quoted in Giovanni Lombardi, 100.

78. Giovanni Bocca, in *L'Europeo* (February 26, 1956); quoted in Lombardi, 100.

79. See *Conversazioni con Danilo Dolci*, 66.

80. "Dolci vs. Far Niente," *Time* (February 20, 1956), 32.

81. Maria Brandon-Albini, "Un Gandhi Chrétien Chez Les 'Bandits' de Sicile: Danilo Dolci," *Les Temps Modernes*, no. 124 (May 1956): 1642–55.

82. Ibid., 1655.

83. See *Conversazioni con Danilo Dolci*, 70ff.

84. Gianfranco Corsini, "Dieci Vincitori al 'Premio Viareggio,'" *L'Ora* [?] (July 27, 1958).

85. For an excellent article comparing Dolci's oral histories with those compiled by other socially committed intellectuals during these years, see Adriana Chemello, "'Storie di vita' da Scotellaro a Dolci," *Rassegna della letteratura italiana* (January–August 1980).

86. Danilo Dolci, *Report from Palermo*, trans. P. D. Cummins, 5, 81, 182–83, 159, 230. I have slightly modified the translation of the excerpt beginning with "My wife was cooking . . . "

87. Arnaldo Geraldini, "'Inchiesta a Palermo' è un'opera di scienza," *Corriere della Sera* (May 8, 1958).

88. "'L'Osservatore Romano' protesta per l'assoluzione di Dolci e Carocci: intervento Vaticano nella vertenza," *Corriere della Sera* (May 8, 1958).

89. See for instance Stuart Woolf, *A History of Italy, 1700–1860* (New York: Methuen, 1979), 21–26.

90. For a more detailed account of Dolci's conflicts with the Catholic Church, see McNeish, xiii–xiv, 116, 234ff.

91. Danilo Dolci, "Cosa è pace?" in *Esperienze e riflessioni*, 230–31.

92. Interviews with Danilo Dolci, Partinico, Italy (May–June, 1986).

93. Danilo Dolci, ed., *Una politica per la piena occupazione* (Torino: Einaudi, 1958), 1.

94. Ibid., 7ff.

95. See *Conversazioni con Danilo Dolci*, 74–77.

96. Silone to Dolci (January 8, 1958). Original in Dolci Papers, Mugar Memorial Library, Boston University (hereafter Dolci Papers, Boston University).

97. Danilo Dolci, "Testo della dichiarazione resa da Danilo Dolci il 16 Gennaio 1958, a Palermo, in seguito alla comunicazione ufficiale dell'assegnazione del Premio Lenin per la pace" (January 16, 1958), 2. Dolci Papers, Boston University.

98. See the letters from Capitini to Dolci in Aldo Capitini, *Lettere a Danilo Dolci* (Il Ponte, 1969), 7–10.

99. Danilo Dolci, "Schema della relazione per il Congresso per la Pace di New Delhi," June 16–18, 1962 (Partinico: Centro Studi e Iniziative, 1962), cicl. 218, 2–6; in Archives, Centro Studi; "Foreign delegates begin talks on ways to banish nuclear arms," *Hindustan Times* (June 16, 1962).

100. See Danilo Dolci, "Dalle Vecchie Strutture alle Nuove," in *Esperienze e riflessioni*, 257ff.

101. Danilo Dolci, "Ai Più Giovani," in *Esperienze e riflessioni*, 221–24.

102. Danilo Dolci, "Schema della relazione per il Congresso per la Pace di New Delhi," 3–4.

103. Danilo Dolci, "Cosa è pace?" in *Esperienze e riflessioni*, 239.

104. Danilo Dolci, "The Premises of the Work," in Mary Taylor, ed., *Community Development in Western Sicily: An Introduction to the Centro Studi* (Partinico: Centro Studi e Iniziative, June 1963), 14; in Archives, Centro Studi.

105. Martin Clark, *Modern Italy, 1871–1982* (London: Longman, 1984), 355.

106. Schneider and Schneider, 132.

107. "Appunti per gli amici" (newsletter of the Centro Studi, published monthly in Partinico (hereafter "Appunti per gli amici"), nos. 15ff. (1960–64); "Programmi Semestrali" (Centro Studi e Iniziative, July–December 1961); in Archives, Centro Studi.

108. Lorenzo Barbera, *Consuntivo del lavoro di sviluppo di comunità a Roccamena dal Luglio 1960 al Giugno 1961* (Partinico: Centro Studi e Iniziative, 1961), cicl. 178; and Ruth Hemmi, *Rapporto sul lavoro a Trappeto dall'Agosto 1960 al Luglio 1962* (Partinico: Centro Studi e Iniziative, 1962), cicl. 225; in Archives, Centro Studi.

109. Mangione, 50.

110. I am basing my description here on my own observation of Dolci in 1986, on my interviews with his coworkers, and on the detailed testimonials given during the 1960s by Jerre Mangione and James McNeish in their books.

111. McNeish, 192.

112. Danilo Dolci, "Paper Presented before the International Liaison Committee of Organizations for Peace," Basel, Switzerland (August 19–20, 1960); reprinted in *Outlaws*, 295.

113. This generalization is based on interviews with fourteen of Dolci's coworkers, from those who worked with him in Palermo during the 1950s, to members of the Centro Studi in the 1960s, to Dolci's associates in the 1970s and 1980s: Franco Alasia, Paola Buzzola (Barbera), Orazio De Guilmi, Michael Fähndrich, Franco LaGennusa, Francesco Grimaldi, Alberto L'Abate, Pino Lombardo, Rosaria Martinetti, Albrecht Müller-Schöll, Carlo Presciuttini, Eliana Riggio, Justin Vitiello, Renata Zwick-Rubino. Seven of these individuals were sharply critical of Dolci's role as a leader. For two personal testimonials written during the 1960s by individuals highly sympathetic to Dolci (yet nonetheless cataloguing his bitter conflicts with his coworkers), see James

McNeish, xiv, 91, 147–48, 171, 183, 188, 193–96, 224–26, 240–44; and Jerre Mangione, 22, 39, 45, 52, 71, 121ff., 148, 183, 188, 238, 269, 273, 284–91, 347.

114. Interviews with Danilo Dolci, Partinico, Italy (May–June, 1986).

115. Eduard Watjen, quoted in Mangione, 289.

116. Interview with Alberto L'Abate, Florence (March 9, 1986).

117. Danilo Dolci, *Spreco.*

118. See Francesco Renda, *Storia della Sicilia dal 1860 al 1970,* vol. 3 (Palermo: Sellerio, 1987), 434–36; 486–93.

119. Ibid., 436–38.

120. Interviews with Danilo Dolci, Partinico, Italy (May–June, 1986).

121. See for instance Pino Arlacchi.

122. For a vivid account of Carnevale's career, see Carlo Levi, *Le parole sono pietre* (Torino: Einaudi, 1955). See also Pantaleone, 117–55, 212–31.

123. See Schneider and Schneider, 183–84.

124. See Pantaleone, 135–41.

125. "Intermediario costoso il consorzio per gli espropriandi," *L'Ora* (August 16, 1962); G. F. P., "La diga e la mafia," *L'Unità* (September 9, 1962); see also Danilo Dolci, *The Man Who Plays Alone,* trans. Antonia Cowan (London: MacGibbon & Kee, 1968), 65ff.

126. "Minacce ed incendi a Partinico per bloccare la diga sullo Jato," *L'Ora* (August 17, 1961); "Un'altro attentato della mafia per le dighe," *Il Giorno* (August 24, 1961). See also McNeish, 199.

127. "Superati gli ostacoli concesso l'appalto ma i lavori di costruzione non iniziano," *Giornale di Sicilia* (February 2, 1962); Danilo Dolci, *The Man Who Plays Alone,* 66–67.

128. Danilo Dolci, *The Man Who Plays Alone,* 68.

129. Dolci to Giulio Pastore (Aug. 7, 1962); reprinted in "Appunti per gli amici," no. 22, cicl. 231 (September 7, 1962); in Archives, Centro Studi.

130. "Appunti per gli amici," no. 22, cicl. 231 (September 7, 1962); in Archives, Centro Studi.

131. Interviews with Danilo Dolci, Partinico, Italy (May–June, 1986).

132. "Appunti per gli amici," no. 22, cicl. 231 (September 7, 1962); and "Riunione per un movimento generale per la diga" (Partinico: Centro Studi e Iniziative, August 10, 1962), cicl. 228; in Archives, Centro Studi.

133. *Conversazioni con Danilo Dolci,* p. 82.

134. Ibid., 81; Danilo Dolci and Franco Alasia, "La mafia come impedimento allo sviluppo nella zona dello Jato," cicl. 335 (Partinico: Centro Studi e Iniziative, 1964), 9–10; in Archives, Centro Studi.

135. Quoted in McNeish, 210.

136. Ibid., 213, 215.

137. "Appunti relativi alla diga sul fiume Jato," cicl. 226 (Partinico: Centro Studi e Iniziative, 1962); "Nota sul Centro Studi e Iniziative di Partinico" (Partinico: Centro Studi e Iniziative, 1977); in Archives, Centro Studi.

138. Danilo Dolci, "La riconquista dell'acqua" (Partinico: Centro Studi e Iniziative, 1988); in Archives, Centro Studi.

139. Enzo di Pasquale, "Acqua, digiunano in mille," *Giornale di Sicilia* (January 24,

1988); Ettore Boffano, "Dolci: 'La gente può vincere la piovra,'" *Stampa Sera* (January 25, 1988): 9; Giorgio Petta, "Le campagne finiranno per appassire," *La Sicilia* (January 29, 1988).

140. Serra's account is quoted in Danilo Dolci, *Verso un mondo nuovo* (Torino: Einaudi, 1965 [hereafter *Verso un mondo nuovo*]), 281–83.

141. "Nota sul Centro Studi e Iniziative di Partinico" (1977); interview with Franco LaGennusa, a Dolci coworker and a member of the Jato Irrigation Consortium; Trappeto (June 12, 1986).

142. Pantaleone, *Mafia e politica* (1962).

143. Danilo Dolci, *The Man Who Plays Alone*, 205–42.

144. Ibid., 321.

145. Ibid., 206.

146. *Conversazioni con Danilo Dolci*, 88; see also Danilo Dolci, *The Man Who Plays Alone*, 302.

147. Danilo Dolci, *The Man Who Plays Alone*, 250.

148. "Danilo Dolci denunciato per vilipendio alle istituzioni," *Il Giornale del Mezzogiorno* (January 19, 1966); "Sbagliata la denuncia contro Dolci," *L'Ora* (January 20, 1966).

149. Danilo Dolci, *The Man Who Plays Alone*, 274–76.

150. Ibid., 242.

151. Correspondence between Moro and Mattarella, quoted from newspaper accounts, and reprinted in Danilo Dolci, *The Man Who Plays Alone*, 242.

152. Ibid., 301; Pantaleone, 94–116.

153. See Giuseppe Mammarella, *L'Italia contemporanea (1943–1985)* (Bologna: Il Mulino, 1985), 310–12, 349, 351, 394–95, 462, 468, 484, 492. For a concise account (and *exposé*) of Leone's career by a leading Italian journalist, see Camilla Cederna, *Giovanni Leone: La carriera di un presidente* (Milano: Feltrinelli, 1978).

154. Danilo Dolci, *The Man Who Plays Alone*, 352–361.

155. See Billy J. Chandler, *King of the Mountain: The Life and Death of Giuliano the Bandit* (Dekalb: Northern Illinois University Press, 1988); and Pantaleone, 155–82; Renda, 277–286; Finley, Smith, and Duggan, 216.

156. Danilo Dolci, *The Man Who Plays Alone*, 362.

157. Ibid., 367.

158. *Conversazioni con Danilo Dolci*, 92.

159. "Volpe era mafioso," *L'Ora* (February 9, 1977); "Aveva detto che l'ex-deputato DC era mafioso—Danilo Dolci assolto dall'accusa d'aver calunniato Calogero Volpe," *Corriere della Sera* (February 9, 1977); reprinted in Danilo Dolci, *Il ponte screpolato* (Torino: Stampatori, 1979 [hereafter *Il ponte screpolato*]), 38.

160. Danilo Dolci, *Il ponte screpolato*, 38.

161. For a revealing study of political corruption in Southern Italy, see James Walston, *The Mafia and Clientelism* (New York: Routledge, 1988).

162. See the correspondence in Aldo Capitini, 3–12.

163. Dolci funded these travels by writing lengthy articles for the left-wing Palermo newspaper *L'Ora*, describing in detail his reactions to what he saw—from the streets of New York to the rural villages of Senegal.

164. Interviews with Danilo Dolci, Partinico, Italy (May–June, 1986).

165. See for instance *Verso un mondo nuovo; Esperienze e riflessioni*, 257ff.; and *Conversazioni con Danilo Dolci*, 93–109.

166. *Conversazioni con Danilo Dolci*, 98.

167. See *Verso un mondo nuovo*, 153ff.; *Conversazioni con Danilo Dolci*, 101.

168. See *Esperienze e riflessioni*, 279; *Conversazioni con Danilo Dolci*, 105.

169. Danilo Dolci, "In America . . . " *L'Ora* (April 8, 11, 12, 17, and 18, 1961).

170. Danilo Dolci, "In URSS," reprinted in *Verso un mondo nuovo*, 35–96.

171. Interviews with Danilo Dolci, Partinico, Italy (May–June, 1986).

172. Russell to Dolci (June 27, 1962); Dolci to Russell (Aug. 6, 1962); in Dolci Papers, Boston University.

173. Russell to Dolci (September 6, 1962); in Dolci Papers, Boston University.

174. Sergio Talenti, "Danilo Dolci Nobel per la pace?" *Paese Sera* (April 26, 1965).

175. See Bertrand Russell, *War Crimes in Vietnam* (London: Allen & Unwin, 1967), 125ff.

176. See Ronald W. Clark, *The Life of Bertrand Russell* (London: Jonathan Cape and Weidenfeld & Nicholson, 1975), 623–28.

177. Dolci to Russell (August 16 and October 12, 1966); Russell to Dolci (September 15 and October 21, 1966); in Dolci Papers, Boston University.

178. *Conversazioni con Danilo Dolci*, 113–15.

179. "Appunti per gli amici" (Partinico: Centro Studi e Iniziative, October–November 1967), cicl. 435; in Archives, Centro Studi.

180. "Per il Vietnam una marcia che attraverserà l'Italia," *L'Unità* (October 17, 1967).

181. "Appunti per gli amici" (1967).

182. "Antiwar Marchers in Rome Scuffle with Police Outside U.S. Embassy," *New York Times* (November 30, 1967).

183. Aldo Paladini, "Dolci risponde su politica di opposizione alla violenza," *Vie Nuove* (December 7, 1967), 8.

184. "Conclusi i '50 giorni di pressione' delle zone colpite dal terremoto in Sicilia," A.N.S.A. (Servizio Italiano) (November 3, 1968); Gianni Lo Monaco, "Piano di Dolci per le zone terremotate," *Paese Sera* (September 17, 1968).

185. "Una emittente clandestina a Partinico lancia continui appelli per i terremotati," *La Stampa* (March 26, 1970); "Trasmette da ieri 'radio terremotati,'" *Il Giornale D'Italia* (March 26, 1970).

186. Interviews with Danilo Dolci, Franco LaGennusa, Rosaria Martinetti, Francesco Grimaldi; Partinico, Italy (May–June, 1986).

187. Interviews with Danilo Dolci, Partinico, Italy (May–June, 1986). Dolci's personal life also underwent a major transition during these years. In 1973, after twenty years of marriage, he and his wife Vincenzina Mangano separated. Two years later, Dolci met Elena Norman, a Swedish social worker who had come down to work at the Centro Studi as a volunteer, and they were married in 1976. They established their residence back on the hilltop in Trappeto, near the old Borgo di Dio, and subsequently had two children.

188. This "economic miracle," fueled initially by the Marshall Plan and subsequently encouraged by low labor costs and cheap energy supplies, had produced an average annual growth-rate of 8.1 percent in industrial production, a rate comparable only to

those of the other two losers of World War II, Japan and Germany. In 1967—to take one indicative example—the Turin-based automobile firm, FIAT, was selling more cars in Europe than any other company. See Martin Clark, 348ff.

189. The Italian political system, with its weak executive and continual reshuffling of parliamentary governments, had proved more sturdy in structure than superficial appearances suggested. It was dominated by the Christian Democratic party, which enjoyed the backing of the Vatican, the United States, and a large proportion of the Italian middle class. Yet Italian politics had also witnessed a steady "drift to the left"—a process in which Christian Democratic politicians were increasingly forced to cooperate with Italy's main left-wing parties (the Socialists and Communists) in order to remain in power. A peculiar equilibrium had emerged, in which the Communists (who claimed roughly a third of the popular vote) followed a policy of constructive opposition; their avowed aim was not to precipitate a revolutionary crisis but rather to be assimilated gradually into the governmental machinery of the existing republic. See Giuseppe Mammarella; and Norman Kogan, *A Political History of Postwar Italy* (New York: Praeger, 1981).

190. See for instance Arturo Carlo Jemolo, *Questa repubblica: dal '68 alla crisi morale* (Firenze: Felice Le Monnier, 1981); Alain Touraine, *The May Movement,* trans. Leonard F. X. Mayhew (New York: Random House, 1971), esp. 147ff.; Alberto Ronchey, *Accadde in Italia: 1968–1977* (Milano: Garzanti, 1977).

191. See for instance Peter Lange and Sidney Tarrow, eds., *Italy in Transition* (London: Frank Cass & Co., 1980); Alessandro Silj, *Never Again without a Rifle: The Origins of Italian Terrorism,* trans. Salvator Attanasio (New York: Karz, 1979); Alberto Martinelli and Gianfranco Pasquino, eds., *La politica nell'Italia che cambia* (Milano: Feltrinelli, 1978); Umberto Romagnoli and Tiziano Treu, *I sindacati in Italia: storia di una strategia, 1945–1976* (Bologna: Il Mulino, 1977), 80ff.

192. *Conversazioni con Danilo Dolci,* 110–11, 122–23.

193. Interviews with Danilo Dolci, Partinico, Italy (May–June, 1986).

194. See for instance Gianni Rodari, "Che tipo di scuola volete? Rispondono madri e figli," *L'Ora* (July 6, 1973). See also Danilo Dolci, *Chissà se i pesci piangono* (Torino: Einaudi, 1974); and *Il ponte screpolato.*

195. *Conversazioni con Danilo Dolci,* 123.

196. Danilo Dolci, *Il ponte screpolato,* 32–35, 45–49; Franco Alasia, "Cronologia Essenziale" (Partinico: Centro Studi e Iniziative, 1985).

197. Interviews with Danilo Dolci, Partinico, Italy (May–June, 1986); Franco Alasia, "Cronologia Essenziale."

198. See for instance Maria Montessori, *Education and Peace* (Chicago: Henry Regnery Co., 1972); and Elizabeth G. Hainstock, *The Essential Montessori* (New York: Mentor, 1978).

199. See for instance Paulo Freire, *Pedagogy of the Oppressed,* trans. Myra Bergman Ramos (New York: Continuum, 1970). See also Henry A. Giroux, *Theory and Resistance in Education: A Pedagogy for the Opposition* (South Hadley, Mass.: Bergin & Garvey, 1983); and Beatrice and Ronald Gross, eds., *Radical School Reform* (New York: Simon & Schuster, 1969).

200. Interview with Renata Zwick-Rubino, Partinico (June 10, 1986).

201. Interviews with Danilo Dolci, Partinico, Italy (May–June, 1986).

202. *Conversazioni con Danilo Dolci,* 135.

203. Ibid., 133, 134.

204. Ibid., 134.

205. Ibid., 141.

206. Excerpted from "Educational Planning for the Future," in Danilo Dolci, *The World Is One Creature,* trans. Justin Vitiello (New York: Amity House, 1984), 169–70. I have slightly modified the translation in a few places.

207. For a sensitive (but extremely hermetic) overview of Dolci's poetry, see Giuseppe Fontanelli, *Danilo Dolci* (Firenze: La Nuova Italia, 1984).

208. Danilo Dolci, *Palpitare di nessi* (Roma: Armando, 1985), 243–44.

209. Ibid., 118.

210. Danilo Dolci, "In Questo Frammento," in *Creatura di creature,* 80.

211. See Danilo Dolci, *La comunicazione di massa non esiste* (forthcoming).

212. Seminar with Danilo Dolci, Berkeley, California (February 1984).

213. Danilo Dolci, *La creatura e il virus del dominio* (Latina: L'Argonauta, 1987), 99.

214. For an excellent account of the Frankfurt School's history and theoretical contributions, see Martin Jay, *The Dialectical Imagination* (Boston: Little, Brown, 1973).

215. See for instance *Conversazioni con Danilo Dolci,* 139ff.

216. See Danilo Dolci, *Palpitare di nessi,* 115ff., 170–75, 184ff., 229ff; *La comunicazione di massa non esiste,* 7, 19, 25–33, 62ff; *La creatura e il virus del dominio,* 99ff.

217. E. P. Thompson, "Deterrence and Addiction," in *Beyond the Cold War,* 23.

218. See Danilo Dolci, *La creatura e il virus del dominio,* 47–57, 95ff., 133ff.

219. *Conversazioni con Danilo Dolci,* 154.

220. Adriano Baglivo, "Padrini in sciopero a Palermo," *Corriere della Sera* (May 5, 1986).

221. Interview with Orazio de Guilmi, Trappeto (June 12, 1986).

222. Interview with Alberto L'Abate, Florence (March 9, 1986).

223. Interview with Pino Lombardo, Santa Ninfa, Sicily (June 3, 1986).

224. Interviews with Franco LaGennusa, Trappeto, Italy (May–June, 1986).

225. Interviews with Dolci's coworkers, 1985–87.

226. Carlo Levi, "Open Letter to the Men and Women of Partinico" (September 8, 1962). Original in Dolci Papers, Boston University.

Conclusion

1. Alfred North Whitehead, *Process and Reality* (New York: Free Press, 1957 [1929]), p. 400.

2. See for instance Dorothy V. Jones, *Code of Peace: Ethics and Security in the World of the Warlord States* (Chicago: University of Chicago Press, 1991), chap. 2.

3. See Martin Ceadel, *Pacifism in Britain, 1914–1945* (Oxford: Clarendon Press, 1980); Peter Brock, *Twentieth-Century Pacifism* (New York: Van Nostrand Reinhold, 1970); Lawrence S. Wittner, *Rebels against War: The American Peace Movement, 1941–1960* (New York: Columbia University Press, 1969); and Katsuya Kodama and Unto Vesa, eds., *Towards a Comparative Analysis of Peace Movements* (Aldershot, England: Dartmouth, 1990).

4. For a discussion of Toynbee's and Morgenthau's views on spheres of influence, and on seeking a comprehensive agreement between the United States and the Soviet Union, see Chap. 2, above. Churchill remained to the end of his days a fervent advocate of *Realpolitik,* but he also tempered this stance with public appeals for conciliatory approaches between the superpowers, and for seeking a full-scale diplomatic settlement, as in the following statement he made in a 1950 speech:

> The idea appeals to me of a supreme effort to bridge the gulf between the two worlds [of the superpowers] so that each can live its life, if not in friendship, at least without the hatreds of the Cold War. . . . [While] I believe there is time for a further effort for a lasting and peaceful settlement, I cannot feel that it is necessarily a long time. . . . Above all things, we must not fritter it away. (Winston Churchill, "On European Unity and Settlement with Russia," reprinted in *Bulletin of the Atomic Scientists* 6 (June 1950): 170. See also Joel Rosenthal, *Righteous Realists: Political Realism, Responsible Power, and American Culture in the Nuclear Age* (Baton Rouge: Louisiana State University Press, 1991)

5. See for instance Kenneth Kipnis and Diana T. Meyers, eds., *Political Realism and International Morality: Ethics in the Nuclear Age* (Boulder, Colo.: Westview Press, 1987); Peter Calvocoressi, *A Time for Peace: Pacifism, Internationalism, and Protest Forces in the Reduction of War* (London: Hutchinson, 1987); April Carter, *Peace Movements: International Protest and World Politics since 1945* (London: Longman, 1992).

6. Václav Havel, *Disturbing the Peace,* trans. Paul Wilson (New York: Knopf, 1990), 180–81.

7. Václav Havel, "From a New Year's Day Speech," *New York Review of Books* (February 15, 1990): 22.

8. At one level, the implicit debate here appears to parallel one of the classic political "disputes" of the modern world: the clash between Burke and Robespierre, between conservative paternalism and the radical egalitarianism of the French Revolution. In fact, however, the confrontation is even more complex than that, for Burke believed in a society that fused both hierarchy and small, self-governing communities; while Robespierre, despite his egalitarianism, ruthlessly drew political power into the centralized command of his Committee of Public Safety.

Another misleading historical parallel is the one between Thompson and Dolci and the nineteenth-century anarchists; for revolutionary theorists like Bakunin showed a similar distaste for the massive structures of the nation-state, and a similar attraction for a broad-minded internationalism of free individuals. Thompson and Dolci, however, were quite different from those anarchists. They disagreed with the anarchists' rigid distinction between state and society, and rejected the idea that smashing the structures of the state would somehow liberate the latent creative forces in society. Instead, their analyses were more subtle, more tortured, more complex and ambiguous. There could be no question of smashing anything, they believed, for state and society were mutually interpenetrating, like the parts of a living organism. Thus, the goal had to be approached with infinitely more delicacy and patience, and with a primary emphasis on respecting those humane values that provided the only reliable guideposts in an otherwise tentative and groping endeavor.

9. George Orwell, *Nineteen Eighty-Four* (Oxford: Clarendon Press, 1984 [1949]).

10. Thompson and Dolci would no doubt have agreed strongly with the observation that Orwell made as early as 1949:

My recent novel [*Nineteen Eighty-Four*] is NOT intended as an attack on Socialism or on the British Labour Party (of which I am a supporter) but as a show-up of the perversions to which a centralized economy is liable. . . . The scene of the book is laid in Britain in order to emphasize that the English-speaking races are not innately better than anyone else and that totalitarianism, *if not fought against,* could triumph anywhere. (George Orwell, "Letter to Francis A. Henson," June 16, 1949; from *In Front of Your Nose: The Collected Essays, Journalism, and Letters of George Orwell, 1945–1950,* vol. 4, ed. Sonia Orwell and Ian Angus [New York: Harcourt, Brace & World, 1968], 502 [emphasis in original])

11. Danilo Dolci, *Per l'approfondimento dell'iniziativa antifascista* (Partinico: Centro Studi e Iniziative, 1972), 4, 6, 13.

12. E. P. Thompson, *Double Exposure,* 147.

13. See for instance Kenneth N. Waltz, *Theory of International Politics* (Reading, Mass.: Addison-Wesley, 1979); Hidemi Suganami, *The Domestic Analogy and World Order Proposals* (Cambridge: Cambridge University Press, 1989), chaps. 8 and 9; and Johan Galtung, *The True Worlds: A Transnational Perspective* (New York: Free Press, 1980), esp. 305ff.

14. Jean Bethke Elshtain, "Realism, Just War, and the Witness of Peace," in *Power Trips and Other Journeys: Essays in Feminism and Civic Discourse* (Madison: University of Wisconsin Press, 1990), 154. See also Hedley Bull, *Hedley Bull on Arms Control,* selected by Robert O'Neill and David N. Schwartz (New York: St. Martin's, 1987); and Martin Wight, *Power Politics,* ed. Hedley Bull and Carsten Holbraad (Leicester: Leicester University Press, 1978).

15. See the lucid discussion and bibliography in Phillip Taylor, *Nonstate Actors in International Politics: From Transregional to Substate Organizations* (Boulder, Colo.: Westview, 1984). See also A. J. R. Groom and Paul Taylor, eds., *Frameworks for International Cooperation* (New York: St. Martin's Press, 1990); Rudiger Jutte and Annemarie Grosse-Jutte, eds., *The Future of International Organization* (New York: St. Martin's Press, 1981); and Andrew M. Scott, *The Dynamics of Interdependence* (Chapel Hill: University of North Carolina Press, 1982).

16. See for instance the two studies by the political scientist Ernst B. Haas, the first of which reflects a relatively optimistic assessment in 1958, the second a more chastened analysis two decades later: Ernst B. Haas, *The Uniting of Europe: Political, Social, and Economic Forces, 1950–1957* (Stanford: Stanford University Press, 1958); and *The Obsolescence of Regional Integration Theory* (Berkeley: University of California Institute of International Studies, 1975).

17. See the detailed discussion of these kinds of "multi-level" solutions in Suganami.

18. Johan Galtung, *The True Worlds: A Transnational Perspective* (New York: Free Press, 1980), 347.

19. See for instance Ernst B. Haas, "The Collective Management of International Conflict," in United Nations Institute for Training and Research, *The United Nations and the Maintenance of International Peace and Security* (Dordrecht, The Netherlands: Martinus Nijhoff, 1987), 39ff.; James N. Rosenau and Ernst-Otto Czempiel, eds., *Governance without Government: Order and Change in World Politics* (New York: Cambridge University Press, 1992); and Robert E. Riggs and Jack C. Plano, *The United Nations: International Organization and World Politics* (Pacific Grove, Calif.: Brooks/

Cole, 1988). For a more optimistic view about the plausibility of world federalism, see David W. Felder, *How to Work for Peace* (Tallahassee: Florida A & M University Press, 1991), 45–56.

20. See the excellent discussion in Suganami, chap. 9; and Stanley Hoffmann, *Duties beyond Borders: On the Limits and Possibilities of Ethical International Relations* (Syracuse: Syracuse University Press, 1981), chap. 5. See also Inis L. Claude, Jr., *States and the Global System: Politics, Law, and Organization* (New York: St. Martin's Press, 1988); and Richard A. Falk, *The Promise of World Order: Essays in Normative International Relations* (Philadelphia: Temple University Press, 1987).

21. For a sampling of this vast literature see for example Donald J. Ortner, ed., *How Humans Adapt: A Biocultural Odyssey* (Washington, D.C.: Smithsonian Institution Press, 1983); Joseph Lopreato, *Human Nature and Biocultural Evolution* (Boston: Allen & Unwin, 1984); Arthur L. Caplan, ed., *The Sociobiology Debate* (New York: Harper & Row, 1978); and Louise S. Spindler, *Culture Change and Modernization* (New York: Holt, Rinehart, & Winston, 1977).

22. Immanuel Kant, *Perpetual Peace,* ed. Lewis White Beck (New York: Liberal Arts Press, 1957 [1795]).

23. Marc Bloch, *Strange Defeat* (New York: W. W. Norton & Co., 1968), 173.

24. E. P. Thompson, "Deterrence and Addiction," in *Beyond the Cold War,* 21.

25. *Conversazioni con Danilo Dolci,* 58–59.

26. Kenneth E. Boulding, *Stable Peace* (Austin: University of Texas Press, 1978).

27. Michael Howard, *The Causes of Wars and Other Essays* (Cambridge, Mass.: Harvard University Press, 1983), 61–62.

28. Ibid., 62

29. Ibid.

30. Michael Howard was by no means alone in using the word "power" in this way; in fact, his use of the word arguably reflects the most prevalent "common-sense" meaning of the term, as well as the word's most common connotation in scholarly discussions. In the *Encyclopedia of Philosophy,* for instance, power is defined along exactly the same lines: "A, by his power over B, successfully achieved an intended result r; he did so by making B do b, which B would not have done but for A's wishing him to do so; moreover, although B was reluctant, A had a way of overcoming this." Stanley I. Benn, "Power," in Paul Edwards, ed., *The Encyclopedia of Philosophy,* vol. 5 (New York: Macmillan, 1972 [1967]).

31. Leo Szilard, "Shall We Face the Facts?" *Bulletin of the Atomic Scientists* 5 (October 1949): 273.

32. The terms I use in making this distinction are, I realize, highly ambiguous. What constitutes the dividing line between "persuasion" and "manipulation?" Can "persuasion" be a form of coercion? These are extremely complex questions, which have been discussed at length by philosophers and sociologists. The sociologist Steven Lukes offers the following thoughtful discussion of the subject:

> "The question of whether rational persuasion is a form of power . . . [inclines me to answer] both yes and no. Yes, because it is a form of significant affecting: A gets B to do or think what he would not otherwise do or think. No, because B autonomously accepts A's reasons, so that one is inclined to say that it is not A but A's reasons, or B's acceptance of them, that is responsible for B's change of course. I

suspect that we are here in the presence of a fundamental (Kantian) antinomy between causality, on the one hand, and autonomy and reason, on the other. I see no
way of resolving this antinomy: there are simply contradictory conceptual pressures
at work. (Steven Lukes, *Power: A Radical View* [London: Macmillan, 1974],
32–33)

For an equally subtle discussion of the concept of manipulation, see Joseph Femia,
Gramsci's Political Thought (Oxford: Clarendon Press, 1981).

33. Here, I am deliberately diverging from the discussion of power put forth by Steven Lukes in his excellent study, *Power: A Radical View*. Lukes takes to task Hannah
Arendt and Talcott Parsons for seeking a concept of power based on cooperation rather
than conflict (chap. 5). Arendt and Parsons, he argues, have simply defined out of existence all forms of power that involve conflict, and have focused too narrowly on cases
in which an underlying concord or perceived harmony of interests already exists.

Nevertheless, while his criticisms of Arendt and Parsons are persuasive, Lukes himself tends to downplay excessively those important cases in which people resolve their
conflicts through bargaining and compromise. He seems to assume that these kinds of
accommodation are really (beneath the surface) expressions of domination by one party
over the other. Thus, for Lukes, the exercise of power seems unavoidably to entail an
unequal result, in which one group "wins," or at least loses less than the other. This, I
think, is too narrow and conflictual a concept of power. It fails to include those important interactions in which conflict exists, *and* concessions are made by both sides,
in the name of a common higher interest in reaching agreement. Although bargaining
sometimes leads to unequal deals, there is no reason why *all* such forms of cooperative
conflict-resolution should necessarily lead to unequal or "unfair" results.

34. Ernst B. Haas, "The Collective Management of International Conflict," 55–56.

35. For a sampling of the extensive scholarly literature on international organization
and conflict-resolution, see Hans Morgenthau, *Politics among Nations* (New York:
Knopf, 1961); Kenneth Waltz, *Theory of International Politics;* Glenn H. Snyder and
Paul Diesing, *Conflict among Nations* (Princeton: Princeton University Press, 1977),
esp. chaps. 2 and 3; James N. Rosenau and Ernst-Otto Czempiel, eds., *Governance
without Government: Order and Change in World Politics;* Robert O. Keohane, "Reciprocity in International Relations," *International Organization* 40 (Winter 1986); Dorothy V. Jones, *Code of Peace;* Robert Jervis, "Cooperation under the Security Dilemma,"
World Politics (January 1978); Robert C. North, *War, Peace, Survival: Global Politics
and Conceptual Synthesis* (Boulder, Colo.: Westview Press, 1990).

36. On both the theory and the practice of United Nations police forces, see F. T. Liu,
United Nations Peacekeeping and the Non-Use of Force (Boulder, Colo.: L. Rienner,
1992); Steven Luper-Foy, ed., *Problems of International Justice* (Boulder, Colo.: West-
view Press, 1988); Augustus R. Norton and Thomas G. Weiss, *U.N. Peacekeepers:
Soldiers with a Difference* (New York: Foreign Policy Association, 1990); Robert E.
Osgood, *An International Military Force in a Disarming and Disarmed World* (Washington: Institute for Defense Analyses, 1963); Indar Rikhye and Kjell Skjelsbaek, eds.,
*The United Nations and Peacekeeping: Results, Limitations, and Prospects: The Les-
sons of 40 Years of Experience* (New York: St. Martin's, 1991); Adam Roberts and
Benedict Kingsbury, eds., *United Nations, Divided World: The UN's Role in International Relations* (Oxford: Clarendon Press, 1988); Anthony Verrier, *International*

Peacekeeping: United Nations Forces in a Troubled World (Harmondsworth: Penguin, 1981); Richard S. Williamson, *The United Nations as Peacekeeper* (Washington, D.C.: Dept. of State, 1989).

On the equally complex subjet of international arbitration, see A. O. Adede, *The System for Settlement of Disputes under the United Nations Convention on the Law of the Sea: A Drafting History and Commentary* (The Hague: M. Nijhoff, 1987); Thomas M. Franck, *Judging the World Court* (New York: Priority Press, 1986); Hurst Hannum, *Autonomy, Sovereignty, and Self-Determination: The Accommodation of Conflicting Rights* (Philadelphia: University of Pennsylvania Press, 1990); Gerald Rabow, *Peace through Agreement: Replacing War with Non-Violent Dispute-Resolution Methods* (New York: Praeger, 1990); Gregory A. Raymond, *Conflict Resolution and the Structure of the State System: An Analysis of Arbitrative Settlements* (Montclair, N.J.: Allenheld, Osmun, 1980); Thomas L. Saaty and Joyce M. Alexander, *Conflict Resolution: The Analytic Hierarchy Approach* (New York: Praeger, 1989).

37. Stanley Hoffmann, *Duties beyond Borders: On the Limits and Possibilities of Ethical International Relations,* 205.

38. For an excellent discussion of the role of education in promoting cooperative politics, see Elise Boulding, *Building a Global Civic Culture: Education for an Interdependent World* (New York: Teachers College Press, 1988). See also Elise Boulding, Clovis Brigagao, and Kevin Clements, eds., *Peace Culture and Society: Transnational Research and Dialogue* (Boulder, Colo.: Westview Press, 1991); Linda R. Forcey, ed., *Peace: Meanings, Politics, Strategies* (New York: Praeger, 1989); Richard Smoke and Willis Harman, *Paths to Peace: Exploring the Feasibility of Sustainable Peace* (Boulder, Colo.: Westview Press, 1987); W. Scott Thompson et al., eds., *Approaches to Peace: An Intellectual Map* (Washington, D.C.: United States Institute of Peace, 1991).

39. *Newsweek* (November 26, 1984), 57.

40. *Conversazioni con Danilo Dolci,* 153–54. I have condensed my translation and paraphrased Dolci in a few places here, seeking to remain faithful to the spirit of this striking passage.

BIBLIOGRAPHY

Note: I have divided this bibliography into five sections—one on each of the four figures in this study, along with a section on the Cold War era, international cooperation, and general sources. For purposes of brevity, I am only listing here the texts actually used or cited by me.

1.1 Louise Weiss (Unpublished Sources)

The private papers of Louise Weiss are currently being held in the Département des Manuscrits at the Bibliothèque Nationale in Paris. A portion of these papers has been catalogued and bound into sixty-nine volumes, under the heading "Nouvelles Acquisitions Françaises, Legs 1977, Cotes 17794–17862." A second (and still larger) collection of documents was acquired by the Bibliothèque Nationale in 1983, after Weiss's death. These materials are still being sorted and are held in "Legs 1983, Don 84-06."

The Bibliothèque du Parlement Européen in Luxembourg and the Bibliothèque Marguerite Durand in Paris have amassed valuable collections of newspaper clippings on Weiss's career. Original prints of Weiss's documentary films are stored in the Archives du Film, Bois D'Arcy, France.

1.2 Louise Weiss (Primary Sources)

Auriol, Vincent. *Journal du Septennat, 1947–1954,* vol. 7 (Paris: Armand Colin, 1971).

Bloch, Marc. *Strange Defeat,* trans. Gerard Hopkins (New York: Norton, 1968).

Bouthoul, Gaston, and René Carrère. *Le défi de la guerre, 1740–1974* (Paris: Presses Universitaires de France, 1976).

Brissaud, Jean-Marc. *Eléments pour une nouvelle politique étrangère* (Pau: Front National, Université d'Eté, September 1985).

De Sa Rego, Carlos, "Le parapluie de l'Oncle Sam a perdu ses charmes," *Libération* (February 16, 1987).

Evrigenis, M. Dimitrios. *Commission d'enquête sur la montée du Fascisme et du racisme en Europe: Rapport sur les résultats des travaux* (Luxembourg: Parlement Européen, 1985).

Le Pen, Jean-Marie. *Pour la France: Programme du Front National* (Paris: Albatros, 1985).

Monnet, Jean. *Memoirs,* trans. Richard Mayne (London: Collins, 1978).

Office for Official Publications of the European Communities. *Steps to European Unity* (Luxembourg, 1985).

Sondages: Revue Française de l'opinion publique, no. 2 (1951); no. 3 (1956); no. 2 (1957).

Time (January 28, 1980) (European ed.).

Weiss, Louise. "Ce que dit Tchitchérine," *L'Europe Nouvelle* 1, no. 51 (December 17, 1921): 1627.

———. "Trotsky parle," *L'Europe Nouvelle* 1, no. 51 (December 17, 1921): 1620.

———. "Le tsar famine," *L'Europe Nouvelle* 1, no. 51 (December 17, 1921): 1648.

———. "Notre bilan," *L'Europe Nouvelle* 6, no. 52 (December 29, 1923): 1654.

———. "1925, l'année de Locarno," *L'Europe Nouvelle* 8, no. 410 (December 26, 1925): 1723.

———. "Entre le Traité de Versailles et le Pacte," *L'Europe Nouvelle* 8, no. 399 (October 10, 1925): 1338.

———. "Du Traité de Versailles au Pacte Kellogg," *L'Europe Nouvelle* 11, no. 550 (August 25, 1928): 1142.

———. "Remarques sur la co-existence des civilisations primitives et de la civilisation occidentale," *Revue des Travaux de l'Académie des Sciences Morales et Politiques* (1954): 83–93.

———. "Visite de l'IFP aux Instituts de Recherches en Scandinavie," *Guerres et Paix* 1967/2.

———. *Mémoires d'une Européenne,* vol. 1, *Une petite fille du siècle, 1893–1919* (Paris: Albin Michel, 1968).

———. "Voyage de Louise Weiss aux Etats-Unis (February–April 1968)," *Guerres et Paix* 1968/4.

———. *Mémoires d'une Européenne,* vol. 2, *Combats pour l'Europe, 1919–1934* (Paris: Albin Michel, 1969).

———. *Mémoires d'une Européenne,* vol. 3, *Combats pour les femmes, 1934–1939* (Paris: Payot, 1970).

———. *Mémoires d'une Européenne,* vol. 4, *Le sacrifice du Chevalier, 1939–1940* (Paris: Albin Michel, 1971).

———. *Lettre à un Embryon* (Paris: Julliard, 1973).

———. *Mémoires d'une Européenne,* vol. 5, *La résurrection du Chevalier, 1940–1944* (Paris: Albin Michel, 1974).

———. *Mémoires d'une Européenne,* vol. 6, *Tempête sur l'occident, 1945–1975* (Paris: Albin Michel, 1976).

———. "Allocution de la doyenne d'age," *Débats du Parlement Européen* (July 17, 1979): 6.

———. "Qui sont les victimes?" *Le Figaro* (June 4, 1981).

1.3 France—Weiss (Secondary Sources)

Adereth, M. *The French Communist Party: A Critical History, 1920–1984* (Manchester: Manchester University Press, 1984).

Agulhon, Maurice, and André Nouschi. *La France de 1940 à nos jours* (Paris: Nathan, 1984).

Barrows, Susanna I. *Distorting Mirrors: Visions of the Crowd in Late-Nineteenth-Century France* (New Haven: Yale University Press, 1981).

Betts, Raymond. *Assimilation and Association in French Colonial Theory, 1890–1914* (New York: Columbia University Press, 1961).

———. *Tricouleur: The French Overseas Empire* (New York: Gordon & Cremonesi, 1978).

Bourdet, Claude. *L'Afrique du nord et nous* (Paris: Burin-Martinsart, 1973).

———. *L'aventure incertaine: De la résistance à la restauration* (Paris: Stock, 1975).

Capelle, Russell B. *The MRP and French Foreign Policy* (New York: Praeger, 1963).

Feld, Werner J., ed. *Western Europe's Global Reach* (New York: Pergamon, 1980).

Flynn, Gregory, et al. *Public Images of Western Security,* Atlantic Papers no. 54/55 (Paris: Atlantic Institute for International Affairs, 1985).

Fontaine, Pascal. *Le Comité d'Action pour les Etats-Unis d'Europe de Jean Monnet* (Lausanne: Centre de Recherches Européennes, 1974).

Ginsberg, Roy H. *Foreign Policy Actions of the European Community* (Boulder, Colo.: L. Rienner, 1989).

Girardet, Raoul. *L'idée coloniale en France de 1871 à 1962* (Paris: La Table Ronde, 1972).

Graham, B. D. *The French Socialists and Tripartisme, 1944–1947* (Toronto: University of Toronto Press, 1965).

Greilsammer, Alain. *Les mouvements fédéralistes en France de 1945 à 1974* (Paris: Presses d'Europe, 1975).

Grosser, Alfred. *French Foreign Policy under De Gaulle* (Boston: Little, Brown, 1967).

Haas, Ernst B. *The Uniting of Europe* (Stanford: Stanford University Press, 1958).

Hoffmann, Stanley. *Decline or Renewal? France since the 1930s* (New York: Viking, 1974).

Howorth, Jolyon. *France: The Politics of Peace* (London: END, 1984).

Kemp, Tom. *Economic Forces in French History* (London: Dennis Dobson, 1971).

Klein, Jean. "Mythes et réalités de la défense de l'Europe," *Politique Etrangère,* no. 2 (Summer 1983): 315–40.

———. "Le débat en France sur la défense de l'Europe," *Stratégique* (1984): 8.

Kolodziej, Edward A. *French International Policy under De Gaulle and Pompidou* (Ithaca: Cornell University Press, 1974).

Lerner, Daniel, and Raymond Aron, eds. *France Defeats EDC* (New York: Praeger, 1957).

Lipgens, Walter. *A History of European Integration, 1945–1947,* vol. 1, trans. P. S. Falla and A. J. Ryder (Oxford: Clarendon Press, 1982).

Martin-Pannetier, Andrée. *La défense de la France* (Paris: Charles-Lavauzelle, 1985).

Mayeur, Jean-Marie, et al. *Histoire du peuple Français: Cent ans d'esprit républicain,* vol. 5 (Paris: Nouvelle Librairie de France, 1965).

Mayne, Richard. *The Recovery of Europe* (New York: Harper & Row, 1970).

Mendl, Wolf. *Deterrence and Persuasion: French Nuclear Armaments in the Context of National Policy* (London: Faber, 1970).

Noguères, Henri, et al. *Histoire de la résistance en France, de 1940 à 1945,* 5 vols. (Paris: Robert Laffont, 1981).

Paxton, Robert O. *Vichy France: Old Guard and New Order, 1940–1944* (New York: Columbia University Press, 1972).

Pickles, Dorothy. *The Government and Politics of France,* vol. 2 (London: Methuen, 1973).

Said, Edward. *Orientalism* (New York: Pantheon, 1978).

Salvadori, Massimo. *L'alternativa dell'Europa* (Bari: Laterza, 1985).

Schmidt, Hans A. *The Path to European Union* (Westport, Conn.: Greenwood Press, 1981).

Sorum, Paul C. *Intellectuals and Decolonization in France* (Chapel Hill: University of North Carolina Press, 1977).

Thornton, A. P. *The Imperial Idea and Its Enemies* (New York: St. Martin's Press, 1985).

Tilly, Louise A., and Joan W. Scott. *Women, Work, and Family* (New York: Holt, Rinehart & Winston, 1978).

Watt, Donald C. *Too Serious a Business: European Armed Forces and the Approach to the Second World War* (London: Temple Smith, 1975).

Weber, Eugen. *France, fin de siècle* (Cambridge, Mass.: Belknap Press, 1986).

Willis, F. Roy. *Italy Chooses Europe* (New York: Oxford University Press, 1971).

Willis, F. Roy, ed. *DeGaulle: Anachronism, Realist, or Prophet?* (New York: Holt, Rinehart, & Winston, 1967).

Zeldin, Theodore. *France, 1848–1945: Ambition, Love, and Politics,* vol. 1 (Oxford: Clarendon Press, 1973).

2.1 Leo Szilard (Unpublished Sources)

The private papers of Leo Szilard are held by the Special Collections Department at the Central Library of the University of California, San Diego. They include his voluminous correspondence; drafts of articles, essays, and speech texts; selections of newspaper and magazine articles on Szilard and his work; transcripts of radio and television debates in which he participated; and a vast quantity of personal notes and memoranda in which he worked out his ideas before circulating them among close friends. Selections from his private papers have been published in 1969, 1978, and 1987 (see section 2.2 below, under the names Gertrud Szilard, Helen S. Hawkins, and Spencer R. Weart).

2.2 Leo Szilard (Primary Sources)

Aron, Raymond. "The Atomic Bomb and Europe," *Bulletin of the Atomic Scientists* 6 (April 1959): 110–14.

Branyan, Robert L., and Lawrence H. Larsen, eds. *The Eisenhower Administration, 1953–1961: A Documentary History,* vol. 2 (New York: Random House, 1971).

Brodie, Bernard. *The Absolute Weapon* (New York: Harcourt, Brace & Co., 1946).

Bundy, McGeorge. *Danger and Survival* (New York: Random House, 1988).

Byrnes, James F. *All in One Lifetime* (New York: Harper & Row, 1954).

Churchill, Winston. "On European Unity and Settlement with Russia," *Bulletin of the Atomic Scientists* 6 (June 1950): 170.

Clark, Grenville, and Louis B. Sohn. *World Peace through World Law* (Cambridge, Mass.: Harvard University Press, 1958).

Current Biography (1947).

Ehrenberg, W. "Maxwell's Demon," *Scientific American* 217, no. 5 (November 1967): 103–10.

Hawkins, Helen S., G. Allen Greb, and Gertrud W. Szilard, eds., *Collected Works of Leo Szilard,* vol. 3, *Toward a Livable World: Leo Szilard and the Crusade for Nuclear Arms Control* (Cambridge, Mass.: MIT Press, 1987).

Khrushchev, Nikita. *Khrushchev in New York* (New York: Crosscurrents Press, 1960).

———. *Khrushchev Remembers,* trans. Strobe Talbott (Boston: Little, Brown, 1974).

Mabley, Jack. "Mabley's Report: Atom Expert's Plan to Avert All-Out War," *Chicago's American* (February 1962).

Mannheim, Karl. *Ideology and Utopia* (New York: Harcourt, Brace, & World, 1936).

Masters, Dexter, and Katherine Way, eds. *One World or None* (New York: McGraw Hill, 1946).

Morgenthau, Hans. "On Negotiating with the Russians," *Bulletin of the Atomic Scientists* 6 (May 1950): 143.

Nathan, Otto, and Heinz Norden, eds. *Einstein on Peace* (New York: Avenel Books, 1960).

Oppenheimer, Robert. "Physics in the Contemporary World," *Technology Review* (February 1948).

Smith, Alice K., and Charles Weiner, eds. *Robert Oppenheimer: Letters and Recollections* (Cambridge, Mass.: Harvard University Press, 1980).

Sorensen, Theodore C. *Kennedy* (New York: Harper & Row, 1965).

Szilard, Gertrud W., and Bernard T. Feld, eds. *Collected Works of Leo Szilard: Scientific Papers* (Cambridge, Mass.: MIT Press, 1972).

Szilard, Leo. "Calling for a Crusade," *Bulletin of the Atomic Scientists* 3 (April–May 1947): 102–6, 125.

———. "The Physicist Invades Politics," *Saturday Review of Literature* 30 (May 3, 1947): 7.

———. "Letter to Stalin," *Bulletin of the Atomic Scientists* 3 (December 1947): 347–49, 376.

———. "Comment to the Editors," *Bulletin of the Atomic Scientists* 3 (December 1947): 350, 353.

———. "The AEC Fellowships: Shall We Yield or Fight?" *Bulletin of the Atomic Scientists* 5 (June–July 1949): 177–78.

———. "America, Russia, and the Bomb," *New Republic* 121 (October 31, 1949): 11–13.

———. "Shall We Face the Facts?" *Bulletin of the Atomic Scientists* 5 (October 1949): 269–73.

————. "Can We Have International Control of Atomic Energy?" *Bulletin of the Atomic Scientists* 6 (January 1950): 9–12, 16.

————. "The Diary of Dr. Davis," *Bulletin of the Atomic Scientists* 6 (February 1950): 51–57.

————. "Security Risk," *Bulletin of the Atomic Scientists* 10 (December 1954): 384–86, 398.

————. "The First Step to Peace," *Bulletin of the Atomic Scientists* 11 (March 1955): 104.

————. "Disarmament and the Problem of Peace," *Bulletin of the Atomic Scientists* 11 (October 1955): 297–307.

————. "How to Live with the Bomb and Survive: The Possibility of a 'Pax Russo-Americana' in the Long-Range Rocket Stage of the So-Called Atomic Stalemate," *Bulletin of the Atomic Scientists* 16 (February 1960): 59–73.

————. "To Stop or Not to Stop," *Bulletin of the Atomic Scientists* 16 (March 1968): 82–84, 108.

————. "Political Settlement in Europe," *New Republic* 145 (October 9, 1961): 15–19.

————. "The Mined Cities," *Bulletin of the Atomic Scientists* 17 (December 1961): 407–12.

————. *The Voice of the Dolphins* (New York: Simon & Schuster, 1961; repr., Stanford, Calif.: Stanford University Press, 1992).

————. "Are We on the Road to War?" *Bulletin of the Atomic Scientists* 18 (April 1962): 23–30.

————. "Minimal Deterrent vs. Saturation Parity," *Bulletin of the Atomic Scientists* 20 (March 1964): 6–12.

————. "The 'Sting of the Bee' in Saturation Parity," *Bulletin of the Atomic Scientists* 21 (March 1965): 8–13.

————. "Reminiscences," ed. Gertrud Weiss Szilard and Kathleen R. Winsor; in Donald Fleming and Bernard Bailyn, eds., "The Intellectual Migration: Europe and America, 1930–1960," *Perspectives in American History,* vol. 2 (Cambridge, Mass.: Charles Warren Center for Studies in American History, 1968).

Szilard, Leo, et al. "U.N.in Cuba" (Letter to the Editor), *Bulletin of the Atomic Scientists* 19 (April 1963): 33.

Time (October 3, 1960; October 10, 1960).

Von Neumann, John. "Can We Survive Technology?" *Fortune* (June 1955): 106ff.

Wagar, W. Warren. *H. G. Wells: Journalism and Prophecy* (Boston: Houghton Mifflin, 1964).

Weart, Spencer R., and Gertrud Weiss Szilard, eds. *Collected Works of Leo Szilard,* vol. 2, *Leo Szilard: His Version of the Facts* (Cambridge, Mass.: MIT Press, 1978).

Wells, H. G. *The Open Conspiracy: Blue Prints for a World Revolution* (London: V. Gollancz, 1929).

York, Herbert F. *Making Weapons, Talking Peace: A Physicist's Odyssey from Hiroshima to Geneva* (New York: Basic Books, 1987).

2.3 USA—Szilard (Secondary Sources)

Bloomfield, Louis P., Walter C. Clemens, Jr., and Franklyn Griffiths, eds. *Khrushchev and the Arms Race: Soviet Interests in Arms Control and Disarmament, 1954–1964* (Cambridge, Mass.: MIT Press, 1966).

Blumberg, Stanley A., and Gwinn Owens. *Energy and Conflict: The Life and Times of Edward Teller* (New York: G. P. Putnam's Sons, 1976).

Fermi, Laura, *Illustrious Immigrants* (Chicago: University of Chicago Press, 1968).

Fleming, Donald, and Bernard Bailyn, eds. *The Intellectual Migration: Europe and America, 1930–1960* (Cambridge, Mass.: Harvard University Press, 1969).

Gabor, Dennis. "Leo Szilard," *Bulletin of the Atomic Scientists* 39 (September 1973): 52.

Goodell, Rae. *The Visible Scientists* (Boston: Little, Brown, 1975).

Griffith, Robert, and Athan Theoharis, eds. *The Specter: Original Essays on the Cold War and the Origins of McCarthyism* (New York: New Viewpoints, 1974).

Habermas, Jürgen. *Theory and Practice* (Boston: Beacon Press, 1973).

Halasz, Nicholas and Robert. "Leo Szilard: The Reluctant Father of the Atomic Bomb," *New Hungarian Quarterly* (1974).

Hewlett, Richard G., and Oscar E. Anderson. *The Atomic Shield* (University Park: Pennsylvania State University Press, 1962).

———. *The New World, 1939–1946* (University Park: Pennsylvania State University Press, 1962).

Hughes, H. Stuart, *Consciousness and Society* (New York: Vintage Books, 1958).

Kahan, Jerome. *Security in the Nuclear Age* (Washington, D.C.: Brookings Institution, 1975).

Lanouette, William, with Bela Silard. *Genius in the Shadows* (New York: Scribner's, 1993).

McCagg, William O., Jr. *Jewish Nobles and Geniuses in Modern Hungary* (New York: Simon & Schuster, 1958).

Medvedev, Roy. *Khrushchev*, trans. Brian Pearce (Oxford: Basil Blackwell, 1982).

Mosse, George L. *The Crisis of German Ideology* (New York: Grosset & Dunlap, 1964).

Newhouse, John. *Cold Dawn: The Story of SALT* (New York: Holt, Rinehart, & Winston, 1973).

Rhodes, Richard. *The Making of the Atomic Bomb* (New York: Simon & Schuster, 1986).

Rotblat, Joseph. *Pugwash—the First Ten Years* (London: Heinemann, 1967).

———. *Scientists, the Arms Race, and Disarmament* (Paris: UNESCO, 1982).

Sherwin, Martin J. *A World Destroyed* (New York: Vintage Books, 1977).

Shils, Edward. "Leo Szilard: A Memoir," *Encounter* 23, no. 6 (December 1964): 35–41.

Sims, Jennifer E. *Icarus Restrained: An Intellectual History of Arms Control, 1945–1960* (Boulder, Colo.: Westview, 1990).

Smith, Alice K. "The Elusive Dr. Szilard," *Harper's Magazine* 201 (July 1960).

———. *A Peril and a Hope* (Chicago: University of Chicago Press, 1965).

Struve, Walter. *Elites against Democracy: Leadership Ideals in Bourgeois Political Thought in Germany, 1890–1933* (Princeton: Princeton University Press, 1973).

Wittner, Lawrence S. *Rebels against War: The American Peace Movement, 1941–1960* (New York: Columbia University Press, 1969).

3.1 E. P. Thompson (Unpublished Sources)

E. P. Thompson loaned me copies of unpublished essays and out-of-print manuscripts dating from the 1950s and beyond. Mary Kaldor, one of the cofounders of END, allowed me access to her voluminous private archives on END, held in Brighton, England; these archives contain correspondence, committee minutes, newspaper clippings, internal circulars and memoranda, and drafts of speeches and essays by major figures in END.

The Press Library at the Royal Institute for International Affairs (Chatham House) in London possesses an exhaustive and extremely well-organized collection of contemporary newspaper clippings. For the present study, I made considerable use of the files under the heading "Security-Disarmament (Atomic)."

3.2 E. P. Thompson (Primary Sources)

Articles cited from the following periodicals and newspapers:

Daily Telegraph
END Journal
Financial Times
Guardian
In These Times
New Statesman
New York Times
Observer
San Francisco Chronicle
Sunday Telegraph
Time (periodical)
Times (London)
Tribune

Althusser, Louis. *For Marx* (New York: Vintage Books, 1970).
———. *Reading Capital* (London: New Left Books, 1970).
Anderson, Perry. "The Left in the Fifties," *New Left Review* 29 (January–February 1965).
———. "Socialism and Pseudo-Empiricism," *New Left Review* 35 (January–February 1966).
———. *Arguments within English Marxism* (London: New Left Books, 1980).
Artmann, Danielle, ed. *Samizdat '86: The Moscow Trust Group* (London: END, 1986).
Bahro, Rudolf. *Building the Green Movement,* trans. Mary Tyler (London: GMP Publishers, 1986).
———. *The Alternative in Eastern Europe* (London: Verso/New Left Books, 1979).
Baldwin, Hugh, and END Hungary Working Group, eds. *Documents on the Peace Movement in Hungary* (London: END, 1986).
Bulkeley, Rip. *The Valley Path: CND and the Cold War* (Oxford: Fox & Lantern Press, 1985).
Coates, Ken. *The Most Dangerous Decade* (Nottingham, England: Spokesman, 1984).

Duff, Peggy. *Left, Left, Left: A Personal Account of Six Protest Campaigns, 1945–65* (London: Allison & Busby, 1971).

Endpapers, nos. 1–7 (Nottingham, England: Spokesman, 1982–84).

Flynn, Gregory, and Hans Rattinger, eds. *The Public and Atlantic Defense* (London: Rowman and Allanheld, 1985).

Furtado, Jean. *Turkey: Peace on Trial* (London: END, 1983).

Harford, Barbara, and Sarah Hopkins, eds. *Greenham Common: Women at the Wire* (London: Women's Press, 1984).

Havel, Václav. *Living in Truth,* ed. Jan Vladislav (London: Faber, 1986).

Howard, Michael. *The Causes of Wars and Other Essays* (Cambridge, Mass.: Harvard University Press, 1983).

Jones, Mervyn. *Chances* (London: Verso, 1987).

Kaldor, Mary. "Beyond the Blocs: Defending Europe the Political Way," *World Policy Journal* 1, no. 1 (Fall 1983).

Kaldor, Mary, and Paul Anderson, eds. *Mad Dogs: The U.S. Raids on Libya* (London: Pluto Press, 1986).

Kavan, Jan, and Zdena Tomin, eds. *Voices from Prague: Documents on Czechoslovakia and the Peace Movement* (London: Palach Press, 1983).

Konrad, George. *Antipolitics,* trans. Richard E. Allen (New York: Quartet Books, 1984).

———. "The Post-Yalta Debate" (interview by Richard Falk and Mary Kaldor), *World Policy Journal* (Summer 1985).

Köszegi, Ferenc, and E. P. Thompson. *The New Hungarian Peace Movement* (London: END, 1983).

Labour Party National Executive Committee. *Defence and Security for Britain* (London: Labour Party, 1984).

Lambert, John, ed. "Talking Peace: The Inside Story of the European Nuclear Disarmament Conventions," *Agenor 97* (June–July 1986).

New Left Review, ed. *Exterminism and Cold War* (London: Verso, 1982).

Sandford, John. *The Sword and the Ploughshare: Autonomous Peace Initiatives in East Germany* (London: END, 1983).

Saville, John, and Ralph Miliband, eds. *Socialist Register 1976* (London: Merlin Press, 1976).

Thompson, Ben. *Comiso* (London: END, 1982).

Thompson, Edward P., ed. *The Railway: An Adventure in Construction* (London: British-Yugoslav Association, 1948).

———, ed. *The Yorkshire Voice of Peace* 2, no. 1 (1953).

———. *William Morris: Romantic to Revolutionary* (London: Lawrence & Wishart, 1955).

———. "Socialist Humanism," *New Reasoner* (Summer 1957).

———. "Agency and Choice," *New Reasoner* (Summer 1958).

———. "The New Left, *New Reasoner* (Summer 1959).

———. "The Point of Production," *New Left Review* 1 (January–February 1960).

———. "Revolution," *New Left Review* 3 (May–June 1960).

———. "Revolution Again," *New Left Review* 6 (November–December 1960).

———. *The Making of the English Working Class* (New York: Vintage, 1966 [1963]).

————. *Warwick University Ltd.* (Harmondsworth, England: Penguin, 1970).

————. "The Moral Economy of the English Crowd in the Eighteenth Century," *Past and Present,* no. 50 (1971).

————. *Whigs and Hunters* (Harmondsworth, England: Penguin Books, 1975).

————. "Interview with E. P. Thompson," *Radical History Review* 3 (Fall 1976): 4.

————. *William Morris: Romantic to Revolutionary* (New York: Pantheon, 1976).

————. *The Poverty of Theory and Other Essays* (London: Monthly Review Press, 1978).

————. "Recovering the Libertarian Tradition" (interview), *Leveller* 22 (January 1979).

————. *Writing by Candlelight* (London: Merlin Press, 1980).

————. *Beyond the Cold War* (New York: Pantheon, 1982).

————. *Infant and Emperor: Poems for Christmas* (London: Merlin Press, 1983).

————. *Double Exposure* (London: Merlin Press, 1985).

————. *The Heavy Dancers* (London: Merlin Press, 1985)

————, ed. *Star Wars* (New York: Pantheon, 1985).

————. *The Sykaos Papers* (London: Bloomsbury, 1988).

Thompson, Edward P., and John Saville, eds. *Reasoner,* nos. 1–3 (1956).

Thompson, Edward P., and Dan Smith, eds. *Protest and Survive* (Harmondsworth, England: Penguin, 1980).

————. eds. *Prospectus for a Habitable Planet* (Harmondsworth, England: Penguin, 1987).

Thompson, Edward P., and T. J. Thompson, eds. *There Is a Spirit in Europe: A Memoir of Frank Thompson* (London: Gollancz, 1947).

Williams, Raymond, ed. *May Day Manifesto* (Harmondsworth, England, Penguin, 1968).

3.3 England—Thompson (Secondary Sources)

Abelove, Henry. "Review Essay on 'The Poverty of Theory,'" *History and Theory* 21, no. 1 (1982): 132–42.

Ash, Timothy Garton. *The Polish Revolution* (New York: Charles Scribner's Sons, 1983).

Byrne, Paul. *The Campaign for Nuclear Disarmament* (London: Croom Helm, 1988).

Ceadel, Martin. *Pacifism in Britain, 1914–1945* (Oxford: Clarendon Press, 1980).

Cornforth, Maurice, ed. *Rebels and Their Causes* (London: Lawrence and Wishart, 1978).

Dahrendorf, Ralf, and Theodore C. Sorensen. *A Widening Atlantic? Domestic Change and Foreign Policy* (New York: Council on Foreign Relations, 1986).

Dalton, Russell J., and Manfred Kuechler, eds. *Challenging the Political Order: New Social and Political Movements in Western Democracies* (New York: Oxford University Press, 1990).

Desan, Suzanne. "Crowds, Community, and Ritual in the Work of E. P. Thompson and Natalie Davis," in Lynn Hunt, ed., *The New Cultural History* (Berkeley: University of California Press, 1989).

Dougherty, James E., and Robert L. Pfaltzgraff, Jr., eds. *Shattering Europe's Defense Consensus* (Washington, D.C.: Pergamon-Brassey's, 1985).

Innes, Joanna, and John Styles. "The Crime Wave: Recent Writing on Crime and Criminal Justice in Eighteenth-Century England," *Journal of British Studies* 25 (October 1986): 380–405.

Jenkins, Peter. *Mrs. Thatcher's Revolution: The Ending of the Socialist Era* (Cambridge, Mass.: Harvard University Press, 1988).

Johnstone, Diana. *The Politics of Euromissiles* (London: Verso, 1984).

Jungerman, John A. *The Strategic Defense Initiative: A Primer and Critique* (La Jolla, Calif.: Institute on Global Conflict and Cooperation, 1988).

Kaldor, Mary, ed. *Europe from Below: An East-West Dialogue* (London: Verso, 1991).

Kaldor, Mary, and Richard Falk (with the assistance of Gerard Holden). *Dealignment: A New Foreign Policy Perspective* (Oxford: Basil Blackwell, 1987).

Kaye, Harvey J. *The British Marxist Historians* (Cambridge: Polity Press, 1984).

Kaye, Harvey J., and Keith McLelland, eds. *E. P. Thompson: Critical Perspectives* (Philadelphia: Temple University Press, 1990).

Kolodziej, Edward A., and Robert A. Pollard. "The Uneasy Alliance: Western Europe and the United States," *Wilson Quarterly* 7, no. 5 (Winter 1983): 112–20.

Kuhlman, James A., and Louis J. Mensonides, eds. *Changes in European Relations* (Leyden, The Netherlands: A. W. Sijthoff, 1976).

Mastny, Vojtech. *Helsinki, Human Rights, and European Security* (Durham, N.C.: Duke University Press, 1986).

McConnell, Scott. "The 'Neutralism' of E. P. Thompson," *Commentary* (April 1983).

Mercer, Paul. *Peace of the Dead: The Truth behind the Nuclear Disarmers* (London: Policy Research Publications, 1986).

Miller, William L., et al. *How Voters Change: The 1987 British Election Campaign in Perspective* (Oxford: Clarendon Press, 1990).

Minnion, John, and Philip Bolsover. *The CND Story* (London: Allison & Busby, 1983).

Myrdal, Alva, et al. *Dynamics of European Nuclear Disarmament* (Nottingham, England: Spokesman, 1981).

Overy, Bob. *How Effective Are Peace Movements?* (Montreal: Harvest House, 1982).

Palmer, Bryan. *The Making of E. P. Thompson* (Toronto: New Hogtown Press, 1981).

Parkin, Frank. *Middle-Class Radicalism* (Manchester: Manchester University Press, 1968).

Penning-Rowsell, Edmund. "The Remodeling of Morris," *Times Literary Supplement* (August 11, 1978): 913–14.

Rose, Clive. *Campaigns against Western Defence* (London: Macmillan, 1985).

Sked, Alan, and Chris Cook. *Postwar Britain: A Political History* (Sussex: Harvester Press, 1979).

Stansky, Peter. "The Protean Victorian," *New York Times Book Review* (May 15, 1977).

Taylor, Richard, and Colin Pritchard. *The Protest Makers* (Oxford: Pergamon, 1980).

Thies, Wallace J. *The Atlantic Alliance, Nuclear Weapons & European Attitudes,* Policy Papers in International Affairs no. 19 (Berkeley: University of California, Institute of International Studies, 1983).

Ulam, Adam B. *Dangerous Relations: The Soviet Union in World Politics, 1970–1982* (New York: Oxford University Press, 1983).

Weschler, Lawrence. *Solidarity* (New York: Simon & Schuster, 1982).

Widgery, David. *The Left in Britain* (Harmondsworth, England: Peregrine Books, 1976).

"William Morris: Romantic to Revolutionary" (anonymous review), *Times Literary Supplement* (July 15, 1955): 391.

Wright, Gordon. *The Ordeal of Total War, 1939–1945* (New York: Harper and Row, 1968).

Young, Nigel. *The Contemporary European Antinuclear Movement: Experiments in the Mobilization of Public Power* (Oslo: International Peace Research Institute, 1983).

4.1 Danilo Dolci (Unpublished Sources)

The private papers of Danilo Dolci are currently being held by the Mugar Memorial Library at Boston University, which acquired them in 1982. They contain Dolci's correspondence, drafts of essays and memoranda, documents pertaining to the administration of the Centro Studi e Iniziative, and newspaper clippings covering the entire period since 1952.

Dolci's personal archive in Partinico holds an exhaustive collection of committee minutes, cyclostyled reports, and internal circulars covering the activities of the Centro Studi from 1958 to the present.

4.2 Danilo Dolci (Primary Sources)

Articles cited from the following periodicals and newspapers:

"Appunti Per Gli Amici" [Newsletter of Dolci's Centro Studi]
Corriere della Sera
L'Europeo
Il Giornale del Mezzogiorno
Giornale di Sicilia
Il Giornale d'Italia
Il Giorno
New York Times
L'Ora
Paese Sera
Rassegna della Letteratura Italiana
Scuola e Città
La Sicilia
La Stampa
Stampa Sera
Les Temps Modernes
Time
L'Unità
Vie Nuove

Bini, P. *Il mezzogiorno nel parlamento repubblicano (1948–1972)*, vols. 1, 2, 4 (Milano: Giuffré Editore, 1978).

Capitini, Aldo. *Lettere a Danilo Dolci* (Firenze: Il Ponte, 1969).

Dolci, Danilo. *Fare presto (e bene) perché si muore* (Firenze: La Nuova Italia, 1953).

———. *Banditi a Partinico* (Bari: Laterza, 1955).

————. *Una politica per la piena occupazione* (Torino: Einaudi, 1958).

————. *Report from Palermo,* trans. P. D. Cummings (New York: Orion Press, 1959).

————. *Spreco: documenti e inchieste su alcuni aspetti dello spreco nella Sicilia occidentale* (Torino: Einaudi, 1960).

————. *Outlaws,* trans. R. Munroe (New York: Orion Press, 1961).

————. *Verso un mondo nuovo* (Torino: Einaudi, 1965).

————. *The Man Who Plays Alone,* trans. Antonia Cowan (London: MacGibbon & Kee, 1968).

————. *Chissà se i pesci piangono* (Torino: Einaudi, 1974).

————. *Esperienze e riflessioni* (Bari: Laterza, 1974).

————. *Non esiste il silenzio* (Torino: Einaudi, 1974).

————. *Racconti siciliani* (Torino: Einaudi, 1974 [1963]).

————. *Il ponte screpolato* (Torino: Stampatori, 1979).

————. *Sicilian Lives,* trans. Justin Vitiello (New York: Pantheon, 1981).

————. *Creatura di creature* (Venezia: Corbo e Fiore, 1983).

————. *The World Is One Creature,* trans. Justin Vitiello (New York: Amity House, 1984).

————. *Palpitare di nessi* (Roma: Armando, 1985).

————. *La creatura e il virus del dominio* (Latina: L'Argonauta, 1987).

————. *La comunicazione di massa non esiste* (forthcoming).

Freire, Paulo. *Pedagogy of the Oppressed,* trans. Myra Bergman Ramos (New York: Continuum, 1970).

Gramsci, Antonio. *La questione meridionale* (Roma: Editori Riuniti, 1966).

Impastato, Felicia B. *La mafia in casa mia* (Palermo: Arci Donna, 1986).

Levi, Carlo. *Le parole sono pietre* (Torino: Einaudi, 1955).

Montessori, Maria. *Education and Peace* (Chicago: Henry Regnery Co., 1972).

Russell, Bertrand. *War Crimes in Vietnam* (London: Allen & Unwin, 1967).

Silone, Ignazio. *Vino e pane* (Milano: Mondadori, 1955).

Spagnoletti, Giacinto. *Conversazioni con Danilo Dolci* (Milano: Mondadori, 1977).

Taylor, Mary, ed. *Community Development in Western Sicily: An Introduction to the Centro Studi* (Partinico: Centro Studi e Iniziative, June 1963).

4.3 Italy—Dolci (Secondary Sources)

Alongi, Giuseppe. *La maffia* (Palermo: Sellerio, 1977 [1886]).

Arlacchi, Pino. *La mafia imprenditrice* (Bologna: Il Mulino, 1983).

Banfield, Edward C. *The Moral Basis of a Backward Society* (New York: Free Press, 1958).

Banfield, Edward C., and James Q. Wilson. *City Politics* (Cambridge, Mass.: Harvard University Press and MIT Press, 1963).

Barzini, Luigi. "Godfathers and Sons," *New York Review of Books* (June 10, 1982).

Berta, Giuseppe. *Le idee al potere* (Milano: Edizioni di Comunità, 1980).

Blok, Anton. *The Mafia of a Sicilian Village, 1860–1960* (New York: Harper & Row, 1974).

Casucci, Costanzo, ed. *Interpretazioni del fascismo* (Bologna: Il Mulino, 1982).

Cederna, Camilla. *Giovanni Leone: La carriera di un presidente* (Milano: Feltrinelli, 1978).

Centorrino, Mario, and Emanuele Sgroi, eds. *Economia e potere mafioso in Sicilia* (Milano: Giuffré, 1984).

Chemello, Adriana. " 'Storie di vita' da Scotellaro a Dolci," *Rassegna della Letteratura Italiana* (January–August 1980).

Chubb, Judith. *Patronage, Power, and Poverty in Southern Italy* (Cambridge: Cambridge University Press, 1982).

Clark, Martin. *Modern Italy, 1871–1982* (London: Longman, 1984).

Clark, Ronald. *The Life of Bertrand Russell* (London: Jonathan Cape and Weidenfeld & Nicholson, 1975).

Cornelisen, Anne. *Women of the Shadows* (New York: Pantheon, 1976).

Finley, M. I., Denis Mack Smith, and Christopher Duggan. *A History of Sicily* (London: Chatto & Windus, 1986).

Fontanelli, Giuseppe. *Danilo Dolci* (Firenze: La Nuova Italia, 1984).

Galtung, Johan. "Gandhi, Dolci e noi," *Il Ponte* 13, no. 3 (March 1957): 359–67.

Giroux, Henry A. *Theory and Resistance in Education: A Pedagogy for the Opposition* (South Hadley, Mass.: Bergin & Garvey, 1983).

Gross, Beatrice and Ronald, eds. *Radical School Reform* (New York: Simon & Schuster, 1969).

Hainstock, Elizabeth G. *The Essential Montessori* (New York: Mentor, 1978).

Jay, Martin. *The Dialectical Imagination: A History of the Frankfurt School and the Institute for Social Research, 1923–1950* (Boston: Little, Brown, 1973).

Jemolo, Arturo Carlo. *Questa repubblica: dal '68 alla crisi morale* (Firenze: Felice Le Monnier, 1981).

Kogan, Norman. *A Political History of Postwar Italy* (New York: Praeger, 1981).

L'Abate, Alberto, and Giorgio Mugnanini. "Danilo Dolci—Apostle of Nonviolence," *Mankind* 2, no. 7 (February 1958).

Lange, Peter, and Sidney Tarrow, eds. *Italy in Transition* (London: Frank Cass & Co., 1980).

Lombardi, Giovanni. "Il caso Dolci visto attraverso la stampa," *Scuola e Città* (March 31, 1958): 98ff.

Mammarella, Giuseppe. *L'Italia contemporanea* (Bologna: Il Mulino, 1985).

Mangione, Jerre. *A Passion for Sicilians: The World around Danilo Dolci* (New York: William Morrow, 1968).

Martinelli, Roberto, and Gianfranco Pasquino, eds. *La politica nell'Italia che cambia* (Milano: Feltrinelli, 1978).

McNeish, James, *Fire under the Ashes* (London: Hodder & Stoughton, 1964).

Nott, Kathleen. "Danilo Dolci: Nonviolence in Italy," *Commentary* (February 1961): 119–26.

Pantaleone, Michele. *Mafia e politica* (Torino: Einaudi, 1962).

Podbielski, Gisèle. *Twentyfive Years of Special Action for the Development of Southern Italy* (Milano: Giuffré, 1978).

Renda, Francesco. *Storia della Sicilia dal 1860 al 1970,* vol. 3 (Palermo: Sellerio, 1987).

Romagnoli, Umberto, and Tiziano Treu. *I sindacati in Italia: storia di una strategia, 1945–1976* (Bologna: Il Mulino, 1977).

Ronchey, Alberto. *Accadde in Italia: 1968–1977* (Milano: Garzanti, 1977).

Sabetti, Filippo. *Political Authority in a Sicilian Village* (New Brunswick, N.J.: Rutgers University Press, 1984).

Scarpinato, Roberto, ed. *Mafia, partiti, e pubblica amministrazione* (Napoli: Jovene, 1985).

Schmidt, Steffen W., Laura Guasti, Carl H. Landé, and James C. Scott, eds. *Friends, Followers, and Factions: A Reader in Political Clientelism* (Berkeley: University of California Press, 1977).

Schneider, Jane, and Peter Schneider. *Culture and Political Economy in Western Sicily* (New York: Academic Press, 1976).

Silj, Alessandro. *Never Again without a Rifle: The Origins of Italian Terrorism,* trans. Salvator Attanasio (New York: Karz, 1979).

Tarrow, Sidney. *Peasant Communism in Southern Italy* (New Haven: Yale University Press, 1967).

———. *Between Center and Periphery* (New Haven: Yale University Press, 1977).

Touraine, Alain. *The May Movement,* trans. Leonard F. X. Mayhew (New York: Random House, 1971).

Vitiello, Justin. "Danilo Dolci—Nonviolence in Sicily," *Resurgence* (September–October 1983).

West, Anthony. "Man's Inhumanity to Man," *New Yorker* (February 20, 1960): 156ff.

Woolf, Stuart. *A History of Italy, 1700–1860* (New York: Methuen, 1979).

5.1 Cold War Era

Ambrose, Steven E. *Rise to Globalism* (Harmondsworth, England: Penguin, 1980).

Chomsky, Noam. *Towards a New Cold War* (New York: Pantheon, 1982).

Chomsky, Noam, and Edward S. Herman. *The Washington Connection and Third World Fascism* (Boston: South End Press, 1979).

Cohen, Bernard C. *The Public's Impact on Foreign Policy* (Boston: Little, Brown, 1973).

Deutscher, Isaac. *Stalin: A Political Biography* (New York: Oxford University Press, 1949).

Etzold, Thomas H., and John Lewis Gaddis, eds. *Containment: Documents on American Policy and Strategy, 1945–1950* (New York: Columbia University Press, 1978).

Fleming, Denna F. *The Cold War and Its Origins, 1917–1960* (New York: Doubleday, 1961).

Ford, Gerald R. *The Vladivostok Negotiations and Other Events,* IGCC Policy Papers no. 2 (San Diego: University of California, Institute on Global Conflict and Cooperation, 1986).

Gaddis, John L. *The Long Peace* (New York: Oxford University Press, 1987).

Gorbachev, Mikhail S. *Toward a Better World* (New York: Richardson & Steirman, 1987).

Halle, Louis J. *The Cold War as History* (London: Chatto & Windus, 1967).

Halliday, Fred. *The Making of the Second Cold War* (London: Verso, 1983).

Hammond, Paul Y. *Cold War and Détente* (New York: Harcourt Brace Jovanovich, 1975).

Hammond, Thomas T., ed. *Witnesses to the Origins of the Cold War* (Seattle: University of Washington Press, 1982).

Kahan, Jerome. *Security in the Nuclear Age* (Washington, D.C.: Brookings Institution, 1975).

Kauffmann, William W., ed. *Military Policy and National Security* (Princeton: Princeton University Press, 1956).

Kennan, George F. *The Nuclear Delusion: Soviet-American Relations in the Nuclear Age* (New York: Pantheon, 1982).

Kissinger, Henry A. *Nuclear Weapons and Foreign Policy* (New York: Harper & Bros., 1957).

Kolko, Gabriel, and Joyce Kolko. *The Limits of Power: The World and United States Foreign Policy, 1945–1954* (New York: Harper & Row, 1972).

LaFeber, Walter. *America, Russia, and the Cold War, 1945–1984* (New York: Alfred A. Knopf, 1985).

Maddox, Robert S. *The New Left and the Origins of the Cold War* (Princeton: Princeton University Press, 1973).

Maier, Charles S., ed. *The Origins of the Cold War and Contemporary Europe* (New York: New Viewpoints, 1978).

Mates, Leo. *Nonalignment: Theory and Current Policy* (Dobbs Ferry, N.Y.: Oceana Publications, 1972).

Mills, C. Wright. *The Causes of World War Three* (New York: Simon & Schuster, 1958).

Nixon, Richard M. *The Real War* (New York: Warner Books, 1980).

Orwell, George. *In Front of Your Nose: The Collected Essays, Journalism, and Letters of George Orwell, 1945–1950,* vol. 4, ed. Sonia Orwell and Ian Angus (New York: Harcourt, Brace & World, 1968).

———. *Nineteen Eighty-Four* (Oxford: Clarendon Press, 1984 [1949]).

Pipes, Richard. *US-Soviet Relations in the Era of Detente* (Boulder, Colo.: Westview Press, 1981).

Schurmann, H. Franz. *The Logic of World Power* (New York: Pantheon, 1974).

Schwartz, Steven. *A Nuclear Weapons Primer: A Supplement to the UCSC Nuclear Information Handbook* (Santa Cruz: University of California, Adlai E. Stevenson Program on Nuclear Policy, 1986).

Sharnik, John. *Inside the Cold War* (New York: Arbor House, 1987).

Sivard, Ruth L. *World Military and Social Expenditures, 1986* (Leesburg, Va.: World Priorities Publications, 1986).

Steel, Ronald. *Pax Americana* (New York: Viking, 1967).

Talbott, Strobe. *Endgame: The Inside Story of SALT II* (New York: Harper & Row, 1979).

Terkel, Studs. *The Good War: An Oral History of World War II* (New York: Pantheon, 1984).

Thompson, Kenneth W. *Cold War Theories* (Baton Rouge: Louisiana State University Press, 1981).

Ulam, Adam B. *Expansion and Coexistence: Soviet Foreign Policy, 1917–1973* (New York: Praeger, 1974).

Urban, George R., ed. *Detente* (London: Temple Smith, 1976).

U.S. Arms Control and Disarmament Agency. *World Military Expenditures and Arms Transfers, 1986* (Washington, D.C.: Government Printing Office, 1986).

U.S. Army War College, ed. *National Security and Detente* (New York: Thomas Y. Crowell, 1976).

Wegs, J. Robert. *Europe since 1945* (New York: St. Martin's Press, 1984).

Williams, William A. *The Tragedy of American Diplomacy* (New York: Dell, 1962).

Wohlstetter, Albert. "The Delicate Balance of Terror," *Foreign Affairs* 37, no. 2 (January 1959).

5.2 International Cooperation

Adede, A. O. *The System for Settlement of Disputes under the United Nations Convention on the Law of the Sea: A Drafting History and Commentary* (The Hague: M. Nijhoff, 1987).

Art, Robert, and Kenneth Waltz, eds. *The Use of Force,* 2d ed. (Lanham Md.: University Press of America, 1983).

Bailey, Kathleen C. *Doomsday Weapons in the Hands of Many* (Urbana: University of Illinois Press, 1991).

Bose, Anima, ed. *Peace and Conflict Resolution in the World Community* (New Delhi: Vikas, 1991).

Boulding, Elise. *Building a Global Civic Culture: Education for an Interdependent World* (New York: Teachers College Press, 1988).

Boulding, Elise, Clovis Brigagao, and Kevin Clements, eds. *Peace Culture and Society: Transnational Research and Dialogue* (Boulder, Colo.: Westview Press, 1991).

Boulding, Kenneth E. *Stable Peace* (Austin: University of Texas Press, 1978).

Brock, Peter. *Twentieth-Century Pacifism* (New York: Van Nostrand Reinhold, 1970).

Bull, Hedley. *Hedley Bull on Arms Control,* selected by Robert O'Neill and David N. Schwartz (New York: St. Martin's, 1987).

Calvocoressi, Peter. *A Time for Peace: Pacifism, Internationalism, and Protest Forces in the Reduction of War* (London: Hutchinson, 1987).

Carter, April. *Peace Movements: International Protest and World Politics since 1945* (London: Longman, 1992).

Claude, Inis L., Jr. *States and the Global System: Politics, Law, and Organization* (New York: St. Martin's Press, 1988).

Deutsch, Karl, and Stanley Hoffmann, eds. *The Relevance of International Law* (Garden City, N.Y.: Anchor Books, 1971).

Elfstrom, Gerard. *Ethics for a Shrinking World* (New York: St. Martin's, 1990).

Elshtain, Jean Bethke. *Women and War* (New York: Basic Books, 1987).

———. *Power Trips and Other Journeys* (Madison: University of Wisconsin Press, 1990).

Falk, Richard A. *The Promise of World Order: Essays in Normative International Relations* (Philadelphia: Temple University Press, 1987).

Felder, David W. *How to Work for Peace* (Tallahassee: Florida A and M University Press, 1991).

Fischer, Dietrich, Wilhelm Nolte, and Jan Oberg, eds. *Winning Peace: Strategies and Ethics for a Nuclear-Free World* (New York: Crane Russak, 1989).

Forcey, Linda R., ed. *Peace: Meanings, Politics, Strategies* (New York: Praeger, 1989).

Franck, Thomas M. *Judging the World Court* (New York: Priority Press, 1986).

Galtung, Johan. *The True Worlds: A Transnational Perspective* (New York: Free Press, 1980)

———. *There Are Alternatives! Four Roads to Peace and Security* (Nottingham, England: Spokesman, 1984).

Groom, A. J. R., and Paul Taylor, eds. *Frameworks for International Cooperation* (New York: St. Martin's Press, 1990).

Haas, Ernst B. *The Uniting of Europe: Political, Social, and Economic Forces, 1950–1957* (Stanford: Stanford University Press, 1958).

———. *The Obsolescence of Regional Integration Theory* (Berkeley: University of California, Institute of International Studies, 1975).

———. "The Collective Management of International Conflict," in United Nations Institute for Training and Research, *The United Nations and the Maintenance of International Peace and Security* (Dordrecht, The Netherlands: Martinus Nijhoff, 1987).

Hannum, Hurst. *Autonomy, Sovereignty, and Self-Determination: The Accommodation of Conflicting Rights* (Philadelphia: University of Pennsylvania Press, 1990).

Hanrieder, Wolfram F., ed. *Global Peace and Security: Trends and Challenges* (Boulder, Colo.: Westview Press, 1987).

Henkin, Louise, et al. *Right vs. Might: International Law and the Use of Force* (New York: Council on Foreign Relations, 1991).

Hoffmann, Stanley. *Duties beyond Borders: On the Limits and Possibilities of Ethical International Relations* (Syracuse: Syracuse University Press, 1981).

Jervis, Robert. "Cooperation under the Security Dilemma," *World Politics* (January 1978).

Jones, Dorothy V. *Code of Peace: Ethics and Security in the World of the Warlord States* (Chicago: University of Chicago Press, 1991).

Jutte, Rudiger, and Annemarie Grosse-Jutte, eds. *The Future of International Organization* (New York: St. Martin's Press, 1981).

Kant, Immanuel. *Perpetual Peace,* ed. Lewis White Beck (New York: Liberal Arts Press, 1957).

Keohane, Robert O. "Reciprocity in International Relations," *International Organization* 40 (Winter 1986).

Kipnis, Kenneth, and Diana T. Meyers, eds. *Political Realism and International Morality: Ethics in the Nuclear Age* (Boulder, Colo.: Westview Press, 1987).

Kodama, Katsuya, and Unto Vesa, eds. *Towards a Comparative Analysis of Peace Movements* (Aldershot, England: Dartmouth, 1990).

Kothari, Rajni, et al. *Towards a Liberating Peace* (Tokyo: United Nations University Press, 1988).

Leyton-Brown, David, ed. *The Utility of International Economic Sanctions* (New York: St. Martin's, 1987).

Liu, F. T. *United Nations Peacekeeping and the Non-Use of Force* (Boulder, Colo.: L. Rienner, 1992).

Luper-Foy, Steven, ed. *Problems of International Justice* (Boulder, Colo.: Westview Press, 1988).

Luttwack, Edward N. *Strategy: The Logic of War and Peace* (Cambridge, Mass.: Belknap Press, 1987).

Maxwell, Mary. *Morality among Nations: An Evolutionary View* (Albany: State University of New York Press, 1990).

Morgenthau, Hans. *Politics among Nations,* 3d ed. (New York: Alfred A. Knopf, 1961).

Nakarada, Radmila, and Jan Oberg, eds. *Surviving Together: the Olof Palme Lectures on Common Security* (Aldershot, England: Dartmouth, 1989).

Nardin, Terry, and David R. Mapel, eds. *Traditions of International Ethics* (Cambridge: Cambridge University Press, 1992).

North, Robert C. *War, Peace, Survival: Global Politics and Conceptual Synthesis* (Boulder, Colo.: Westview Press, 1990).

Norton, Augustus R., and Thomas George Weiss. *U.N. Peacekeepers: Soldiers with a Difference* (New York: Foreign Policy Association, 1990).

Osgood, Robert E. *An International Military Force in a Disarming and Disarmed World* (Washington, D.C.: Institute for Defense Analyses, 1963).

Peterson, M. J. *The General Assembly in World Politics* (Boston: Allen & Unwin, 1986).

Rabow, Gerald. *Peace through Agreement: Replacing War with Non-Violent Dispute-Resolution Methods* (New York: Praeger, 1990).

Raymond, Gregory A. *Conflict Resolution and the Structure of the State System: An Analysis of Arbitrative Settlements* (Montclair, N.J.: Allenheld, Osmun, 1980).

Reiss, Mitchell. *Without the Bomb: The Politics of Nuclear Non-Proliferation* (New York: Columbia University Press, 1988).

Riggs, Robert E., and Jack C. Plano. *The United Nations: International Organization and World Politics* (Pacific Grove, Calif.: Brooks/Cole, 1988).

Rikhye, Indar, and Kjell Skjelsbaek, eds. *The United Nations and Peacekeeping: Results, Limitations, and Prospects: The Lessons of 40 Years of Experience* (New York: St. Martin's, 1991).

Roberts, Adam, and Benedict Kingsbury, eds. *United Nations, Divided World: The UN's Role in International Relations* (Oxford: Clarendon Press, 1988).

Rosenau, James N., and Ernst-Otto Czempiel, eds. *Governance without Government: Order and Change in World Politics* (New York: Cambridge University Press, 1992).

Rosenthal, Joel H. *Righteous Realists: Political Realism, Responsible Power, and American Culture in the Nuclear Age* (Baton Rouge: Louisiana State University Press, 1991).

Saaty, Thomas L., and Joyce M. Alexander. *Conflict Resolution: The Analytic Hierarchy Approach* (New York: Praeger, 1989).

Schelling, Thomas C. *Arms and Influence* (New Haven: Yale University Press, 1966).

Scott, Andrew M. *The Dynamics of Interdependence* (Chapel Hill: University of North Carolina Press, 1982).

Smith, Michael J. *Realist Thought from Weber to Kissinger* (Baton Rouge: Louisiana State University Press, 1986).

Smoke, Richard, and Willis Harman. *Paths to Peace: Exploring the Feasibility of Sustainable Peace* (Boulder, Colo.: Westview Press, 1987).

Snyder, Glenn H., and Paul Diesing. *Conflict among Nations* (Princeton: Princeton University Press, 1977).

Suganami, Hidemi. *The Domestic Analogy and World Order Proposals* (Cambridge: Cambridge University Press, 1989).

Taylor, Phillip. *Nonstate Actors in International Politics: From Transregional to Substate Organizations* (Boulder, Colo.: Westview Press, 1984).

Thompson, Kenneth W. *Morality and Foreign Policy* (Baton Rouge: Louisiana State University Press, 1980).

Thompson, W. Scott, et al., eds. *Approaches to Peace: An Intellectual Map* (Washington, D.C.: United States Institute of Peace, 1991).

United Nations Department for Disarmament Affairs. *The United Nations and Disarmament, 1945–1985* (New York: United Nations, 1985).

———. *Confidence and Security-Building Measures in Asia* (New York: United Nations, 1990).

United Nations Institute for Training and Research. *The United Nations and the Maintenance of International Peace and Security* (Dordrecht, The Netherlands: M. Nijhoff, 1987).

U.S. Helsinki Watch Committee. *From Below: Independent Peace and Environmental Movements in Eastern Europe and the U.S.S.R.* (New York: Helsinki Watch Committee, 1987).

Verrier, Anthony. *International Peacekeeping: United Nations Forces in a Troubled World* (Harmondsworth, England: Penguin, 1981).

Wallop, Malcolm, and Angelo Codevilla. *The Arms Control Delusion* (San Francisco: Institute for Contemporary Studies, 1987).

Waltz, Kenneth N. *Man, the State, and War: A Theoretical Analysis* (New York: Columbia University Press, 1959).

———. *Theory of International Politics* (Reading, Mass.: Addison-Wesley, 1979).

Walzer, Michael. *Just and Unjust Wars* (New York: Basic Books, 1977).

Warner, Daniel. *An Ethic of Responsibility in International Relations* (Boulder, Colo.: L. Rienner, 1991).

Wells, Robert N., Jr., ed. *Peace by Pieces—United Nations Agencies and Their Roles* (Metuchen, N.J.: Scarecrow Press, 1991).

Weston, Burns H., ed. *Alternative Security: Living without Nuclear Deterrence* (Boulder, Colo.: Westview Press, 1990).

Wight, Martin. *Power Politics,* ed. Hedley Bull and Carsten Holbraad (Leicester, England: Leicester University Press, 1978).

Williamson, Richard S. *The United Nations as Peacekeeper* (Washington D.C.: Department of State, 1989).

5.3 General Subjects

Barraclough, Geoffrey. *An Introduction to Contemporary History* (Harmondsworth, England: Penguin, 1967).

Bellah, Robert N. *Beyond Belief: Essays on Religion in a Post-Traditional World* (New York: Harper & Row, 1970).

———. *Habits of the Heart* (Berkeley: University of California Press, 1985).

Caplan, Arthur L., ed. *The Sociobiology Debate* (New York: Harper & Row, 1978).

Davidson, Basil. *Scenes from the Anti-Nazi War* (London: Monthly Review Press, 1980).

Delzell, Charles F. *Mussolini's Enemies* (Princeton: Princeton University Press, 1961).

Femia, Joseph. *Gramsci's Political Thought* (Oxford: Clarendon Press, 1981).

Fischer, Louis, ed. *The Essential Gandhi* (New York: Vintage, 1962).

Fussell, Paul. *The Great War and Modern Memory* (New York: Oxford University Press, 1975).

Gamson, William A. *The Strategy of Social Protest* (Homewood, Ill.: Dorsey Press, 1975).

Gerth, Hans H., and C. Wright Mills, eds. *From Max Weber* (New York: Oxford University Press, 1946).

Inglehart, Ronald. *Culture Shift in Advanced Industrial Society* (Princeton: Princeton University Press, 1990).

Jäckel, Eberhard. *Hitler's World View: A Blueprint for Power* (Cambridge, Mass.: Harvard University Press, 1972).

Kolakowski, Leszek. *Main Currents of Marxism,* vol 3, trans. P. S. Falla (Oxford: Clarendon Press, 1978).

Lopreato, Joseph. *Human Nature and Biocultural Evolution* (Boston: Allen & Unwin, 1984).

Lukes, Steven. *Power: A Radical View* (London: Macmillan, 1974).

Manuel, Frank E., and Fritzie P. *Utopian Thought in the Western World* (Cambridge, Mass.: Belknap Press, 1979).

Mosse, George L., ed. *International Fascism: New Thoughts and New Approaches* (London: Sage Publications, 1979).

Nagler, Michael. *America without Violence* (Covelo, Calif.: Island Press, 1982).

Nolte, Ernst. *Three Faces of Fascism* (New York: Holt, Rinehart & Winston, 1965).

Ortner, Donald J., ed. *How Humans Adapt: A Biocultural Odyssey* (Washington, D.C.: Smithsonian Institution Press, 1983).

Spindler, Louise S. *Culture Change and Modernization* (New York: Holt, Rinehart, & Winston, 1977).

Stern, Fritz. *The Politics of Cultural Despair: A Study in the Rise of the Germanic Ideology* (New York: Doubleday, 1961).

Taylor, A. J. P. *The Struggle for Mastery in Europe, 1848–1918* (Oxford: Clarendon Press, 1954).

———. *Bismarck: The Man and the Statesman* (New York: Alfred A. Knopf, 1969).

Thucydides. *The Peloponnesian War,* trans. Benjamin Jowett (Oxford: Clarendon Press, 1900).

Tocqueville, Alexis de. *Democracy in America,* vol. 2, trans. Henry Reeve (New York: Alfred A. Knopf, 1945 [1835]).

Whitehead, Alfred North. *Process and Reality* (New York: Free Press, 1957 [1929]).

INDEX